WHEN THINGS
W GO rong

WHEN THINGS
GO
Wrong

Organizational Failures and Breakdowns

Helmut K. Anheier
Editor

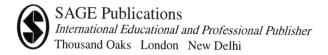
SAGE Publications
International Educational and Professional Publisher
Thousand Oaks   London   New Delhi

For information:

SAGE Publications, Inc.
2455 Teller Road
Thousand Oaks, California 91320
E-mail: order@sagepub.com

SAGE Publications Ltd.
6 Bonhill Street
London EC2A 4PU
United Kingdom

SAGE Publications India Pvt. Ltd.
M-32 Market
Greater Kailash I
New Delhi 110 048 India

Printed in the United States of America

Library of Congress Cataloging-in-Publication Data

Main entry under title:
    When things go wrong: Organizational failures and breakdowns /
edited by Helmut K. Anheier.
        p.   cm.
    Includes bibliographical references and index.
    ISBN 0-7619-1047-6 (acid-free paper)
    ISBN 0-7619-1048-4 (pbk.: acid-free paper)
    1. Business failures.   2. Bankruptcy.   I. Anheier, Helmut K., 1954–
HG3761 .W46   1999
658.4—ddc 21   98-25537

This book is printed on acid-free paper.

99 00 01 02 03 04 05 7 6 5 4 3 2 1

Acquiring Editor:	Marquita Flemming
Editorial Assistant:	MaryAnn Vail
Production Editor:	Wendy Westgate
Production Assistant:	Stephanie Allen
Copyeditor:	Linda Gray
Typesetter/Designer:	Lynn Miyata
Indexer:	Molly Hall

Contents

Acknowledgments   ix

⌘ PART I: Introduction

1. Organizational Failures, Breakdowns, and Bankruptcies:
   An Introduction   3
   HELMUT K. ANHEIER
   Rutgers University, New Jersey

   LYNNE MOULTON
   Rutgers University, New Jersey

⌘ PART II: Organizations and Failure

2. Costly Information: Firm Transformation, Exit,
   or Persistent Failure   17
   LYNNE G. ZUCKER
   University of California, Los Angeles

   MICHAEL R. DARBY
   University of California, Los Angeles

3. Decision Overreach as a Reason for Failure:
   How Organizations Can Overbalance   35
   DAVID WILSON
   Warwick Business School, England

   DAVID J. HICKSON
   Bradford Management Centre, England

   SUSAN J. MILLER
   Durham University, Durham, England

4. "Tales From the Grave": Organizations' Accounts
of Their Own Demise   51

   MARK HAGER
   Indiana University of Pennsylvania, Pennsylvania

   JOSEPH GALASKIEWICZ
   University of Minnesota, Minnesota

   WOLFGANG BIELEFELD
   University of Texas, Dallas

   JOEL PINS
   University of Minnesota, Minneapolis

5. Organizational Coping, Failure, and Success:
Academies of Sciences in Central and Eastern Europe   71

   RENATE MAYNTZ
   Max-Planck-Institute, Cologne

🔁 PART III: The Political Economy of Failure and Bankruptcy

6. Successful Failure: An Alternative View of
Organizational Coping   91

   WOLFGANG SEIBEL
   University of Konstanz, Germany

7. Veiled Politics: Bankruptcy as a Structured
Organizational Field   105

   KEVIN J. DELANEY
   Temple University

8. The Politics of Blame Avoidance:
Defensive Tactics in a Dutch Crime-Fighting Fiasco   123

   MARK BOVENS
   Utrecht University, Netherlands

   PAUL 't HART
   Leiden University, Netherlands

   SANDER DEKKER
   Leiden University, Netherlands

   GERDIEN VERHEUVEL
   Leiden University, Netherlands

9. Creating the Agents of Corporate Rescue:
   Professionalization of Insolvency   149
   > TERENCE C. HALLIDAY
   > *American Bar Foundation*
   >
   > BRUCE G. CARRUTHERS
   > *Northwestern University*

⌸ PART IV: The Cognitive Construction of Failure

10. Prosaic Organizational Failure   179
    > LEE CLARKE
    > *Rutgers University, New Jersey*
    >
    > CHARLES PERROW
    > *Yale University*

11. Permanent Failure and the Failure of
    Organizational Performance   197
    > MARSHALL W. MEYER
    > *University of Pennsylvania*

⌸ PART V: Structural Failures

12. Success and Failure in Institutional Development:
    A Network Approach   215
    > FRANK P. ROMO
    > *State University of New York at Stony Brook*
    >
    > HELMUT K. ANHEIER
    > *Rutgers University*

13. Stalemate: A Structural Analysis of Organizational Failure   241
    > HELMUT K. ANHEIER
    > *Rutgers University*
    >
    > FRANK P. ROMO
    > *State University of New York at Stony Brook*

ꙮ PART VI: CONCLUSION

14. Studying Organizational Failures   273

HELMUT K. ANHEIER
Rutgers University

LYNNE MOULTON
Rutgers University

References   291
Index   309
About the Editor   312
About the Contributors   313

Acknowledgments

The idea to pull together a volume on current research on the types, causes, and outcomes of organizational failures goes back to a conversation Paul DiMaggio and I had several years ago while taking a stroll on the Princeton campus. Paul, as inspiring as ever, suggested the idea to the Editorial Board of the *American Behavioral Scientist,* which then invited me to edit a special issue of this journal of the topic. The present volume is in many ways an expansion of the efforts that initially flowed into the journal issue, and it is only fair to say that without Paul's crucial support and encouragement neither would have happened. The same is true when it comes to Lynn Moulton's contribution. She did much to keep the project alive and organized, and she provided critical substantive and editorial input on virtually all chapters in the book. Special thanks, too, go to Marquita Flemming and her superb staff at Sage.

The editorial work for this book was supported by a grant from the Dean of the Faculty of Arts and Sciences of Rutgers University. This support is gratefully acknowledged.

PART I

Introduction

Organizational Failures, Breakdowns, and Bankruptcies

An Introduction

HELMUT K. ANHEIER
LYNNE MOULTON

1

The themes of failure, breakdown, disintegration, decline, and bankruptcy have fascinated social scientists for a long time. Indeed, there is a rich research tradition going back well to the founding period of economic, sociological, and political science. Examples include (a) Durkheim's analysis of anomie and pathological forms of the division of labor, (b) Marx's work on class structures, (c) Weber's theme of contradictions between forms of rationality, (d) Pareto's model of elite circulation and the erosion of centralized power, (e) Toynbee's study of the disintegration of civilizations, and (f) Schumpeter's analysis of the potential paralysis of capitalist society. To a large extent, their concern was the massive reorganization that occurred during the transition from preindustrial to industrial societies, and the consolidation of the capitalist market economy.

Although this comparative-historical perspective is continued in works such as Smelser's (1962) breakdown model of the normative order, Geertz's (1963) notion of "involution," or Kennedy's (1987) study on *The Rise and Fall of Great Powers* and Huntington's (1996) *Clash of Civilizations,* most recent research on failure and decline has adopted a much narrower focus. Increasingly, organizational failure became largely the concern of bankruptcy law, operations research, and corporate decision-making models. Moreover, research tends to be strongly firm centered and focused on efficiency and other performance criteria.

This analytic focus is not surprising given the frequency of business failure. In the United States from 1985 to 1995, an average number about 70,000 businesses failed each year (U.S. Bureau of the Census, 1997, table 852). Although on an annual basis, businesses fail at a rate of only 1 per 100, the number of firm closures represents nearly 40% of the number of business starts during that period (U.S. Bureau of the Census, 1997, table 852). Most of these firms file for bankruptcy, and each year between 1985 and 1995, an average of 56,164 businesses sought protection under Chapters 7, 9, 11, or 12 of the 1978 Bankruptcy Reform Act (U.S. Bureau of the Census, 1997, table 856). Also during this time period, an average of 4,208 firms were merged with, or bought by, other companies—a threefold increase from 1985 to 1996 (U.S. Bureau of the Census, 1997, table 859). In contrast to businesses, failure of government entities seems much rarer. Municipalities filed for bankruptcy at an average rate of 10 per year from 1985 to 1995 (U.S. Bureau of the Census, 1997, table 856).

In general, studies of failure deal with its causes. Research either (a) highlights failure as a consequence of external factors, such as decline in available resources and organizational carrying capacity, greater competition, changes in niche dimensions and density (Baum & Singh, 1994; Hannan & Carroll, 1992; Sheppard, 1995; Swaminathan & Wiedenmayer, 1991), isolation (Baum & Oliver, 1991), and more unexpected events such as catastrophes and jolts (Meyer, 1982), or (b) explores failures as a consequence of internal factors, such as bad corporate decisions, mismanagement, disputes and in-fighting, and lack of organizational slack (Levy & Merry, 1986; Mintzberg, 1990).

Typically, the concern in the management literature with failure and bankruptcy takes the form of "rise-and-fall" books, in which scholars examine the failure of particular, usually large, corporations such as RJR Nabisco (Burrough & Helyar, 1990), General Motors (Keller, 1989), E. F. Hutton (Sterngold, 1990), Eastern Air Lines (Robinson, 1992), IBM (Carroll, 1993), or Orange County, California (Jorion, 1995). In the past, management textbooks largely ignored explicit discussion of organizational failure (Feldman & Arnold, 1983; Hunsaker & Cook, 1986; Huse & Bowditch, 1977; Schermerhorn, Hunt, & Osborn, 1988). Decline, unplanned change, and environmental changes that could lead to organizational demise were mentioned in passing as potential problems about which managers must be aware and should plan for. More recently, however, some analysts are paying attention to the potential for decline and "termination" throughout the organizational life cycle, although failure is exclusively defined as a finite event, resulting in firm closure (Bartol & Martin, 1994). In this literature, potential for failure is treated as part of organizational process, yet failure itself is not seen as the complex process that researchers in this volume describe. Against this background, the collection of essays in this book goes beyond the current emphasis on managerial and legal concerns and explores the broader organizational, political, cognitive, and structural aspects of failures. We will briefly discuss each aspect in turn.

▓ ORGANIZATIONAL ASPECTS

In contrast to work focusing on singular, large-scale corporate failures, organizational theorists treat creation, growth, decline, and death as part of the organizational life cycle (Cameron, Kim, & Whetten, 1987; Whetten, 1987). Within this cycle, each stage of organizational development includes characteristic crises such as leadership problems or coordination difficulties, which in turn trigger typical responses—for example, delegation or decentralization (Kimberly & Miles, 1980). Sometimes, reactions to actual or perceived crises lead to wrong, even "fatal" decisions, leading to a downward spiral, whereby organizations pass through various distinct phases from early impairment to marginal existence and a death struggle (Hambrick & D'Aveni, 1988). Each phase is characterized by progressive deterioration of performance, slack, and environmental conditions. Similarly, Staw, Sandelands, and Dutton (1981) diagnose typical threat-rigidity behavior among organizations prior to massive failure, whereby inflexible reactions to perceived problems trigger the actual crisis. Other authors investigate distinct phases of the organizational life cycle. For example, Carroll and Delacroix (1982) and Brüderl and Schüssler (1990) attribute failure to organizational newness and "adolescence."

▓ POLITICAL ASPECTS

In this perspective, organizations are seen as political entities that compete for advantages within a larger political economy inhabited by different institutions and constituencies. Political reasons for failure emphasize the notion of legitimacy as a major resource for organizational survival and underscore the importance of organizational strategies. Linz and Stepan (1978), who introduce a model for the breakdown of democratic regimes, present one of the key examples of this research. In this model, the legitimacy of a regime depends on its efficacy (the ability to formulate solutions to perceived problems) and its efficiency (the ability to implement formulated solutions), and all three interact to influence the likelihood of stability or breakdown.

For example, the fragmentary party system, and the basic cleavages of the political order (democratic, communist, authoritarian) of the

Weimar Republic in Germany overlapped with regional, religious, and economic interests on the one side and complex interpersonal social structures of elites, disloyal elites, and counterelites, as well as loyal and disloyal oppositions, on the other (Lepsius, 1978). This complex political system reduced the regime's legitimacy and made effective and efficacious solutions impossible, thereby contributing to further tendencies toward instability and, ultimately, breakdown. Likewise, O'Donnell's (1973) classic study of party competition in Argentina reports on a political contest among major players in what he called "the impossible game," in which "both winners and losers must lose" (p. 175). Lewis (1990) describes the subsequent stalemate in Argentina's political system, leading to erosions in governmental legitimacy.

▦ COGNITIVE ASPECTS

Studies focusing on the cognitive aspects deal with questions of perception, identification, and declaration of failure. Why do some failures appear as obvious and "expected" (e.g., the breakup of Yugoslavia, most airline bankruptcies), whereas others, such as the failure of the Soviet Union; the insolvency of Orange County, California; or the numerous failures of savings and loan associations in the late 1980s, do not? Research in this field highlights the importance of routines, blueprints of interpretation, and dispositions toward organizing. Billings, Milburn, and Schaalman (1980) introduce a model of crises perception as discrepancies between unusual and unexpected "triggering events" and "standard operations" that then lead to organizational decision making under high uncertainty and time pressure, ultimately making miscalculations and wrong decisions more likely. Of importance in this context are routine-based repertoires of crisis management as well as crisis plans that try to anticipate "triggering events" to preempt the development of organizational disasters.

Analyzing organizational behavior, psychologists such as Kets de Vries and Miller (1984) identify certain "cultural elements" and "dispositions" among managers and CEOs that make failure more likely. For example, the paranoid organization is suspicious of the internal and external environment and shows a high degree of speculative mistrust combined with hypersensitivity toward alleged threats and overconcern with hidden motives. At the other extreme is the carefree, overconfident organization, seemingly invincible to inside and outside challenges. Both types are prone to failure, as the history of organizational disasters would amply demonstrate.

▦ STRUCTURAL ASPECTS

The structural approach differs from other work on organizational failure by going beyond the utilitarian, efficiency-oriented calculus of management and economic literature. It differs from political and cognitive perspectives by looking at sets of actors and organizations and the network ties among them. The failures occur in the *social fabric* of organizations and groups, and such failures may not necessarily coincide with situations of economic distress and vice versa. Implicitly, this type of work goes back to the work of sociologist Georg Simmel who suggested that the tendency of failure is the result of both simple and complex, sometimes counteracting, relational components of the social structure. For Simmel, societies negotiate a quantitative relation between "harmony and disharmony, association and disassociation, favor and disfavor, to achieve identifiable structures" (Simmel, 1968, p. 187, first author's translation). We find similar formulations in the work of Rokkan (1975), who suggested that societies and institutions must find upper and lower ceilings of conflict and discontent, and in the essay by Hirschmann (1981) on "exit" and "loyalty" in organizational settings, whereby participants confronting a situation perceived as unsatisfying can either leave (exit) or remain loyal. In general, this type of work suggests that societies and organizations are conglomerates of conflict and support relations, as well as of positive and negative affect and indifference. Although the substantive meaning of the relative balance among these relations depends on actual contexts and task environments, significant imbalances may lead to failures.

Consider the following examples to illustrate the structural approach to failure. Useem (1985) describes the extreme tension between administration and inmates, which, in the end, led to the 1980 New Mexico prison riot. Even though conflicts were intense, no general cleavage structure developed, and the social organization among inmates remained highly fragmentary and weak. In a situation loaded with actual and potential conflicts, realignments among antagonistic cliques of prisoners accounted for both the chaotic leadership and the extreme violence of the uprising, and, ultimately, made the rapid disintegration of the social structure more likely.

Compare the New Mexico case with Crozier's (1974) analysis of two professional groups to explain the low performance of French public corporations in the field of technological innovation and improvement. Crozier shows that the higher-status *polytechniciens* control rewards, whereas the lower-status mechanical engineers control everyday work operations, the major source of uncertainty in the organization. In the absence of status mobility, each can only block the other's attempts at change because cooperation means that one group has to give up what it presently uses to keep the other at bay. Thus, the *polytechniciens* adjust themselves to irrelevance, whereas the engineers are content with improvisation and the preservation of outdated technology. It is a situation in which two endogamous, antagonistic status groups, locked in a stalemate, are unable to dissociate. Each group possesses half of what is needed to solve the stalemate; yet it is this half that it needs to keep the other group at bay.

Finally, contrast both cases to Romo's (1986; Romo & Anheier, 1991) study of the social structure of an elite psychiatric institution. Here, a seemingly innocent personnel matter brought underlying interpersonal conflicts among staff and between staff and patients to the open. In the subsequent dispute, emerging alliances involving groups of junior staff and patients were unable to overcome the dominant contest of some junior and senior staff members for leadership. In the end, staff members who had challenged the leadership were expelled from the institution, resulting in a radical contraction and realignment of the social structure, thereby changing the organization and its objectives in significant ways.

OVERVIEW

The chapters in this volume are examples of current scholarship on each of these four aspects of organizational failure. They cover a range of organizational forms—that is, for-profit corporations, government agencies, and nonprofit organizations—and offer evidence both cross-nationally and over time.

In their chapter on "Costly Information: Firm Transformation, Exit, or Persistent Failure" Lynne G. Zucker and Michael R. Darby examine organizational aspects of failure and successes. It is a commonplace, they argue, that successful firms are those that continue to satisfy the demands of their "environment" via profitability, innovation, and productivity. They unfold this notion by examining success, or failure, as the outcome of investment (or lack of investment) in acquiring and using new information. In their study of pharmaceutical firms, they offer an example of a field in which recent dramatic changes in science and technology have sharply highlighted causes of firm failure. Zucker and Darby find that successful firms make large investments in information and technology in two ways. First, aggressive innovators, usually new and small firms, invest in the initial development of new information. Second, large and previously successful firms, with significant capital to invest, adopt the innovations as a warrant against obsolescence. Significantly, these firms move toward adoption only after the risks of innovation have been borne by other firms. Investment in such costly information is, then, a necessary yet not sufficient condition for firm success. Firm failure, on the other hand, may be caused by delaying or refusing to adopt new technology or, especially, to acquire new information.

Underlying all organizational failures (and, of course, successes) are streams of decisions—some good, some bad. David Wilson, David J. Hickson, and Susan J. Miller in "Decision Overreach as a Reason for Failure: How Organizations Can Overbalance" explore the "outliers" in this universe: large-scale, faulty decisions with adverse, often dramatic consequences leading to an organization's quick demise. They use two case studies to illustrate the decision-making process and consequent actions that lead to such rapid failure. What is at issue here is not a technical or operational calamity but managerial overreach: The organization simply goes too far to survive. Although theories of organizational failure usually deal with unexpected occurrences and other triggering events, subsequent actions, and their ultimate consequences in terms of success and failure, the authors here signal the importance of how such actions may be planned to begin with, often in much detail and with great care, yet lead to unanticipated consequences that finally threaten the organization's survival.

In their chapter " 'Tales From the Grave': Organizations' Accounts of Their Own Demise," Mark Hager, Joseph Galaskiewicz, Wolfgang Bielefeld, and Joel Pins present one of the few studies that explore reasons for failure by interviewing former managers. The authors compare this data with the rich information provided by a multiyear panel study of nonprofit organizations. Exit interviews conducted during the course of the study allowed researchers to detail "inside" explanations for organizational death. The authors describe and categorize these reasons and compare events in organizational survivors with those in failures. They find that organizations die in many different ways but that current theories do indeed provide valid ways of categorizing and dissecting these failures. Market problems, internal disruptions, and the like were predictably frequent causes of failure. Surprisingly, a large number reported that "mission completion," as opposed to "failure," underlay the organizations' death. This is a situation not commonly addressed by theory, as the authors point out. More broadly, the authors demonstrate that new organizations often fail precisely because they are new, thereby giving more credibility to the "liability of newness" thesis (see Brüderl & Schüssler, 1990).

Struggles with unanticipated changes and consequences are the topic in Renate Mayntz's chapter on "Organizational Coping, Failure, and Success: Academies of Sciences in Central and Eastern Europe." She explores how organizations cope with massive external threats to their very survival in a political economy that has radically changed within a short period of time. She finds that contingency and strategic choice perspectives of organizational coping are complementary and concludes that organizational success or failure are functions of the nature and intensity of the environmental challenge and of the organizational response to it. Prior to the regime changes in Central and Eastern European countries, the Academies of Sciences enjoyed a good "fit" with the institutional environment of the Socialist regimes, characterized by centralized state control, hierarchical division of labor, concentration of similar tasks in one large organization, and a Soviet-type academy model. After the regime changes, however, the academies experienced dramatic incongruence with the new democratizing political systems. Mayntz argues that the political history of each country was important in producing varied meanings of regime change. Academies adjusted more easily to the changing environmental conditions during and after the transformations of the early 1990s in countries where the academy model was part of a general loss of national independence, where there was a history of "Western" scientific tradition, and where there was an established intellectual reform movement.

Two chapters highlight the political aspects of organizational failure. First, Wolfgang Seibel, in "Successful Failure: An Alternative View of Organizational Coping" challenges the often unspoken assumption that efficiency and effectiveness are in fact prerequisites for continued organizational survival. Similar to the question posed by Meyer and Zucker (1989), he asks why some organizations can permanently fail yet continue to mobilize resources at rates much higher than suggested by economic rationality. A common explanation is that these organizations represent stakeholders' inability to exercise control, either because of a lack of information or because of problems in enforcing performance standards. The failure, however, is a "temporary" condition, because stakeholders will eventually gain control and rescue the organization from eventual death. Seibel argues that this may not always be true. He offers two cases— German programs for battered women's aid and for handicapped training— that persistently fail in attaining usual standards of efficiency, effectiveness, and accountability. Yet they are provided with continued support, even though the failure is well-known and persistent: They are "successful failures." Seibel effectively argues that in such cases overriding stakeholder interests may be better served by failure than by success. Failing organizations may help keep a troubling issue out of the public eye and create the illusion that something is being done; they may function to support ideological positions or keep otherwise troublesome constituencies at bay.

Kevin J. Delaney's contribution, "Veiled Politics: Bankruptcy as a Structured Organizational Field," offers a strong lesson not only in the politics of organizational failure but also in the complicated semantics sometimes involved in labeling organizational behavior. Bankruptcy regulations in commercial law, he suggests, initially designed as mechanisms for "orderly failure," are increasingly used as part of political strategies. Corporations use bankruptcy as an organizational response to otherwise insoluble problems. Far from spelling the demise of an organization, it may prove to be a salvation. Delaney extensively documents and describes his argument that bankruptcy is another branch of organizational politics. He then extends his reasoning to depict the larger organizational field that has developed around the industries in which, in particular, megabankruptcy are most frequent. The strength of these fields has made bankruptcy a viable alternative to many other potential solutions to problems that are (or would be) more transparent and accountable.

Two chapters take a more ecological approach in their political analysis of organizational failure by describing how various aspects of the institutional environment shape the representation of failure and political and legal responses to it. First, Mark Bovens, Paul 't Hart, Sander Dekker, and Gerdien Verheuvel, in "The Politics of Blame Avoidance: Defensive Tactics in a Dutch Crime-Fighting Fiasco," develop a typology of defensive tactics employed by policy elites to deflect blame for policy fiascoes. They make a distinction between program and political failure and proceed to show how the consequences of program failure rest at least partially on how the failure is represented politically. Although their analysis of the Dutch interregional criminal investigation team's dissolution shows that many political scandals do not unfold in a linear way, Bovens et al. argue that each chronological step of fiasco construction is associated with a set of defensive tactics meant to avoid blame.

In "Creating the Agents of Corporate Rescue: Professionalization of Insolvency," Terence C. Halliday and Bruce G. Carruthers analyze the process of privatizing bankruptcy through the professionalization of insolvency practice in England in the late 1980s. They demonstrate the complementary qualities of the co-optation and state sponsorship models of professionalization through their analysis of the political process leading to the 1986 Insolvency Act. In this case, the State's interest in sponsoring a hybrid profession of insolvency practitioners to improve "market morality" corresponded well with the desire among insolvency practitioners for a more cohesive professional identity. Halliday and Carruthers conclude that the institutions set up to deal with corporate failure reflect not only the interests of the various parties to the debate but also reflect prevailing political ideologies and their interpretations of what causes corporate failure in the first place. Under Thatcher conservatism, "statutorily guided self-regulation" through the professionalization of insolvency practitioners reflects a broad commitment to improving market morality and to a growing interest in "saving" failing companies.

Lee Clarke and Charles Perrow's chapter, "Prosaic Organizational Failure," deals with cognitive aspects of organizational failure. To avert failure, organizations must create plans for action in the face of foreseeable contingencies. They argue that organizational failure, far from being precluded, may often be a *result* of these plans, particularly in rare-event scenarios with little or no actual experience to go by. The authors suggest that under these conditions, plans frequently become "fantasy documents," providing detailed and extensive response strategies for situations that, ultimately, cannot be delineated. Organizations believe these representations and ignore contrary experience. Thus, such plans may primarily serve legitimizing functions by providing management and clients with comforting "cognitive blueprints," irrespective of the organization's ability to adapt to critical situations.

In his chapter, "Permanent Failure and the Failure of Organizational Performance," Marshall W. Meyer extends the work he began with Lynne G. Zucker in *Permanently Failing Organizations* (Meyer & Zucker, 1989) by examining the performance basis on which organizations are deemed to be permanently failing. He argues that most existing measures of performance are inadequate evaluations of actual performance, which tends to "lie ahead and beyond measurement." Not only do organizations sometimes fail at failure because they become fixed in patterns of low performance, but their managers also tend to fail to measure performance. The challenge facing managers and researchers is figuring out if, how, or when the seemingly endless determinants of performance actually contribute to organizational success and profitability. Measuring everything, using old or new measures, is not the solution to this challenge, claims Meyer, because most performance outcomes are realized only in the future. Performance outcomes can be projected or predicted but not measured directly. Firms must rely on "second-best measures" of current and past performance, which may or may not be good indexes of performance.

Finally, the two chapters by Frank P. Romo and Helmut K. Anheier use a structural, network approach to organizational failure. In the first chapter, "Success and Failure in Institutional Development: A Network Approach," they analyze two competing perspectives—Michels's (1962) oligarchy thesis and Olson's (1971) free rider thesis—on success and failure patterns in organizational development. Using blockmodel analysis of interorganizational networks, they find that the underlying relational structures of support and conflict among the organizations involved contributed to the success or failure of each development. Overall, their results give more credibility to Michels's oligarchy thesis, which links oligarchic tendencies to success in organizational development. They suggest, however, that cultural and cognitive factors as well as path dependencies can swamp interorganizational dynamics that would otherwise lead to either success or failure. They conclude that rational economic behavior may prove inadequate in accounting for differences in organizational development. Otherwise, the organization that failed should have succeeded, and the one that succeeded should more likely have failed. Behind these seemingly paradoxical outcomes are nonetheless self-interested actors, oriented not at maximizing some abstract notion of economic returns but pursuing objectives that, deeply embedded in the culture of the organizational field, appear rational to them, based on conceptions that are taken for granted and that remain unchallenged.

In their second chapter, on "Stalemate: A Structural Analysis of Organizational Failure," they explore the phenomenon of stalemate against the backdrop of different types of failures in organizational settings. In stalled social organizations, groups tend to support those who oppose them and to contend with those who give support. Thus, neither "exit" nor "voice" become clear and unambiguous alternatives in terms of organizational behavior. Using data from various case studies, they look at the characteristics of stalemate relative to breakdown, factionalism, and permanent failure. The defining characteristic of stalemate is the significant overlap between strategic areas of interest and areas of conflict among the parties involved. Stalled social structures are prone to goal displacement, severe constraints on coalition formation and conflict mediation, high degrees of inertia, and a slow, frequently drawn-out process of decline and dissolution. Stalled organizations reveal a sense of "false loyalty" among participants and are kept together by what makes the organizations fail.

▓ CONCLUDING COMMENTS

Over the last 10 or so years, research on organizational failure has gathered momentum. Based on "thick descriptions" of organizational case studies and, increasingly, on larger, quantitative analyses, researchers have introduced various theories, more often complementary than competing with each other. These theories, often in the form of empirical generalizations, have no intention of adding up to a "grand theory of organizational failure," nor are they likely to do so. The phenomenon of failure in organizations is too multifaceted for this task, and theories are best when they highlight organizational, economic, political, or cognitive aspects, or some subset of these, without trying to become too encompassing and therefore overly abstract.

Undoubtedly, future work in this field will broaden our empirical knowledge and improve current theoretical understanding. Toward this process, we suggest three avenues that may be important to explore in this respect. First, we need a better understanding of the phenomenon of failure as such. From the chapters presented in this volume, it becomes clear that "failure" is a relative concept. For one, it seems relative to the expectations and strategies of the various stakeholders putting a claim on the performance of the organization. Moreover, failure is relative to notions of success as well as to organizational maintenance. And if failure is relative in its meaning and implications, so is success. Organizations are rarely monolithic entities, and their success and failure implies an underlying question that analysts must bring to the forefront: successful for whom, a failure for whom?

Second, the relativity of the term notwithstanding, can we develop "yardsticks" and sets of indicators for organizational failure and success; and indeed, studies in the field often operate with either implicit or explicit measures of performance or "states." Nor do measures necessarily have to restrict themselves to monetary indicators such as profitability, return-on-investment, or similar ratios. Structural sociology has developed initial measures for failure tendencies in social networks based on positive and negative affect (Anheier, 1994a), as well as overall measures for structures of opportunity and constraints in organizational fields (Burt, 1992). The challenge for future research in this field is to combine economic and noneconomic performance measures to assess organizational tendencies toward success and failure.

Finally, we need to acknowledge that the reasons organizations fail may be different from how they fail and what "failed state," if any, they will ultimately obtain. Failures can be the result of various simple and complex structural processes and sometimes counterveiling tendencies, which may result in different types of failure over time. In other words, we have to differentiate between failure as process and failure as an outcome. Then we will be in a better position to understand how some failures become successful and how some initial successes can turn into failures. We will return to these issues in the concluding chapter of this book.

PART II

Organizations and Failure

Costly Information

Firm Transformation, Exit, or Persistent Failure

LYNNE G. ZUCKER
MICHAEL R. DARBY

> It must be remembered that there is nothing more difficult to
> plan, more doubtful of success, nor more dangerous to manage
> than the creation of a new system. . . . The hesitation arises . . .
> from the general skepticism of mankind which does not really
> believe in an Innovation until experience proves its value.
>
> —Niccolo Machiavelli, *The Prince*, (1947, p. 15)

When information needed to make "smart" decisions about adoption and implementation of innovation is costly to obtain, evaluate, or use, we expect that firms will vary significantly in the amount of information they are willing to invest in acquiring or using (Darby, 1976). To acquire and use information and estimate its value to the firm, specific

AUTHORS' NOTE: This research has been supported by grants from the Alfred P. Sloan Foundation through the NBER Research Program on Individual Technology and Productivity, the National Science Foundation (SES 9012925), the University of California Systemwide Biotechnology Research and Education Program, and the University of California Pacific Rim Research Program. We are indebted to a talented team of postdoctoral fellows Zhong Deng, Julia Liebeskind, and Yusheng Peng and research assistants Jeff Armstrong, Rajesh Chakrabatri, Yui Suzuki, Akio Tagawa, Maximo Torero, and Alan Wang. This article is a part of the NBER research program in productivity. Any opinions expressed are those of the authors and not those of the National Bureau of Economic Research.

intellectual human capital, or at least access to specific intellectual human capital, may be necessary (Zucker, 1991a).

In the case of scientific breakthrough innovations, those with the most information about these discoveries are the scientists actually making them. This information constitutes intellectual human capital retained by the discovering scientists (Zucker, Darby, & Brewer, 1994). Few scientists know the new techniques, and it takes considerable time for other scientists to learn the techniques in the laboratories of the discovering scientists (as collaborators or as graduate and postdoctoral students); hence, there is transient scarcity of this embodied know-how at the time of a major breakthrough in science (Zucker, Darby, & Armstrong, 1994; Zucker, Darby, & Brewer, 1994).[1] When these discoveries have immediate commercial value, as in the cases of semiconductors and biotechnology (Teitelman, 1994), the discovering scientists have commercially valuable information that is initially very costly for others to obtain.

Incumbent pharmaceutical firms with substantial assets are motivated to redeploy these assets to perform effectively under changed circumstances (Zucker & Darby, 1995a). Unlike other industries in which firms become "permanently failing," such as electric railways—due in part to heavy sunk costs in assets that are difficult to redeploy (Hilton & Due, 1964; Meyer & Zucker, 1989)—many pharmaceutical firms had high levels of investment in intellectual human capital at the time of the breakthrough discoveries and were able to successfully redeploy these assets either by retraining the scientists or by replacing those resistant to the new techniques (Zucker & Darby, 1995a). Incumbent firms continue this transformation process. A recent article on SmithKline Beecham's research and development (R&D) chief, George Poste, explores his attempts to turn around a company that is now the tenth largest in drug revenues, down from third in 1989:

> Poste [hired] "bio-informaticians," who are equipped with powerful computers to help locate genes by searching for patterns in DNA sequences. . . . Since becoming boss, he has cut the R&D organization by nearly a quarter, axing 1,300 people who he felt were redundant or had not signed on to his vision. (Flynn, 1996, p. 81)

Our theory is simple. Obtaining, evaluating, and using breakthrough discoveries in science rests on information that is costly: (a) to obtain and evaluate the information, prior investment in science is required; (b) to obtain access to tacit knowledge of top scientists making these discoveries, trust is generally necessary because intellectual property cannot be formally protected at early stages of discovery (Zucker & Darby, 1995b;

Zucker, Darby, Brewer, & Peng, 1996); and (c) to use the information requires major redeployment of assets with significant downside risk if the discovery fails to produce the promised results or produces unexpected results (e.g., new product liability problems). These generalizations hold true at the level of the individual scientist, the university department, and the firm; in general, those individuals and organizations who enter a new scientific arena risk less or are less risk averse than those who do not.

The amount of accumulated assets prior to the innovation creates a paradoxical effect: Those with more assets are unlikely to waste them by refusing to transform in the face of a superior innovation, but because they have more at risk, because of systematic biases toward overestimating downside risk under uncertainty, or both (Tversky & Kahneman, 1974), those with more assets are likely to lag behind those with fewer assets, waiting to see the revealed benefits. Once they do adopt, their higher level of accumulated assets may enable them to "catch up" to the early adopters. To apply these ideas directly to incumbent pharmaceutical firms, those with strong prior R&D are expected to adopt recombinant DNA techniques and to become actively involved in producing biological-based drugs, but they are also expected initially to lag significantly behind the new start-up firms.

▦ INVESTMENT IN INFORMATION SEEKING AND EVALUATION BY INCUMBENT FIRMS

We expect differential abilities to detect, evaluate, and implement performance-enhancing innovations depending in part on the investment that firms have made in intellectual human capital in the past.[2] This investment not only has the virtue of improving identification of innovation, firms also have a wider range of choices about potential strategic alternatives that otherwise may exist in the firm's environment without being detected. Once choices are identified, this same intellectual human capital can be employed to evaluate, discriminating between innovations likely to improve firm performance if adopted and those not likely to do so.

In Table 2.1, the world's leading firms in drug development are listed in order of the number of R&D drugs in 1981-1982, and their investment in intellectual human capital is indicated by their research intensity, measured by R&D expenditures and these expenditures per employee. For the U.S. firms with R&D expenditure data broken out for 1984, we can see that contemporary performance in terms of producing new drugs, here chemical compounds, is not particularly related to investments in intellectual human capital/information detection and evaluation made by these firms. The firm ranked second in the world, Bristol-Meyers, has relatively low

TABLE 2.1 World's Leading Companies in the Development of
New Drugs in 1981-1982: Analysis of Research and
Development Intensity

			1984	
Company	Country	Number of R&D Drugs	R&D Expenditures ($ millions)[a]	R&D Expenditures/ Employee ($ thousands)[a]
Roche	Switzerland	100		
Bristol-Myers	United States	82	214.2	6.3
Hoechst	Germany	73		
Merck & Co.	United States	72	396.0	11.8
American Home Products	United States	66	184.6	0.4
Upjohn	United States	64	264.0	12.0
Johnson & Johnson	United States	56	420.9	5.4
Eli Lilly	United States	56	330.0	11.4
Ciba-Geigy	Switzerland	49		
Roussel-Uclaf	France	48		
Sandoz	Switzerland	47		
Boehringer-Ingelheim	Germany	45		
Rhône-Poulenc	France	43		
Bayer	Germany	42		
Schering-Plough	United States	42	165.3	6.4
Meiji-Seika	Japan	42		
Dow-Chemical	United States	41		
Takeda	Japan	41		
Warner-Lambert	United States	41	198.4	4.4
Beecham	United Kingdom	40		

SOURCE: California Department of Commerce (1986, tables 11 and 12) and our calculations.
NOTE: Tables have not been updated for this reprinting of the 1996 article.
a. Research and development expenditures for 1984 were not available for the non-U.S. firms and Dow-Chemical.

research intensity compared with Merck, Upjohn, and Eli Lilly. American Home Products, ranked fifth, has the lowest research intensity, falling below even Warner-Lambert, which is ranked 19th of 20 firms worldwide.

It seems likely, then, that it is not simply profitability that leads to the decision to invest in information gathering and evaluation via intellectual human capital but, rather, that investing and maintaining information systems for innovations reflects higher expectations of the frequency and importance of change in the industry—here, specifically science-driven technological change. Thus, the size and intensity of the R&D effort, not the characteristics of the firm itself, should predict whether firms will take the next strategic steps to decide whether or not to actually discover/ engineer new biologicals itself, to become involved in other aspects of biologicals production such as manufacturing or marketing, and/or to invest in firms involved in biologicals in some way. Firms that invest more in these intellectual human capital-based detection and evaluation systems are likely to respond earlier and more effectively to the transformation in drug discovery and formulation caused by the genetic engineering revolution.

But mechanisms to gather information are real investments and incur costs even during periods when innovations become less frequent: Thus, as innovations increase in both frequency and importance, more information-gathering mechanisms will be associated with improved performance (on average); as innovations decrease on those dimensions, fewer information-gathering mechanisms will be associated with improved performance (less sunk cost). To the extent that the demand for information is highly variable or that within-firm information risks systematic bias from internal politics as in performance evaluation of professionals, it will tend to be subcontracted out rather than built up within the firm (Darby, 1976; Hanson, 1995; Zucker, 1991a). For example, the leading incumbent pharmaceutical firms have long invested in relationships with top scientists, both as consultants and as recipients of funding for basic research (e.g., the original discovery of DNA) even during periods of low discovery rates in basic science. These scientists can be thought of as subcontractors to detect significant changes in basic science that might prove relevant to the firms.

We believe that similar processes must be important in other industries. Examining the minicomputer, cement, and airline industries, Tushman and Anderson (1986) report that, empirically, technological breakthroughs can either increase or decrease the risks faced by incumbent firms according to whether the breakthroughs are initiated within or without the incumbent industry and, further, that these effects decrease over successive discontinuities. We would interpret these findings as reflecting whether the breakthroughs occur in fields of science or technology in which the incumbent firms find it rational to invest in intellectual human capital capable of recognizing and using the breakthroughs. Where breakthroughs have already occurred, incumbent firms are more likely to choose to acquire such competence and hence will be less threatened by successive breakthroughs.

▦ NATIONAL LEVELS IN BIOSCIENCE AND FIRM TIES TO INTELLECTUAL HUMAN CAPITAL

Although information seeking and evaluation are necessary conditions to internal transformation, they is not sufficient: Incumbent firms must decide to employ or otherwise access the intellectual human capital that embodies the new breakthrough technology (Zucker, Darby, & Armstrong, 1994; Zucker, Darby, & Brewer, 1994). Both the tacit nature of this knowledge at the beginning of the breakthrough period and the demand for trust to protect valuable scientific discoveries make working relationships with scientists necessary.

Two kinds of working relationships appear to be the most common methods: top scientists moving from universities to firms ("affiliated") or conducting joint research projects at the bench science level between these "star" discovering scientists, many of whom remain at the university, and scientists working at the firm ("linked"). We identify a subset of these relationships that occur between the worldwide star bioscientists, those with over 40 genetic sequence discoveries or 20 articles reporting such discoveries by 1990 in *GenBank,* and firms (Bilofsky & Burks, 1988; *GenBank,* 1990). Increases in the intensity of these working scientific relationships, as measured by the number of joint research articles between affiliated or linked star scientists and other firm scientists, result in significantly higher firm productivity, at least for linked stars in our initial empirical test limited to California (Zucker, Darby, & Armstrong, 1994).

Star scientists are not evenly distributed across the world; their location depends on the size of the scientific base and supporting scientific infrastructure in bioscience in each of the countries. Table 2.2 shows the general distribution, with the United States clearly dominant and Japan second, although Japan has only about half of the expected stars based on a straight population-base prediction when compared with the United States. Similarly, Germany and France also have about half of the expected stars relative to the United States; the United Kingdom looks somewhat stronger, although if the net out-migration of star bioscientists is taken into account (see tables in Zucker & Darby, 1996, in press), the findings echo those from Japan, Germany, and France.

Ties to firms (including both affiliated and linked) vary even more strikingly across countries. The third column in Table 2.2 shows that a higher percentage of stars in Japan are ever "tied" (affiliated or linked) to firms than in the United States, whereas less than a third as many stars are tied to firms in the United Kingdom and none in France and Germany.

Most of the firms are pharmaceutical firms or small, new biotechnology firms. One measure of the intensity of their scientific research is their R&D expenditure per employee. Table 2.2 continues our analysis by examining changes over time in R&D expenditures and labor compensation per employee in drugs for the four countries where data are available (Danzon & Percy, 1995). Relative to the United States, in 1981 drug firms in Germany spent about three quarters as much on R&D per employee,

TABLE 2.2 The International Competitive Arena: Star Bioscientists' Commercial Involvement, R&D Expenditures in Drugs per Employee, Employee Compensation in Drugs

				Expenditures per Employee in Medicine and Drugs						
Nation or Region	Stars			R&D Expenditures[a]			Labor Compensation[a]			
	Total[b]	Tied[c]	% Tied	1981	1985	1990	1975	1980	1985	1990
United States	207	69	33.3	100.0	100.0	100.0	100.0	100.0	100.0	100.0
Japan	52	21	40.4	—[d]	—	—	—	—	—	—
Other APEC[e]	24	1	4.2	—	—	—	—	—	—	—
France	25	0	0.0	63.2	56.6	50.8	76.5	89.0	84.5	86.1
Germany	24	0	0.0	77.4	77.5	50.7	71.0	67.6	64.2	65.4
Switzerland	15	3	20.0	—	—	—	—	—	—	—
United Kingdom	31	3	9.7	66.6	62.1	54.2	56.7	61.3	68.8	78.0
Other Europe[f]	30	3	10.0	—	—	—	—	—	—	—
Rest of world[g]	9	0	0.0	—	—	—	—	—	—	—
Total world	417	100	24.0	—	—	—	—	—	—	—

SOURCES: Zucker and Darby (1996, table 3) and calculations of the authors; Danzon and Percy (1995, tables 12c and 14), based on the Organization of Economic Cooperation and Development (OECD), Structural Analysis (STAN) Industrial Database, April 1993.
NOTE: Tables have not been updated for this reprinting of the 1996 article.
a. Indices relative to the United States deflated by gross domestic product deflators and converted at purchasing-power parity exchange rates.
b. Unique stars ever publishing in a given country.
c. Number of stars in the country who ever published as or with an employee of a new biotechnology enterprise (NBE) in the same country. For grouped entries, the sum of these numbers.
d. — = data not available.
e. Other Asia Pacific Economic Cooperation (APEC): Australia and Canada.
f. Other Europe: Belgium, Denmark, Finland, Italy, The Netherlands, and Sweden.
g. Rest of world: Israel and the U.S.S.R.

whereas the level of spending was about two thirds in France and the United Kingdom. Relative spending dropped across the board to approximately half of U.S. levels by 1990, dropping rather precipitously between 1985 and 1990 in Germany. Labor compensation in 1975 relative to the United States was hovering at around three quarters for France and Germany and at about half for the United Kingdom; by 1990, France had risen to 86% of the U.S. level, while the United Kingdom had risen to over three quarters. Germany declined slightly in labor compensation relative to the United States.

Not shown in Table 2.2 is what was happening to the levels of R&D spending in the pharmaceutical industry in the United States: By 1987, the average drug R&D per employee in the United States had nearly doubled its 1981 value, and it continued its steady climb, up another 40% by 1990. Much of the increase in the United States was due to the new biotechnology firms that continued to make heavy R&D investments relative to other pharmaceutical companies; whereas the biotech industry made on average a 23% increase in R&D between 1993 and 1994, the leading incumbent pharmaceutical company, Merck, made only a 9% increase between 1992 and 1993 (Lee & Burrill, 1995, figure 1).

▦ LAG BY INCUMBENT FIRMS IN TIES TO STARS AND IN GENETIC SEQUENCE PATENTS

Because incumbent firms face greater downside risk than new biotech start-ups, we expect that they will lag behind the new firms in their use of the breakthrough techniques. We have analyzed the pattern of both ties to star scientists and patenting over time for U.S. firms, comparing incumbent pharmaceutical firms with new biotechnology firms.

Table 2.3 compares the history of ties between stars and firms by examining publication counts of affiliated or linked stars over time between dedicated biotech firms, major incumbent firms, and other incumbent subunits. In other research, we have found that the number of publications in these bench-level working relationships predicted higher subsequent firm productivity in terms of products in development, products on the market, and employment growth in the firm (Zucker, Darby, & Armstrong, 1994). Thus, firms with access to leading-edge science as evidenced by such affiliations and linkages perform significantly better than the vast majority of enterprises that lack such access.

We examine the intensity of ties between stars and firms for the periods 1976 to 1980, 1981 to 1985, 1986 to 1990 in Table 2.3. During the first 5 years of the biotech revolution, only one well-known new biotechnology firm had the intellectual human capital that we are measuring here. In the second 5 years, 17 firms had demonstrated substantial access to intellectual human capital, of which almost 24% were major pharmaceutical firms and the remainder were new biotechs. Quantitatively, the pharmaceuticals lagged further, however, with all 97 articles by affiliated stars being published by stars affiliated with new biotech firms and only 19% of 52 linked articles linked to pharmaceutical firms.

In the third 5-year period, 1986 to 1990, summarized in Table 2.3, there appears to be evidence of a general catch-up effort by pharmaceutical firms. Pharmaceutical firms began to have star scientists publishing as their employees (11%), and their share of linked articles rose to 24% (excluding the nascent group of incumbent firms in other industries with significant scientific capital).

Table 2.4 presents a similar pattern of results in the area of patent production. However, the timing is somewhat later: Although the science diffused rapidly in the late 1970s in terms of initial publications of stars,

TABLE 2.3 Publications by Stars Affiliated With or Linked to U.S. Firms

Variables	Number of Firms	Publication Counts of Stars			
		Affiliated Stars	Linked in BEA[a]	Linked in Other U.S.[b]	Linked Foreign[c]
1976 to 1980					
Dedicated biotech firms	1	9	0	0	0
Major pharmaceutical firms	0	0	0	0	0
Other incumbent subunits	0	0	0	0	0
Total for all firms	1	9	0	0	0
1981 to 1985					
Dedicated biotech firms	13	97	20	12	10
Major pharmaceutical firms	4	0	2	7	1
Other incumbent subunits	0	0	0	0	0
Total for all firms	17	97	22	19	11
1986 to 1990					
Dedicated biotech firms	19	68	16	30	6
Major pharmaceutical firms	8	8	3	9	4
Other incumbent subunits	3	0	2	2	0
Total for all firms	30	76	21	41	10
1976 to 1990					
Dedicated biotech firms	22	174	36	42	16
Major pharmaceutical firms	9	8	5	16	5
Other incumbent subunits	3	0	2	2	0
Total for all firms	34	182	43	60	21

SOURCE: Zucker and Darby (1995a).
NOTE: Tables have not been updated for this reprinting of the 1996 article.
a. The firm's location and that of the university, research institute, or hospital with which the star is affiliated are in the same functional economic area as defined by the U.S. Bureau of Economic Analysis (BEA).
b. The star is located in a university, research institute, or hospital in a different U.S. BEA area.
c. The star is located in a foreign university, research institute, or hospital.

patenting of genetic sequences did not boom until the mid 1980s in the United States. *GenBank* has data on 3,353 patents granted through the end of 1990, of which we were able to link 611 or 18.2% of the world total to 21 of the 34 firms examined in Table 2.3.[3] Table 2.4 provides annual data for total numbers of genetic-sequence patents granted to the major pharmaceuticals with ties to stars, ties to the corresponding dedicated biotech firms, and their sum. For purposes of rough comparisons with Table 2.3, we again add the values for 1980 to 1985, 1986 to 1990, and 1980 to 1990. Again, we find that the major pharmaceuticals lagged behind the dedicated biotech firms but then began catching up quickly in the late 1980s: They had only 8.7% of total patents for 1980-1985, but

TABLE 2.4 Worldwide Genetic-Sequence Patents Granted to U.S. Firms With Affiliated or Linked Stars, 1980-1990

Period	Major Pharmaceutical Firms	Dedicated Biotech Firms	All Firms
1980	0	2	2
1981	0	4	4
1982	4	17	21
1983	0	9	9
1984	1	29	30
1985	4	34	38
1986	3	49	52
1987	10	18	28
1988	45	101	146
1989	43	152	195
1990	7	79	86
1980 to 1985	9	95	104
1986 to 1990	108	399	507
1980 to 1990	117	494	611

SOURCE: Zucker and Darby (1995a) and *GenBank* (August 15, 1995).
NOTE: Tables have not been updated for this reprinting of the 1996 article.

this rose to 21.3% in 1986 to 1990. Given an average lag of perhaps 2 years between application and granting of the patent, this performance is even more remarkable.

As we have shown, although the incumbent pharmaceutical firms are closing the gap in the United States, even the most transformed incumbent firms still lag the new biotechnology firms in detection, evaluation, and use of the breakthrough discoveries. To assess the effects of these lags, we examine the performance of incumbent firms relative to the new biotechnology firms in drug discovery in biologicals, examining biological drugs receiving FDA (Food & Drug Administration) approval on the market in the United States through 1994, and then turn to a more general comparison of overall performance of worldwide pharmaceutical firms judged most productive in 1981, adding in the new biotech firms with products on the market by the end of 1993.

▒ EFFECTS ON PRODUCTIVITY OF THE FIRM

In Zucker and Darby (1995a), we identified nine major American incumbent pharmaceutical companies that appeared by 1990 to be successful in transforming their technological identity in drug discovery to biotechnology. These firms were identified on the basis that one or more star scientists were working as or with employees of the firm and that the firm was assigned patents for genetic-sequence discoveries. Based on other work (Zucker & Darby, 1996), we expect this pattern to be associated with both more important research on the part of the star scientists themselves and greater firm success as measured by numbers of products in development and on the market and by growth in employment.

If we are correct that this is a dominant technology, then we would expect that these nine firms would have done relatively well in recent years compared with those with no evidence of successful transformation. By and large, this is borne out by the firms' experience in the first half of the 1990s. By the end of 1995, despite a wave of consolidation in the pharmaceutical industry, five of the firms continued as successful major American pharmaceutical firms with no change in control (although some of them had themselves made significant acquisitions).[4] Another firm's major pharmaceutical operations were transferred to a joint venture formed by its chemical-company parent and one of the five firms just mentioned.[5] One of the remaining three firms merged into a major European pharmaceutical firm that itself had successfully transformed to biotechnology, and the merged firm is one of the world's leaders in biotech.[6] A second entered into a merger with a European firm with the resulting firm's ownership equally divided by the stockholders of the two merging firms.[7] Control of the last firm was acquired by one of the other major European pharmaceutical groups, but it remains a separate American enterprise with substantial public ownership.[8] The biotechnological research thrust of the entire group is built around the American corporation.

To explore the net effect of strategic decisions by firms on their productivity in producing and/or licensing, manufacturing, or marketing new biologicals, and on the overall productivity of these firms, we now turn to a comparison among major incumbent pharmaceutical firms worldwide, as identified earlier in Table 2.1. In Tables 2.3 and 2.4, we have documented systematic differences in the strategies concerning adoption of new breakthrough technology by incumbent pharmaceutical firms and by new biotechnology firms in the United States. Incumbent pharmaceutical firms lag in adoption but also show their ability to redeploy their assets effectively and quickly once they judge that the value of the breakthrough discoveries has been established.

In Table 2.5, we examine the 18 companies that obtained licenses for the first 21 new biological entities licensed for U.S. marketing, as well as the other companies from Table 2.1. There is considerable diversity of experience among the companies listed in Table 2.1. Among the 20 leading companies identified in 1981-1982, only 9 had any new biological

TABLE 2.5 New Biological Entities Approved for the U.S. Market by 1994

Company[a]	Country	Year of First[b]		Number of Biologicals[c]		Year(s) of FDA Approval of Biologicals
		Star's Article	Genetic-Sequence Patent in U.S.	Discovered[d]	Licensed Manufactured, Marketed[e]	
Roche	Switzerland					
Hoffman-La Roche		89	86		1	86
Genentech, Inc.		79	82	7		82, 85, 86, 87, 89, 90, 93
Bristol-Myers	United States		88			
Hoechst	Germany		89			
Roussel-Uclaf						
Merck & Co.	United States	87	86		1	86
American Home Products	United States		89			
Genetics Institute		84	88	1		86
Upjohn	United States	86	82			
Johnson & Johnson	United States					
Ortho Biotech Group				1	1	86, 90
Eli Lilly	United States	85	84	1	1	87, 92
Ciba-Geigy	Switzerland		88			
Chiron (Cetus)		82	85	3		86, 92, 93
Sandoz	Switzerland					
Boehringer-Ingelheim	Germany		88			
Rhône-Poulenc-Rorer	France/U.S.		89			

Company	Country	Star's Article	Patent in U.S.	d	e
Bayer	Germany		90		
Miles, Inc.			90		93
Schering-Plough (DNAX)	United States	82	87	1	86
Meiji Seika	Japan		88		
Dow-Chemical	United States				
Takeda	Japan	83	87		
Warner-Lambert	United States				
Beecham	United Kingdom				
SmithKline Beecham		86	89	1	89
Amgen	United States		88	2	89, 91
Baxter International	United States				
Baxter Healthcare				1	92
Berlex Biosciences	United States	89		1	93
Biogen	United States	83	85	1	86
Cytogen	United States			1	92
Immunex	United States		88	1	91
Inteferon Sciences	United States	83		1	89
Molecular Biosystems	United States			1	94

SOURCES: Our calculations; Lee and Burrill (1995); Pharmaceutical Manufacturers Association (1993).

NOTE: Tables have not been updated for this reprinting of the 1996 article.

a. Companies are those listed in the United States or their successors in the human therapeutics industry plus all other firms with new biological entities approved for marketing in the United States.

b. These data are currently available only through 1990 (our relational database described in Zucker, Darby, & Brewer, 1994, and Zucker, Darby, & Armstrong, 1994, is currently being updated through 1995). The Star's Article column gives the date of the first article (through 1990) authored by a star as or with an employee of the company. The Patent in U.S. column gives the year of the first genetic-sequence patent in the United States assigned to the company.

c. These companies may have new biological entities approved for marketing in their home or other markets but not in the United States, which arc not counted in this table.

d. These numbers are for new biological entities approved for marketing in the United States that were discovered at the firm regardless of where they are manufactured and marketed directly by the firm or licensed to other firms.

e. These numbers are for new biological entities approved for marketing in the United States that were not discovered at the firm but are manufactured and/or marketed by the firm under license from another firm.

entities licensed for U.S. marketing by 1994—7 if we exclude the 2 with biologicals only because of late acquisitions of dedicated biotech companies. One more preexisting pharmaceutical company and 7 other dedicated biotech companies complete the list bringing products of the new technology to market.

Also in Table 2.5, subsidiaries and majority-owned firms with licensed biologicals are indented below their parents. In the case of Chiron, Genentech, and Genetics Institute, this ownership or control was acquired after their first new biological entities in the table were licensed for U.S. marketing. Clearly, a strategy that we have only briefly mentioned—adopting the breakthrough discoveries primarily through purchase of one or more dedicated biotech firm—was also actively pursued. Note that the incumbent firms who did not have star bioscientists tied to them through affiliation or linkage were more likely to acquire a dedicated biotechnology firm.

Some firms are quite successful relative to their competitors, sometimes in drug discovery, other times in licensing, manufacturing, and marketing these new discoveries. In Table 2.6 we can see the striking effects. Actively "downsizing" in both R&D and manufacturing in 1995-1996 was the former power house, Hoechst, and recent mergers included Upjohn. Others have failed, such as American Cyanamid that was acquired by American Home Products, and although only 20 years out from the founding of Genentech, others already appear to be on their way to permanently failing status.

Boehringer-Ingelheim, Rhône-Poulenc, Bayer, Dow-Chemical, SmithKline Beecham, Baxter, and Hoechst all have low performance relative to the top firms. Clearly, the order of top-performing pharmaceutical firms has been profoundly disturbed by the genetic revolution. Of the new dedicated biotech firms, the ones that are profitable have largely been acquired as they required more capital than they were able to raise by other means (with the major exception being Amgen); other new firms still talk primarily in terms of the "burn rate" of their capital, and some continue to show strongly negative earnings as a percentage of sales.

▓ SUMMARY AND IMPLICATIONS

Preference for science-based drug discovery is revealed in both the amount and percentage devoted to R&D functions of the firm. Incumbent firms in the United States and elsewhere with such preferences are more likely to invest in top scientists at the leading edge of the breakthrough discoveries and to move to capture quickly, through patenting or other means, the intellectual property created. National research funding policy condi-

TABLE 2.6 Earnings as a Percentage of Sales for Major Pharmaceutical Firms, 1987 and 1994

Company	Country	Earnings as a Percentage of Sales 1987	1994	Source Code
Roche	Switzerland	6.5	19.4	b
Hoffman-LaRoche		18.3	15.6	a
Genentech, Inc.				
Bristol-Myers Squibb	United States	13.1	15.4	a
Hoechst	Germany	4.1	2.8	b
Roussel-Uclaf		4.8	11.2	b
Merck & Co.	United States	17.9	20.0	a
American Home Products	United States	16.8	17.0	a
Genetics Institute		−0.7	−14.4	d
Upjohn	United States	12.1	15.0	a
Johnson & Johnson	United States	10.4	12.8	a
Ortho Biotech Group			12.8	d
Eli Lilly	United States	17.7	22.5	a
Ciba-Geigy	Switzerland	3.6	8.7	b
Chiron		16.1	6.6	c
Sandoz	Switzerland	7.0	10.9	b
Boehringer-Ingelheim	Germany		4.0	b
Rhône-Poulenc Group	France	3.9	4.7	b
Bayer	Germany	3.3	4.5	b
Miles, Inc.			1.1	d
Schering-Plough	United States	11.7	19.8	a
Meiji-Seika Kaisha Ltd.	Japan	1.1*		b
Dow-Chemical	United States	9.3	4.7	a
Takeda	Japan	6.0*	6.5*	b
Warner-Lambert	United States	8.5	10.8	a
Beecham	United Kingdom	9.6		b
SmithKline Beecham			1.8	b
Amgen	United States	−10.4	19.4	c
Baxter International	United States	5.3	6.4	a
Baxter Healthcare			6.4	d
Berlex Biosciences	United States	n/a	n/a**	
Biogen	United States		−3.1	c
Biogen N.V.		−180.7		b
Cytogen	United States	−36.7	−1,334.7	c
Immunex	United States	−1.6	−22.9	c
National Patent Development	United States	9.3	−6.8	a
Interferon Sciences				
Molecular Biosystems	United States	24.9	−214.0	c

NOTE: Tables have not been updated for this reprinting of the 1996 article.
a. *Moody's Industrial Manual 1988* and *Moody's Industrial Manual 1995.*
b. *Moody's International Manual 1988* and *Moody's International Manual 1995.*
c. *Moody's OTC Industrial Manual 1988* and *Moody's OTC Industrial Manual 1995.*
d. *Bioscan,* various issues, 1988 to 1995.
*Japanese fiscal year figures for April 1 of indicated year through March 31 of following year.
**Privately held.

tioned the number of top scientists available at the time of the break-through, and the subsequent speed of ramp up as the importance of the breakthrough was recognized.

Within the United States, incumbent firms were slower to commer-cialize these new discoveries than new biotechnology firms, in part because the breakthroughs were made in California universities that had heavily invested in molecular biology and the major incumbent pharma-ceutical firms were located primarily in New Jersey and surrounding states. Little or no—and to a lesser extent, slow—use of the breakthrough discoveries resulted in generally lower performance compared with those firms who adopted more fully and faster. Few large incumbent firms actually went out of business during the 20 years since commercialization began, but many merged or became low performing. As we begin to unravel the process of transferring scientific discovery to the firm, we also tell the story of the profound effects that basic science in a span of 20 years has wrought in a major international industry. The lag generated by downside risk to firms with significant assets has a telling effect, but whether that effect is permanent for incumbent firms depends on whether they are willing to make the transition to the new technology and on the strategy of conversion that they choose. The rest of our story has yet to be written, but given the costly information problem, we expect that incumbent firms who choose to incorporate the new discoveries internally will be more successful in identifying, evaluating, and using the next major breakthrough discovery and continuing to prosper with new radical changes in technological regime.

▨ NOTES

1. This is not simply "tacit knowledge" but, rather, knowledge that has initial tacit properties that may or may not remain as the knowledge becomes routinized as "normal science."

2. Firms are not motivated to seek information about innovations unless innovations have occurred with a high degree of frequency and were often important in improving performance in the past. Thus, the past *is* prologue in the sense of making rational certain investments in information gathering.

3. We matched genetic-sequence patents to 8 of the 9 major pharmaceutical firms and to 13 of the 22 dedicated biotech firms, but found no genetic sequence patents for the 3 other new biotech subunits (NBSs). Of course, the latter group was late on the scene and may appear in patent data after the 1990 cutoff in the data that we have so far analyzed.

4. Abbott Laboratories, Schering-Plough (DNAX Research Institute sub-sidiary), Eli Lilly and Co., Merck & Co., and Monsanto Company (G. D. Searle subsidiary).

5. E. I. Du Pont, Biotechnology Systems formed joint venture with Merck & Co. called Du Pont Merck Pharmaceuticals Co. (January 1991).

6. SmithKline Beckman merged into Beecham Group plc to form SmithKline Beecham plc (July 1989).

7. Upjohn Co. merged in fall 1995 with Pharmacia AB of Sweden to form Pharmacia & Upjohn, Inc. (a Delaware corporation based in London and traded in New York, London, and Stockholm).

8. In August 1990, Rhône-Poulenc Group merged its human pharmaceutical business with the Rorer Group, which was named Rhône-Poulenc Rorer, Inc. The Rhône-Poulenc Group holds about 68% ownership in Rhône-Poulenc Rorer, Inc., with the remaining 32% of the shares trading on the NYSE. The Rhône-Poulenc Group has a strong, independent presence in veterinary and agricultural applications of biotechnology.

Decision Overreach as a Reason for Failure

How Organizations Can Overbalance

3

DAVID WILSON

DAVID J. HICKSON

SUSAN J. MILLER

The senior management team of a small brewery in England was contemplating expansion. This family-owned firm had experienced steady growth of sales for its beers throughout the previous 10 years. Most of the directors favored expanding the company, and an unanticipated opportunity to purchase a relatively huge additional brewing plant seemed too good to miss. A vigorous future seemed to stretch ahead. Problems then began to arise, especially cash flow problems, which overwhelmed management. The decision that had purported to drive the company forward could be seen to have done exactly the opposite. It brought a takeover that meant the end of the firm as an independent entity.

This is one of 55 cases of strategic decision making (Miller, Hickson, & Wilson, 1993) currently being studied in an attempt to explain more fully the success or failure of decisions. It was the particular characteristics of this brewery decision that drew attention to it beyond the generality of cases. The decision not only went too far but also went beyond reversal. This chapter discusses the likely constituents and causes of what is called *decision overreach*.

AN ABSENCE OF OVERREACH

There are tangential references in the literature to overreach, but we could find no studies that address the concept directly. Only a few may be thought to have touched on it, if their ideas are stretched to serve that supposition. Greenwood and Hinings (1993), for example, argue that broad "archetypes," such as patterns of beliefs among managers or strategic recipes, can be taken so far as to lead to decision failure, and Dutton and Duncan (1989) focus on the faults of strategic planning. Nutt (1986) emphasizes the role of key executives in holding the process within reach, and Huff and Reger (1987) point to information and decision support systems as keeping things under control. Miller (1990) analyzes how implementation can take a decision forward out of the "failure zone," but not how it gets into that zone.

Nor have others who have searched through and synthesized published research come up with any concept of this kind. Hickson (1987) reviews what had been written on managerial decision-making processes, the subject of decision, and the decision itself. He includes incrementalism, edging forward little by little, but no mention is made of the contrasting big move, let alone of any concept of a decision that goes too far. Listing those few studies that have ventured to project from process to performance, Rajagopalan, Rasheed, and Datta (1993) show that varying combinations of consensus, drive from the top, and decision speed are held to have affected economic and other performance criteria, yet again, they do not mention any concept remotely like overreach. Laroche (1995) takes a more interpretive stance, preferring to regard the idea of a decision as a representation by managers of what they think they are doing, a way "to organize the flow of action" as "participants make their way in the organizational mess." However, nothing emerges from this perspective either, nothing about how decisions that are "socially represented" might be taken too far in this socially constructed reality. The scale and the scope of managerial imagination are not mentioned at all.

Overreach is not to be confused with technical disasters such as the sinking of the Titanic, Three Mile Island, Bhopal, and Chernobyl (e.g., Perrow, 1984; Smith, 1995; Turner, 1978). A managerial overreach, not an operational calamity, is the concern of this chapter

CASES OF OVERREACH

As already stated, attention was drawn to decision overreach by the case of the brewery, conspicuous among the 55 decisions being studied in 14 public and private sector organizations, large and small. These decisions were a representative one third of the 150 cases covered by the "Bradford Studies" (see Cray, Mallory, Butler, Hickson, & Wilson, 1988; Hickson, Butler, Cray, Mallory, & Wilson, 1986). That original research traced and compared processes up to the point of decision—that is, to when implementation was authorized. Data had been collected during the later 1970s and early 1980s. The subset of 55 were revisited during 1990 to 1993 to obtain data on what happened subsequently, during implementation and afterward. The 55 case histories cover periods ranging from 15 to 20 years.

Preparatory to the second period of data collection, telephone inquiries revealed that there were still senior executives in each organization, or otherwise locatable, who recalled meeting members of the research team during the original investigation, who had been closely involved personally in what had happened since then, and who were willing to talk about it.

The interviews with them were semistructured, commencing with a general history of how the decision had been implemented, the sequence of subsequent events, and a listing of who and which departments or other interests from the managerial echelons had been involved. This also included external interests, such as suppliers, customers, and competitors. Interviews continued with open questions about the success of the decision and reasons for success (or lack of it). A number of rating scales were completed, the results of which are not pertinent to this chapter. Typically, interviews lasted from 1 to 2 hours, and some were longer. The essentials of what was said were noted on semistructured interview guides rather than using a tape recorder; earlier experience had shown that informants were frequently reluctant to record occasionally sensitive material verbatim. Where available, archival data such as internal reports and documents were also examined.

Discovering what came to be called overreach was a case of classic serendipity. There was no such idea in mind when the research began. Cases had been analyzed and reanalyzed, discussed and rediscussed, many times. Gradually, they had been grouped in terms of their successfulness, or lack of it, in implementation and the subsequent outcomes. There were quite a number of failures or, at least, performances disappointing to the managements responsible. There were various kinds of production problems, market changes, failures to sell, and lack of profitability. Yet the decision by the brewery was none of these. The market generally was good, and sales were rising. The problem was simply the purchase of a huge additional plant. Again and again, discussion returned to the case history, until it was recognized for what it was and thereafter seen in a fresh light.

Then, reexamination of the other 54 cases in this light, deliberately seeking any more instances of overreach, found 1 other decision in an engineering factory with similar features, although not so pronounced as in the brewery. The brewery decision remains the exemplar, the extreme, or what can be termed an *ideal type*.

The two firms in which the overreach decisions were made are given the fictitious names of Thomson, the brewery, and Jacobite, the engineering factory. In addition to the managers interviewed during 1978 and 1977 in the firms, respectively, about the original making of the decisions (Hickson et al., 1986), those now interviewed during 1990 and 1992 were, in Thomson, two of the small number of directors—being the former managing director (or president), who was visited at his home, and the former financial controller, who was seen at the firm to which he had moved. In Jacobite, they were the financial controller, the commercial manager, the quality control manager, and the former chairman and managing director (president) who, too, was visited at home. Some were seen once; others more than once. All had been included among the original informants. The two case histories are as follows.

Thomson

Thomson was formed early in the 19th century as a small family-owned brewery. When first visited, it still employed only 35 people and was producing only a small quantity of beer. However, demand for quality beer was increasing rapidly, so the firm's owners and managers were considering what could be done to expand production. During these deliberations, an opportunity arose to purchase a closed-down brewery some distance away. This would increase capacity to almost eight times current production, and there was some doubt whether or not this relatively colossal increase was manageable and necessary. Doubts were short-lived, however. Only one nonexecutive director stood his ground in opposition and resigned. The cost of acquiring this eightfold capacity was substantially less than the cost of even just doubling production on the existing site. Furthermore, it could be acquired right away, avoiding prolonged construction. The only problem was raising the money. The banks were unhappy because Thomson already had a substantial overdraft and they felt that the company had not really fully worked through the financial implications. There was no sufficiently detailed business plan or profitability projection. Eventually, one bank was persuaded to finance the acquisition.

Problems began to arise, however, within months of the start of production. The volume of beer could be brewed and got out, but the scale of what had been taken on proved too great to manage. In a plant of this size, more technical problems arose than had been anticipated. The boiler and the lifting gear were unreliable. The effluent treatment plant became inadequate for this volume under stricter government regulation.

But more than anything, the inflow of revenue at this scale of operation was slower and with smaller margins than Thomson's management, used to a much smaller and tighter operation, had envisaged. They did not have enough capital to finance themselves through the resultant cash flow crisis. In brief, over several years, this led to their succumbing to successive takeovers and their brand's being absorbed into the capacity of a larger competitor. They had overbalanced in reaching for such an immense relative increase in production volume, when they might have sustained a lesser increase.

Ten years after the decision to buy the additional brewery, Thomson was reduced to a nominal shell of a firm with only a little symbolic specialist brewing in their original tiny premises. They were back to where they started, but minus their independence.

Jacobite

Jacobite had long held a premier position supplying components mainly to a small number of well-known industrial buyers that assembled Jacobite's precision engineering items into household name products. Their decision was a relatively massive investment in new buildings to house a new plant.

Pressed by rising demand, top management had debated ways of adding to existing space and so embarked on a series of costing exercises. These involved consultation with external organizations such as banks, major customers, and equipment suppliers, as well as with the internal functions of production, planning, engineering, sales, and finance. Discussions were led by Jacobite's vigorous chairman, who was closely involved personally. It was decided to build an extensive new factory on a contiguous site. This was a big decision in two ways. First, it assumed an increase in sales volume of up to 50% and, second, it was expensive, incurring substantial debts for the company to pay for it. All senior managers in Jacobite were in favor of the decision. Confidence in the future was high.

However, sales volumes peaked at no more than a 20% increase, whereas several years of economic recession forced drastic cost cutting. Jacobite was threatened with closure as capital ran out. The large site and premises, with the production equipment that had been installed, were unsustainable. Financial collapse was only narrowly averted, under new ownership, by halving the premises and radically changing ways of working.

The bulk of the older buildings were sold, and all the manufacturing equipment was moved into the newer buildings. Just-in-time production and cell-form manufacturing on more modern equipment replaced previous large batch and mass production methods. Soon, 200 employees were turning out what 700 had done before. From one point of view, this was a turn-around success story. From another, the company had come close to collapse because it had gone too far in expanding production floor space beyond what was needed. The original premises with relatively small improvements could have been big enough for the new equipment and production methods.

There was in Jacobite, unlike Thomson, an element of market miscalculation, but as in Thomson, the scale of their move was relatively too big.

■ CONSTITUENTS OF DECISION OVERREACH

What do these two cases have in common? First, the move that was made was relatively huge, disproportionate, more so for Thomson than for Jacobite. Second, it was irreversible, wholly so for Thomson, which could not recoup and was reduced to a mere front organization, not quite so irrevocably for Jacobite. Disproportionality and irreversibility appear to be the two characteristics that distinguish overreach.

Disproportionality denotes the scale of the move decided on, relative to the size and scope of the organization. It could be regarded as inherent in any doubling or more than doubling of ongoing activity or capacity. It corresponds to Ross and Staw's (1993) description of "the sheer size of the venture relative to the total size of the firm" (p. 723). The means of assessing disproportionality may vary from sector to sector and from organization to organization, but both cases reported here were described as being for high stakes. At Thomson, the owner-managers were venturing their entire company from the start. The stakes could not have been higher. They took on no less than eight times their firm's previous capacity, wholly disproportionate. Jacobite did not go anything like so far. Although they more or less doubled their manufacturing capacity, they did survive—just—the subsequent crisis. Had they reached further they would have probably gone under.

Irreversibility is the second constituent of overreach. It is the critical one for failure. Conceivably, a decision that was only disproportionate might succeed if all went well. Conceivably, too, such a decision might not become catastrophic even should all not go well *provided* it was possible to draw back, to retract. But when in each case reported here all did not go well, management was in an irreversible situation. At Thomson, this was wholly so, for their new plant's previous ties with sales outlets had been severed, and without these it was unsalable. In England, each main brewery controlled inns and public houses and so ensured basic direct sales, as distinct from those through the wider retail trade. So

Thomson was stuck with its acquisition. Jacobite's decision was not so absolutely irreversible. By halving premises (a reverse sidestep, so to speak), reducing the workforce from 750 to 200 employees, and rethinking and reequipping its production operations, the company was able to get by.

OVERREACH AS A SPECIAL CASE

Our database contains four other decisions by manufacturers that turned out very badly but that did not have the features of overreach. In the first case, a huge multinational, one of the leaders in an oligopolistic world market, a decision was taken to back the development of a new material in which their established principal product would be used, alongside their other continuing main outputs. After the investment of tens of millions of pounds over many years and an apparently initially successful marketing, it eventually became clear that technical limitations to the new material would restrict its use to far less than had been assumed. So the rights to it were sold off to other firms for limited purposes.

A manufacturer of industrial chemicals decided to add to its product range a new chemical of a kind it had not handled before. The market looked promising. However, development and manufacturing costs were higher than expected, and it took longer than expected to reach a financially worthwhile volume of production. Before this was attained, if it ever could have been, cost cutting and a change in market strategy closed down this emerging product. Another poor decision by the management of the same company was to purchase land adjacent to their main industrial site on the presumption that it would be needed to expand their plant. Although plans for expansion were drawn up, the land was found to be difficult to build on, and it proved cheaper to buy an existing extra plant elsewhere and rent the land for farming.

Fourth, a manufacturer of model kits decided to add to its largely plastic-based kits a range made in a specific type of wood. Additional premises were rented on a government-subsidized, employment-creating scheme. But the wood, which had to be imported, proved to be diseased, and simultaneously, demand for wooden kits began to tail off. The costs of the extra premises could not be sustained. Fortunately, they had been rented, not bought, and although the terms of the state subsidy required each tenant to find a substitute tenant if they withdrew, a substitute was found.

All these four cases were run-of-the-mill failures. They failed, or at least underperformed, because of technical or market reasons or both. Relative to the business concerned, they were significant and serious, yet still well within the means of the firms. They were not disproportionate.

Nor were they irreversible. What was done could be disposed of or closed down, and without undue strain or undue risk.

Many important bad decisions have also been made much of in the literature. For example, Hage (1980) cites Ford's failed Edsel car, IBM's mistaken computer choices, and Du Pont's Corfam shoe as instances of American high-risk decisions that did not come off. Valentin (1994) describes the failure of a rapid expansion of retail outlets by Boise Cascade Corporation, also in the United States, within an increasingly "unwieldy conglomerate."

Overreach is something distinct from this more usual genre of failure. It is a special case of failure. It is probably not a common reason for failure, and it is not a necessary element in failure. It is one in which disproportionality and irreversibility stand out and magnify the risk. Many decisions go wrong because of technical difficulties or market shortfalls such as beset Thomson and Jacobite, and others do so because of the kind of overwhelming financial squeeze that was the principal cause of calamity for both firms, but it was the disproportionality and irreversibility of what they did that laid them open, unduly so, to these perils.

They could not be accused of poor management generally. Both managements had a creditable record. Their other decisions that were studied went well. Thomson had, while still small, computerized and begun laboratory-based quality control in a way that was advanced for a small brewery. Jacobite set up a new marketing department and introduced new material into its components, and it, too, had computerized. Neither firm appeared to be in the condition of continual poor performance, vividly depicted by Meyer and Zucker (1989) as "permanent failure." Their managements were not breaking out of that condition, which these authors hypothesize can be a successful breakout but that can equally be an "outright failure." The decisions in Thomson and Jacobite were not of that kind. Theirs were moves from a successful position to take advantage of buoyant demand. It was more likely that past success disposed their managements to the "immoderation" of risky, proactive innovation, as against the caution that can also follow success, according to Miller (1994). Even so, overreach is not just another name for bad management.

Nor is overreach the same as escalation. Escalation of commitment means going on and on, usually in a multichoice escalation, as Lipshitz (1995) has defined it, or perhaps a single-option escalation along a path without turnings, as he contends occurred in American decisions on Operation Desert Storm in the Gulf War with Iraq in 1990. Something of the sort happened also in the 1980s with the burgeoning aspirations and costs of the Expo 86 exhibition intended to boost the standing and economy of British Columbia in Canada (Ross & Staw, 1986). This is the "pouring good money after bad" fiasco, getting ever deeper into the "big muddy" (Staw, 1976). It is persisting with a course of action that seems to be going wrong in the hope that more effort and resources will put it right—whereas overreach is not escalation, but one big move.

Nor is it a big move into the unknown. The managements of Thomson and Jacobite knew very well what they were about. Between them, they each had decades of experience in their industries, and what they did was nothing new. They were doing exactly what the famous counsel given by Peters and Waterman (1982) would have had them do—"stick to the knitting" that they knew so well. It was the disproportionality of what they did that took them out of their depth and its irreversibility that prevented Thomson—and Jacobite almost—from getting back out.

In short, an overreach decision has a relative scale and an irretrievability that marks it out from the commonplace extension of core business. That more usual extension is likely to bolster survival, according to Mitchell and Singh (1995), whereas overreach jeopardizes survival.

CONTRIBUTORY FACTORS

Were there any circumstances that may have disposed the managements of Thomson, and to a lesser extent Jacobite, to decide on a step too far? Were there factors that disposed them and not other firms to overreach? For as mentioned earlier, their businesses were not in difficulties. They were not precipitated into rash moves by crises. Ruling that out, therefore, what else could have contributed?

First, both companies were on the small side. Then, these decisions were taken quickly and with a lack of foresight. Finally, did overfamiliarity carry with it an intrinsic overconfidence? These four probable contributory factors are now considered:

1. Management size
2. Decision process duration
3. Lack of foresight
4. Overfamiliarity

We do not suppose this list is exhaustive. It is what attracts attention in the two cases of overreach examined here.

Management Size

Thomson had 35 employees and Jacobite came down to 200, although when the decision was made, they had close to 750. But each firm was small enough for each top management echelon to be small, half a dozen men at most, dominated at Thomson by two cousins from the owning family, especially the elder, and at Jacobite by the strong, driving figure of the chairman and managing director who had led the way for decades. Did mutual supportiveness and pressure in small groups with years of stable membership engender blinkered "groupthink," as Janis (1972) called it? At Jacobite, there were no doubts about the decision that was taken. At Thomson, a third cousin who expressed doubts was overridden and left the scene.

Eisenhardt and Bourgeois (1988) found evidence in microcomputer firms that power sharing by CEOs and a consequent minimum of interpersonal competitive politics were associated with good performance. However, it might be that in the overreach cases, the men at the very top dominated the small managerial cadres too much, although it is difficult to be conclusive about this.

In any case, the managements of small organizations are less able to accumulate resources that are not immediately used in the conduct of everyday business. They have little "organizational slack" (March & Simon, 1958, p. 126). Large organizations can build up slack and so go further before their managers begin to go too far. This accords with Singh's (1986) study of organizational performance (using data from 173 U.S. and Canadian managers). He found that the key variables contributing to good performance were slack and decentralization. So small firms are less buffered by reserves, as the managements of Thomson and Jacobite found to their cost.

Decision Process Duration

The 150 decisions studied by Hickson et al. (1986) were arrived at, on average, in 12.4 months, and so, almost exactly, were those reported by Mallory (1987) and by Hickson and Arruda (1996). Against this strongly supported mean for British managements, the two overreach decisions are very quick. From earliest recalled mention of the possibility to the decision (that is, to implementation's being agreed and authorized) each took 3 months, only a quarter as long. Speed may also be haste. Thomson's managing director at the time said, in retrospect, "Really, we seized an opportunity rather than made a planned decision. . . . We felt we could hardly turn it [the purchase of the brewery] down. We were planning to spend £150,000 expanding our own brewery and the acquisition only cost £115,000."

Eisenhardt (1989) shows startlingly fast decisions in her eight microcomputer businesses, in times ranging from 1.5 to 12 months. The contrast with the range from 1 month up to 48 months, 4 years, reported by Hickson et al. (1986) is striking. All eight cases reach a decision in less than the Hickson et al. (1986) mean time. For Eisenhardt (1989), speed is good in a "high-velocity environment." However, that is what limits generalization of her finding. Speed is not necessarily good everywhere. Thomson and Jacobite were in vigorous but not dynamically "high-tech" industries. Beyond that, they were in a different society. The faster American approach to management compared with the British is consistently asserted (see Hickson & Pugh, 1995, for summary portraits of both).

Hence, it is more likely that speed in the overreach decisions allowed vital information to be overlooked or insufficiently considered. Although in Eisenhardt's (1989) particular industry, "fast decision makers use more, not less, information," that was almost certainly not so in Thomson and Jacobite.

Lack of Foresight

Moving fast, perhaps in haste, also leaves little time for "prévoyance," as the French doyen of management writers Fayol (1949) put it—in other words, less time to plan and foresee.

As noted, Thomson's decision was opportunist rather than planned. They never foresaw their difficulty in managing the transition from a very small capacity to a larger volume, especially how much working capital would be needed and that getting it would mean loss of control over the business. Jacobite management was more careful, with the chairman involved in every detail, even to personally designing the pattern of the tiling in the new canteen. However, this care and concern detail had to with the planning of the form of the new premises and the laying out within them of the existing production technology. It did not extend to foreseeing coming radical changes in technology or to widely scanning the market because they relied on broad assurances by their main industrial buyers of continuing and larger orders, without themselves checking further.

Small Management Size, Short Decision Duration, and Lack of Foresight Acting Together?

Here, the likely interaction of size, duration, and prévoyance becomes evident. If the organization is small, there is less slack in every sense to enable prévoyance. There is less money to pay for research or advice; fewer individuals to prepare financial, capacity, or sales forecasts; and fewer people or none with the specialist training required for these tasks. It is also likely that there is no one at the top of the organization sufficiently removed from daily operational problems to enable strategic-level assessments to be made free of day-to-day distractions, and "groupthink" may trap those involved. If, then, the decision is made in a short time, and especially if in haste, a thorough scan of what lies ahead and an attempt to think as carefully as possible about whatever may be plannable are even less likely. Therefore, small size, short duration, and scanty planning are likely to act together in creating the circumstances in which management is most prone to decision overreach.

The contrast can be seen in the other poor decisions in manufacturers among our own cases, where lack of success was not due to overreach. The two new product launches were in much larger companies, took much longer to make (between 3 and 4 years), and were comprehensively planned. Although the decision in one of the same companies to purchase adjacent land was made more quickly, the land had always been there, physically visible every day, and this simple contingency purchase did not require any detailed data or planning. All three failed, nevertheless. The point is that there were no factors conducive to failure through overreach.

The fourth decision, venturing into wooden model kits made in additional premises, did, however, show predisposing features. It was in a relatively small business of 300 employees. It was made very quickly, in no more than a month or so. It was opportunistic, prompted by the sales director's chancing on cheap assignments of wood more than by carefully weighing the merits of the venture. Perhaps management was lucky. Had it not been that the first deliveries of wood were diseased, would they have gone on too far? Had it not been that the state offered subsidized buildings for rent, would they have bought premises rather than renting and found it more difficult to draw back? Was this an overreach might-have-been?

Overfamiliarity

The final contributory factor we have suggested as disposing a management to decision overreach is overfamiliarity. This is more speculative. We have no explicit evidence for it. It appears a self-evident concomitant of the other three factors.

The decisions in Thomson and Jacobite were an extension or expansion of the existing core businesses that managers knew well. None of these decisions moved outside the accustomed "knitting" (Peters & Waterman, 1982). Unlike the Boise Cascade Corporation that changed the pattern in the knitting by shifting its building materials division from principally wholesale supplies into consumer do-it-yourself retailing

(Valentin, 1994), Thomson and Jacobite went on doing exactly as they had always done. Their managements knew all about brewing and engineering. They were not newcomers to the business and had many years of successful decision making behind them. All had been in the industry and the firm for a long time, most of them for life.

Could it have been that, as a result, they were less alert to the novel, nonproduct elements in what they decided? Probably they were overconfident. Probably, too, this led to what has been termed "risky shift" decision making (Stoner, 1968), a shared state of mind that shifts attention from the degree of risk entailed and so is more open to failure. So those in control of Thomson and Jacobite underrated or did not sufficiently reckon with the risks inherent in what they meant to do. They risked too much because they knew too well. They were overfamiliar with their businesses.

Doing more of the same has been proposed by many authors, such as Quinn (1980), as a recipe for achieving progressive and relatively less risky change. The reasoning is that the more familiar managers are with their products and markets, the less the uncertainty associated with strategic change. If this is in general a good thing, then there can be too much of it. Sticking to what is familiar can carry with it the bounding of awareness. Managers and organizations can become locked into particular frames of reference. These can bind awareness, effectively preventing managers from seeing what might go wrong until it is too late. They can also lead, perhaps, to what Grinyer and McKiernan (1994) term the "hubris" effect. This happens when successful managements, as those of Thomson and Jacobite were, develop pride in their ways of doing business and assume that these will always work in the future. Such misplaced confidence may be a result of managers' being too familiar with a business and not questioning their actions until after substantial commitments have been made. They do not see that their "sense making" may be gradually ceasing to make sense (Weick, 1995).

CONCLUSION

The two cases of failure described in this chapter are at the decision level of analysis. They are examples of failure by managers in exercising "strategic choice" (Child, 1972). Although there are only two such cases in our sample, we cannot avoid the conclusion that analyzing failure at the decisional level can help understanding of organizational failure. In each case, the outcome of the particular decision imperiled the whole organization. Perhaps overreach decision processes are the most likely to

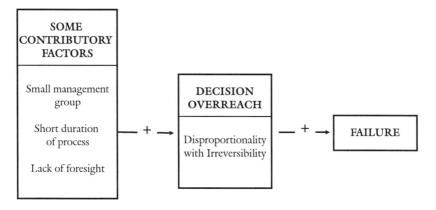

Figure 3.1. A Model of Overreach

threaten the survival of the whole organization. The other cases of decision failure in our sample never threatened overall survival of the firm, despite being severe setbacks in their own right. They failed because of one or more of the predisposing factors cited by Zucker (1991b), which include little or no investment in new technology, inadequate investment in research and development, and failing to achieve sufficient market penetration through advertising or brand strength. The two overreach patterns of failure are different, in that these "usual" factors for failure are not present in either case.

Figure 3.1 diagrams the model of overreach deduced from our cases. It postulates that both disproportionality and irreversibility are necessary, neither being sufficient on its own. It implies that there will be multiple factors contributing—in other words, a multivariate explanation—and stipulates the four factors identified in this chapter without being able, from just two cases, to estimate their proportionate contributions.

Both the cases analyzed come from manufacturing organizations. Are manufacturers more prone to overbalance in this way? We have no cases of overreach from 31 decisions in service organizations, but 2 come from 24 decisions in manufacturers. In the absence of a broader study of manufacturers, we cannot be sure of any predilections. However, given that comparatively more decisions in manufacturers require substantial capital investment in tangible assets such as buildings and plants (e.g., Hickson et al., 1986; Pettigrew & Whipp, 1991), these may be more open than most decisions to being irrevocably overblown.

It is tempting to speculate about the influence of leadership on the contributory factors. The popular press and much management literature (e.g., Bryman, 1992; Shackleton, 1995) make much of the leader as a cause for failure (and success) of an organization. According to this view, failure is an attribute of the individual rather than a decisional or organizational feature. Wise leaders bring success, and poor leaders make foolish and ill-informed judgments, increasing the likelihood of failure. There is some limited evidence of this from our two cases. In Jacobite, the strong driving influence of the chairman and managing director was a key component of the strategic choice made. In the brewery (Thomson), leadership was shared between two powerful cousins from the owning family. In both cases, these leaders held sway over only small top-management groups. There was little countervailing power to redirect the choices made. They were unlikely to bring in outsiders to dilute the overfamiliarity with the industry. As Strebel (1995) argues, if organizations are going to avoid failure, they need entrepreneurial champions to maintain innovation and creativity. We would add that organizations may be at risk from "blinkered champions" whose parameters are too focused or short-term.

Lindblom (1959) and Quinn (1978) both advocated incremental steps for reducing uncertainty in decision processes. Such small steps also build in the ability to retract the decision should it begin to go off course. It has never been possible to define how big or how small an incremental step is. However, it is possible in the overreach cases to see what it is not. The eightfold and twofold increases decided on in Thomson and Jacobite were not on the scale of increments on what had been done before. They were on a far larger proportionate scale. They correspond rather to Ross and Staw's (1993) description of one-way big steps that, once the organization has got moving, are almost impossible to stop.

Seeing failure at the decision level of analysis allows us to see more than the polar extremes of market selectivity (survival of the fittest firms) on the one hand, and the individual characteristics of effective leaders on the other. Of course, we need more cases of overreach to generalize, but in the two presented here, the prevailing patterns for avoiding this kind of failure are not to act too hastily, to plan carefully so that all aspects can be considered, and not to rely on too much personal knowledge derived from previous experience. This seems to be especially so for smaller organizations.

These findings might even be taken to imply that restless entrepreneurs and strong charismatic leaders may make for a colorful scenario, but they are likely to risk overbalancing the organization. Is uncertainty reduction in organizations best achieved after all by cooler, impersonal means?

"Tales From the Grave"

Organizations' Accounts of Their Own Demise

MARK HAGER
JOSEPH GALASKIEWICZ
WOLFGANG BIELEFELD
JOEL PINS

Although there has been an increase in scholarly interest and writing on the subject of organizational mortality or failure (see Carroll & Hannan, 1995; Hannan & Carroll, 1992), little of this has dealt systematically with nonprofit organizations (see Baum & Oliver, 1991; Bielefeld, 1992, 1994; Bowen, Nygren, Turner, & Duffy, 1994, chap. 6; Selle & Oymyr, 1992; Singh, Tucker, & House, 1986, for exceptions). This is unfortunate, because the nonprofit sector faced a series of financial constraints brought on by cutbacks in public expenditures during the Reagan administration, continued low levels of public expenditures during the Bush administration, and recessions in the early 1980s and 1990s. In addition, the sector's mission and accountability have increasingly been scrutinized by the public, by government, and by business (Estes, Binney, & Bergthold, 1989; Goss, 1993), and major institutional funders have,

AUTHORS' NOTE: Funding for this research was provided by the Nonprofit Sector Research Fund of the Aspen Institute, the National Science Foundation, the Northwest Area Foundation, the Program on Nonprofit Organizations at Yale University, and the University of Minnesota Graduate School. Thanks to Phuong Phan, Yoshito Ishio, Alisa Potter, Naomi Kaufman, and Kay Schaffer for their capable research assistance.

in some cases, reevaluated and changed their funding priorities (Millar, 1991; Millar & Moore, 1991).

Data gathered as part of a panel study of the nonprofit sector in Minneapolis-St. Paul, Minnesota, between 1980 and 1994 (Galaskiewicz, 1985, 1990; Galaskiewicz & Bielefeld, 1990, in press) provide an opportunity to examine nonprofit mortality (see also Bielefeld, 1994). This is one of the few studies in the United States that has followed a broad-based population of nonprofit organizations over an extended period of time and the only one we know of that returned to conduct exit interviews with those organizations that ceased to operate during the course of the study. After discussing the concept of death and reviewing the literature explaining death, we will describe our data in detail and commence with our analysis. First, we describe the different ways in which organizations in our panel "died." Second, we compare the organizations that ceased operations with those that survived for four time periods. Third, we summarize some of the reasons for organizational closing provided by those affiliated with the dead organizations.

▨ THE CONCEPT OF ORGANIZATIONAL DEATH

The prevalence of life cycle and ecological models of change in organization science has produced several generations of theorists who think and write about organizations in terms of life metaphors (Tsoukas, 1991; Van de Ven & Poole, 1995). According to many accounts, organizations are born, grow, age to adolescence and maturity, become set in their ways, and eventually die. Although organizations certainly are not alive in any meaningful biological sense, few people question the use of these metaphors in describing organizational life cycles (for an exception, see Young, 1988). Nonetheless, our metaphors strongly condition how we think about organizations. Theorists are preoccupied with when organizations are "born," what species they are (their forms), and when they have changed enough to be termed *dead*.

The vagaries of biological metaphors aside, the concept of "death" for an organization is not as straightforward as one might assume. It could be argued that an organization is dead when it ceases operation, loses its corporate identity, loses the capacity to govern itself, or experiences any combination of these situations. Multiple criteria are needed, because many organizations continue to operate beyond what might be considered a terminal event (e.g., bankruptcy, loss of the corporate charter, a change in ownership, etc.). Marple (1982) notes that from 1865 to 1910, most small railroad companies were absorbed into railroad empires. Because few railroads died outright, the only meaningful way to study railroad death is to account systematically for the mergers. Is merger a death? Freeman, Carroll, and Hannan (1983) addressed this issue in their study of newspapers and labor unions. Organization exits from these populations were coded according to whether the exit was due to dissolution or merger. In their stochastic models, merger rates are initially lower than dissolution rates; however, merger rates exceeded dissolution rates within 10 years. They conclude that mergers and dissolutions are different, although they both happen in theoretically predictable ways, given the age, size, and structure of the organization.

It is also important not to equate death with failure. Carroll and Delacroix (1982) note that "many merger partners are highly successful." They explain that "success makes these organizations attractive candidates for merger opportunities. Consequently, the death of a formal organization does not logically imply anything about its previous failure or success in performance" (p. 170). Some organizations close when their mission is fulfilled, further confounding researchers who look for the bullet that ended the organization.[1]

Milofsky (1987) argues that neighborhood-based organizations may decide to close if this action is in the best interest of the community. "Organizational death," he writes, "may be a viable solution to certain problems as long as it contributes to the overall well-being of the community" (p. 278). On the other hand, some organizations seem to be "permanently failing" (Meyer & Zucker, 1989), yet continue to operate for years on end.

Clearly, the definition of organizational death is not without its difficulties. In the course of our research, we made the distinction between organizational transformation and closure. On the one hand, when an organization was removed from the panel, because it merged with another organization, left the area, was acquired (but retained its governance structure), or changed status (e.g., nonprofit to for-profit), we referred to that organization as *transformed*. On the other hand, those organizations that truly disbanded—that is, ceased operations altogether or dissolved their board of directors—were referred to as *closed*. In this chapter, we focus our attention principally on the latter and equate death with closure.

WHY DO ORGANIZATIONS DIE?

Empirical literature suggests a host of reasons why organizations close, including youth (Carroll, 1983; Carroll & Delacroix, 1982), adolescence (Brüderl, Preisendörfer, & Ziegler, 1992; Brüderl & Schüssler, 1990), density and competition (Carroll & Hannan, 1989; Hannan & Carroll, 1992; Swaminathan & Wiedenmayer, 1991), size (Freeman et al., 1983; Wholey,

Christianson, & Sanchez, 1992), and lack of institutional linkages (Baum & Oliver, 1991). These causes can be roughly divided into internal and environmental (external) factors, depending on whether the cause stems from the organization itself or from the environment in which it is embedded.

Internal Causes of Organizational Failure

Numerous studies of nonprofit populations have found that organizational age and size are directly related to organizational survival (Baum & Oliver, 1991; Bielefeld, 1994; Bowen et al., 1994; Selle & Oymyr, 1992; see also Singh et al., 1986); however, few studies have examined *why* age and size increase the chances of survival. In 1965, Stinchcombe (1965) wrote a profoundly influential essay that argued why younger organizations die sooner than older organizations. In sum, he argued that younger organizations have less experience, fewer slack resources, fewer constituencies that could rally behind it in support, and less social capital (networking) than older organizations. It is not so much that the organization is young per se but that it has not yet acquired the capital, knowledge, and resources that enable older organizations to ride out hard times. The key is routinization, and the ability of an organization to overcome the "liability of newness" is directly related to the establishment of routine and reliable personnel-personnel and personnel-client relationships.

Hannan and Freeman (1984) agree that organizations with high reliability, a low variance in performance, and high accountability—the ability to account rationally for organizational actions—are less likely to die. They argue that this makes an organization more legitimate and thus less likely to be "selected out" of the population. As organizations get older, they learn how to reproduce structure and thus become more legitimate, albeit also more structurally inert. Hannan and Freeman go on to argue that the worst thing an older organization can do is try to change itself. At that point, it sets the "liability of newness clock" back to zero.

In sum, many researchers have found an inverse relationship between organizational death and both size and age. We interpret this in two ways. First, conditions in younger and smaller organizations are in flux. Thus, operating procedures, personnel, and even goals are constantly changing. The organization is unable to establish routines and values (Tushman & Romanelli, 1985). This takes its toll internally, but it also means that the organization has yet to establish its legitimacy. Second, managers in younger and smaller organization have less expertise and thus are less able to control their organization. They don't have the capacity to resolve conflicts and power struggles, to properly conduct financial affairs, or to create a sense of shared values in the organization in terms of clarity of mission. Because the situation is so much in flux and managers lack expertise, organizations that are smaller and younger are more likely to cease operations.

External Causes of Organizational Failure

Organizational ecologists have been very successful in explaining organizational births and deaths. By now, students are familiar with the relationship between population density and organizational births and deaths (see Hannan & Carroll, 1992, for an overview of this literature). The denser the population of organizations, the higher the birth rate until at a certain point births drop off and the rate of organizational death increases. In other words, the relationship between density and birth rates is nonmonotonic with the form of an inverted U, whereas the relationship between density and death rates is nonmonotonic with the form of a U. Ecologists argue that the first effect is due to the increasing legitimacy of a specific organizational form as the population increases, which in turn encourages more new organizations to come on board. The latter is due, first, to the liability of newness (Stinchcombe, 1965) and, second, to population density reaching the carrying capacity. At this point, organizational death is an adjustment to the limited stock of resources in a given environmental niche and increased competition (Hannan & Carroll, 1992). Thus, as population fields become more crowded, the increased competition results in organizations' dying.

Alternatively, there may be a change in market conditions. The demand for goods and services can change over time, and if the demand for an organization's goods and services decreases, the organization can suffer severe hardships (Delacroix, Swaminathan, & Solt, 1989). For nonprofits, this translates into fewer consumers of organizational services, decreased program service revenues, fewer major funders available, decreased contributions, or some combination of these losses. Because these organizations can receive contributions from third parties, conditions in their donor markets are as important as conditions in their consumer markets. Shifts in demand for nonprofit goods and services can come about for a number of reasons—emergence of new social problems, changes in government priorities, and so on.

Resource-dependence theory emphasizes organizational adaptation (or lack thereof) to environmental contingencies. The emphasis here is on environmental scanning and strategic action (Burt, 1983a; Pfeffer & Salancik, 1978). Resource-dependence theory is concerned with critical resource flows—information, money, referrals, moral support—and argues that, to succeed, organizations need to take actions to ensure that they have access to these resources. An important consideration, therefore, is whether or not an organization formulates and successfully carries out co-optation strategies. Although reference to strategies calls to mind internal factors, the theory focuses on organizational control of external constraints and opportunities. Resource-dependence theory leads us to expect that those organizations that establish and maintain relationships with their communities, funders, other service providers, and professional associations would, as a consequence, be more likely to survive.

However, institutional theory has also addressed the issue of organizational survival. Baum and Oliver (1991) argue that

> an organization is more likely to survive if it obtains legitimacy, social support, and approbation from external constituents of its institutional environment. This external legitimation elevates the organization's status in the community, facilitates resource acquisition, and deflects questions about an organization's rights and competence to provide specific products or services. (p. 187)

The key is for organizations to accrue the referents of legitimacy that would signal to the broader community that it is a credible and trustworthy organization and a worthy recipient of community support (see also Suchman, 1995). Consequently, organizations that are externally legitimated are more likely to survive.

Institutional theory is also sensitive to the normative controls that external actors can exercise over nonprofits. DiMaggio and Powell (1983) describe how organizations are influenced by governmental agencies, funders, professional associations, and others in their social networks. To this list we might add the mass media, local politicians, parent organizations, and other nonprofit organizations. DiMaggio and Powell were particularly concerned about how these external actors often force organizations to adopt forms that conform to external expectations but that are highly inefficient for the organization. To the extent that organizations are vulnerable to the normative control of external actors, the nonprofit's autonomy is threatened and so is its survival.

In sum, we can differentiate four broad environmental influences on organizational survival. (a) Ecological theory highlights the importance of competition and the carrying capacity of resource environment. (b) Market theory focuses on the demand for organizations' goods and services. (c) Resource-dependency theory examines how well organizations maintain contacts with key funders, interlock with competitors, share information, and stay connected to developments in the community and in professional associations. Finally, (d) institutional theory points to the importance of a positive image and legitimacy and the dangers of becoming too vulnerable to outside normative controls.

▒ DATA, METHODS, AND VARIABLES

We developed a population of public charities for the Minneapolis-St. Paul metropolitan area from the *Cumulative List of Organizations* published by the Internal Revenue Service. This publication lists all the organizations given public charity status under IRS code 501(c)(3) and the city or town where they were headquartered. It was current for October 31, 1979. We identified all the organizations headquartered in the Twin Cities five-county metro area (Anoka, Dakota, Hennepin, Ramsey, and Washington Counties). We excluded private and corporate foundations (although community and operating foundations were included) and churches, congregations, assemblies, and any other explicitly religious organizations (although we included organizations that provided charitable services that were affiliated with some church or denomination—e.g., the University of St. Thomas or Lutheran Social Services). Altogether we had 1,601 organizations in our sampling frame.

We grouped organizations into functional categories (e.g., health/welfare, education, legal, housing/urban development, mass media, recreational, cultural, civic, environmental, and miscellaneous) assigning organizations on the basis of name and descriptions that were available in community directories. If we were still unsure about an organization, we called it. If that failed, we assigned it to an "unidentified" category. After all organizations had been grouped, we drew a one-in-five (20%) stratified systematic sample. This produced a target of 326 organizations to interview in 1980.

We interviewed 229 organizations in late 1980 and early 1981 (70.2%). Most of the missing organizations simply could not be located, or we were unable to track down a contact person even though we were able to find an address for the organization (typically a private residence). Forty-two organizations in 1980 fell into that category. The other organizations were truly defunct; and some were only paper organizations (e.g., trusts). A small minority, 15, refused to be interviewed.

Of the original 229 nonprofits interviewed in 1980-81, we reinterviewed 201 in late 1984 and early 1985 and 174 in late 1988 and early 1989. In 1993 and 1994, we returned to the field and interviewed 162 organizations. By the end of our study period—early 1995—155 organizations were still in our panel. Thus, we had five points in time: 1980 (229 organizations), 1984 (201 organizations), 1988 (174 organizations), 1992 (166 organizations), and 1994 (155). This results in an attrition rate of 32.3% with 74 organizations exiting our panel.

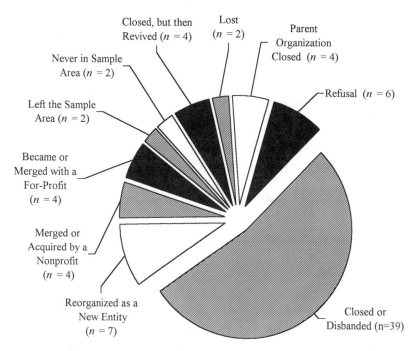

Figure 4.1. Representation of the Distribution of Exits From Panel
(*N* = 74)

Figure 4.1 provides an overview of those organizations that exited our panel. Clearly, organizations left the panel in a variety of different ways. For example, an organization "closed or disbanded" when a knowledgeable informant (usually the former top administrator or a former board member) verified that two conditions had been met: no program or board activity had occurred during the previous year and none was expected during the following year. Informants felt comfortable with these criteria and all felt that our definition of death (or termination) corresponded to their definition—that is, that organizations we believed to be dead were believed to be dead by our informants.

Organizations also left the panel for other reasons as well. In some cases, organizations were transformed into new organizational entities. Transformation can range from legal redefinition of an organization to a change significant enough to justify the claim that a "different" organization has emerged and replaced its predecessor (Wilson, 1985). One example is when a nonprofit organization changes its status to a for-profit organization. Although the legal change is clear, the "new" organization may or may not operate essentially the same as it did while it was a nonprofit.

One might suspect that the existence of new ownership rights would lead to operational differences, but this is an empirical question. The same kinds of considerations are relevant for mergers or acquisitions. These can be very complex phenomena, whose study in the nonprofit sector is just beginning (Singer & Yankey, 1991; Wernet & Jones, 1992). From the legal standpoint, again, things are relatively clear; an organization ceases to exist. However, even though ownership rights are not an issue, the same resources either may or may not exist in their previous (or any) form.[2]

Looking at Figure 4.1, we see that little more than half (39) that fell out of the study did so due to outright closure. Six left due to refusal. Seven nonprofits reorganized into new entities, most often into churches or government agencies. Four merged with or were acquired by other nonprofit organizations. Another four became or merged with for-profit organizations. Two organizations relocated to other areas, and another two were found to have never actually been based in Minneapolis-St. Paul.[3] Four organizations ceased operations to the extent that we were convinced that they should be dropped from the sample, but they later revived. Four more organizations closed because of the closure of a parent organization. The fate of at least two nonprofits is unknown because they disappeared without a trace between waves of data collection.

In 1995 we initiated exit interviews with the 47 organizations that closed (including those for which the parent organization closed and those that revived). As of the writing of this chapter, we have been able to collect data on 34 of the 43 closed organizations and 1 of the 4 that came back to life. We interviewed either the former executive director or administrator or a prominent board member. We chose not to conduct interviews with organizations that changed status, merged with other organizations, refused to be interviewed, or otherwise exited the panel. This resulted in a response rate of the targeted population of 74.5%.

Following a period of open-ended questions about the factors influencing an organization's decision to close, we handed respondents two sets of stimuli. The first was a list of factors compiled by the researchers that listed organizational characteristics that might contribute to the demise of an organization. These factors included organization size, age, financial condition, personnel capabilities, staff conflict, power struggles, clarity of mission, personnel loss and turnover, changes in goals, and other. We also included a category for organizations that closed because they believed that they had achieved their mission. The second set of stimuli was a list of factors that listed environmental conditions and changes that have been listed in the organization literature. These factors include isolation, crises of legitimacy, decreased donor demand, decreased consumer demand, external normative control, and other.

■ PREDICTORS OF ORGANIZATION SURVIVAL

Because we had a panel study, we were able to identify the organizations that were most likely to fail. We particularly wanted to see if we could replicate the age and size effects found in other studies. We also included several control variables: (a) whether the organization provided health or welfare services or both, educational services, cultural services, or other services and (b) the extent to which the organization depended on private donations, public grants, or service fees.

The organization's size was measured by tallying the total income from 16 sources for 1979 and 1980: private/community foundations, individuals, businesses/corporations/corporate foundations, federated donors, trusts/bequests, net income from special benefit events, federal government grants/contracts, state government grants/contracts, county government grants/contracts, city government grants/contracts, membership dues, interest/dividends/rents, net income from sale of assets, net income from sale of unrelated services, program service revenue, and other.[4] We subsequently converted these sums to 1982 dollars, took the average for the two years, and computed the natural logs ($\ln\text{Revenu}_{80}$).

We measured the extent to which firms depended on different funding sources. We expected that organizations that were highly dependent on funding streams that shrank over the 12-year period would be less likely to survive. From inspection of cross-sectional sample surveys for 1980, 1984, 1988, and 1992 (see Hager & Jorgensen, 1996), we learned that government funding as a percentage of total nonprofit income went down between 1980 and 1988 and then increased slightly in 1992, whereas private donations increased as a percentage of total nonprofit income between 1980 and 1984 but then decreased in 1988 and rose again in 1992. Finally, earned income as a percentage of total income declined slightly between 1980 and 1984, increased between 1984 and 1988, and then dipped slightly in 1992, returning to 1980 levels. Thus, being dependent on one funding stream in 1980 (e.g., government funding) could have contributed to an organization's demise, whereas being dependent on another (e.g., earned income) could have contributed to its survival.

To measure dependency on earned income, we added up revenues from program service fees, membership dues, and net earnings from the sale of unrelated services and divided by Revenu_{80} (PctFees_{80}). To measure dependency on private donations and grants, we tallied revenues from individual donations, corporate gifts and grants, foundation grants, trusts and bequests, special fund-raising events (net income), and grants from federated fund drives (e.g., United Way) and divided by Revenu_{80} (PctPriv_{80}). Finally, to measure dependency on government funding, we

TABLE 4.1 Logistic Regression Explaining Organizational Survival, 1984, 1988, 1992, and 1994

	Dependent Variables											
	$Survive_{84}$			$Survive_{88}$			$Survive_{92}$			$Survive_{94}$		
Independent Variables	b	SE	sig	b	SE	sig	b	SE	sig	b	SE	sig
Age_{80}	.127	.084	.129	.076	.038	.047	.049	.025	.052	.054	.024	.026
$lnRevenu_{80}$	1.24	.345	.000	.595	.156	.000	.440	.123	.000	.357	.113	.001
$Hlth/Wel_{80}$	2.37	1.65	.150	.816	.864	.345	.630	.716	.379	−.058	.590	.922
$Educ_{80}$	2.11	1.46	.148	.153	.753	.838	.124	.628	.843	−.823	.516	
$Cultur_{80}$	2.36	1.88	.210	.274	1.02	.789	−.181	.837	.829	−1.21	.723	.093
$Other_{80}$	1.88	1.42	.184	.368	.808	.648	.171	.674	.800	−.489	.558	
$PctPriv_{80}$	−.089	1.88	.962	−.450	1.15	.695	−1.38	1.02	.176	−1.67	1.01	.098
$PctPubl_{80}$	−3.05	2.04	.134	−1.13	1.19	.344	−.699	1.06	.509	−.596	1.03	.565
$PctFees_{80}$	−.789	1.81	.663	.190	1.12	.865	−.218	.981	.824	−.377	.971	.698
Constant	3.18	4.54	.483	−2.30	1.43	.107	−1.24	1.20	.300	−.071	1.10	.949
Model c^2	39.67 (p = .000)			34.67 (p = .000)			36.19 (p = .000)			39.66 (p = .000)		
Percentage correct predicted	95.4			89.7			84.6			83.6		
N	195			195			195			195		

NOTE: N = 202.

tallied revenues from grants and contracts from all governmental sources and divided by $Revenu_{80}$ ($PctPubl_{80}$).[5]

We computed the age of the organization back dating from 1980 (Age_{80}). We also collected data on organizations' primary activities. In 1980, we found that 31.9% ranked health/welfare services ($Hlthwel_{80}$), 28.4% educational services ($Educ_{80}$), 6.6% recreational services ($Recreat_{80}$), 10.9% cultural activities ($Culture_{80}$), 2.2% legal services ($Legal_{80}$), 6.1% housing and urban development ($Housing_{80}$), 4.4% science ($Scien_{80}$), 7.9% organizational development ($Orgdev_{80}$), and 10.9% other services ($Other_{80}$) as their top priority. The percentages add up to more than 100%, because several organizations listed more than one activity as "primary." Because of the small number of organizations in a number of our categories, we recoded $Recreat_{80}$, $Legal_{80}$, $Housing_{80}$, and $Orgdev_{80}$ as $Other_{80}$.

Table 4.1 presents the results of the analysis. In this table, we analyze only 202 cases. We eliminated cases that left our panel because they refused to participate in later years; were lost; were never in or left the sample area; merged or were acquired; or reorganized as a church, for-profit, or government agency. The dependent variables in all our equations were dichotomous, with 1 indicating that the organization survived and 0 indicating that it closed. There were four logistic regression equations, because we were predicting survival (or death) at four points in time:

1984, 1988, 1992, and 1994. There were several ways to do this analysis; the simplest was to regress survival on organizational variables measured in 1980 for each of the four years.

As found in previous studies, the older and larger the organization, the more likely it was to survive the panel period. Organizational size ($lnRevenu_{80}$) was significant in predicting survival between 1980 and 1984. Organizational size and age (Age_{80}) were significant in predicting survival between 1980 and 1988. Organizational size was significant in predicting survival between 1980 and 1992, but age was significant at only the .06 level. Finally, organizational size and age were significant in predicting survival between 1980 and 1994. In other words, smaller organizations and younger organizations were more likely to disband between 1980 and 1994; neither dependency on fees, private donations, or government funding nor activity area had any effect on the likelihood of survival.

▦ RESULTS FROM EXIT INTERVIEWS

The preceding results are consistent with what we found in the literature and tell us which organizations died (smaller and/or younger organizations). But why were these organizations more likely to die? One strategy for understanding nonprofit death in more detail was to go directly to the individuals who were with the organization when it died and ask them.

Internal Factors

Organizations that closed were asked to rank the internal factors that influenced the decision to dissolve the organization. Table 4.2 reports the frequencies for the top three ranks for each of the response categories. We grouped options into six clusters:

1. Size (organization too small, organization too large)
2. Age (organization too young)
3. Instability (personnel loss and turnover, goal changes)
4. Managerial expertise (financial difficulties, personnel capabilities, conflict among staff, power struggles, unclear mission)
5. Success (organization completed its mission)
6. Other

Organizational size was cited by a significant number of organizations as contributing to their closure: 37.1% of the respondents said that being

TABLE 4.2 Internal Factor Rankings (in percentages)[a]

	Rank #1	Rank #2	Rank#3	Rank #4	Contributing Factor (Percentage Yes)
Organization Size					
Too small	17.1	20.0	17.1	0.0	54.2
Tool large	2.9	0.0	2.9	0.0	5.8
Organization Age					
Too young	5.7	8.6	2.9	0.0	17.2
Instability					
Personnel loss and turnover	11.4	8.6	8.6	5.7	34.3
Goal changes	2.9	5.7	0.0	0.0	8.6
Managerial Expertise					
Financial difficulties	20.0	14.3	8.6	2.9	45.8
Personnel capabilities	5.7	2.9	11.4	2.9	22.9
Conflict among staff	0.0	2.9	2.9	2.9	8.7
Power struggles	2.9	2.9	0.0	8.6	14.4
Unclear mission	2.9	0.0	0.0	5.7	8.6
Success					
Organization completed mission	17.1	2.9	5.7	5.7	31.6
Other	14.3	14.3	5.7	2.9	37.2

NOTE: a. $N = 35$.

too small was either the most or second most important reason for closing. In contrast, only 2.9% said that being too large was most or second most important. Age was also cited as important: 17.2% said that being too young was either the most or second most important reason for closing.

A moderate number of respondents thought that instability was a problem: 20% cited personnel loss and turnover as the most or second most important factor leading to closure, and 8.6% cited changes in goals as either the most or second most important factor explaining their closure. The most important managerial factor by far was financial difficulties: 34.3% said that this was the most or second most important factor in explaining closure. After this, not many of the managerial variables were frequently cited. Only 8.6% cited personnel capabilities as the number one or two reason for closure; 2.9% cited conflict among staff as important; 5.8% cited power struggles; and 2.9% cited unclear mission.

Surprisingly, 20% said that the first or second most important reason for their closing was that their organization completed its mission. Finally, 28.6% cited some other reason for their organization closing.

External Factors

The external factor instrument differed slightly from the internal factor instrument. Whereas the internal instrument listed a host of single factors, the external instrument grouped two to four issues under five major headings. Respondents were asked to check off any factors that contributed to their closing. First, we asked about donor and consumer demand. For the former, respondents could choose two categories:

1. Decreased contributions from funders, whether by conscious choice or by changes in giving guidelines or priorities
2. Fewer major funders available

For the latter, respondents could choose three categories:

1. Decreased program service revenues
2. Fewer consumers of services
3. The changed nature of the service environment

The frequency of responses on each of these items is given in Table 4.3. Decreased contributions was cited by 14.3% and fewer major funders available was cited by 28.6%; 22.9% said that there were decreased program service revenues, 25.7% said that there were fewer consumers of their services, and 20.0% said that the nature of service delivery had changed significantly.

We next asked about organizations' social capital. Organization representatives were presented these five response categories:

1. The organization lost contact with funders.
2. Few board members were members of other nonprofit boards.
3. The organization failed to make connections with complementary organizations or lost critical connections with the local community.
4. The organization was unable to share information and resources with other nonprofit organizations or to establish joint programs.
5. Organization staff did not hold membership in professional associations or task forces.

TABLE 4.3 Distribution of External Factors Influencing the Closure of Nonprofit Organizations (in percentages)[a]

	Contributing Factor (percentage yes)
Decreased Donor Demand	
Decreased contributions	14.3
Fewer major funders available	28.6
Decreased Consumer Demand	
Decreased program service revenues	22.9
Fewer consumers of services	25.7
Changing nature of service environment	20.0
Isolation	
Lost contact with funder	17.1
No board member on other NPO boards	2.9
Disconnected from Community	17.1
Low information sharing with other NPOs	2.9
Staff not active in professional associations	0.0
Crisis of Legitimacy	
Criticized by outsiders	17.1
Perceived as different somehow	5.7
Perceived as unimportant	37.1
External Normative Control	
Overregulation by business or government	5.7
Outsider influence over operations	17.1
Other	
Parent organization closed	11.4
Miscellaneous other	14.3

NOTE: a. $N = 35$.

Organizational isolation is perceived as a less salient issue than some of the more tangible issues in other sections. Six organizations (17.1%) felt that they had lost contact with funders. Only 2.9% of the organizations felt that they lacked interlocking directorates or shared too little information with other nonprofits. Six organizations (17.1%) felt that their loss of connection with the community had a deleterious effect on the organization. No organization felt that the lack of staff membership in professional associations was connected to their organization's demise.

The next cluster of items pertained to the image or legitimacy that the organization enjoyed in the broader community. We presented respondents with three prompts:

1. The organization suffered from the criticisms or negative opinions held by important outsiders.
2. The organization suffered from the perception that it had become different in some way.
3. The organization suffered from the perception that it was not needed or important.

Over one third (37.1%) of the organizations claimed that the outside perception that their organization was not needed or important was a critical determinant of their dissolution. Although the other two prompts received fewer marks, they add credence to the conclusion that nonprofit survival largely depends on a positive image and a viable public mission.

We then asked about the potential debilitating effects of outside control and regulation. Respondents were presented with two options:

1. The organization was threatened by increased regulation by government or by associated businesses or corporations.
2. The organization experienced undue influence by outsiders in internal operations.

The second issue was interpreted in ways that we did not foresee when we created the response categories. Few people (5.7%) perceived that their organization was a victim of regulation. However, six organizations cited outsider influence on internal operations as a factor influencing the demise of the organization (17.1%). Although the question was created with media representatives and politicians in mind, nearly all of the organizations marking this response noted that their organization was a victim of the control of strong-willed members of their board of directors.

Finally, four organizations closed due to the dissolution of a parent organization, and seven organizations (20.0%) cited other factors as the primary external cause of the demise of their organization. Other external factors included the saturation of a service population and a generational shift in attitudes toward public participation.

▨ EXPLAINING SIZE AND AGE FACTORS

In both the logistic regression analysis and in the interviews, it was clear that age and size were important factors in organizations' closing. Yet why were size and age important? Several reasons were cited in our introductory comments, but it still is not clear why these factors should be so critical in explaining who lives and dies. Given that many—but not all—our respondents said that age and size were important, we have an opportunity to see which other factors are correlated with these two responses. In other words, by taking the 35 organizations that died as our units of analysis, we can see which other factors were cited by those respondents who said that size and age were important in explaining why their organizations closed.[6]

Table 4.4 presents the results, and the results are easy to summarize.[7] Organizations that gave "being too small" as a reason for their demise were also more likely to say that being disconnected from their community was a serious problem. No other item was correlated with "being too small." Furthermore, organizations that gave "being too young" as a reason for their demise were more likely to say that being disconnected from their community or being isolated from other nonprofit organizations was a serious problem. These findings could be taken as support for Stinchcombe's (1965) earlier argument that the liability of newness is due to younger organizations' not having the linkages to their environment that they need to survive. Finally, organizations that said that they were "too young" were also more likely to say that they had too few customers for their services.

CONCLUSION

Throughout the course of this study, we were struck that no two organizations died in the same way. That is, each organization had a unique set of circumstances that led to the decision to close. Nonetheless, the received theory on the causes of organizational demise provided effective categories that resonated with the experiences of nonprofit representatives who described the events surrounding the closing of their organization.

Looking at internal factors cited as contributing to closure, we found that personnel loss and turnover as well as financial difficulties were the two most frequently cited internal reasons cited for closure. We also found that a significant portion—about one fifth—closed because they had completed their mission. Whether this is a true representation of sentiments or a rationalization of failure, it points to the need for organizational scientists to question the assumption that a dissolving organization is a failing one. Similarly, it questions the assumption that organizations that complete their missions embrace new missions in order to survive (Blau, 1955; Sills, 1957). Other managerial issues, such as conflict and power struggles and the routinization of a clear mission and goals, were not seen as that important.

Consistent with the expectation that market conditions affected closure, we found that a large number of organizations reported a decrease in donor demand or a decrease in consumer demand for their services.

TABLE 4.4 Zero-Order Correlations Between Being Too Small, Being Too Young, and Internal and External Factors

Construct	Indicators	Being Too Small	Being Too Young
Instability			
	Personnel loss and turnover	−0.062	−0.169
	Goal changes	−0.129	−0.139
Managerial Expertise			
	Financial difficulties	0.151	0.191
	Personnel capabilities	0.090	−0.067
	Conflict among staff	−0.129	0.131
	Power struggles	−0.117	0.031
	Unclear mission	−0.129	0.131
Decreased Donor Demand			
	Decreased contributions	0.047	0.248
	Fewer major funders	−0.054	0.048
Decreased Consumer Demand			
	Decreased service revenues	−0.183	−0.067
	Fewer consumers of services	0.277	0.426*
	Changing service environment	0.029	−0.038
Isolation			
	Lost contact with funders	−0.039	−0.006
	No board boundary spanners	−0.187	−0.078
	Disconnected from community	0.417*	0.598***
	Low information sharing with other NPOs	0.157	0.377*
Crisis of Legitimacy			
	Criticized by outsiders	−0.039	0.195
	Perceived as different somehow	−0.021	−0.112
	Perceived as unimportant	0.112	0.278
External Normative Control			
	Overregulation by business or government	0.226	−0.112
	Outsider influence over operations	0.113	0.195

NOTE: $*p < 0.05$; $***p < 0.001$.

Social capital (or social isolation) did not seem as important. Although staying connected to the community and funders were cited as important by some, interlocking directorates, networking with other nonprofits, and participation in professional associations were all seen as unimportant in explaining closures.

Clearly, our respondents felt that organizational legitimacy was critical. The largest percentage of respondents said that being perceived as unimportant or nonessential was an important factor in their deciding to close down their operation. However, they did not think that overregulation by businesses or government or the influence of outsiders on the organization had much effect on their closing.

Finally, our analysis shed some light on why being new or small was such a liability for organizations. Nonprofits that said that smallness was a problem also said that being disconnected from the community was a problem, and organizations that said that newness was a problem said that being disconnected and not sharing information with other nonprofit organizations was a problem as well. Thus, it appears that there may be a network story behind the age and size effects on survival. The newer and smaller organizations had difficulty getting tied into the community, and lacking social capital, these organizations were more likely to disband. In their recent review of research on the ecology and evolution of organizational populations, Amburgey and Rao (1996) note that "ecological research on mortality has tended to overlook how existing organizations are relationally embedded in social networks" (p. 1274). Our conclusions point to the need for additional research on the role of information and resource networks, community embeddedness, and other vehicles of social capital in overcoming the liabilities of youth and small size among nonprofit organizations.

NOTES

1. Of course, there are also many examples of organizations that achieve their goals and then reorganize and continue to exist, pursuing new goals and with a new mission—for example, the March of Dimes' succession of goals from polio eradication to foci on other childhood maladies (Sills, 1957).

2. Nonprofit organizations can remain separate legal entities even though they are "owned" by another for-profit or nonprofit. In the cases in which this occurred (as measured by the presence of a separate governing board of directors), the organization was still considered "alive" and it was not excluded from the panel. In cases in which an organization merged or was acquired by another organization and forfeited its board, it was considered by us to be dead.

3. One organization, based in New York City, filed its paperwork to maintain its nonprofit status in the home state of its president. The organization fell into our sample because the president in the late 1970s happened to live in our sampling area. However, his successor lived in another state. Consequently, the paperwork for the organization moved with the new president and the organization no longer existed as a Minnesota nonprofit. The other organization was a Minnesota nonprofit but never began operations sufficiently to the point where its organizers considered it as a founding. They referred to the enterprise as "a waste of the fee for filing for nonprofit status." Consequently, we consider the organization as never established as a nonprofit.

4. In 1979-80, 7.0% of the cases had missing data for one or more of these items. We used data for 1984 (converted to 1980 dollars) to replace missing data for 1980. After these substitutions and tallying up across the 16 revenue streams, we had missing data for only 1.7% of the cases.

5. Government funding comes in many different forms. In our interviews, we instructed respondents to differentiate between reimbursements to clients (e.g., Medicaid and Medicare) and grants and contracts. The former was counted as program service revenue and the latter as donated income. Our rationale was that the latter funding decision was made by an agency rather than the consumer and should thus be considered part of the institutional environment rather than the technical.

6. The zero-order correlation between "being too small" and "being too young" was .417 ($p = .013$).

7. We recoded the internal factors so that if a respondent said the factor was important at all, it was scored a 1 and a 0 otherwise. Thus, all our variables were dichotomous.

Organizational Coping, Failure, and Success
Academies of Sciences in Central and Eastern Europe

RENATE MAYNTZ

5

🔲 TROUBLESOME ENVIRONMENTS AND ORGANIZATIONAL CHANGE

The relationship between organizations and their environments has been a prominent theme in organizational analysis ever since organizations have been conceived of as social systems. But there have been very different approaches in studying this relationship. In the 1960s and early 1970s, the then-dominant structural approach, embodied especially in the Aston program,[1] focused on the correspondence between specific types of organizational structure and the characteristics of their environment: What kind of organizational structure fits a given kind of environment? The structural contingency model (Lawrence & Lorsch, 1967) was applied mainly to firms, and technological innovations and changing market demands figured as the most relevant environmental aspects.

Contingency theory was soon criticized for neglecting the influence of strategic choice on the part of management (Child, 1972). Deliberately setting itself off from contingency theory, a new school of organizational thought conceived of the organization as an actor responding to environmental opportunities and restrictions (Crozier & Friedberg, 1977). This is also the perspective in Pfeffer and Salancik's (1978) resource-dependence model, despite the book's misleading title (*The External Control of Organizations*). In this tradition of strategic organizational action, the "coping paradigm" can be located, only that "coping" is generally related to *threatening* situations in particular. But the emphasis on strategic action, or coping, is not an *alternative* to contingency theory; it can most fruitfully be used as a complementary approach, as this chapter shall try to demonstrate.

Following Schimank and Stucke (1994, pp. 16-17), coping can be distinguished from prevention on the one hand and from fatalistic suffering on the other hand. It is an active kind of response to perceived threats, particularly threats emanating from the environment. Coping strategies seek either to influence the environment such as to eliminate a threat or to adapt to the changed external circumstances in such a way as to ensure the persistence of the organization as a functioning whole. Going beyond an abstract classification of troublesome environmental changes in terms of increasing complexity, dynamics, or restrictiveness (e.g., Emery & Trist, 1965), one might distinguish four major types of environmental threats: resource scarcity, task obsolescence, positional challenges, and imposed structural changes. Each and every one of these threats may, if coping fails, become a challenge to the very survival of an organization. But such extreme threats, particularly if they appear unexpectedly and come to a head rapidly, are relatively rare events. The radical regime change in the Central and Eastern European (CEE) countries that posed such a threat to many organizations affords a rare occasion to study the behavior of organizations in severe crisis situations.

The events that can endanger the very survival of an organization obviously vary with its character. State-financed scientific organizations, our object in the research to be reported here, are not exposed to the same threats as private firms or research institutes living off the market for contract research. At first sight, publicly financed educational and scientific organizations may appear especially vulnerable because they depend on a single source of support—that is, the state. But in the case of a large and prestigious organization such as a national academy of the sciences, it takes something like a major political earthquake to cause it serious trouble. This, however, is exactly what happened to the academies in the CEE countries when the latter underwent a radical regime change at the end of the 1980s. How did these scientific organizations respond to the challenge, and what determined the outcome in terms of organizational survival and change?

In posing these questions, two theoretical issues are raised. The first concerns the determinants of coping strategies. Here, we assume that not only organizational characteristics but also external conditions affect the choice of coping strategies. This is evident to the extent that the *opportunities* for coping vary from situation to situation. But there may also exist a more general relationship between environmental characteristics and an organization's readiness to engage in coping. In this connection, it has for instance been suggested that active coping presupposes the perceived ability to control events, whereas extreme threats are met by holding fast to standard operation procedures, thus leading to organizational rigidity and the centralization of decision powers (Hermann, 1963).

The second theoretical issue concerns the determinants of coping success. What counts as "success," of course, needs to be defined, and there are several different indicators one might wish to consider; the same is true of the complementary concept—failure. Leaving this aside for the moment, the question is whether success or failure is a direct consequence of organizational coping reactions, as models of strategic choice sometimes seem to imply. Here, our assumption is that success or failure is a function *both* of the nature and intensity of the environmental challenge and of the organizational responses to it. There are troubles so severe that no conceivable kind of organizational response can ensure even bare survival; but in many crisis situations, environmental conditions and organizational characteristics together define a kind of survival corridor[2] that permits, but whose existence by no means guarantees, successful coping.

ACADEMIES IN SOCIALIST SOCIETIES: FIT BETWEEN ORGANIZATION AND ENVIRONMENT

In the socialist countries of Central and Eastern Europe, the science system was structured by and large in the same way: The universities served mainly educational purposes, industrial research was largely organized in so-called branch institutes, and state-financed basic and problem-oriented research was concentrated in national academies. A national academy of sciences is mainly a large holding organization for state- financed research institutes (mostly in the natural sciences), but the academy has individual members, too, which means that the academy is also a learned society with both full and "corresponding" members. This group of academicians is neither restricted to members of the academy institutes, nor are all scientists with a leadership function in an academy institute necessarily personal members of the academy (i.e., academicians, in this terminology).

The organization of state-financed basic and problem-oriented research in national academies is a Soviet invention. The Russian Academy of Sciences (RAS) was founded by Peter the Great as a "society of scientists" and served certain advisory functions to the government. At the beginning of the 20th century, Russian scientists pleaded for the establishment of research institutes in the framework of the academy, but by the time of the revolution in 1917, the RAS had only one research institute and five laboratories. Soon afterward, the buildup of the academy to become the major organization of state-financed research started; in 1940, it counted already 78 research institutes.[3]

The academy model developed in Soviet Russia was subsequently extended to other Soviet Republics, including the three Baltic states after they had been forcibly integrated into the Soviet Union. The various regional academies in the Soviet Union formed an interrelated and, in part, functionally differentiated system directed by the Soviet Academy of Sciences in Moscow (the former RAS; the Russian Soviet Republic did not then have a separate academy). After World War II, all East and Middle European satellite countries sooner or later copied the Soviet model of research organization. Most of these countries used to have academies in the form of learned societies, but their universities were the major sites of basic research. To that extent, they stood in the West European tradition. The introduction of the Soviet model of science organization, in which academies served as the major institutions of state-financed research, broke with that tradition. In the highly developed Western industrial countries, academies typically continued to exist as learned societies, and state-supported nonuniversity research organizations grew up outside of them. Thus, in Germany the Kaiser-Wilhelm-Gesellschaft, founded in 1911 and continued after World War II as Max-Planck-Society, has become the largest German organization doing basic research. Even the English Royal Society, which played a significant role in the development of the experimental natural sciences in the 17th and 18th centuries did not grow into a large research organization; instead, the promotion of basic and problem-oriented basic research became the task of the various British research councils (Braun, 1997).

There is an evident fit between the Soviet type of research organization and the state socialist society. Centralized state control, division of labor, and the concentration of similar tasks in one large organization have been the principles underlying the structure of socialist economies. The concentration of basic and problem-oriented research of most or even all disciplines in one large organization is fully congruent with these principles. Also, the Soviet-type academy is directly subject to state control and thus conforms to the hierarchical governance mode, whereas the traditional learned societies were based on the principle of scientific self-organization.

But more than a congruence of organizational principles is involved when we speak of a basic fit between state socialism and the academy model of research organization. In "scientific" socialism, science was considered the basis of production and planned innovation. Its key function in the process of societal reproduction and development gave science a special prestige and justified both an elite status of scientists and special state support to scientific research. The view that the reproduction process is scientifically based justified a high share of research and development (R&D) personnel among the gainfully employed and thus explains the overexpansion of R&D staff in socialist compared with Western capitalist countries. Along the same line, Organization for Economic and Cooperative Development (OECD) experts remark that the Russian science and technology (S&T) base was extremely large by comparative international standards, whether in terms of employment, number of establishments, or resource commitment as a share of gross national product (GNP), and that this expansion of S&T institutions was driven by political rather than economic forces (OECD, 1994, pp. 15-16).

The assumption that the promotion of science serves to advance production implies a linear model of technological development. This model links basic and applied research and the practical application of research results in one causal chain. This linear model came to supplant the earlier image of a vertical rank order relationship between theory (philosophy) and practice in the course of the 19th century, a shift related to the transition from a stratified to a functionally differentiated society (Mayntz, 1997). There are, however, different modes of relating the various functional subsystems to each other, and this is reflected in different versions of the linear model. In Western democratic market societies, the functional subsystems are supposed to adapt spontaneously to each other, following rules of exchange; in state socialist societies, in contrast, the functional subsystems are coordinated by a central authority. In the Western type of society, basic research, the first link in the chain, is the driving force of the process of technological development; this version of the linear model is fittingly called a "science push model." It is based on the assumption, formulated maybe most clearly by President Roosevelt's science adviser Vannevar Bush at the end of World War II, that scientific research is most creative and productive when it is left to follow its own dynamic (Bush, 1945/1960). This implicit theory largely guided Western science policy during the first two postwar decades. In contrast, the view that scientific research must be politically directed toward desirable ends goes hand in hand with a "demand pull model," in which desired applications drive the search for knowledge. This version of the linear model lay at the base of science policy in socialist countries, where research was centrally planned and organized as part of the societal production and reproduction process.[4] The academy model—that is, the concentration of research in one large, specialized, and politically controlled organization—is thus closely linked to a particular view of the function of science in a planned society and the proper relationship between knowledge production and application.

■ THE CHALLENGE OF RADICAL REGIME CHANGE

The chain reaction of reforms and—mostly rather peaceful— revolutions that swept Central and Eastern Europe toward the end of the 1980s undermined the basic logic of the academy model of research organization: It no longer "fit" the changed sociopolitical environment. This incongruence spelled a serious challenge to the academies of sciences in the postsocialist CEE countries. Their fate, however, was extremely varied. In this chapter, the challenge will first be sketched in more detail. We then turn to the coping reactions of the academies and the transformations they underwent. The basis of this analysis are data from a large, comparative empirical study of the transformation of former socialist academies of sciences in the CEE reform states,[5] as well as from an in-depth study of the transformation of the former East German Academy of Sciences (Mayntz, 1994a).

The challenge faced by the academies of the reform states derived mainly from three related changes in the environment of the science system at large. The first and most fundamental of these was the regime change itself, notably the abolition of the Communist party's political monopoly and claim to comprehensive central control, and the introduction of market principles in the economy. Where production is no longer politically controlled and market principles come to reign, the justification for claims of centralized research planning is lost. Where different functional subsystems of society are granted a certain autonomy, the science system, too, is emancipated from central control and is at the same time exposed to market forces. For industrial research, which was largely privatized[6,] this meant that its fate became closely tied to the (negative) development of the production sector; the two other sectors of the science system suffered from the state's financial problems through budget cuts.

A second, related, change has taken place at the level of political priorities. This change followed from the difficult economic situation in which all transformation societies find themselves and that has given priority to economic survival and the avoidance of social unrest, leaving little room for future-oriented investments. The economic problems besetting the transformation societies are such that science, and particularly basic research, can do little for their solution. So far, the former socialist countries try to solve their economic problems mainly by offering cheap labor for mass production rather than by high-tech production and innovation. At the same time, the newly opened frontiers obviate the former need to reinvent Western technological achievements that could not be imported because of the Western embargo or due to the shortage of hard currencies. Both developments have lowered the demand for R&D and detract from the practical value of science. Science, therefore, does not receive a privileged treatment anymore. Science budgets have been cut overproportionately, and issues of institutional reform are treated slowly and sometimes erratically.

The third factor is a parallel development at the level of values. The high prestige enjoyed by science as long as it was considered the functional basis of progress and the prime condition of reaching and even overtaking the capitalist countries of the West has decreased with the erosion of the belief in all forms of central planning. The shift toward more individualistic values of personal well-being has reinforced this decrease in the value of knowledge.

The effects of these contextual changes for the national academies are to some extent contradictory, because they have, on one hand, produced welcomed opportunities, but on the other hand, they have caused serious trouble. Although the legal and institutional changes have generally increased the independence of science, especially of basic research within and outside of universities, and have thus enlarged the scope for action enjoyed by scientific institutions, the economic situation and the attendant financial difficulties have seriously restricted this scope. Thus, the right to select research topics independently is of little practical value when institutes and scientists are forced, for financial reasons, to concentrate on work for which they can get a contract or grant, and the new freedom to travel comes to naught where there is no money to pay for it. In fact, scarce financial resources are a problem afflicting all of the still existing academies in the CEE countries today. But there are also environmental threats to the formerly privileged position, the functional identity, and even the organizational survival of the academies. The changes we observe, therefore, are only partly "reforms" in the sense of improvements and, in many respects, merely adaptations to a troublesome situation.

▓ INSTITUTIONAL CHANGES: GENERAL TENDENCIES

The institutional changes we observe are the combined effect of spontaneous reform movements within the science system and of science policy decisions. The general direction of the changes reflects basic structural tensions inherent in the Soviet model of organizing the science system. Thus, the political control to which science had been subjected provoked demands for autonomy and participation, both at the level of institutions and of individual scientists. The dominant position of the national academy was severely criticized by university representatives, especially where the universities traditionally had played an important role in research. In general, the efforts to reform the science system were strongest in countries where before the regime change in the late 1980s and early 1990s there had already existed an intellectual opposition of a certain strength and outspokenness—something that held true for Poland, Hungary, and the CSSR, but not, for instance, for communist East Germany and for the various Soviet republics.

The most important institutional changes in the ex-socialist science systems can be briefly summarized in six points:

1. Central control and political guidance of the science system have greatly diminished, even if not entirely disappeared. This is in large part an effect of the political regime change—the loss in directive capacity of the former ruling party, the introduction of a multiparty system, and the limitations in government powers resulting from a democratic constitution. But scarce financial resources and shifting political priorities have also played a role. Often, the independent status that science has gained is even written into law. An important consequence is the academy's official freedom to define its own research program.

2. In many ex-socialist countries, the national academy of sciences has lost its privileged position within the science system, both with respect to its science policy functions and with respect to its position vis-à-vis the universities. Formerly, the academies were heavily involved in developing the national research plans. Now, the locus of science policy-making has shifted to government agencies; in several cases, ministries responsible for science policy and the promotion of research have been newly formed. Academy institutes can no longer claim preferential treatment. Universities who used to feel underprivileged as research sites have been able to improve their status and have often been less afflicted by financially motivated personnel reductions than academies. The cooperative relations of academy institutes with universities do not seem to have noticeably intensified; at times it seems that there is even more competition now, especially when both types of institution look to the same sources for research grants.

3. The academy leadership has lost much of its programmatic steering function for the academy institutes, and within limits, the same is true for the relationship between institute leaders and individual scientists or

research teams. Thus, the process of decentralization observed under Point 1 at the national level continues at the intraorganizational level. This is in part a deliberately planned change and finds expression for instance in the establishment of new participatory (democratic) procedures and bodies. In part, however, it is an unintended side effect of the weakening of the leadership's resources and in particular of the scarcity of centrally available funds, which forces institutes and individual scientists to engage in fund-raising activities for themselves by themselves.

4. Whereas before the regime change the academy typically served both as a research organization and a learned society, these two components now tend to become more distinctly separate. Even when the national academy still serves both functions, the institutes now tend to have a representative body of their own that fulfills coordination and strategic guidance functions that pertained to the academy leadership before.

5. Competition for resources, not only between the different sectors of the science system but also between different institutes and research teams, has been introduced as a measure to increase the overall quality of research. The institutional form in which this takes place is typically the establishment of national research funds. In several countries, these funds dispose of a growing share of the total R&D budget. Expert scientists play a crucial role in these funds. In principle, this mode of R&D financing increases the autonomy of the science system.

6. At least in the first phase of the reforms, the academies have programmatically emphasized their basic research orientation. This reorientation is at least in part a reaction to the strong pressure toward applied research that characterized socialist science policy especially during the 1980s.[7] A basic research orientation can contribute to the autonomy of science, because it diminishes its dependence on specific user groups in defining research goals. At the level of individual institutes, the basic research orientation was reinforced by evaluation procedures giving priority to theoretical importance and cognitive innovation of research and by the chance to acquire grants from (possibly foreign) funds favoring basic over applied research. On the other hand, the need to find additional income from contract research has sometimes induced institutes to engage in more applied research than they would have done otherwise.[8] Whether for political or for economic reasons, science policy in some CEE countries now appears to shift again to a stronger emphasis on the practical applicability of science.

By and large, the institutional changes summarized in these six points have evidently served to reestablish the "fit," or congruence, between the organization of the science system and the new sociopolitical regime.

From the viewpoint of postsocialist science policy, these changes are considered reforms, but this is not necessarily the viewpoint of the national academies, for whom these changes meant not only more autonomy but also some loss of status and some ambiguity as to their major task; for some academies, they even spelled a threat to their very survival.

▧ THE THREAT TO SURVIVAL: VARIATIONS IN THE ENVIRONMENTAL CHALLENGE

The reform tendencies summarized in the previous section did not necessarily imply a threat to the academy model of research organization as such. Nevertheless, the survival of the existing academies was seriously challenged in several of the reform states, and several of the former academies have in fact suffered radical changes in their functional identity and/or organizational integrity.

In East Germany, the academy was completely dissolved. Of its 60 research institutes, only 21 survived as organizations (mostly with reduced personnel); 6 were simply closed down, and the research potential of the remaining institutes was radically restructured (Mayntz, 1994b, p. 195). The learned society did not survive either, and only a small minority of its members were later asked to join the newly founded Berlin-Brandenburgische Akademie der Wissenschaften. In the Czech Republic, the learned society was dissolved as part of the academy in 1992 and reestablished a year later as a private association, whereas the academy continues as a research organization.[9] In the three Baltic Republics, in contrast, the academy was divested of its research institutes, which have typically become subject to the jurisdiction of a ministry. Although these academies thus lost their function as research organization, they continue as learned societies, and sometimes still serve as spokespersons and interest representatives for their former institutes. To take the research institutes away from the academy was also debated in other countries, especially in the Czech and Slovak Republics, in Hungary, and in Poland; here, however, the academies eventually retained both of their previous functions, although they did undergo serious reforms. In the other CEE countries, and notably those that were formerly part of the Soviet union, the academies suffered and continue to suffer from crippling financial problems, but their functional identity and organizational integrity were not seriously challenged. Structural changes that did take place (over and beyond "reforms" of the type described in the previous section) are closely linked to the disappearance of the centralized Soviet academy system.

These differences point to the fact that what, on the surface, looks like a basically similar kind of environmental change, is in fact a variable. A number of identifiable external factors have influenced the survival chances of a given national academy. The three most important ones are connected with the history of the countries concerned. Among these, the *political history* of the CEE countries stands out, because it imparted widely varying meanings to the regime change.

East Germany, where the academy suffered the worst fate of all,[10] had become separated from West Germany in 1945. In the context of *perestroika,* the regime change of 1989 opened the way to German reunification. Legally construed as accession of the former German Democratic Republic (GDR) to the Federal Republic of Germany, reunification meant that East German institutions had to be adapted to West German structures. As a major organization of nonuniversity research, the East German academy of sciences was incompatible with these structures. This incompatibility was the main argument for dissolving the academy.

In the case of the three Baltic Republics, it was again their political history that provided the motive for a radical break with the Soviet model. These three countries had been incorporated against their will into the Soviet Union, and a Soviet type academy had subsequently been imposed on them. It was thus part of the act of national liberation that a new model of research organization was chosen.

In countries such as Poland, Hungary, and the Czech and Slovak Republics, the academy appeared similarly as a legacy of the past regime, but as these countries had not formally lost their national independence, the reform movement lacked the pronounced anti-Soviet impulse of the Baltic Republics. In these countries, another aspect of their past played an important role—that is, the *existence of a well-remembered "Western" tradition of science organization.* In the newly independent Soviet Republics Russia, Ukraina, and Belorus, this factor was absent, and this clearly contributed to the basically unchallenged persistence of the academy model of research organization in these countries.

A third differentiating factor has already been alluded to briefly—that is, *the existence of an intellectual reform movement (opposition) of significant strength* before the onset of the political transformation. Such a reform movement, or intellectual elite, typically included parts of the scientific establishment. After the regime change, this group gained political influence. Thus, science policy came to be developed by a coalition of politicians and scientists with shared political convictions. Academy scientists in countries such as Hungary and Poland participated actively in developing far-reaching academy reforms and were able, by the same token, to counter more radical demands; in Lithuania, academy scientists who shared the political elite's anti-Soviet impetus were instrumental in preparing the law that took the research institutes away from the academy. In East Germany, in contrast, the fate of the academy was decided mainly by West German policymakers, and not even East German politicians rallied to its rescue.

▨ COPING STRATEGIES

The general direction of the institutional changes in the science system of the former socialist societies is in accordance with the overall change in societal governance they are undergoing. Subjectively, however, these changes were experienced as a radical modification, if not a complete breakdown, of the familiar order. Such situations are ripe with both opportunities and threats. In many CEE countries, the opportunities appeared more important in the beginning, notably the opportunity for the national academy and its research institutes to gain more autonomy. Soon, however, the threats began to outweigh the opportunities. As shown in the previous section, many academies faced a, more or less pronounced, challenge to their organizational (functional and structural) identity or even their survival, as a consequence of reform plans pursued both by representatives of the universities and by the new political elite. Even those academies that maintained their organizational integrity suffered from the financial problems that followed from severe cuts in state budgets and the sudden and sharp decrease in external demand for contract research, especially on the part of industry. Together, this meant a shortage or even complete lack of money for investments in the research infrastructure, the need to reduce personnel, the inability to pay decent salaries to the research staff, and a sharply decreasing attractiveness of a career in science both for existing qualified researchers and for new recruits.

A fundamental challenge to its identity or even survival could be countered only by the leadership of the academy—that is, by the corporate actor "academy" itself, while coping with the financial shortage also involved the mesolevel of academy institutes and the microlevel of academy scientists. The choice of coping strategies to deal with the different kinds of threat at the different organizational levels is an important determinant of the final outcome of the transformation.

As shown in the previous section of this chapter, the continuation of the national academy of sciences was deliberately put into question in about half of the CEE countries. The intensity of this challenge varied, but so did the readiness of the academy leadership to support far-reaching reforms and even a basic transformation. Thus, in the Baltic countries, the transformation of the academies to mere learned societies and the transfer of the former academy institutes to the jurisdiction of ministries did not meet with strong resistance on the part of the scientific establishment. In Hungary, Poland, and the Czech and Slovak Republics, the academies successfully resisted the challenge to their organizational integrity and functional identity. Two main factors can explain this outcome. The first is successful coalition building with state actors, a strategy available only because in these countries, a political bond existed between the reform forces in politics and in science. Even so, however, the political support game was difficult to play for the representatives of science, because political power now tends to be more diffuse and science lacks a strong political anchor and a powerful lobby. The second factor that contributed importantly to the successful mastering of the survival crisis was the readiness of the academy leadership in these countries to support far-reaching internal reforms, both in the policy-making and the implementation phases. By doing so, the academy leadership could counter major criticisms that served to justify plans to divest the academies of their research institutes in the interest of increased efficiency and scientific innovation.

In the formerly socialist East Germany, where the academy also strove to maintain its organizational integrity in a vastly changed political environment, a similar readiness to embrace internal reforms did not have the same effect because the main argument for the dissolution of the academy was its institutional incompatibility with the structure of the West German science system and not its relative inefficiency (which rather served to justify subsequent personnel reductions). Even more important, however, for the academy's final defeat in its struggle for survival was that the first of the two promising strategies, coalition building with the new political elite, failed in the East German case for a number of interrelated reasons. To begin with, no bond from former times of political opposition joined the academy leadership and the new political elite. This is obvious insofar as the dominant policymakers were West Germans rather than East Germans, but it also holds for the new East German government. Although the new government represented the democratic opposition movement, a church-centered, relatively small, and not very visible group compared with the opposition movements that had existed in Hungary, the CSSR and Poland, the East German scientific establishment in general and the academy leadership in particular had been, by and large, loyal supporters of the socialist regime. For this reason, there existed few personal ties and little mutual sympathy between the academy and the new East German political elite, and the first (and last) freely elected government of the GDR gave less than wholehearted support to the academy. In addition to these objective difficulties, the academy leadership also failed to appreciate these complexities of the situation and to anticipate the "frame switch" from political reforms to unification by accession. It concentrated its efforts on the reform of its statutes when it should have searched for political allies and sought support from West German scientific organizations such as the Max-Planck-Society where for several reasons it had little chances of getting it.[11] Thus, strategic mistakes were made and may have influenced the outcome, the dissolution of the academy.[12]

Survival threat and financial troubles were two largely unrelated challenges. Thus, in Russia, where the academy was never seriously challenged as such, it suffered particularly high budget cuts. Because the financial trouble that now afflicted them had very little to do with the previous performance of the academies, their willingness to accept and even voluntarily initiate reforms was not able to neutralize the basic threat in the form of financial shortage. And even where coalition building with the new political elite was feasible, it could not offset the negative effects of the economic crisis. The academies as corporate actors thus could do little to ameliorate their financial situation by attempting to influence their environment; they had to seek ways to adapt by trying to minimize the damage.

One strategy of adaptive coping was rationalization to save money and increase productivity; this strategy was chosen for instance by the Czech academy where personnel reduction was not passively suffered but actively embraced as a means to increase effectiveness. Selective budget cuts according to a systematic evaluation of institutes make up a related strategy. A different strategy, typical especially for the Russian academy, is followed where academies allot budgets to the institutes on the basis of their (nominal) personnel strength, thus impeding the making of personnel cuts and leaving the institutes to their own devices in trying to survive on the basis of manifestly insufficient resources.

In the transformation process, the survival of individual institutes is not fully tied to the survival of the academy as an organization. In principle, the academy may be dissolved as such, but some or even all of its institutes may well survive. On the other hand, the persistence of the academy does not necessarily ensure the survival of all of its institutes. The impotence of the academy as corporate actor to ensure the survival, let alone the well-being of the institutes leads to a de facto decentralization, reducing the internal control capacity of the academy as a consequence of its loss of control over its environment. As a consequence, academy institutes could, and had to, develop their own coping strategies. The political and economic changes did not affect all academy institutes in a given country in the same way,[13] and there is a great variety in the amount of resource cuts they had to cope with. But by and large, it was the same bundle of coping strategies that could lead to a (relatively) successful adaptation to a threatening situation: (a) One strategy was to change the institute's research profile in accordance with changes in external demand and criteria of relevance. (b) A second strategy was to reduce personnel selectively so as to keep a maximum of the productive researchers and create openings for young scientists. A repeated evaluation of scientists helped in this effort. (c) Finally, institutes could actively look for "new customers" and for new sources of income. At least the first and the third of these strategies can, however, have dysfunctional consequences for the quality of research. This is true for instance if additional income is generated by renting part of the institute's premises or by engaging in commercial activities or if in the search for new customers, the institute's own research program is compromised. Although some institutes—for instance, in Poland—have tried it, there is also little scientific reward in turning to teaching and training. Strategies ensuring the short-term survival of an institute may thus prove dysfunctional for the quality of science in the long run.

It may seem surprising at first sight that at the lowest organizational level, the individual scientist—the weakest actor of all—appears to have the largest scope for coping. In contrast to the larger social units, individuals have, above all, an exit option: They may look for other jobs in their own or in foreign countries, in science or in some other field. Of course, the aggregate effect of this individual strategy is at least potentially dysfunctional for the higher-level units and the science system at large, especially because the younger and better qualified scientists tend to be the most mobile and thus contribute to the "brain drain" phenomenon. Sometimes, individual scientists also have better opportunities to find funds from other sources: National and international grants are normally negotiated, applied for, and given to individual researchers or small teams rather than to an institute, let alone an academy. But again, at the unit level of the institute, the successful acquisition of grants and contracts by its members is a double-edged sword. On the one hand, this is an important source of income and is a way to supplement scarce salaries. On the other hand, this form of successful coping implies a de facto decentralization to the level of small groups or teams within the institute and a consequent fragmentation of its program structure and weakening of the leadership's directive capacity with respect to the choice of research topics.

☷ CONCLUSION

The preceding analysis has fully supported the initial hunch that the "fit" (contingency) and "strategic choice" perspectives are not mutually exclusive but, rather, complementary. In our case, radical regime change has destroyed the previously existing fit between the academy model of research organization and its sociopolitical environment, and the ensuing incongruence stimulated conscious efforts at institutional change. The general direction of institutional reform reflects basic tensions inherent in the former (congruent!) model of science organization in socialist societies. This underlines the important fact that an organizational form that is congruent with a given (here, sociopolitical) environment is not necessarily harmonious in itself.

Where the reforms succeeded, they reestablished something like a new situation of congruence. But this was not primarily the result of organizational coping. Some forms of organizational coping have in fact delayed rather than promoted adaptation, whereas political interventions have in many instances served to fit the science system to the new sociopolitical conditions. Coping that is successful according to some of the possible criteria is therefore not the only, or even the major, mechanism bringing about congruence between organizations and environment—an insight that must go against the grain of all evolutionary approaches in organizational theory but that rings a familiar bell to the political scientist.

Turning now to the specific questions asked at the beginning of the analysis, it is hardly feasible to summarize the empirical findings by pointing to a small set of factors responsible for either "success" or "failure" in coping. This has much to do with the ambiguity of organizational survival as a criterion of success or failure. In some cases in which the national academy did not survive in its previous form, this was not considered as a failure by the academy researchers who rather supported such plans. On the other hand, some forms of organizational survival may be qualified as cases of coping failure—for example, where an academy persists and has formally even kept most of its personnel, but at the same time, its research effectiveness has radically eroded. If maintenance of research effectiveness, however difficult to assess, is used as a criterion, the transformation of the East German academy, which did not survive as an organization, might even be called a success. Organizational integrity, staff maintenance, and performance are three different criteria of success that are not highly correlated; each is affected by different external forces and can be countered by different coping strategies. Coalition building with the political elite is particularly relevant to ward off a survival threat, whereas adaptation to changed demands for research outputs is more important in dealing with budget problems.

But whatever the outcome and whatever the factors explaining it, the fate of each academy is clearly the *joint* result of a particular external situation. The same holds for the choice of organizational strategies, which were clearly influenced by what the environment offered—or excluded—in terms of strategic options; coalition building can again serve as an illustration. It may be due to the *political* origin of the environmental changes that factors rooted in the political history of a given country played such an important role in shaping not only available strategic options but the very goals pursued by external (political) and organizational (academy scientists and leaders) actors. The observation, on the other hand, that organizational success or failure is the result of coping attempts taking place at several organizational levels at the same time is not a unique feature of our particular case but can be generalized to other organizations and other types of situation. However, the relatively great scope for autonomous coping efforts at the level of individual academy institutes, and individual scientists or research groups, is clearly related to the erosion of formerly strict hierarchical relations. As was pointed out, this erosion, although partly the effect of deliberate decentralization, followed also from the *corporate actor's* inability to ward off the trouble. Although this stands in contrast to the thesis that perceived inability to control threatening events (helplessness) results in organizational centralization and rigidity, it is in accordance with the widespread experience that in highly threatening and turbulent situations, such as a revolution or defeat in war, the erosion of larger, hierarchical structures is what typically happens.

▓ NOTES

1. For a summary review see Pugh and Hickson (1976).
2. This concept plays a focal role in the study by Wolf (1995).
3. Information by Elena Mirskaya, Moscow.
4. It does not contradict the validity of this statement to observe that the scientific establishment in socialist societies was actively involved in the process of research planning. Political control was not a simple top-down process but contained elements of bottom-up processes of planning within the politically defined framework of binding values and goals. A detailed description of this control structure for East Germany can be found in Kocka (1997).
5. The results of this study, performed by a network of researchers from the corresponding CEE countries under the coordination of Peter Weingart, Uwe Schimank, and myself and partly financed by the German Ministry of Research

and Technology, have in part already been published (see Mayntz, Schimank, & Weingart, 1995). A second phase of the joint project, consisting of case studies of the fate of three academy institutes per country, has been concluded in 1996 (see Mayntz, Schimank, & Weingart, 1998). The draft chapters of this publication, written by Julita Jabletzka, Stanislaw Provaznik, Petr Machleidt, Adolf Filacek, György Darvas, Eduar Sarmir, Stefan Zajac, Gennady Nesvetailov, Elena Miskaja, and Kostadinka Simeonova, form part of this chapter's database.

6. For Russia, see for example Couderc (1996).

7. In some countries, notably Romania, the imperative demand that science must be directly useful even became a threat to the very existence of the academy, which lost control over its institutes in 1974 and could not even elect new members to the learned society, being considered recalcitrant to demands for full political control over, and practical usefulness of, all scientific research. After the regime change, Romanian research institutes were in contrast required to perform mainly basic research to qualify for membership in the revived academy. See the (unpublished) case study report by Zaman, Sandu, and Dacin (1995), *Transformation der Rumänischen Akademie.*

8. This pressure was, of course, much stronger in the case of formally privatized research institutions, especially formerly state financed branch institutes that used to serve industry; see Couderc (1996) for details on Russia.

9. Information in a letter by A. Filácek and P. Machleidt.

10. Note should be taken that this is not the same as saying that the East German research potential suffered the greatest losses; as shown in more detail in Mayntz (1997), this is definitely not the case.

11. The importance of the definition (or interpretation) of the situation as a factor in making strategic choices has repeatedly been noticed (e.g., Lyles & Mitroff, 1980; Milliken, 1990).

12. For a more detailed analysis see Mayntz (1994a).

13. For a systematic analysis of the varied fates of East German academy institutes see Wolf (1995).

PART **III**

The Political
Economy of
Failure and
Bankruptcy

Successful Failure

An Alternative View of Organizational Coping

6

WOLFGANG SEIBEL

It is acknowledged in current organization theory that the morphology of efficient organizations may vary (Williamson, 1985). It is also theoretical common sense that organizational stability may be enhanced by niches of intraorganizational inefficiency in the form of organizational slack (Cyert & March, 1963). Moreover, it is acknowledged that single organizations may survive despite permanent inefficiency or failure (Leibenstein, 1978; Meyer & Zucker, 1989). The present article argues that relevant theory has to explain why resources can be continuously mobilized despite permanent failure. It is stated that, at the microlevel, a prerequisite of reliable failure is that *principals* as providers of resources are interested in low performance of their *agents*. Furthermore, it is stated that this kind of perverse interest requires ideologies as coping mechanisms, given the dilemma of interest in failure, on one hand, and the values of modern organizational culture based on efficiency and accountability, on the other hand. The basic hypothesis is that the homogeneity and ubiquitousness of means-and-end efficiency in modern organizational culture bear the risk of problem overload and that niches of reliable organizational inefficiency may function as a buffer mitigating that risk. Accordingly, reliable organizational failure may be a prerequisite of successful coping and risk reduction. Success may mean failure—and vice versa. Finally, as far as the macrolevel is concerned, it is stated that neither the private for-profit nor the public sector is likely to provide a stable environment for interest in failure and appropriate ideological coping mechanisms. Instead, there is good reason to assume the nonprofit or "third" sector provides all that it takes to secure successful organizational failure.

▨ WHY SHOULD PRINCIPALS CONTRIBUTE RESOURCES TO PERMANENTLY FAILING ORGANIZATIONS?

In available theory, the phenomenon of low-performance-high-persistence organizations is being explained by the failure of those in charge of the organization—owners, shareholders—to enforce their prerogatives in running the organization (Meyer & Zucker, 1989). Implicitly, this is a principal-agent perception of organizational management. As principals, we may conceive those controlling strategic resources of the organization while conceding performance control to "agents" (Fama, 1980; Ross, 1973). In a market economy, stockholders are the textbook case of principals, whereas the role of agents is assumed by managers. In the public sector, the principals are formed by the public at large and their representatives, whereas the agent function is performed by bureaucrats.

Suppose, however, that the principals loose control over organizational performance. In this case, why should they continue to contribute resources to it? One conventional answer points to information asymmetries (Arrow, 1963; Pauly, 1968). The agents—for example, managers—may not tell the truth about the organization's performance, and they are most likely inclined to be dishonest when performance is poor and the likelihood of the truth being discovered is small. In the business world, however, the hard indicators of performance—namely, figures on profit and losses—will ultimately unveil the truth. But as long as measurement of organizational performance is blurry, information asymmetries between principals and agents may persist. For instance, if the quality of services is hard to evaluate either because reasonable scales of measurement do not exist or because the person who purchases a good or service is not the consumer (as in the case of day care services; cf. Hansmann, 1980), the principals have no sound basis for their judgment on performance. Under such circumstances, the agent's incentive to tell the truth about poor performance is substantially weakened.

In this perspective, information asymmetry implies moral hazard and the persistence of a low-performance organization is conceived as the result of adverse selection: Those contributing resources are not aware of the real performance and those running the organization, behind a veil of ignorance, are constantly cheating. Consequently, low-performance organizations may persist, or even worse, because of lower production costs, they may supersede high-performance organizations (Akerlof, 1970). Still, this means to suppose that those contributing resources to the organization are interested in both high performance and complete information about performance. Accordingly, the public at large may insist on appropriate regulation or different kinds of counterincentives to opportunistic behavior behind the shield of information asymmetry.

The weakness of this kind of theorizing is that it does not allow for the assumption of reliable failure. In this perspective, organizational failure remains an accidental phenomenon nobody can definitely count on. As long as the principals of all kinds—shareholders, consumers, the public at large—are assumed to be interested in both high performance and in complete information on the actual degree of performance, failure cannot be assumed to be definitely "permanent." By the same token, however, one may assume failure to be a permanent pattern of organizational behavior if one could assume the principals' being interested in both low performance and ignorance on the actual degree of performance. How can we conceivably substantiate such an assumption? In what follows, I start with two illustrative cases.

▦ TWO EXAMPLES: HELP FOR BATTERED WOMEN, TRAINING AND EMPLOYMENT OF THE HANDICAPPED

Since the mid-1970s, the former West Germany and West Berlin have witnessed a growing number of houses for battered women. Feminism has strongly influenced both the founding and the organizational behavior of those institutions, most of which label themselves *"Autonome Frauen-häuser"* (Autonomous Women's Houses). *Autonomy* above all means independence from public authorities. Furthermore, the Autonomous Women's Houses (AWHs) observe several principles of self-guidance such as job rotation and suppression of formal hierarchy and professionalism. Work in the Houses is not defined as service but as solidarity among women. Finally, the AWHs intend to be "political" institutions not only providing help but also struggling against patriarchate as such.

The actual organizational behavior of the AWHs is characterized by substantial tensions between the feminist guidelines and the necessities of organizational goal attainment. Goal attainment not only requires traditional forms of organizational fitness and efficiency but also financial support from public authorities. The AWHs must struggle for survival and public subsidies. Accordingly, they have to address public authorities asking for public money. This fact alone is being perceived as partial surrender to the patriarchate. Moreover, the ideology of "autonomy" weakens the organizational strength of the AWHs, which in turn makes public authorities in the perception of the houses' leaders precisely as overwhelmingly strong as the feminist prejudices suppose. Ironically, the AWHs would have the chance to get more stable funding if they would accept being classified as "establishments" according to the Federal Social Help Act (*Bundessozialhilfegesetz* or BSHG). But the feminist leaders of the AWH movement reject this funding model in that such a status would individualize the collective phenomenon of patriarchate and male oppression and undermine the autonomous status of the houses. The AWHs are also reluctant to accept formal prescriptions of accountancy linked with the provision of public subsidies. Although these prescriptions—such as standards of minimal professional qualification, nomination of staff members representing the House vis-à-vis the authorities, equipment of the houses, and so on—belong to regular bureaucratic routine and may even be in the interests of the women seeking shelter, the AWHs try to escape from any external control at all. What they desire is the squaring of the cycle—a statutory funded independence.

Not surprisingly, this attitude creates permanent conflicts with the subsidy-giving authorities. Payments are seriously delayed, and much energy is absorbed in endless quarrels. The closed-minded attitude of the AWHs results in a self-fulfilling prophecy. Every exigency or reaction of the grant-giving authorities is a priori perceived as "bureaucratic" and oppressive and has to be rejected. If, due to this noncooperative behavior, the authorities refuse to do this or that or even stop payment, this is proof of the initial suspicion. And because in the perception of the authorities, the AWHs turn out to be dubious and untrustworthy institutions, the authorities feel obliged to exert even more rigid control.

As far as the internal side is concerned, rejection of professionalism and formal hierarchy is the crucial problem. Job rotation and fluctuating employment of staff members have a negative impact on the spirit of the houses. Frustration and burnout syndrome prevail (Steinert, 1988). The more frustration, the more fluctuation among staff members—another vicious circle. This situation sometimes causes conflicts between the staff and the board of an AWH. Whereas staff members tend to emphasize a rigorous rejection of formal professionalism and hierarchy, the board often emphasizes a certain organizational soundness as a prerequisite for successful work and successful dealing with public authorities. Such attitudes of the boards are often criticized by staff members as bureaucratic or even authoritarian. It is obvious that these internal conflicts weaken the overall position of the AWHs.

Another quasi-unsolvable problem in modern capitalism is employment of mentally or physically handicapped people. Nonetheless, a great attempt to solve this problem was made in West Germany with the Gravely Handicapped Persons Act (*Schwerbehindertengesetz*) of 1974. The law established so-called Workshops for Handicapped Persons (*Werkstätten für Behinderte*) whose purpose was to combine personal care for handicapped people with the improvement of their labor skills, with the aim to integrate them into the regular labor market. These workshops are nonprofit institutions in the form of charitable associations or limited-liability corporations. The idea was that the workshops would be partially sustained by public subsidies but mainly funded through their own entrepreneurial activities.

However, self-funding by the sale of products never became an important part of the workshops' resource mobilization. Entrepreneurial activity including marketing and sales strategies never has been developed (cf. Arnold, 1990). In fact, all the workshops are completely dependent on public subsidies and long-term contracts with customers, who use the weak position of the workshops to achieve low price levels. Thus, the simulation of the market forces to familiarize handicapped persons with the requirements of the regular labor market does not work. What is more, labor within the workshops is extremely poorly paid (150-400 deutschmarks or $100-$270 per month).

As far as staffing of the workshops is concerned, the law prescribes a double qualification of a manager. He or she has to have an economic as well as a psychological or pedagogical degree. But 15 years after the law was put into practice, only a minority of the managers had that double qualification (Arnold, 1990).

The workshops' boards of directors are mainly composed of representatives of subsidy-giving authorities, including the two Christian churches. They have no incentive to exert serious control over the workshops. They either keep a low profile or try to sharpen their profile through the amount of money they are able to mobilize for the organization.

In general, internal management as well as external control of the workshops is weak. The lack of business administration skills of the managers and the overrepresentation of public subsidy givers on the workshop's board make illusive any hopes of entrepreneurial behavior. The managements' behavior is entirely shaped by more or less sustained funding from public authorities. Instead of entrepreneurial spirit, a rent-seeking mentality is prevailing.

INTEREST IN FAILURE, INTEREST IN IGNORANCE

One may assume two kinds of principals and two kinds of interests. The first category of principals are those immediately responsible for the

TABLE 6.1 Principals' Interest in Inefficiency and in Ignorance of Inefficiency

	P1 (Board)	P2 (Public)
AWH		
I1	1	3
I2	2	4
WHP		
I1	5	7
I2	6	8

NOTE: AWH = Autonomous Women's Houses; WHP = Workshops for Handicapped Persons; I1 = Interest in inefficiency; I2 = Interest in ignorance of inefficiency; P1 = Principal 1: the boards; P2 = Principal 2: the public.

organization, typically board members. The second category is the public at large. There are also, we assume, two categories of interests. The first category is interest in organizational weakness, inefficiency, and so on. The second category is interest in ignorance about inefficiency. The two kinds of interests seem to be mutually exclusive. But they are not necessarily. Interest in inefficiency may be veiled by preference falsification (Kuran, 1995). One may assume organizational inefficiency to be the hidden preference of board members and the public. In a modern organizational culture, however, nobody can ever admit to be interested in inefficiency without violating the general values of organizational modernity. What board members and the public probably do is make others and themselves believe that organizational inefficiency, if existent at all, is a randomly occurring phenomenon that does not affect general organizational soundness and efficiency. As we know from research on cognitive dissonance and its social consequences (Festinger, 1957; Kuran, 1995, pp. 181-184), this is the way we try to reconcile values and actual behavior. Interests in inefficiency and interests in ignorance about inefficiency may occur simultaneously or separate of each other. Both kinds of interests may also serve as functional equivalents.

Given two kinds of principals, two kinds of interests, and two cases, we may draw an eight-field matrix (see Table 6.1).

In the case of AWHs, board members have no a priori interest in organizational inefficiency (Cell 1), but they are prevented from insisting on efficiency by ideological constraints. Accordingly, we may assume the AWH board members to be interested in ignorance of how weak the houses' performance really is (Cell 2). Patterns of justification will emerge to avoid or mitigate cognitive dissonances. They will probably include the pretense of nonapplicability of regular standards of efficiency and accountability due to an assumed incompatibility of "solidarity" and "altruism," on one hand, and organizational efficiency and accountability, on the other hand.

Still talking about the AWHs, why should the general public be interested in organizational inefficiency (Cell 3)? Suppose violence against women is a ubiquitous phenomenon: What results could be expected from efficient institutional arrangements to fight against it? Probably efficient management would reduce short-range organizational survival to a matter of standard operating procedures. Efficient management would, consequently, result in more available time and energy for strategic issues, and it would use time and energy skillfully and efficiently for that purpose. Efficient management would publicly reveal the ubiquitousness of a phenomenon that is subject to public reticence. It would remind a male-dominated public how recklessly males are treating women, and it would remind society of the inappropriate funding for those institutions that take care of what, presumably, is just the tip of the iceberg when it comes to violence against women. Why should a male-dominated public be interested in such kind of efficiency?

But why should the public be interested in ignorance of the inefficiency of the AWHs (Cell 4)? As long as there is some acknowledgment that male violence against women is something society should take care of, it is good to know that something is being done. To acknowledge openly how poorly AWHs are performing would cause serious cognitive dissonances. According to different ideological stances, it would either mean to acknowledge that a serious societal problem is rather insufficiently being dealt with or that something that in own's one perception is not a serious problem at all is subject to waste of money and human energy. One psychological compromise we might be inclined to accept is, as long as there is some acknowledgment that male violence against women is something society should take care of, it is good to know that something is being done, regardless of how it is being done and how efficiently it is being done.

In the case of the Workshops for Handicapped Persons (WHPs), one may assume direct interests of board members in organizational inefficiency (Cell 5). Unlike the board members of the AWHs, WHP board members are representatives of subsidy-giving authorities or other institutions relevant for resource mobilization (such as parties or churches). WHP board members are gatekeepers in terms of resource mobilization. They have an incentive to keep the organization dependent on their own discretion because this is what enhances their own prestige and power. Prestige and power are also enhanced by the network of dignitaries of local and regional social policy in which the boards of social service institutions of significant size are important nodes. Efficient WHP management would put this arrangement into jeopardy. It would destabilize existing networks as well as undermine the role of board members as influential gatekeepers in terms of resource mobilization. Efficient management would try to diversify resource mobilization and to avoid or to break up one-sided dependencies of certain subsidy givers. Why should board members be interested in such kind of efficiency?

But why should board members be interested in ignorance of the inefficiency of the WHPs (Cell 6)? Presumably, knowledge instead of ignorance would destabilize the network arrangement of the boards. If everyone would know about the inefficiency of the organization, general mistrust would prevail among the board members. Whether or not one of the board members would blow the whistle would be essentially uncertain. This kind of mistrust and uncertainty would destroy the basis of networking. Accordingly, board members must be essentially interested in sustaining the illusion that decent work is being done. What is more, they too have to keep their cognitive dissonances under control. Whether vis-à-vis their fellow board members or vis-à-vis themselves, they have to keep compatible the values of charity and social help, on one hand, and the values of organizational modernity, on the other hand. Thus, why should WHP board members be interested in the sad truth about performance?

But why should the public at large be interested in inefficient WHPs (Cell 7)? Ultimately, as in the case of the AWHs, efficiency would reduce the chance to escape some puzzling truths. Unlike AWHs, however, WHPs have no serious funding problem, and their task is not subject to ideological dispute. Care for the handicapped is widely acknowledged as a legitimate task of appropriate institutions. The peculiarity of the WHPs, however, is their ambitious goal. Integrating the handicapped into the labor market is a useless attempt in an era of mass employment that has characterized the European situation since the mid-1970s. To maintain an unattainable goal and to reduce the social and political costs of its unattainability is the main challenge connected to the WHPs. Efficient management of the workshops would increase the risk that the unattainability of their goals become obvious. Skillful managers would try to make the workshops relatively independent from the networks of well-established sponsoring through public and semipublic channels. Given the low degree of competitiveness of its workforce, the workshops could not rely on the market as a strategic source of revenues. Fund-raising would have to be diversified. Unlike fund-raising through the established networks, however, the new strategy would have to address a comparatively anonymous public, and it would have to be intensified. Skillful management would remind the public of its special obligation toward the handicapped. The public, thus, would be invited to spend more money for something unachievable without having a moral basis to reject such a request. Why should the public be interested in this kind of efficiency?

By the same token, one can assume the public at large to be interested in ignorance of the workshops' inefficiency (Cell 8). Given the remembrance of what was euphemistically called euthanasia during the Nazi period, the German public at large is definitely committed to the idea that economic and political strain should not affect the well-being of the weakest and handicapped members of society. To abandon officially the WHP's ambitious goal is thus subject to ideological constraints. What can be abandoned, however, is the quest for truth when it comes to the workshops' performance. The cognitive dissonances between the moral obligation toward the handicapped and the discernment of the uselessness of the workshops' endeavor may be mitigated just by the illusion that the workshops are doing a decent job. Thus, why should the public at large be interested in the truth about the workshops' poor performance?

THE STRUCTURAL AND IDEOLOGICAL PREREQUISITES OF SUCCESSFUL FAILURE

How can we generalize the findings on persistent failure in the cases we have examined in the previous section? First, both the AWHs and WHPs are in a peripheral position outside the dominant spheres of the public and the private sector. Actually, both are nonprofit institutions. Therefore, they are relatively remote from both fiscal auditing and public attention.

Within that framework, the core mechanism making the principals continue to provide resources to permanently failing organizations is based on a combination of interests and ideologies.

First, one prerequisite of continuous resource mobilization despite low performance is that the principals at both levels (board and public) are interested in failure rather than in achievement of the organization they are in charge of. Efficient management may jeopardize informal social networks that are crucial to resource mobilization. Efficient managers will tend to make the organization independent from resource constraints (Pfeffer & Salancik, 1978, pp. 106-110). They will, therefore, necessarily violate the interests of those who primarily use the organization for the purpose of social networking. Consider the board of trustees of an organization with the trustees being the organization's main funders: The trustees' interest in networking is being best served through the organization's tight dependence of the funds the trustees themselves provide. At least, the trustees cannot be expected to encourage those determined to loosen that dependence.

Second, another prerequisite of continuous resource mobilization despite low performance is that the principals at both levels (board and public) prefer not being confronted with dilemmas that the organization has to cope with. Consider the organization's job being something terrible, disgusting, or just puzzling. Again, the mere remoteness from public attention may facilitate forgetting about those jobs. But efficient managers, even in a peripheral position, will focus on the organization's strategic weakness as far as public attention is concerned. Why, then, not prefer weak instead of strong managers in charge of puzzling problems, supposing that strong and efficient agents could remind the principals to provide more resources for appropriate solutions?

Third, the interests in low instead of high performance have to be reconciled with the values of organizational modernity based on the principles of efficiency and accountability. It is here where the role of myths and ideology has to be considered (Meyer & Rowan, 1977; Starbuck, 1982). In the cases examined in the previous section, the evaluation of performance was subject to an ideology based on values— such as charity, solidarity, altruism—which, to some degree at least, protect the organization against the "inappropriate" application of efficiency and accountability standards. The values themselves have to symbolize something that the principals hold in high esteem, something subject to nostalgia or other kinds of myths (such as charitable purposes or one's own youth in case of alumni clubs). More generally, ideologies have to mitigate the cognitive dissonances caused by the gap between poor performance and the standards of organizational efficiency and accountability.

Presumably, interests and ideologies are mutually dependent. The interest in low degrees of organizational performance causes the need for justifying ideas. But the ideas would not create a stable veil of ignorance if they were not based on interests. Thus, ignorance itself is what those providing resources have to be interested in. One can hardly imagine permanent failure without demand for ignorance.

▓ WHY THE NONPROFIT SECTOR PROVIDES A STABLE ENVIRONMENT FOR SUCCESSFUL FAILURE

The probability of reliable failure according to what had been outlined in the previous section would increase if

- organizations find themselves in a peripheral position outside the dominant spheres of the public and the private sector;

- those providing resources to the organization are interested in failure rather than in achievement;

- those providing resources to the organization prefer not to be confronted with dilemmas the organization has to cope with;

- plausible ideologies are available that protect the organization against the "inappropriate" application of efficiency and account-ability standards, thus mitigating the cognitive dissonances caused by the gap between poor performance and the standards of organi-zational efficiency and accountability;

- demand for ignorance is satisfied, which stabilizes the illusion of the compatibility of organizational performance and the standards of organizational efficiency and accountability.

Neither private enterprises nor public bureaucracies provide an envi-ronment in which a critical mass of these prerequisites is likely to occur. In both sectors, the logic of competition and hierarchy creates intolerable uncertainty as soon as the principles of efficiency and accountability are challenged. Even if one admits these values are mainly myths and ceremo-nies (Meyer & Rowan, 1977), one cannot afford to abandon them. The values of efficiency and accountability provide the cultural backbone of organizational modernity. This is why one may imagine inefficiency and general failure to occur randomly and exceptionally. To imagine failure to be a systematic element of organizational culture, however, would appear as the pandemonium of essential uncertainty.

The following will state that the institutional sphere between the market and the state may be interpreted as that stable niche where permanently failing organizations have a solid chance to survive. This sphere—usually called nonprofit sector or just "third sector"—provides both the structural and the cultural (mental and cognitive) prerequisites of reliable organizational failure.

Nonprofit institutions have a precarious structure of resource mobi-lization. The mobilization of monetary resources is restricted by what is being called the nondistribution constraint. The "nonprofit" status means that money cannot be mobilized from investors looking for capital assets. At the same time, statutory money is also absent. Unlike public bureau-cracies, nonprofit institutions cannot count on steady financing through public budgets. Given this precarious situation, nonprofit institutions can survive only if they develop appropriate and, possibly, stable structures of alternative resource mobilization (Gronbjerg, 1993). Because the nonpersonal and anonymous structures of the market and the state are not available, personal networks are the main structural compensation (cf. Pfeffer & Salancik, 1978, pp. 161-175). The leaders of nonprofit institutions try to bind potential donors and sponsors or their representatives to the organization through co-opting them into the boards of directors or trustees. These boards represent the characteristic governance structure of nonprofit institutions.

However, the boards also provide an opportunity structure for the enhancement of prestige and local or regional power (Middleton, 1987), which is, indeed, the only inducement a nonprofit institution can provide to its active sponsors. The mere existence of the board is basic to this opportunity structure of prestige and power. Thus, the opportunity structure itself is independent from the respective organization's performance. What is more, high performance may even negatively affect the power-related opportunity structure of a board of directors or trustees. Efficient management may not only jeopardize informal social networks, it may also make the organization independent from single sources of monetary support. Such attempts to reach flexibility and independence are likely to violate the interests of those who primarily use the organization for networking, because these interests are best being served through enduring dependence of a given nonprofit organization from a given set of sponsors.

A similar pattern holds for the mobilization of labor resources. Due to the monetary constraints, nonprofit institutions suffer from a competitive disadvantage regarding salaries and wages. The compensation is what is being called making a virtue out of necessity: Nonprofit institutions may indeed define themselves as "something special," meaning an organizational phenomenon that, fortunately, belongs neither to the cold and hostile world of profit making nor to the anonymous world of the leviathan and its giant bureaucracy.

The ideological halo surrounding a nonprofit institution may fulfill a multiple function. First, it may attract a labor force adherent to the very antiprofit-antibureaucracy ideology, willing to work in a friendly environment for relatively low wages. Second, it may attract a voluntary workforce with no special ideological commitment whose compensation is not money but the good feeling of doing good (Karylowski, 1982). Third, it may attract donations, because people prefer to give to an organization that is forced to keep its surplus instead of distributing it to asset owners. Fourth, the idea of a nonprofit institution being something special may cause an image according to which the usual criteria of efficiency and accountability are not applicable to this unique type of organization.

When it comes to performance control, the nonprofit sector is indeed structurally remote from public attention. Because individual payments to nonprofit institutions are typically made as voluntary donations, the general public does not focus the taxpayer's sharp eye on the nonprofit sector. In fact, although heavily dependent on public support, nonprofit institutions remain private institutions in the common sense as well as in the legal sense. Nonprofit leaders are neither elected by the public nor formally accountable to it. No general accounting office regularly examines nonprofit institutions even if they are heavily subsidized through public money. Thus, unlike the situation in the public sector, the absence of control through a competitive market is substituted neither by control through hierarchy and formal rules nor by control through public attention.

Finally, there is empirical evidence that Western democracies delegate especially puzzling problems to nonprofit institutions: The integration of the handicapped into the labor market, especially in periods of high unemployment rates; the unemployment of young and unskilled workers with its consequences for social peace and urban security; the upkeep and maintenance of satisfying hospital care with justifiable rates of government subsidies and at affordable insurance premiums; the changing gender relationship with eroding ideological justification of sex discrimination and the consequences for economic and political life; the changing structure of the family with a growing number of both double-income, no-kids couples and single-parenthood and its consequences for social integration of children or retirement pensions; the demographic changes with fewer young and more old people with its consequences for retirement pensions, health insurance, home care, and hospital care for the elderly—all these problems are far from being neatly solved according to means-end rationality. As recent data show (Salamon & Anheier, 1996), nonprofit institutions hold an unproportionately large share of related social services and infrastructure.

Why is this so? Suppose many of the above problems are particularly pressing: Why delegate them to an institutional segment whose resource dependency, governance structure, and ideology imply weak rather than strong performance? It is here, we suppose, where an interest in illusion on organizational performance is located. It is not just that board members of nonprofit institutions as principals may be interested in weak performing managers as agents, because otherwise the networking function of the board could be put in jeopardy. Also we may assume the public at large to be interested in weak rather than strong organizational structures when coping rather than problem solving is requested. Nonprofit institutions may be especially suited to cope with the contradictions of organizational modernity. According to the logic of modernity and its intrinsic principles of organizational efficiency and accountability, we refuse to accept both problem nonsolving and organizational failure as standards of responses to problems of any kind. When it comes to unsolvable problems, the competitive advantage of nonprofit institutions as opposed to public sector and private sector institutions is that they may function as placebo arrangements (Seibel, 1989). They may symbolize problem solving while solving nothing at all. They may pretend to be not just as efficient but even more efficient than private or public institutions when it comes to the delivery of certain services while being definitely inefficient and unaccountable.

Nonprofit institutions provide all that it takes to secure this kind of coping arrangement. Because of their unique kind of resource mobilization through personal networks, nonprofits may decouple persistence from performance (cf. Meyer & Zucker, 1989, pp. 91-118). Because of their peripheral position outside the dominant spheres of the public and the private sector, nonprofit institutions are relatively remote from critical public attention. Because of their neither-private-nor-public status, they may build up an ideology based on principles—such as charity, solidarity, altruism—that not only have a prominent place on the societal value scale but that also, to some degree, protect the organization against the "inappropriate" application of efficiency and accountability standards. Because of both their peripheral position and their ideological halo, nonprofit institutions have a psychological advantage when just cushioning rather than solving problems is a feasible option.

This is not to say that nonprofit institutions will be necessarily inefficient and unaccountable. There is sufficient empirical evidence that nonprofit institutions may achieve outstanding performance. However, the argument is that the nonprofit sector as such provides a stable and friendly environment for low-performance-high-persistence organizations. The stability of the nonprofit or third sector is well grounded both in the sphere of interests and in the sphere of values. What is more, the position of a third sector beyond the market and the state limits the risk of spillovers. Reliable failure may be contained through the blurring boundaries between the third sector and the private and the public sector, according to the logic of loose coupling (Glassman, 1973; Weick, 1976). The availability of third sector arrangements, however, may enhance institutional elasticity in general. Societies that encompass a robust third sector may be well tuned to cope with both unsolvable problems and the unintended consequences of collective action.

Veiled Politics

Bankruptcy as a Structured Organizational Field

7

KEVIN J. DELANEY

C asual observers sometimes use the terms *bankruptcy* and *organizational failure* interchangeably. But I have argued in much of my research that at least in the world of megabankruptcy,[1] the filing of a Chapter 11 petition is often a strategic ploy used by management or institutional creditors to force a resolution of an intractable organizational dilemma (see Delaney, 1992a, 1992b, 1994). I have shown that a sociopolitical model provides a useful alternative to economic and legal models for understanding bankruptcy (Delaney, 1994). In short, I have shown that in many major cases, a bankruptcy filing may represent many things *other* than organizational failure. In this article, I will outline the circumstances under which bankruptcy may specifically be a form of what I will call "veiled politics." By this I mean that the bankruptcy arena provides organizations with the opportunity to resolve complex political problems, filling a vacuum left by failed political decision making at a national level, or alternatively, bankruptcy presents organizations with the opportunity to *circumvent* overt political decisions. I will also illustrate how nonbankrupt corporations piggyback their own corporate strategies on the bankruptcy strategies of other firms. Thus, decisions made in individual bankruptcy cases serve to structure nonbankruptcy solutions to similar organizational and political problems.

In the second part of the article, I argue that bankruptcy can be understood as a tightly structured organizational field, exploring why the field may be an attractive environment for corporations in search of solutions to pressing dilemmas. Combining this concept of an organizational field with insights from the sociology of law and the professions, I show that the megabankruptcy field is structured by those with both resources and very specific types of professional knowledge. From this section, it will become clear not only why some organizations prefer bankruptcy but also why using bankruptcy to resolve major social issues represents a threat to democratic decision making. The bankruptcy arena translates political problems that involve individuals and communities in patterns of resolution historically rooted in, and better suited to, the protection of private capital interests and negotiations among large, powerful institutions. The final section of the article addresses the implications of viewing bankruptcy as politics for general theories of organizational failure.

As I build this argument, I draw from an archive of information about large corporate bankruptcies. For all the cases cited in this article, I conducted a review of the business and popular press as well as of published court decisions. In a few cases, I conducted field research at the bankruptcy hearings, particularly those cases from the Southern District of New York. Additional information is drawn from interviews I conducted in New York City with eight leading corporate bankruptcy attorneys. These lawyers provided insights into many of the major cases discussed in this article as well as general observations about the field of large corporate bankruptcy. I am indebted to them for their time and candor.

▦ BANKRUPTCY AS POLITICS BY ANOTHER NAME

If politics is defined as the "striving of groups and individuals to influence the distribution of resources in their favor" (Marger, 1981, p. 26), then bankruptcy court has surely become an arena of politics. Particularly since the Bankruptcy Reform Act of 1978, which opened up the bankruptcy process through a broadened definition of a "claim" against a company (see Delaney, 1992b), more large corporations with complex organizational problems—sometimes completely of their own making and sometimes not—have entered bankruptcy to resolve their dilemmas. At the same time, governmental structures either set the stage for the increasing use of bankruptcy—through broadened bankruptcy legislation, for example—or failed to provide solutions to major national problems caused by, or involving, corporations. In other cases, governmental structures (e.g.,

TABLE 7.1 Select List of Megabankruptcy Cases

Corporation	*Main Issue*
Amatex	Mass injury (asbestos)
Johns-Manville	Mass injury (asbestos)
UNR	Mass injury (asbestos)
A. H. Robins	Mass injury (Dalkon Shield)
Dow Corning	Mass injury (silicone breast implants)
Quanta Resources	Toxic waste site
T. P. Long Chemical	Toxic waste site
Penn Terra	Toxic waste site
Oklahoma Refining Co.	Toxic waste site
Chem-Dyne Corp.	Toxic waste site
Greyhound	Unionized labor
Continental Airlines	Unionized labor
Eastern Airlines	Unionized labor
Braniff	Unionized labor
Texaco	Competitive weapon
BiCoastal	Competitive weapon
LTV	Pension obligations
Pan American Airways	Pension obligations
Trans World Airlines	Pension obligations
Wheeling-Pitt	Pensions/labor
Kaiser Steel	LBO
Resorts International	LBO
Salant Corporation	Junk bonds
Revco	LBO/Junk bonds

Congress) thought they *had* made a decision only to find that another state-sanctioned arena (i.e., the bankruptcy court) provided an alternative means to the corporation's desired end.

Table 7.1 lists some examples in which bankruptcy has been used as veiled politics. This table, by no means exhaustive, illustrates the array of social issues that have found their way into bankruptcy court in the last two decades: litigation over a variety of harmful or deadly products, environmental clean-up costs, battles between unions and management, underfunded pension plans, and soaring health care costs.

Although it may seem counterintuitive to commonsense notions that link bankruptcy to failure, a Chapter 11 filing appears as a potential *solution* to organizations seeking to resolve serious organizational dilemmas. Figure 7.1 illustrates how Chapter 11 bankruptcy can become a form of veiled, or covert, political action. The left-hand column provides examples of the organizational dilemmas that have led firms to consider bankruptcy. As I will show later, each dilemma is intimately connected to political issues and has serious results for wide sectors of society, including not only members of the corporations directly involved but also other corporations with similar dilemmas, and various stakeholders completely external to the corporation, such as consumers of the firm's products or communities where the firm is located. The middle column of the chart illustrates classes of options typically sought by corporations to resolve these dilemmas, listed in the order they are typically pursued. As each stage in the organization's search for a solution becomes blocked, the organization moves down the chain searching for a solution that allows the corporation to survive.

Typically, organizations first try to solve the dilemma internally through accrued resources. If they are unable to do this, often because their resources do not cover the cost of the problem, they look to a "network solution," which entails gaining assistance from other important organizations in their environment, often those with long-standing ties to the corporation. Examples of network solutions might be a long-term bank lender allowing forgiveness or restructuring of a loan, a bank consortium providing a new set of loans, or financial relief from major suppliers or customers, such as restructuring repayment terms or prices.

If the dilemma continues to prove intractable at this stage, perhaps because powerful network members decide the cost of resolution is too high for them to bear or because not all network members can agree on a solution, organizations typically look to the federal or state government for assistance through what I call "overt politics" (e.g., a bailout). If government refuses to provide a solution, the corporation may then play the bankruptcy card. Here, we see bankruptcy as a form of veiled politics; by this I mean it is an attempt to gain a negotiated settlement to a major social issue in a state-sponsored arena (bankruptcy court) after an overt political solution has failed. Here, bankruptcy is used as a corporate strategy, rather than as an admission of organizational failure or decline. Bankruptcy represents a specialized state-sponsored arena in which the organization may resolve its dilemma more favorably than simply continuing business as usual in other organizational environments. Only if veiled politics fail does liquidation, or firm exit, occur. Thus, Chapter 11 bankruptcy is not always a case of organizational failure in that it does not necessarily represent micro- or macroeconomic problems in the typical sense but instead may be used as an alternative forum for political negotiation.

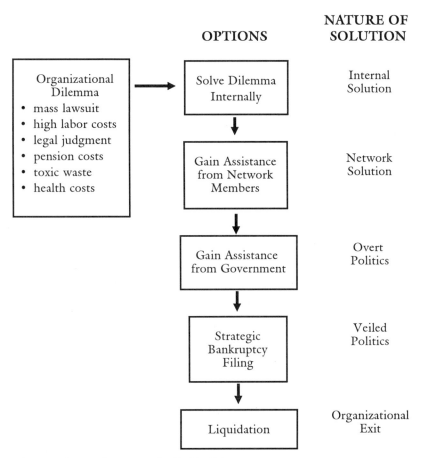

| | **OPTIONS** | **NATURE OF SOLUTION** |

Figure 7.1. Bankruptcy as Veiled Politics

In the remainder of this section, I provide examples of corporations' use of the bankruptcy process to achieve political resolution to major dilemmas. In these cases, bankruptcy is used to fashion political settlements or to circumvent political decisions made in other arenas. A bankruptcy plan may then be used by bankruptcy judges as a basis to fashion settlements in similar cases. Firms that never file bankruptcy also build on bankruptcy strategies—for example, by threatening but never declaring bankruptcy—to gain the advantages afforded by bankruptcy while avoiding some of the costs and stigma of a bankruptcy filing.

Mass injury cases have led to some of the most innovative, and controversial, political settlements in bankruptcy, with the Johns-Manville case leading the way. The asbestos health crisis peaked in the late 1970s as tens of thousands of workers exposed to asbestos and school districts and other organizations that had spent vast amounts of money to remove asbestos from their buildings filed lawsuits against asbestos manufacturers. Manville, the largest and wealthiest of the asbestos firms, first tried to use its own resources to weather the storm. The company also tried to negotiate a network solution in the form of debt restructuring from its lenders but ultimately failed as creditors balked at the size of the debt forgiveness required of them. Manville next took the lead role among asbestos producers in lobbying Congress for a bailout that would bar individual lawsuits and provide governmental funding to help pay for damage (based on the argument that many asbestosis victims suffered exposure in government shipyards). Although Manville lobbied vigorously for its bill, a Senate subcommittee refused to bail Manville out of its dilemma. Manville then *chose* bankruptcy as an alternative route to pursue the political solution it was seeking. In bankruptcy, innovative lawyers and the bankruptcy judge fashioned a collective compensation plan that shields Manville from all future lawsuits (including suits from victims who will develop asbestosis years after the bankruptcy case) and from punitive damages. Barred from suing the firm, victims can draw only from the Manville Trust Fund, which is bankrolled by 10% of Manville's annual profits. The fund has run out of money each and every year because the number and severity of cases has been much higher than was estimated in the bankruptcy plan. For its part, Manville has begun to remake itself as a building products company and can secure lending once again in that lenders now know the firm's asbestos liability is capped.

In many ways, the Manville plan, clearly a work of political negotiation, was modeled on the Agent Orange Fund created in a district court. The Manville plan was then used as a model by other asbestos companies that piggybacked on the Manville solution, either by going into Chapter 11 themselves or by fashioning a similar settlement of their cases without filing bankruptcy. For example, Eagle-Pitcher, a smaller asbestos company, tried to gain a Manville-style solution *without* having to go bankrupt; it simply used the Manville precedent and got a district court judge[2] to consolidate all injury cases into a collective settlement. At the time, asbestos victims complained bitterly that the deal brokered by the judge treated asbestos victims but no other parties, *as if* Eagle Pitcher were in bankruptcy (Feder, 1990, p. D2). Thus, Manville built on the Agent Orange plan and then chartered the political course that similarly situated asbestos corporations, like Amatex, UNR, and Raybestos, followed.

Settlements in other mass injury cases were subsequently modeled on the asbestos experience: A. H. Robins's bankruptcy filing over liability for the Dalkon Shield intrauterine device and Dow Corning's ongoing attempt to gain a settlement for illnesses victims believe were caused by leaking silicone breast implants are just two visible examples. Here, we see corporations following successful bankruptcy strategies of other corporations and bankruptcy judges building on solutions created in other major cases.

In all of these mass injury cases, critical political decisions were made on how to treat current health claimants in the bankruptcy arena (as unsecured creditors) as well as how to treat future victims who did not yet know they had a health problem from a faulty product (in the Manville case, future asbestos victims were represented through a single corporate lawyer, Leon Silverman[3]). Decisions were made by the court on the value of serious injuries and the value of a life. Punitive damages in each case were barred through the reorganization plan, and then future victims—who do not yet know they have been injured—were said to have agreed to barring punitive damages because "their representative" assented to this decision![4]

Here, then, we vividly see bankruptcy as politics. The corporations involved exhausted the various avenues listed in Figure 7.1 but strategically played the bankruptcy card to avoid liquidation. Whether this experience matches the macroeconomic theory of bankruptcy (the process is said to sweep inefficient firms out of the market, allowing efficient firms to reorganize) becomes a moot point in that survival centers more on shrewd political-legal strategy and touches on questions of production efficiency or the quality of managerial decision making about products and markets in, at best, tangential ways.[5] For many of these firms, in fact, one could argue that managers made many monumentally poor decisions or perhaps committed true misdeeds, but through their sheer power and use of the Chapter 11 process, they were able to survive anyway.

In addition to the mass injury cases, bankruptcy has been used as a device to avoid cleaning up toxic waste sites. Quanta Resources used a Chapter 11 filing to abandon an oil tanker contaminated with PCBs in New York Harbor. New York City and New Jersey eventually spent $8 million to clean up the abandoned mess. Quanta abandoned the property, under the Bankruptcy Code, calling the tanker an asset "inconsequential to the value of the debtor corporation." Quanta is just one of several corporations that have abandoned environmental disasters through bankruptcy. T. P. Long and Penn Terra similarly avoided clean-up costs through a Chapter 11 filing.

Underfunded pension funds are arguably a problem caused by poor or deceptive management. However, if a company is large enough, it can use bankruptcy to remedy this problem as well. For example, Eastern Airlines filed for bankruptcy in 1990 and terminated its underfunded pension plan. Eastern eventually paid about 20% of all pension claims, leaving 80% to be picked up by the Pension Benefits Guarantee Corporation (PBGC), the government insurance program for pensions housed in the U.S. Department of Labor. Eastern was not alone in this strategy. Kaiser Steel and LTV both transferred pension obligations to PBGC when the steel industry declined. Pan Am received IRS waivers for 6 straight years allowing it to skip contributions to its pension fund because of financial difficulties. The skipped payments did not help, however, and when Pan Am filed for bankruptcy in 1991, its plan was underfunded by almost $800 million (Ferguson & Blackwell, 1995). In many cases, corporations begin to raid or underfund their pensions in an attempt to survive. Eventually, the strategy reaches its limit and the firm opts for Chapter 11 and attempts to transfer some or all of their pension obligations onto the federal government.[6] A PBGC-sponsored study showed that in the 5 years before a pension plan is terminated, the plan's funding of promised benefits falls from 80% to 40% (see Ferguson & Blackwell, 1995; U.S. General Accounting Office, 1992).[7] Many bankruptcy attorneys see pension cases and bankruptcies designed to reduce health care costs as major contributors of future bankruptcy filings for large corporations.

Corporations have used bankruptcy extensively as a weapon to combat unionized labor, scuttle signed labor contracts, and reduce total labor costs. Greyhound, Continental Airlines, and Eastern Airlines all used Chapter 11 as a weapon against their unions. Claiming that labor costs would soon drive them out of business, these corporations filed bankruptcy and simply repudiated signed labor agreements.[8] They then reorganized with drastically reduced labor costs. Again, the mimicking of bankruptcy strategy can be seen in the labor cases. Throughout its own bankruptcy, Continental Airlines monitored a much smaller bankruptcy case, Bildisco and Bildisco, a New Jersey builder that had declared bankruptcy to rid itself of its union. When the Supreme Court decided in favor of Bildisco, it cleared the way for Continental to emerge from its own bankruptcy with drastically slashed labor costs. According to one of the leading bankruptcy lawyers in the Continental case, the Bildisco decision had put the final stamp of approval on their strategy (personal communication, August 1991). As in the mass-injury examples, other healthier corporations then piggybacked the bankruptcy strategy without actually going bankrupt, this time simply threatening their unions with a bankruptcy filing if did not accept wage and work rule concessions. Eastern copied Continental, and many other airlines held out the specter of bankruptcy to their unionized employees as part of negotiating strategy. Wheeling-Pitt, a large steelmaker, followed the lead of McClouth Steel Products, which used a bankruptcy filing to cut labor costs. In these cases, the bankruptcy settlement of one player in an industry puts pressure on the other more healthy players to adopt similar strategies to compete. In the airline industry, it was the weakest players who first used the bankruptcy strategy. Turning the economic theory of bankruptcy completely on its head, then, bankruptcy becomes a strategic card that helps the *weakest* organizations in a market niche survive, or at least survive for a longer period of time, leading to further instability in the market segment and, potentially, the weakening of stronger players in the industry.

Corporations have even begun using bankruptcy filings, or the threat of filings, against one another. Bicoastal (formerly Singer) and Texaco used bankruptcy as competitive weapons against corporate rivals. Texaco lost a massive judgment to Pennzoil because it had illegally interfered in Pennzoil's planned takeover of Getty Oil. Texaco balked at paying the civil court judgment awarded to Pennzoil for damages incurred by Texaco's interference in the takeover and went bankrupt instead, negotiating better terms for itself against Pennzoil. In effect, Texaco used bankruptcy to circumvent a civil court decision.

Other major corporate problems have found their way to bankruptcy court for settlement. Kaiser Steel, McCall Pattern, Resorts International, and Revco were all leveraged buyouts (LBOs) gone bust. Salant Corporation (maker of Perry Ellis fashions) went the bankruptcy route not once but twice to deal with the debacle caused by its overexpansion through junk bonds. Although these cases are less clearly political than some of the others, they are corporations that by all accounts were mismanaged through risky financial maneuvers yet used bankruptcy to be pulled back from the brink. Orange County California's bankruptcy filing, resulting from overreliance on derivatives, combines politics and economics in a dramatic way as mainstream, local political decisions such as the funding of schools and parks are traded off against the interests of bondholders in the bankruptcy court.

Whether it be abandoning toxic waste sites, trying to cap damage awards from harmful products, or underfunded pension plans, social and political issues are being decided in bankruptcy courts. If bankruptcy is indeed an arena of politics—of claim-staking and claim-making—how does this arena operate? How democratic are the processes that decide the fate of millions of citizens? What players are most influential in structuring outcomes, and why is this setting appealing to institutional actors? In the following section, I argue that the field of megabankruptcy is highly structured by its own history and by certain institutional players and indicate why this field may, under certain circumstances, be appealing to corporations in search of solutions to major organizational crises.

▦ BANKRUPTCY AS A STRUCTURED ORGANIZATIONAL FIELD

Pierre Bourdieu's (1975) notion of an organizational field (Bourdieu & Wacquant, 1992) is useful in understanding the appeal of bankruptcy to corporate actors. An organizational field attempts to capture the idea that organizations operate in a social system that is more than a collection of institutions or a network characterized by dyadic ties between organizations. A field is "clearly constituted by all the positions, relationships, and strategies in which interrelated 'speakers' acquire, from one another and in different quotients, the authority to speak" (Larson, 1990, p. 34). As DiMaggio and Powell (1991) argue, an organizational field cannot be defined a priori but must be understood through empirical investigation. Most important, to borrow from Larson (1990), the field is recognized as a site of competitive struggle over the recognition and monopolization of expert authority.

Figure 7.2 illustrates what I call the megabankruptcy field. The field is clearly recognized by the players involved as an arena with demarcated boundaries as various organizations within the field (e.g., large law firms with bankruptcy practices) recognize other players as being part of the field. Professional expertise, particularly law and financial expertise, is generally necessary to have authority and impact within the field.

The middle circle of Figure 7.2 represents the debtor corporation that files Chapter 11. Certain internal organizational members become key players in bankruptcy, particularly the in-house legal counsel and the top financial management team. The in-house counsel helps management interact with various outside bankruptcy counsel. These outside counsel are the true bankruptcy experts. As I have shown elsewhere, the group of major bankruptcy attorneys is quite small. In my interviews with corporate attorneys in New York City, each attorney typically cited six to eight other major firms (and one lead lawyer at each firm) as key players in most major cases in that district. Each interviewed attorney produced an almost identical list of top experts.

The outside counsel puts into play a series of experts from its own network (e.g., valuation analysts, investment bankers) to assemble strategy and information in the case. Various creditors of the bankrupt firm (mainly commercial banks and insurance companies) also use in-house and outside bankruptcy counsel. Also, included in the bankruptcy field, of course, is the bankruptcy judge. In major jurisdictions, for example the Southern District of New York, certain judges are assigned the most complex cases. Thus, judges often build expertise in large, difficult bank-

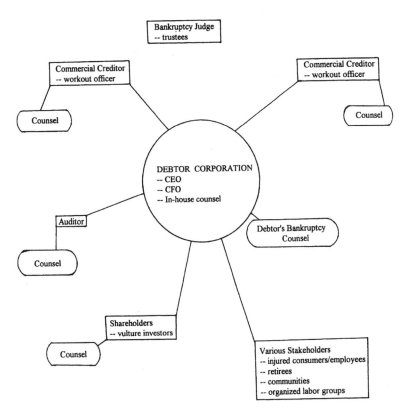

Figure 7.2. The Megabankruptcy Field

ruptcy cases and then build on their accumulated political and legal models to apply and extend solutions from one case to others, as discussed previously. Shareholders are part of the field as well, most notably the "vulture investors," which are investment groups that specialize in buying up the stocks and bonds of bankrupt companies and then use their collective muscle to negotiate a greater payback than their bargain-basement purchase. Various other stakeholders also enter the field depending on the case, including labor groups, consumer groups, and health claimants.

One of the first things you may notice when looking at the megabankruptcy field is that certain interests, to use Galanter's (1974) term, are "repeat players." They stay in the bankruptcy field because it is their raison d'être; they are bankruptcy professionals. Others, however, are one-time players, appearing in bankruptcy court only once, bringing with them no accumulated expertise or connections. Thus, the bankruptcy field is

TABLE 7.2 Power Resources Within the Megabankruptcy Field

	Bankruptcy Knowledge	
	One-Time Player	Repeat Player
Financial resources		
High	Corporate management	Bankruptcy lawyers
		Commercial creditors
		Vulture Investors
Low	Consumers	Bankruptcy judge
	Health claimants	Some unions
	Retirees	(e.g., airline unions)

structured most effectively by repeat players with accumulated knowledge, experience, and connections. These players fight for advantage not just in the particular case of the moment but for future cases where they will have involvement. This helps explain why so few bankruptcy lawyers play both sides of the fence, representing debtors and creditors.

Table 7.2 illustrates one way to think about the power of the various players in the bankruptcy field based on two important dimensions that lend power and authority within the field: knowledge and financial resources. Although corporate management of the debtor corporation may have high resources, they tend to be low on knowledge (within the bankruptcy arena) because they are one-time players; thus, they contract those with high knowledge: bankruptcy attorneys who specialize in debtor representation. The most powerful players *within the bankruptcy field* are likely to be those who are both repeat players and have high resources—in particular the commercial creditors and their counsel. Commercial creditors, because of their numerous lending relationships, are very experienced in the bankruptcy arena in that some percentage of their clients will declare Chapter 11. They appear in bankruptcy court often, unlike corporate management, who tend to experience bankruptcy only the one time they go the Chapter 11 route. As may be obvious, the least powerful players are those who are one-time players (low knowledge) and have fewer resources; these include consumers, health claimants, and retirees.

The bankruptcy field shows certain regularities that reflect its historical place in apportioning assets and debts. Like most areas of commercial law, business bankruptcy had been a somewhat closed field and no one worried greatly about this 20 or 30 years ago. The field was once more limited to technical financial disputes between organizational players battling over the payment of debt. Thus, it is a field designed for corporations and their creditors, with complex procedures centered on the distribution of assets and debts among institutional interests. As new types of cases have entered bankruptcy, bankruptcy judges have struggled to fit new classes of claimants into the old debtor/creditor framework. For example, individual consumers who may one day develop asbestosis from a harmful product are treated as unsecured creditors of the corporation. The field favors financial expertise, financial language, and financial epistemologies. More fundamentally, the field is premised on the protection of private capital interests (Delaney, 1992b).[9]

In the new world of bankruptcy (post-1978 Bankruptcy Reform Act), where nonexperts have seen their interests trampled on, the closed nature of the field becomes of great concern. As Larson (1990) writes of fields,

> [They] are best seen as battlefields, wherein different kinds of experts fight for pre-eminence and where other, "non-expert" forces also intervene. . . . the degree to which these arenas of struggle are open to common citizens is both a measure of democracy and one of the stakes of democratic politics. (p. 35)

Thus, the degree of openness to outsiders becomes a key measure of the democracy within the bankruptcy field.

Nonexperts, however, have a difficult time comprehending the habitus of the bankruptcy field, gaining standing as an "expert voice," and translating their interests into the legal apparatus of bankruptcy. This matters less, perhaps, when large organizations battle one another. But now the fate of women injured by faulty breast implants are decided through bankruptcy. Communities polluted by PCBs attempting to gain redress are shuttled into the bankruptcy court, and unionized workers watch their negotiated contracts torn up before their eyes through a bankruptcy filing.

Only in a closed field developed around financial-legal constructions of knowledge could someone with a lung tumor from asbestos exposure or a woman with silicone leaking throughout her body from a faulty breast implant be transformed into "an unsecured creditor" of the very corporation responsible for their injuries. Formerly litigants in civil court, health claimants are transmuted into unsecured creditors in bankruptcy and their claims against the corporation are put on par with other unsecured loans.

Corporations prefer the organizational field of bankruptcy because they prefer the language of finance to that of expert testimony on personal injuries or unfair labor practices; they prefer a collective settlement funded by a percentage of yearly profits to uncapped litigation; they prefer the prohibition of punitive damages and the treatment of injured individuals as a class of unsecured creditors. However, the very things that make the field appealing to corporations make it an inappropriate place to resolve political issues. When an injured claimant or a labor union are legalistically transmuted into unsecured creditors, we are not just witnessing a handy device for using bankruptcy in a new way. Instead, we are seeing a change in the defining nature of the relationship between the corporation and these other parties. The types of claims injured parties can make, the types of knowledge they can apply and have recognized as legitimate, and the ways of understanding the essence of their dispute have also been changed. They have "become creditors," put on par with institutional creditors who are much more adept at "being creditors."

Although in the short term this use of bankruptcy has surely hurt unorganized and less powerful groups with little expertise in the world of corporate bankruptcy, it is important to recognize that these cases also represent the potential opening up of a formerly closed field, a process that may threaten the very experts that have found the field so appealing in the past. More nonexpert interests have been dragged into bankruptcy court. If labor unions, consumer groups, and environmental activists become repeat players, they will bring their own experts into the field with very different agendas. These groups may gradually begin to gain repeat advantage and divert their resources to advocating change within the field. They may become increasingly successful at shifting the discourse of the field from "convertible subordinated debentures" and "secured credit interests" to "systemic silicone damage," "unfair labor practices," and "PCBs." Some labor unions, in fact, have become more sophisticated in playing the bankruptcy game as they come to understand bankruptcy filings as antiunion strategies. Surely this will have future effects on the field and there may be no turning back. What Bourdieu (1975) calls the *doxa* of the field may be altered: the epistemological system that leads to the recognition of that which is recognized and validated as truth. Larson (1990) has shown that "containing an issue within discursive fields controlled by professionals . . . is an essentially depoliticizing strategy" (p. 39). However, the new presence of unauthorized speakers, nonexperts with political acumen, may transform the field by altering first the discourse of the field, turning it into the locus of a new struggle conceived and understood as a more overt political project. Thus, organizations desperately seeking ways out of dilemmas access an organizational field built to their own specifications yet, at the same time, unwittingly transform the field into something eventually less suited to their designs.

The strategy pursued by corporations may benefit the capital interests and the interests of the experts in the short term but may also represent a threat to expert interests disequilibrating the field in the years to come. The outcome of the politicization of the bankruptcy field remains to be seen.

THE CONNECTION BETWEEN BANKRUPTCY AND FAILURE

Finally, what does viewing bankruptcy as veiled politics conducted in a highly structured field historically rooted in issues of lending mean to general theories of organizational failure? Organizational researchers are very interested in why firms fail, citing things such as managers' inability to cope with rapid change or the population density of a market segment. These approaches probably tell us quite a bit about why everyday firms fail to perform well. But how do these theories of organizational failure match the types of cases I have studied? Most of the firms I've discussed performed miserably in many respects. Several failed to acknowledge major product defects, some were the weakest players in a sheltered oligopoly, others raided their pension funds to bankroll a failing organization. Yet all survived through creative bankruptcies because they had the power, resources, and size to do so. My research leads me to the conclusion that the bankruptcy process represents not the survival of the fittest as economic theories would have it, but the survival of the shrewdest. Simply put, organizations can be very unwise, quite inefficient, or even foolish, yet still survive.

Most important, perhaps, my research serves as a cautionary note to models and theories of organizational failure, reminding us that failure is quite a complicated matter. Organizational models of failure employ what are in reality *indicators* of failure, but we speak globally about "organizational failure" as if it were a unitary term. I would argue that bankruptcy, certainly in the world of large corporations and probably for many smaller businesses as well, is not a useful indicator of failure in that it often represents only the next move in a complex, strategic chess match. But even "disappearance from the marketplace," a typical, and presumably much less contentious indicator of failure, may not indicate what we think it does because those at the top of businesses may gain mightily even as their organizations go out of existence. For example, if a small business shuts down and abandons a toxic waste site, yet the owner has reaped huge rewards for many years, transferring all externalities onto the back of a local community, what exactly has failed? One might say that the organization has failed in that it no longer exists, but alternatively, we might say that the organization served its master very well indeed. Because organizations embody multiple interests and serve multiple purposes for those with stakes in them, it may be misguided to talk about *organizations* failing at all, without first fully accounting for the roster of winners and losers in the organization's demise.

Occasionally, theories of failure try to eliminate cases in which failures are judged "strategic" by the researchers (e.g., Hambrick & D'Aveni, 1988). But if we are theorizing about the meanings and causes of organizational failure, it may not be wise to simply eliminate those failures that trouble unspoken assumptions about the meaning of failure. What does it mean to have a "strategic failure" and how common are strategic failures? Perhaps many organizational failures have at least some strategic component to them if by strategic we mean that as the organization winds down, stakeholders fight for advantage. A more thorough accounting of the interests connected to organizations is needed—an accounting that only begins with owners, managers, and creditors and moves to a very broad conception of organizational stakeholders. By expanding the roster of winners and losers not just to organizations as neutral entities unto themselves but to managers, workers, communities, consumers, and others with stakes in organizations, we may end up with a very different and much broader notion of organizational success and failure. We may find that bankruptcy and failure may at once be a matter of both economics and politics, the two being more inseparable than currently conceived.

▦ NOTES

1. The term *megabankruptcy* carries no precise definition but generally refers to the largest corporate bankruptcy cases.

2. In fact, the judge in this case, Jack Weinstein, made his reputation by ending litigation over the Shoreham nuclear plant and Agent Orange. Eventually, the Eagle-Pitcher consolidation fell apart and the firm finally went through a Manville-style Chapter 11 bankruptcy.

3. Silverman, perhaps best known for his defense of Ivan Boesky in a securities fraud case, reportedly earned $4.5 million in fees for his work representing future asbestos victims and creating the Manville Trust (Labaton, 1990).

4. Whether representing future victims' rights in this way and taking away their right to sue will stand up to judicial review remains an unanswered question.

5. In the Manville case, the folly of this was represented by the court's taking seriously estimates of Manville's revenues for product lines it had *never* engaged in before, projected 20 years into the future.

6. Of late, the Pension Benefits Guarantee Corporation (PBGC) has gotten better at combating this maneuver and has vigorously worked to negotiate some payback from troubled companies. For example, in the Pan Am case, PBGC came to a settlement with Carl Icahn in which he returned $400 million to the pension fund with PBGC making up the remaining deficit (Ferguson & Blackwell, 1995, p. 111).

7. PBGC is currently paying benefits to about 174,000 people in close to 2,000 terminated plans. In 1994, such payments totaled $721 million and terminations increased 30% in just 1 year from 1993 to 1994 (Ferguson & Blackwell, 1995, p. 108; PBGC, 1994, p. 1).

8. Absent a bankruptcy filing, this would have been an unfair labor practice.

9. Many of the lawyers I interviewed complained that bankruptcy judges sometimes act as if their reputation hinges on helping the debtor corporation survive, not wanting to be held responsible for the demise of a major American corporation. Again, this questions how bankruptcy operates according to the economic maxim of survival of the fittest.

The Politics of Blame Avoidance

Defensive Tactics in a Dutch Crime-Fighting Fiasco

8

Mark Bovens
Paul 't Hart
Sander Dekker
Gerdien Verheuvel

Policy fiascoes, unlike natural disasters, cannot be observed by the use of our senses alone. Policy fiascoes are construed. They require the revelation and interpretation of facts and figures. Interpretation, in its turn, requires frames of references, scripts, and arguments. In this respect, it is very important to distinguish between a program and a political failure (Bovens & 't Hart, 1996, pp. 35-36; Edelman, 1977; Mucciaroni, 1990). Roughly, a *program* failure pertains to the technocratic dimension of policy-making and organizational behavior. It occurs when a policy decision, plan, or strategy fails to have the desired impact on target populations or even produces major unintended and unwanted effects. A *political* failure, in contrast, does not involve the social consequences of policies but, rather, the way in which policies are perceived in the court of public opinion and the political arena. In particular cases, these two dimensions need not coincide. A policy may perform reasonably well according to the targets set by their designers but may nevertheless be branded in the media or political arena as a major fiasco. The reverse is possible, too; policies may entail major social costs or conspicuously fail to meet even modest performance standards and yet are not labeled a failure in the political realm.

These discrepancies between technical performance and political perception will worry social engineers and the more instrumentally oriented public administrators. Reaching your targets may not suffice to prevent organizational failure or the termination of funding for your programs. On the other hand it also provides opportunities for more politically adroit policy elites. Unsuccessful programs and organizations may be kept alive through the careful use of political rhetoric and symbols. Either way, the distinction between program and political failure stresses the importance for policy elites to monitor or even join the political processes that lead to the construction of policy fiascoes. These processes invariably involve the attribution of accountability and blame.

Taking political constructivism as its starting point, this chapter analyzes how policy elites may try to defend themselves in the different stages of the politics of blaming that may arise following some initial revelation about damages, deviance, or other evidence of potential organizational or policy fiascoes. First, it provides a provisional theoretical framework for the analysis of defensive tactics. Second, the recent crisis of crime fighting in The Netherlands is introduced and the defensive tactics and arguments of some of the main actors in this major case of organizational failure are presented. The chapter then provides a more extensive typology of the argumentative tactics that can be used by policymakers in the aftermath of organizational failure. It concludes with some general reflections on the use and usefulness of these politics of blame avoidance.

▦ THE POLITICAL CONSTRUCTION OF POLICY FIASCOES

At any point in time in any political system, there are plenty of undesirable and unacceptable social conditions. Likewise, many policies and programs fail to reach their aims, costing a lot more than planned, producing negative unintended effects, and many public officials operating at the borderlines of competent and ethical professional behavior. Yet of all these potential "fiascoes," only a few become labeled as such in the public arena. Many of them go unnoticed or quietly become "causes celébres" only among a small community of insiders.

It is therefore important to understand why some social problems, policy controversies, and failing programs reach the limelight and enter collective memory as fiascoes and others do not (Edelman, 1988). Bovens and 't Hart (1996) have studied the political process of fiasco construction and have argued that full-blown policy fiascoes are those cases in which the dominant public and political view of events is characterized by four related features:

1. Assessing events: A certain set of events or developments has transgressed normal zones of public tolerance and has come to be viewed as highly undesirable. In short, some perceived "damage" to the public interest must be involved—for example, the flooding of a major river system.

2. Identifying agents: The negative events are viewed as a consequence of well-defined acts or omissions by responsible public officials or agencies and are not attributed to a conflux of larger, impersonal forces. In the case of floods, the emphasis is placed not on the unusual amount of rainfall combined with high temperatures in snow covered areas but on the man-made erosion of river banks and the absence of adequate river dikes.

3. Explaining behavior: The crucial acts or omissions producing the negative events are seen as the product of avoidable failures on the part of the people and organizations in question. The absence of high and strong enough river dikes in the case of the floods is viewed as a safety policy failure and attributed to a lack of political leadership in advancing the cause of fiasco prevention in the face of local environmentalist opposition to dike improvement programs.

4. Evaluating behavior: There is a widespread feeling that blame has to be apportioned to those responsible for the course of events. At the same time, there is often intense controversy about who exactly should be blamed for what and what sort of punishment is in order, with different accountability fora mobilizing to assign blame and take sanctions. In the floods case, some may blame the environmentalist groups trading off safety against natural conservation; others point toward local authorities for allowing unprotected river banks to be used for housing and industrial development; yet others blame national government for not stepping in to enforce the public interest.

When these four claims are made persuasively about a certain policy episode, the key policymakers and agencies involved are in for serious trouble. Labeling events as fiascoes (or, with slightly different connotations, "failures," "disasters," "affairs," or "scandals") represents a seductive way of condensing these intricate evaluation questions into a powerful political symbol ('t Hart, 1993). Many ordinary citizens hardly wonder whether social events are caused by choice, chance, or circumstance. In fact, in contemporary western European societies, it is widely assumed that governments should be able to prevent most forms of physical harm and social hardship from occurring. Whenever major disruptions or extraordinary problems occur, many will conclude nearly automatically that some form of mishap must have taken place. Hence, there are many possibilities to create scandal and to target policymakers for severe critique.

In many cases, however, pieces of the argument are missing or intensely contested by various protagonists. Careful investigations of what exactly happened can help only so much, because none of these assertions can be established authoritatively by dispassionate, objective analysis. All of them require an assessment against certain norms and values, and all depend on how the facts of the situation are represented. The construction of policy fiascoes is therefore a highly complex and intensely political process, with parties contesting both the facts of the case and the norms by which the deeds of those involved should be judged. Once events are being construed as fiascoes, questions about accountability and liability force themselves on the public agenda. Who should bear the blame for these negative events? Who shall remedy the victims? Will there be sanctions? The layers of assessing events, identifying agents, and the explanation of their behavior can, therefore, never be separated fully from evaluative issues of guilt and blame. The specter of administrative, legal, or political accountability is always lurking in the background. The attribution of blame is an integral part of the construction and evolution of policy fiascoes. This is the major reason that the public analysis of controversial policy episodes tends to be a highly adversarial process. This is highlighted especially by the behavior of many stakeholders during the "post mortem" period. Many of the officials involved in, or associated with, an alleged fiasco will engage in impression management, shifting of blame, and bureau-political maneuvering.

The Bovens and 't Hart (1996) study focused strongly on the types of frames and arguments used in the professional analysis of policy fiascoes and did not deal with the various tactics and arguments of the policymakers who are involved in the process. In this chapter, we seek to fill part of this gap.[1] We seek to illuminate the public behavior of key policymakers faced with major public criticisms of their performance. What types of defensive tactics can they use? What are their main arguments and excuses when held accountable?

▦ ELITE TACTICS FOR BLAME AVOIDANCE

Understanding the construction of policy fiascoes should take into account how key policymakers and institutions respond to the chorus of criticisms in the mass media and political arenas. Do they take an exclusively defensive stance, do they try to play down the importance of the fiasco or of their contribution, or do they actively seek to escalate the crisis, for example, by "coming out" to tell more, leaking confidential information, or aggressively blaming opponents? There is a fairly extensive but somewhat diverse literature available that can be used to better understand the various tactics of politicians and major civil servants for blame avoidance. There is of course the seminal work of Edelman (1977, 1988) on political language and political symbols. Edelman (1977) discusses a number of classic bureaucratic justifications of governmental policies that recur in response to criticism (pp. 98-102). According to Edelman, "A stock official response to public anxieties is that the action that arouses them is 'routine' " (p. 99). Sometimes, an argument is made that the harm caused by the (failure of) the policy is helpful. In the end, the victims will be better off. When the harm is very great and clear, they can use an even stronger justification and reply that sometimes "it is necessary to destroy in order to save." This is the classic omelet argument, so often incanted in revolutionary situations: "you cannot make an omelet without breaking some eggs." Another stock response, mentioned by Edelman, is the tactic of exaggerating the record. Anticipating criticism, officials make grandiose claims about the positive effects and landmark character of the program or project.

Partly on the basis of Edelman's work, 't Hart (1993) has analyzed the symbolical aspects of crisis management. Bovens (1998) has presented and analyzed, partly on the basis of work by Thompson (1983, 1987), 10 of the most common excuses that employees put forward when held accountable for organizational deviance. Many of these—particularly (a) the excuse of dispensability ("even without my contribution it would have happened"), (b) the excuse of null cause ("I had nothing to do with it"), (c) the excuse of the novus actus interveniens ("I wash my hands of the whole business"), (d) the excuse of ignorance ("I knew nothing of it"), (e) the excuse of superior orders ("I only did what I was told to do"), and (f) the excuse of the lesser evil ("without my contribution, it would have been even worse")—are also used in the political debates about alleged policy fiascoes. Ellis (1994), from whom we take the title of our piece, has focused on one particular presidential tactic for blame avoidance: the use of various subordinates as lightning rods to deflect blame from the presidency.

Focusing on the more argumentative tactics, we have found the work of Schütz (1996) on the defensive self-representation of politicians particularly useful. In a contribution to a book that analyzed how politicians try to maintain their credibility when confronted with a scandal, she discerned seven defensive tactics that can be used consecutively by politicians to defend themselves against allegations, in the media or in political arenas, that they are responsible for the alleged fiasco. The first tactic is denial: the accused politician denies that any negative event has happened. If that is not credible, politicians resort to reinterpretation, which amounts to arguing that the events have happened but should not be seen as negative. Next, they can combat causality, arguing that they did not do it. A fourth tactic is justification, which amounts to arguing that their actions were right or at least in the best interest of everyone. The next tactic is combating capacity, which amounts to arguing that they had no control over their actions. When held fully responsible, they can resort to two additional forms of damage control. They can try to prevent labeling, arguing this was atypical behavior. Finally, they can resort to public repentance and ask for forgiveness (Schütz, 1996, pp. 120-125).

Given our constructivist approach to policy fiascoes, we will concentrate in this chapter on these argumentative tactics. However, there are also a number of nonargumentative tactics that can be applied to avoid blaming. For example, an often-found tactic is that of *remaining silent*. Policymakers can try to stay out of the limelight by not reacting at all, hoping things will blow over or that the media will focus on some of the more vocal actors (Schütz, 1996, p. 125). Among Dutch policymakers, this tactic is often referred to with the phrase: "When you are being shaven, you better sit still." The idea behind this tactic is that reactions will spur extra negative media attention. Also, public reactions may easily backfire if they are not adequate or credible. When they do not succeed and are being called out into the open to defend themselves against allegations of faulty policy-making, policymakers can resort to *evasion*. They can try to evade answering critical questions when interviewed by journalists or interrogated by hearing committees. However, attack is often the best defense. Policymakers will sometimes try to exercise damage control by immediately *initiating an investigation* of their own account. By taking the initiative for an official investigation, they can influence the research agenda and the choice of the analysts and control the timetable. In this way, they can not only silence their critics ("we are already looking into these matters") but also try to keep, or regain, control over the policy agenda. For these reasons, it is a very useful tactic to depoliticize the crisis.

In a fully developed liberal democracy, with attentive newsmedia and active political representatives, policymakers will sooner or later have to resort to tactics of a rather argumentative nature to defend themselves. We will focus on these in our analysis of the case. First, however, we present the outline and context of the case.

▓ THE CRISIS OF CRIME FIGHTING IN THE NETHERLANDS

The Historical Context

Throughout three decades after World War II, crime in The Netherlands was low compared with its neighboring countries. Consequently, crime fighting was largely a depoliticized affair. For a long time, the Dutch police came close to the ideal image outlined for it by one of the fathers of the Dutch police system, the 19th-century liberal statesman Thorbecke who wanted "a police that is seen and heard of as little as possible" (Rosenthal, 't Hart, & Cachet, 1987).

Things started to change in the early 1980s. Drug abuse, drug trade, and drug-related petty crime became the focus of public concern. Steep rises in major crime statistics attracted political attention. In 1990, the major policy plan of the Ministry of Justice was set in an outright alarming tone. It argued that the criminal justice system faced a discrepancy between the increasing demands and its abilities to apprehend, try, and incarcerate criminals, seriously undermining the system's legitimacy. The report highlighted the shortcomings of the system in dealing with organized crime. Police investigators and public prosecutors lacked requisite specialized expertise in accounting, computing, environmental, and fiscal law. Their information about the organization and modus operandi of criminal groups was patchy. Furthermore, the police were constrained by law from using modern surveillance equipment and investigation tactics deemed essential to effectively combat criminal organizations. The then-minister of Justice Hirsch Ballin embarked on a personal crusade to increase police effectiveness and declared a "war on crime."

The major problem was organizational. Although criminal groups increased their scale of operation to local, regional, and international levels, the Dutch police was still organized principally on a local basis, with 148 local forces and a national police comprising 17 districts. News traveled slowly between forces. Cultural barriers against intensified inter-force cooperation were strong. Attempts to reform the 1957 police law and create a unitary police had always failed to gain sufficient support.

However, during the formation of a new Cabinet in the summer of 1989, the decision was finally made to reform the police into 18 regional forces, coming into effect in January 1993.

The IRT

Anticipating the police reorganization, the Justice Department had already taken the initiative to intensify interforce cooperation by forming so-called interregional criminal investigation teams (*IRT's—interregionale rechercheteams*). These were to be elite units devoted exclusively to the fight against large-scale organized crime. They were to contain the necessary mix of police and technical professionals, organized at an appropriately large scale, that could expect to be more effective in preparing the groundwork for a successful prosecution of the more serious criminal groups in the country. One such team, inaugurated in January 1989, involved collaboration between Amsterdam, Haarlem, Utrecht, and Hilversum police forces.[2]

Because the team was focused on penetrating the core of criminal organizations, it operated in the strictest possible secrecy and explored new tactics to obtain information about the organization and modus operandi of major Dutch drugs importers in particular. These new tactics included the use of electronic surveillance equipment, phone tapping, undercover agents, and paid informers. Although formally, the public prosecutor should have a key role in supervising the investigation process, in practice, individual policemen of hard-core units within the IRT were given or acquired considerable discretion in the use of investigation tactics. The perceived need for secrecy to protect the safety of informers was a major reason for a policy of compartmentalizing operational information pursued by some police investigators, even up to the point of not informing their superiors of what exactly they were doing.

While this by itself was a risky way of operating, its vulnerability was increased by a number of factors, including (a) the absence of a legal framework regulating the use of intrusive surveillance and other investigation tactics and thus a considerable risk of prosecutions based on information obtained by the use of these tactics not holding up in court; (b) a lack of a clear investigation policy within the public prosecutor's office and, consequently, large differences of supervision style maintained by individual prosecutors; (c) pervasive speculation about "moles" in the police leaking information to the targets of major criminal investigations, as well as speculation about the use of other forms of "countersurveillance" employed by the criminal opponents of IRT detectives; and (d) tense relations between the constituent forces making up the IRTs, rooted in deep historical and cultural barriers to intensified interforce cooperation.

In Table 8.1, an outline is provided of the main events that caused the issue to flare up. The public debate started with a relatively simple release to the press. On December 7, 1993, it was announced that the Amsterdam-Utrecht interregional criminal investigation team, established in 1989, was to be disbanded. It resulted in capital headlines about police involvement in drug transports, a major parliamentary inquiry, and a crisis of the criminal investigation system. The parliamentary inquiry into investigation methods concerning organized crime revealed that Dutch police authorities had not only authorized the import of hundreds of tons of drugs into the country (many of which found their way to the streets) but in some cases also financed criminal investigations with the revenues of illegal transactions. Also, extensive use had been made of informers, who were often paid substantial sums or allowed to keep the revenues of their illegal transactions. There had been no systematic discussion, authorization, and monitoring of these very controversial methods. Also, it was observed that the criminal investigation process involved many different organizations. As a result, competencies and responsibilities were diffuse, communications faulty, and the criminal investigation system was afflicted by bureaucratic in-fighting, leaks to the press, and personal strife. Finally, administrative, legal, and political authorities had great difficulties in exercising their authority. Police investigators often operated on their own and in secret. By the mid-1990s, the Dutch fight against organized crime had come to be regarded as a major policy fiasco.

▦ ELITE TACTICS FOR BLAME AVOIDANCE: THE IRT CASE

How did the main characters in the case react when the upheaval about the dissolution of the IRT turned into a public scandal? How did they try to diminish the political fallout for themselves or their organization? We have focused on four main characters, two at the local level—Amsterdam chief of police Nordholt and his Utrecht colleague Wiarda—and two at the national level—Van Thijn, erstwhile mayor of Amsterdam and minister of Home Affairs during most of the research period, and Hirsch Ballin, the then-minister of Justice. To complete our picture, we also looked into the defensive behavior of other, less prominently involved officials. We

TABLE 8.1 Chronology

Jan 25, 1989	Official formation of IRT.
Mar 29, 1993	Responsibility for IRT is handed over from Utrecht to Amsterdam. The former IRT-leader Van Lith is being succeeded by Van Kastel.
Nov 8, 1993	The so-called Van Kastel-report appears. In this report an "alarming criminal investigation" is mentioned.
Nov 15, 1993	The public prosecution's office terminates Operation Delta after consultation with the ministers of Justice and Home Affairs.
Dec 7, 1993	Press release concerning the dissolution of the IRT. The Amsterdam police triangle cite the "use of inappropriate and unacceptable investigation methods, for which they could bear no responsibility," as the main reason.
Jan 15, 1994	Van Thijn (former burgomaster of Amsterdam) becomes minister of Home Affairs after the decease of minister Dales.
Jan 22, 1994	Media report on corruption in the police force of Amsterdam. Nordholt calls the allegations of Wiarda "infamous." Wiarda denies the allegations of corruption.
Jan 31, 1994	Establishment of the Wierenga Commission.
Mar 24, 1994	The Wierenga report appears. The Wierenga Commission has found no evidence of corruption within the Amsterdam police force. The true reasons behind the dissolution of the IRT were, according to the commission, tensions within the Amsterdam public prosecution office and the unwillingness of Amsterdam to cooperate with other police forces. Chief Prosecutor Vrakking, Attorney General Van Randwijck, Nordholt, and Van Riessen are being held responsible. Prime Minister Lubbers and Van Thijn immediately announce that there is no talk of resignation of these officials.
Apr 7, 1994	First IRT debate. Motion concerning parliamentary investigation of investigation methods. Ministers of Justice and Home Affairs promise "functioneringsgesprekken" (performance reviews) with those involved.
May 3, 1994	National elections. Conflict between Hirsch Ballin and Van Thijn.
May 20, 1994	News reports on an ongoing authority crisis. The parliament demands a second debate on the IRT concerning the settlement of the IRT affair.
May 25, 1994	Second IRT-debate. Motion declares that Hirsch Ballin and Van Thijn should abstain from further involvement in the IRT-affair.

have concentrated our efforts on those periods in which the public debates were most vehement:

▦ The public debate following the initial dissolution announcement in December 1993

May 27, 1994	Resignation of Hirsch Ballin and Van Thijn.
Jun 1, 1994	Working group preliminary inquiry of investigation methods established by permanent parliamentary commission of Justice, in order to draw up a proposal (motion Dijkstal).
Oct 21, 1994	The working group recommends to start a parliamentary inquiry.
Dec 6, 1994	The chairman of the Second Chamber of Parliament officially installs the parliamentary inquiry commission on investigation methods (Commission Van Traa).
End Dec, 1994	Second Chamber demands clarification of supposed drug transports. The minister of Justice Sorgdrager misinforms the parliament on these drug transports, because the public prosecutor Van Veen did not reveal some classified information to her.
Apr 1995	Investigation of Internal Affairs on the amounts of drugs the CID Haarlem dumped on the market.
Sep 1, 1995	Start of the public hearings by the Commission Van Traa. During the hearings the role of Minister of Justice Sorgdrager is also discussed. According to chief public prosecutor, Blok Sorgdrager (during her time as attorney general) personally consented the passing through of an amount of cocaine. Sorgdrager claims to be ignorant of this.
Oct, 1995	Attorney General Van Randwijck agrees with the ministry of Justice to resign in exchange for a compensation of 7 times his annual pay and another half a million guilders. This arrangement leads to a lot of commotion.
Feb 1, 1996	Publication of the report of the Commission Van Traa.
Mar 25, 1996	Reaction of the Cabinet to the report of the Commission Van Traa. The Cabinet does not want a general prohibition on the letting through of drugs by the police. During the parliamentary debates on the report, the media, as well as certain members of Parliament, demand the resignation of those most responsible in the IRT affair. The Cabinet does not share this view.
Sep 1996	Plans for the implementation of decisions taken in pursuance of the report of the Commission Van Traa. Many members of parliament (among them, members of the Commission Van Traa) are disappointed by the weak measures proposed in plan.

■ The public and parliamentary debates following the publication of the Wierenga Report

■ The parliamentary debates about the institution of a parliamentary inquiry

- ▦ The hearings of the Van Traa Commission
- ▦ The parliamentary debates following the publication of the Van Traa report

The analysis of defensive tactics in the first two periods is based on a content analysis of four Dutch newspapers, two main national dailies (*NRC-Handelsblad* and *De Telegraaf*) and two local newspapers from Amsterdam (*Het Parool*) and Utrecht (*Utrechts Nieuwsblad*). The latter were chosen because of their proximity to the two main policing and political-administrative arenas pitted against each other following the dissolution of the interregional team. For the period of the Van Traa inquiry, we also referred to a number of other newspapers. Furthermore, we analyzed the public hearings of a number of officials by the parliamentary commission of inquiry and the proceedings of the Lower House of the parliamentary debates on the Wierenga and Van Traa reports.

From Program to Political Failure

On November 8, 1993, newly appointed IRT leader Van Kastel submitted a damning report to his Amsterdam superiors, alleging that factions within the team were involved in operations that violated criminal investigation codes. His main worry was the use of the so-called Delta method, which involved the use of informants in providing the police with information about drug import operations, who were monitored by the police but not intercepted in order to enable the informer to rise up the hierarchy. Moreover, the informer was allowed to keep most of the money paid to him by the criminal organization; part of it was used to finance covered police operations. In the process, the police allowed large quantities of soft drugs (cannabis, marijuana) to reach the streets (much later it turned out that the same applied to hard drugs such as cocaine). In response, and after consultation with the ministers of Justice and Home Affairs, the use of the Delta method was terminated on November 15.

The public controversy about crime-fighting methods started when on December 7, 1993, the Amsterdam police "triangle," consisting of Amsterdam burgomaster Van Thijn, chief public prosecutor Vrakking, and police commissioner Nordholt, announced the dissolution of the team, citing its use of inappropriate and unacceptable investigation methods as the main reason. It soon transpired that interpersonal and interforce relations within the team had been highly strained, with hard-line pragmatists in Utrecht and Haarlem opposing due process-oriented formalists in Amsterdam. Refusals to share information were common; mutual distrust was high.

The dissolution announcement—which did not specify the Delta method episode because it was deemed too risky to publicize—triggered a media-amplified war of words between Amsterdam commissioner Nordholt, who took the initiative to dissolve the IRT, and Wiarda, who strongly favored a continuation of the team and its methods and who was outraged about Nordholt's unilateral action. Most of the skirmishes dealt with an assessment of the situation. Wiarda seized the offensive and attacked his opponent vehemently. Within weeks, the *NRC-Handelsblad* (January 22, 1994) reported, without literally citing him, that Wiarda had accused the Amsterdam police force of being infected by corruption up to its highest levels. According to Wiarda this—and not the use of dubious methods—had been the real reason behind the dissolution. Nordholt vehemently denied that corruption had been the cause, using the business as-usual argument: "I do not exclude some corruption; that can be found at every major public institution." He said that he had never in his career experienced such infamous accusations and used the tactic of initiating an investigation. He demanded, and was granted, an official investigation of the allegations by the national police Internal Affairs unit and asked Wiarda to be heard as a witness. He also accused his accuser and said he had contemplated a libel suit against Wiarda for discrediting him and the entire Amsterdam police force. Wiarda was then forced into the defensive. Bolkestein, the leader of the Dutch liberal party, said that Wiarda's career was at stake if he could not substantiate his allegations. Wiarda quickly denied that he had made any specific accusations. He blamed the media for not having cited him correctly and announced taking the *NRC* to court; this never materialized, because it transpired that he had indeed accused the Amsterdam police of corruption in an interview with the regional newspaper *Leeuwarder Courant,* as early as December 1993. Eventually, he was forced to repent in public: "I am sorry that the Amsterdam police department and, thereby the entire Dutch police force, has attracted such damaging publicity. They do not deserve that."

Nordholt, at this stage, was successful in countering the allegations of corruption and skillfully made use of the media to fence off his direct opponent, Wiarda. Wiarda could not substantiate his accusations and subsequently disappeared from the media and remained silent. However, Nordholt did not manage to take away the general impression that the Amsterdam police was to be blamed for the fiasco of the IRT. He did not mention the highly confidential facts contained in the Van Kastel report. Nordholt, however, was backed up by his erstwhile political superior, former Amsterdam burgomaster Van Thijn, who found himself in an awkward role transition having just succeeded the deceased Home Affairs minister Dales a few days earlier.

Another round of defensive tactics, aimed at blame avoidance, can be found after the publication of the Wierenga report, when Parliament started to press for concrete reforms and became strongly dissatisfied with the way the whole affair was handled. This was basically at the national political level and involved Van Thijn and Hirsch Ballin. Faced with an increasingly nasty scandal, the two ministers in charge of the police, Justice minister Hirsch Ballin (Christian Democrats) and Home Affairs minister Van Thijn (Labour) had used the tactic of initiating an investigation and had established an independent commission led by the burgomaster of the city of Enschede Wierenga. Its report appeared on March 24, 1994. It argued that the decision to abolish the team had been wrong and that no illicit methods had been used—again without any mention being made of the Delta method. However, immediately following the report's publication, the press reported from internal police sources that there had been "controlled transports" of major quantities of drugs. During the parliamentary debate about the Wierenga report on April 7, the ministers were summoned to take measures to clean up the mess.

At this second stage, there are several examples of the tactic of combating capacity. Both Van Thijn and Hirsch Ballin, who came increasingly under pressure from Parliament, used the "novus actus interveniens" argument. They argued repeatedly that the police and public prosecutors have "a large measure of independent responsibility" and "should be given ample leeway to fight crime." As mayor of Amsterdam, Van Thijn "had no official responsibility for the investigation of crime." During the April-May 1994 national election campaign, a severe row soured relations between the two ministers. It was triggered by an issue unrelated to the case—abortion and euthanasia. Yet it can be interpreted as an attempt, particularly by Van Thijn, to attack his opponent and to deflect the attention from the criminal investigation issue on which he was vulnerable, given his awkward double role.

The constitutionally prescribed dissolution of the Cabinet in anticipation of the May 3 national elections provided little relief for the two ministers, who by then had developed serious personal and political disagreements, precluding any forceful joint intervention. The new Parliament kept up the pressure. On May 25, 1994, it judged that too little action had been taken and accepted a motion calling on the two ministers to abstain from any further involvement in the affair, turning it over to the prime minister. The result of this parliamentary pressure was the resignation of Hirsch Ballin, followed the same day by Van Thijn.[3]

At this stage, one can find several attempts to prevent labeling. Hirsch Ballin, after being forced to resign, said he would stay on as a member of Parliament: "I am not a damaged man, I won't turn my back on politics with wrath." Van Thijn even published a political biography that covered, and partly justified, his activities in office. He framed his predicament partly as a case of idiosyncrasy and partly as a case of tragic choice. He probably could have saved his political career by citing a highly confidential part of the Wierenga report that caste serious doubts on some of the methods used by the IRT: "How could I have been so stupid. . . . I should never have agreed with the secrecy. I should have insisted on an appropriate way of disclosure" (Breedveld, 1996). He, and the other officials involved, however, had taken a vow of secrecy. At that time, it was thought that revelation of the Delta methods could seriously endanger the lives of various informants and undercover inspectors.

From an Organizational to an Institutional Crisis

Parliament subsequently started its own investigation of the affair, which was elevated in December 1994 to a formal Parliamentary Inquiry (*Parlementaire Enquête*) with quasi-juridical status and procedures. Its televised hearings in the fall of 1995 of a range of police and criminal justice officials caused the affair to resurface in the public domain and revealed much deeper problems in the fight against organized crime than the internal squabbles of a single investigation team. During its investigations, it became clear, for example, that even after the termination of the Amsterdam-Utrecht IRT, the Delta method continued to be used by other police units well after its abolition in Amsterdam and that far more, and more serious, drugs had been brought on the market in this way. In February 1996, the inquiry report was published amid a blaze of publicity. Its main conclusion was that crime fighting in The Netherlands was crippled by a threefold institutional crisis (Enquêtecommissie Opsporingsmethoden, 1996, pp. 420-422):

■ A crisis of *norms.* Police and prosecutors were operating in a legal and normative vacuum left by the government and the legislature. Consequently, there was widespread uncertainty and ambiguity about the appropriateness of various investigation methods, which left room for strongly divergent interpretations by various police units and public prosecutors.

■ A crisis of *organizations.* Crime-fighting tasks, responsibilities, and capabilities were divided across a large number of organizations, without a clear division of labor or effective coordination arrangements existing between them. This set the stage for controversies about who was responsible for what.

▓ A crisis of *authority*. Public prosecutors had in effect lost their grip
on the criminal investigation activities of the police. This was largely
because the public prosecutor's office failed to produce a coherent
and consistently implemented policy on investigation methods. The
problem was exacerbated by the divided police authority structure.

No single actor or agency was held responsible for the development of
this crisis. The inquiry report pointed at a combination of factors, including
overzealous detectives and public prosecutors, a disorganized team structure, bad management at senior levels in the police force and the public
prosecutor's office, a lack of accountability of the police vis-à-vis its
superiors, and legislative negligence. The report rehabilitated the Amsterdam police force and strongly condemned the methods used by the IRT.

The inquiry report soon became the authoritative statement on the
IRT and policing in The Netherlands. Its assessment of the events and its
identification of the main agents and its explanation of their behavior were
hardly questioned. Unlike the Wierenga report, which was seriously
disqualified during the hearings as unfair and unprofessional, Van Traa
and his commission never came under attack. Most of the debates focused
on the issue of blaming. The report contained harsh criticisms of many of
the key agencies and officials involved but did not explicitly call for the
resignations of ministers or other personal sanctions against officials. In
his public statements immediately following the publication of the report,
the inquiry chairman nevertheless made it clear that he thought that
various main actors, especially in the police and public prosecutor's office,
should be punished. When it came to the prospects for ending the crisis,
the inquiry warned that it could not be resolved by a limited number of
dramatic decisions and sweeping reforms. Instead, the report contained a
wide-ranging package of legislative, administrative, and organizational
reforms.

The parliamentary debate about the inquiry report became somewhat
of an anticlimax. Most of the reform proposals were quickly accepted, and
the Justice ministry was instructed to prepare an implementation plan.
Most of the debate focused on two issues: (a) the desirability of sanctions
against officials and (b) the report's proposed legal ban of some of the
most sensitive investigation methods. Not surprisingly, the tactic of
symbolic reform was very prominent in the defense of the then-minister
of Justice, Sorgdrager, who had succeeded Hirsch Ballin in the new
Cabinet. In the major parliamentary debate after the publication of the
report, she cited a series of reforms in the criminal investigation process
that had been initiated over the previous 2 years: "In short, talking about

clear frames for the process and reorganization of criminal investigation, it is apparent that steps have been made. This has also been noticed and acknowledged by the parliamentary inquiry committee. These steps will guarantee that we will never be caught unaware anymore" (TK, Proceedings, May 8, 1996, pp. 383-384).[4]

There were also several instances of scapegoating. Within the Justice Department, several key officials had been ushered out during or following the inquiry, largely under pressure of Justice Minister Sorgdrager (who was politically highly vulnerable because she herself had been a top official within the public prosecutor's office before assuming a Cabinet position in the summer of 1994), who felt she had not been properly advised by her most senior civil servants. However, to the dismay of the inquiry chairman, Parliament was reluctant to instigate tough sanctions against the major protagonists. In the end, Interior Minister Dijkstal, the successor of Van Thijn, announced a "police carousel," whereby many of the leading police chiefs, including the most controversial ones, would be rotated. None of the senior officials involved volunteered to act as a lightning rod, however. Eventually, a number of police chiefs were indeed rotated to other regional police forces. Only a few minor inspectors who had been particularly involved in illegal methods of inquiry were dismissed from their police force.

In sum, the case revealed significant but relatively mild blame avoidance behavior of policy elites. It could not be that the stakes were not high enough to motivate policy actors to go to the brink of propriety to defend themselves. The eventual resignation of two ministers, the dismissal of several senior officials in the Ministry of Justice, and the disconcerting results of the parliamentary inquiry speak for themselves. Also, the corruption charges raised against the senior ranks of the Amsterdam police were hefty, and the force's eventual vindication by the parliamentary inquiry must have come as a relief for commissioner Nordholt. Most important, the crisis of authority over the police in the criminal investigation process severely hurt the standing of the public prosecutor's office and put it under severe pressure to speed up reforms. Despite all this, there was certainly a good deal of animosity between some of the key actors, but there was never the kind of consistent use of scapegoats, lightning rods, and enemy images encountered in other cases of policy failure (Bovens & 't Hart, 1996; Ellis, 1994; Laux & Schütz, 1996).

In this respect, the IRT affair was perhaps not an exemplary but an exceptional case. First of all, the self-restraint displayed by some actors may have been typical for the criminal justice domain in The Netherlands, a sector at the heart of the classical state functions with a relatively low politicization and rather indirect lines of authority and accountability. For example, the notion that by going all out in self-defense the cause of justice might be hurt played a part in Nordholt's and Van Thijn's reluctance to reveal the existence of a secret part of the Wierenga report casting serious doubt on the acceptability of the methods used in the team's Delta project. Getting this information in the public domain could have saved Van Thijn's now aborted political career but was not provided until much later during the parliamentary inquiry. In other policy sectors, where security and legitimacy considerations are less conspicuous and delicate, and political lines of authority and accountability more transparent, we may expect less restraint on the part of elites under media pressure.

Self-restraint may also be a feature of the politics of blame avoidance in The Netherlands as a whole. For one thing, The Netherlands does not have the kind of aggressive tabloids that have destroyed many political careers in England and Germany, for example. The political culture evolves around the perennial need for multiparty consensus building, making the use of offensive tactics against political opponents potentially self-defeating in the long run. Moreover, playing up controversies along ideological or sectarian lines—more prevalent in Belgium and Italy—is considered not done in the predominantly technocratic tradition of depoliticizing controversial issues. Scapegoating and the use of lightning rods are also more difficult in the absence of a spoils system or a political cabinet at the departments. Most of the senior positions in Dutch departments are occupied by professional career civil servants, whose loyalty ultimately lies with their department or the civil service, not with their political superior. In the absence of an extensive system of patronage, few will volunteer to act as a lighting rod and sacrifice their careers.

Also, the relatively mild blame avoidance behavior found in this case may be partly caused by our choice of research material. We have mainly focused on written sources—newspapers, reports of parliamentary debates, and hearings. It may well be that transcripts of interviews on radio and television are a better source of defensive tactics, because of their impromptu and confrontational character.

▨ DEFENSIVE TACTICS AND ARGUMENTS: A TYPOLOGY

The case is very useful, however, to further refine the theoretical framework presented under the heading "Elite Tactics for Blame Avoidance." It provides us with a number of extra tactics and arguments that can be added to the typology of Schütz (1996) to make it more comprehensive. Most tactics turn out to consist of a series of specific arguments and excuses that can be put forward by policymakers to absolve themselves from blame. The case has particularly revealed a series of tactics with an offensive nature. At each of the stages, we found the use of offensive, ad hominem, tactics that were used by the different protagonists to defend themselves against the allegations. Schütz (1996, p. 126) mentioned the use of "counterattacks" but did not extend on them.

On the basis of Schütz (1996), Edelman (1977), and Bovens (1998), we can now present a typology of the most common defensive tactics and arguments that can be found in policy fiasco discourse. We have clustered these tactics and the corresponding arguments according to the four layers of fiasco construction (see Table 8.2) that were distinguished under the heading "The Political Construction of Policy Fiascoes." Conceptually, these defensive tactics and arguments represent more or less linear, chronological steps in the genesis of a political scandal. It is thus assumed that the tactics and arguments first mentioned can be found predominantly during the earlier stages of the unfolding of a political scandal. In reality, we may most likely find more erratic uses of tactics. Many political scandals may not unfold in a linear way. They are often conglomerates of overlapping and interwoven subscandals, as could be seen in the IRT case. The row between Wiarda and Nordholt was in fact a full case within the IRT episode, which in turn was itself a case within the larger fiasco of crime fighting in The Netherlands.

Assessing Events: At the first layer of fiasco construction, that of assessing events, policymakers can try to play down the gravity of the event. To start with, they can argue that nothing happened; the journalists had it all wrong because the alleged negative event just did not occur. This was Wiarda's response when his accusation of corruption backfired: "I have never said that." They can also argue that nothing special happened, claiming the event was a routine matter. This is the business as usual argument, a "stock official response to public anxieties" according to (Edelman, 1977, p. 99) and used by Nordholt in our case. These two arguments are examples of the *denial* tactic.

If denial is not plausible or feasible, they can counterattack and *accuse the accusers.* Sometimes, attack is the best defense. They can, for example, argue that the accusers should be the ones on trial, because they themselves have been engaged in far greater forms of deviance. This was the initial tactic used by Wiarda when confronted by Nordholt's decision to dissolve the IRT.

TABLE 8.2 A Typology of Argumentative Tactics in Blame Avoidance

Fiasco Layer	Tactic	Argument
Assessing events	Denial	Nothing happened
		Business as usual
	Accusing the accuser	They did far worse
	Positive interpretation	No harm resulted
		Harm was negligible
		Harm was compensated
		Omelet argument
	Reframing	It was a success
Identifying agents	Combating causation	Null cause
		Dispensability
		Act of God
	Blaming the messenger	Publicity caused the harm
Explaining behavior	Combating capacity	Ignorance
		Novus actus interveniens
		Superior orders
		Social/political pressure
	Disqualifying the analyst	Unfair investigation
		Unqualified analyst
		Unprofessional report
Evaluating behavior	Justification	Tragic choice
		Lesser evil
	Preventing labeling	Idiosyncrasy
	Scapegoating	Culprit is punished
	Repentance	Public excuses
		Damages
	Symbolic reform	It can't happen again

Third, they can try to portray events in a positive light. This is the tactic of *positive interpretation*. Policymakers can, for example, argue that in fact no societal harm resulted or that the harm done was outweighed by the positive effects of the policy or that victims have been properly compensated. When major social harm is manifest, they can use the "omelet" argument, which amounts to arguing that individual losses are trivial when compared with the overall benefits (Edelman, 1977, p. 100).

The penultimate defensive tactic at this stage is that of *reframing*—arguing that, if seen from a different perspective, the policy has been an overall success. In this tactic policymakers do not reinterpret the facts within the same frame of assessment—as with positive reinterpretation—but they introduce different criteria for success and failure.

Identifying Agents: When it comes to identifying the agents behind the contested events, policymakers can first of all try to *combat causation*. They can deny that they played any part in the causal chain producing the controversy, either because they did not contribute at all ("the excuse form null cause") or only to an insignificant degree ("I was only a small cog in the machine") or because their contribution was minor ("It would have happened anyway") (Bovens, 1998, pp. 113-166). Particularly when they are accused of negligence, policymakers may claim that the negative events were beyond human control, for example, because it was an Act of God (Bovens & 't Hart, 1996, p. 82).

At this layer too, protagonists can resort to an offensive, ad hominem tactic: *blaming the messenger.* One way to do so is to argue that the whistle-blowing, leaks, investigations, or media attention have done more harm to the public interest than the actual policy mistakes. Not the policymaker, but the messenger caused most of the harm. This argument could be heard from the rank and file in the police forces involved in the IRT case. By bringing the Delta method into the open, the Van Traa investigation not only frustrated the fight against crime but also seriously jeopardized the lives of a series of valuable police informers.

Explaining Behavior: At the next layer, that of explaining why they acted in the way they did, policymakers can use the tactic of *combating capacity.* They may admit that they played a role in the causal chain but cite extenuating circumstances to explain their behavior. Or they testify to their original beneficial intentions and thus absolve themselves from blame. This tactic amounts to the French adage of *tout comprendre c'est tout pardonner.* It comes in several forms. Policymakers can use the argument of justifiable ignorance: At the time, the negative consequences of their behavior were wholly unforeseeable—for example, because of the extreme complexity of the process (Bovens & 't Hart, 1996, pp. 80-81). Or they can argue, as did Van Thijn, that there has been a "novus actor interveniens," who, further down the causal chain, had the final and decisive authority. This argument is often used by policy advisers (Thompson, 1983), but it can also be used by policymakers claiming not to have had full authority (for example, because administrative powers were dispersed or decentralized). Those who cannot deny that they had been endowed with discretionary powers can nevertheless argue that their hands were tied, because they acted under superior orders or because they were under tremendous social or political pressure.

At this layer, there is also another ad hominem tactic available. Policymakers can argue that their role and mistakes have been misrepresented in the press or in the official reports, because of the use of partisan, unqualified, or unprofessional analysts. This is the tactic of *disqualifying the analyst*. It was used by Nordholt at several points—in the end with success—to disqualify the conclusions of the report of the Wierenga commission.

Evaluating Behavior: Finally, when it comes to the evaluation of their behavior, policymakers have several defensive tactics at their disposal to absolve them from blame or to control the damage to their political position and personal prestige. First, they can *justify* their actions, by stating that it was right or, at least, inevitable to act in the way they did. Everybody else in their position would, and should, have acted in the same way. They can argue that they had been faced with a tragic choice, a choice between two evils (Bovens & 't Hart, 1996, p. 78; Peters, 1992). Individual policymakers will also often resort to the argument of the lesser evil: They did contribute to the fiasco, but without their contribution, things would have been even worse.

Second, they can try to *prevent labeling*. They can argue that this behavior is by no means typical for them and bring out their track record to prove it. It was just an idiosyncratic event that should not be brought to bear on them (Schütz, 1996, p. 125). Both Van Thijn and Hirsch Ballin used arguments to that effect in the wake of their resignation from office.

In the end, when all other tactics have failed, policymakers can try to exercise damage control through *repentance*. They can publicly admit their failures, ask for forgiveness, and promise that it will never happen again, hoping that by doing so they can clean their slate and clear the way for a continuation of their political careers. This tactic often involves the public offering of excuses or the payment of damages. It can also be applied in the beginning of an affair when all other tactics seem unfeasible at the outset. Thus, a policymaker can try to nip a scandal in the bud, before it even got time to emerge.

A related tactic is *scapegoating*. This involves cases in which chief executives deflect the blame onto subordinates. They are presented to the public at large as the main culprits and are sacrificed through suspension, removal, or dismissal, to satisfy the public need for sanctions and scapegoats. The IRT case provides several examples of this. Sometimes, subordinate administrative officials intentionally act as "lightning rods," as they willingly step forward to divert criticism and to deflect blame away from their political superiors (Ellis, 1994).

Finally, a strategy with a somewhat more offensive nature is *symbolic reform*. Policymakers can try to show their good intentions by announcing major policy or legislative reforms, arguing that it can't happen again because measures have been taken. We saw this argument being used by incumbent Minister of Justice Sorgdrager in the debates about the outcomes of the parliamentary inquiry.

▒ EPILOGUE

The case of the Dutch crime-fighting fiasco and our resulting typology of argumentative tactics raises three different types of questions. First of all, it raises an analytical question: Does this typology help to better describe and understand the political construction of policy fiascoes? The framework presented here is meant to be a heuristic argument; it can be used as a tool for describing and analyzing the political construction of a concrete policy fiasco. It is not meant to be comprehensive; there is much variety in arguments and in the way these arguments are phrased.

This first exploration has uncovered several weak points. Although the various tactics and arguments can be distinguished quite easily analytically, in practice, they sometimes overlap. Most of the tactics and arguments mentioned need further operationalization to be useful for narrative analysis.

What was particularly difficult in this case, was the multilayered and overlapping character. There was no such thing as one fiasco, one particular event that needed to be assessed and justified, but a series of consecutive events caused a chain of allegations and subsequent defensive tactics. For example, Wiarda's allegations of corruption became a fiasco in itself and caused a series of defensive tactics on the part of Wiarda (which resurfaced during the Van Traa hearings).

Also, there was a discrepancy between the parliamentary hearings and proceedings and the media accounts of the various discussions. Journalists, and particularly radio and television reporters, tend to be much more critical and "aggressive" toward the various protagonists than are members of Parliament. Moreover, they tend to focus much more on the issue of personal blame and punishment. A content analysis of defensive routines should therefore not only concentrate on written sources but also, and maybe even predominantly, on transcripts of oral interaction in the media.

How effective are these various tactics and arguments? Which ones help to avoid blame? This empirical-instrumental question cannot be answered, of course, on the basis of one case. Moreover, there are too many intervening variables. It is clear from the case that institutional and political contexts are important. In the Dutch political context, civil servants and magistrates tend to stay out of the limelight and can avoid the media much easier than can politicians. They can afford to use nonargumentative tactics, whereas politicians are daily questioned by the media and political fora. In the absence of a spoils system, there is no direct relationship between the parliamentary evaluation of administrative performance and the career of civil servants. The fate of politicians, however, is in the hands of the accidental majority of Parliament. Timing is very important in that respect. Hirsch Ballin and Van Thijn had the ill luck of being in office at the end of the political cycle. The debates about the Wierenga report were held against the background of the impending elections. This caused them to be more vehement. Sorgdrager and Dijkstal, the successors of Hirsch Ballin and Van Thijn, could get away with a number of mistakes, partly because they were fresh and because the new Parliament gave them the benefit of doubt. Content analysis of media reports cannot get at this intricate question; that will require a more elaborate, multimethod, and comparative research design. It is only appropriate, then, that this chapter ends with a call for a more systematic cross-national study of the politics of fiasco construction.

Finally, there are important issues of a more normative nature. How acceptable are these tactics and arguments in a liberal democracy? We have deliberately refrained from a normative analysis in this chapter, because our main aim was description. However, this does not mean that we assume that each of the tactics and arguments is always morally accept-able.[5] Bovens (1998), in a related but quite different project, has not only presented the 10 most common excuses in cases of organizational deviance but also assessed to what extent they may pass muster to absolve individual officials from moral blame. It turned out that the majority are not, or only in certain circumstances, tenable. Of the excuses discussed here, the excuse of ignorance can, certainly in the case of complex actions and untranspar-ent activities that stretch over the long term and across great distances, cut ice. Then again, it makes quite a difference whether we are assessing the behavior of civil servants or of politicians. In liberal democracies, political responsibility is much more comprehensive—often even border-ing on strict liability—than moral or operational responsibility.

The normative evaluation of policy fiascoes in liberal democracies is usually left to political bodies—except for cases of criminal deviance or civil punitive damages. That is why issues of political construction are so important for students of fiascoes in the first place. Does this mean that the political construction of policy fiascoes is basically a matter of spin-doctoring and image management? For those who fear the Machiavellian or Sophist use of the defensive tactics and arguments, our case provides some consolation. In the end, the facts of the case are not irrelevant. Even the heavy use of sophistry cannot set a bad record straight, provided the political system allows for enough checks and balances. At the early stage of the case, after the Wierenga report, Nordholt and Van Thijn, took most of the blame and were presented as the main causes of the crisis. Nevertheless, they refrained from aggressive rhetorical tactics. Eventually, after the elaborate and careful parliamentary investigations, they were rehabilitated by the Van Traa report. Their decision to dissolve the IRT and to abstain from the Delta method was vindicated. In 1997, in the wake of the whole affair, Wiarda, who had used the most vehement defensive tactics, was subjected to the "police carousel" and quietly transferred from Utrecht to Den Haag. Nordholt, however, retired as he had planned. He was given a statesmanly official farewell party by the city of Amsterdam and the Amsterdam police force, broadcast on national television and visited by all major politicians and magistrates.

NOTES

1. Another important issue in this respect is the role of the media in the process of fiasco construction. An attempt to fill this gap, using the same case, can be found in Bovens, Hart, Dekker, Verheuvel, and De Vries (1998).

2. Following the 1993 reorganization of the police, the team was a joint operation of the regional forces of Amsterdam-Amstelland, Kennemerland, and Gooi and Vechtstreek.

3. This created a constitutional novelty, because technically both ministers already had demissionary status following the dissolution of the Cabinet before the elections. This also explains why Parliament could not move for a straightforward vote of no confidence, because a demissionary Cabinet by definition has an intermediary status pending the formation of a new Cabinet and does not require parliamentary approval (it is therefore assumed to be a caretaker body and is not to take any politically consequential policy initiatives).

4. TK stands for *Tweede Kamer*, the Dutch House of Commons/Second Chamber of Parliament.

5. For a normative analysis of a number of manipulatory tactics, see Goodin (1980).

Creating the Agents of Corporate Rescue

Professionalization of Insolvency

Terence C. Halliday
Bruce G. Carruthers

CREATING AN INFRASTRUCTURE FOR CORPORATE FAILURE

The *behavior* of corporate failure operates within parameters set by an institutional framework that is politically constructed, legally inscribed, and occupationally mediated. Put another way, corporate failure or reconstruction cannot be understood without awareness of the political, legal, and occupational parameters that define what is possible (rules that constrain and enable), what is conventional (current practices within legal constraints), and what is desirable (according to public policy and the incentive systems it has put in place by political manipulations of market relations).

This chapter employs a single case of bankruptcy politics, the English Insolvency Act 1986, to exemplify these general propositions. We shall show that the process of corporate failure and reorganization is politically constructed, through legal means, to advance, among other things, political ideals of corporate and market behavior. The executors of those ideals include not only corporate elites, bankers, and other stakeholders but also professionals—lawyers, accountants, civil servants, and, ultimately, judges.

AUTHORS' NOTE: This chapter draws extensively from Chapter 9 of *Rescuing Business*, by Bruce G. Carruthers and Terence C. Halliday (1998).

The English Insolvency Act offers a particularly dramatic instance of the political and legal construction of corporate failure, for it occurred during Mrs. Thatcher's determined efforts to reconstruct English institutions, most notably through a retraction of the state administrative apparatus and the reinvigoration of market institutions. Concomitantly, therefore, we can observe political ideology coming to terms with occupational aspirations to produce a new legal framework for insolvency, a framework that affected every aspect of corporate decline, failure, or rehabilitation. This contemporary episode shows clearly how much the new institutional order of insolvency depended on the agents of reconstruction—and that, in turn, stimulates a more refined view of professionalization in the late 20th century.

▩ PROFESSIONALIZATION AND AGENCY IN CORPORATE INSOLVENCY

The institutional infrastructure for corporate reorganization results from the confluence of two movements. On the one hand, there is the strong inertial flow of prior law and practice, a set of arrangements that has its entrenched occupational interests, modes of activity, established procedures, and typical outcomes. On the other hand, there can arise active movements for change that stimulate innovation and insurgency at the same time that they provoke resistance and counterattack.

The English statutory reforms of insolvency law and practice brought into the open the interplay of these movements. Four sets of public and private agents negotiated the reconstruction of a new institutional order in a process we call "meta-bargaining" (Carruthers & Halliday, 1998). On the public side, two sets of actors predominated. Mrs. Thatcher's Conservative government and her ministers controlled access to Parliament and through their overwhelming majority in the House of Commons advanced a distinctive ideology of market morality and efficiency that embraced company failure and reorganization. Civil servants, responsible for much bankruptcy administration, could be said to protect a public good at the behest of their government ministers. Yet at the same time they had interests of their own, with their attendant responsibilities and rewards.

On the private side, elite practitioners of insolvency strove for a stable domain of work in which they could effect corporate reconstruction within regulatory structures that protected their reputations and jurisdictions. Before 1985, the division of labor in English insolvency practice was essentially unregulated and open to any practitioners who could persuade clients of their merits. The domain of bankruptcy work, and most especially, that of company rescue, offered a rich opportunity for the jurisdictional control of work. Thus, elite accountants and insolvency practitioners led a powerful thrust for stabilization, via regulatory control, of this arena of professional activity. But the game of corporate liquidation and reconstruction is also of acute interest for creditors and company directors. Their behavior is constrained or enabled by the rules established by insolvency law. Moreover, financial institutions and directors themselves are affected by what players the legal rules permit in the game of company rescue or demise.

But creditors and company directors and managers, too, have acute interests in the legal regime that sets the rules by which they play market games. Moreover, they are significantly influenced by what players the legal rules permit to play the game of corporate rescue or demise.

These four groups engaged in a politics of professionalization from "above" and "below." From above, the government and civil servants sought a reconstituted division of labor, form of practice, and set of procedures that coincidentally expressed government ideology and administrative priorities. From below, professionals and clients pressed their own concept of what form a newly professionalized insolvency practice should take. When the main peak associations of company directors and business discovered the government's proposals, they, too, mobilized energetically to create a gentler regime that softened the obligations of management and the penalties for managerial failure. The resolution of these political-cum-occupational struggles produced the legal regime in which all subsequent company rescue has taken place.

Professionalization From Below and Above

Two broad orientations have characterized theories of professionalization on either side of the Atlantic.[1] Theories of *professional co-optation* dominate Anglo-American scholarship. They postulate that professions drive incessantly to protect or extend their market position. Professionals seek exclusive jurisdictions over work domains, either through market advantages or, more effectively, through state sanction, commonly through licensing (Abbott, 1988; Abel, 1988, 1989; Berlant, 1976; Larson, 1977). In a variant of this utilitarian and instrumentalist model, professions are impelled to status mobility or, at least, status containment (Amark, 1990; Murphy, 1988; Parkin, 1979). Either is achieved through credentialing or recruitment, through state legitimization by means of statutory recognition, or through the respect given the profession by the public or the state in notable matters of public policy (Collins, 1979,

1981). Some of the same logic applies within professions in which specialists more marginal to the profession strive for greater centrality, more lucrative work, and more power to determine their own fates (Halpern, 1992).

Emerging from Continental scholarship is a contrasting line of theory that postulates *state sponsorship* of professions. State-centered theories of professions proceed on the premise that states have their own endogenous interests (Rueschemeyer, 1986; Siegrist, 1986). Primary among these is revenue or taxation (Levi, 1988). But taxation revenue depends on a viable economy, and thus, governments and their executive agencies seek to stimulate taxable economic production (Block, 1987). For example, the Conservative government stated in one of its insolvency policy documents that a primary concern of its department responsible for insolvency law was "to encourage, assist and ensure the proper regulation of British trade, industry, and commerce, and to promote a climate conducive to growth and the national production of wealth" (Insolvency White Paper, 1984, p. 5).

Although state officials may administer the apparatus that advances these goals, they retain an interest in the autonomy and prerogatives of their departments and agencies, together with the security and prospects of their careers. Their bureaucratic interests encompass defense of programs and staff positions. Their career opportunities will proliferate as bureaucracies expand. For both reasons, it can be anticipated that state officials conventionally oppose retrenchment and support expansion of state administrative agencies in insolvency as elsewhere. Civil servants and administrative elites will champion a measure of autonomy from economic and political elites. When a political party takes power, administrative and executive branches of the state may be subject to decisions that conflict with civil service interests, a conflict potentially exacerbated in Britain, where the civil service views itself to be strictly neutral in the implementation of government-sponsored legislation.

Clients, banks, corporate directors, and managers also have strong interests in the quality and efficiency of those professionals on whom they must rely. If the agents of corporate failure and death, or corporate rescue and resurrection, do not perform to standards that market players require, it is not surprising that they, too, may push from below for a reformed professionalism that does meet market demands.

By holding in tension the co-optive and sponsorship models of professionalization, it becomes possible to advance a more refined view of professions' engagement in the institutionalization of not only professions' regulatory and self-governing structures but of the practices over which professionals usually have substantial jurisdictions, including corporate reorganization. The politics of English insolvency law will show that professionalization from below does not simply arise from collective action by professionals, although it usually involves such action. The shape of insolvency law, and professionals' role within it, emerged from a matrix of overlapping interests and conflicts among politicians and civil servants, on the one side, and professionals and their clients, on the other. The institutional framework of insolvency, therefore, results from the negotiation of cross-cutting forces for professionalization that come from above and below. Put differently, the legal parameters of corporate reorganization in part are defined through the dynamics of professionalization, just as the creative use of bankruptcy law (Delaney, 1992b) by professionals provides new techniques of corporate strategy.

▦ THE ENGLISH INSOLVENCY ACT 1986

The English Insolvency Act, passed by Parliament in 1986, carried a substantially larger freight than insolvency law alone, for it was appropriated by the government as part of a campaign to solve problems that Mrs. Thatcher's ministers found in the efficiency and legitimacy of the market. The government's initiatives to reconstruct market institutions included reforms of financial markets, regulation of the City (England's Wall Street), and revisions of company legislation. Although a professional model of self-regulation attends some of these other reforms, professionalization as an instrument—albeit modest—of market reconstruction appeared most strongly in the insolvency proposals. Mrs. Thatcher's government viewed professionalization not simply as a way to regulate a narrow niche in the market for professional services to rescue businesses but, serendipitously, as one means to produce a higher "market morality" (Halliday & Carruthers, 1996).

The major overhaul of English bankruptcy law was initiated by the Labour government in 1977 with the appointment by the secretary of trade and industry of a review committee to conduct a reappraisal of all aspects of the insolvency laws of England and Wales (Cork, 1988; Cork Report, 1982, p. iii). The Insolvency Review Committee was chaired by Kenneth Cork (later Sir Kenneth), Britain's most prominent insolvency practitioner and later lord mayor of London. The committee included prominent representatives from the legal profession, industry, accountancy, and organized labor. The inquiry into insolvency was prompted by a dramatic rise in the number of corporate insolvencies through the 1970s, by some spectacular collapses of companies that threatened to destabilize important sectors of the economy, and by a chorus of consumer complaints about firms that used insolvency to defraud customers. In both individual bankruptcy and corporate insolvency, specialists persuaded the government that the antiquated legislation enacted in the 1880s was not well suited to modern conditions.

The committee sent out requests to hundreds of organizations and individuals. It received a heavy volume of written submissions, and it conducted extensive oral hearings with leading, representative organizations. From these submissions, it sought to elicit grievances and proposals to alleviate them. Conspicuous by their absence, however, were the main representative organizations of industry—the Confederation of British Industry and the Institute of Directors, a lapse that both would come subsequently to regret.

The Cork Report was tabled in Parliament on June 9, 1982 (Insolvency White Paper, 1984). The government responded with its legislative intentions—which effectively also signaled which parts of the Cork Report it accepted—in a White Paper tabled in Parliament and released to the public in February 1984 (Insolvency White Paper, 1984). The White Paper, and the bill that was subsequently introduced into the House of Lords in December 1984, substantially adopted the Cork Committee's recommendations, with some important exceptions. The government's deviations from Cork were widely debated in public and contested in the House of Lords, where the government was defeated on two key measures and forced to amend many more. After a record 1,200 or more amendments, in committee, the Lords, and the Commons, the bill passed in both houses and received Royal Assent on October 30, 1985.[2] It was immediately revised the following year, when provisions concerning company directors' disqualification were spun off into a separate act. The 1986 Insolvency Act and 1986 Company Directors Disqualification Act therefore are the two main products, supplemented by a large amount of secondary legislation, of the 9-year reform process initiated by the establishment of the Cork Committee.

The insolvency legislation must be understood as something more than a narrow technical piece of financial lawmaking. Although both Labour and Conservative governments may initially have conceived its purposes quite modestly, by the time the minister of trade and industry presented the 1984 White Paper, it had become increasingly clear that Conservative policymakers viewed the insolvency bill as one more engine to drive the Tory bid for radical market transformations. Unlikely as it may seem, the Insolvency Bill introduced to Parliament in the autumn of 1984 contained a powerful thrust toward the upgrading of "market morality," efforts directed coincidentally toward improving the quality and probity of company management and toward significantly increasing the quality of professional services in corporate reorganization. Although not expressed so baldly, Mrs. Thatcher's government used a surprising legislative vehicle to further its much broader goal of "cleaning up" markets and making them safe both for investors and for privatization (Halliday & Carruthers, 1996).

Markets function through agents, a proposition not lost on a government committed to reconstruction. Mrs. Thatcher's government therefore incorporated into the legislation another major initiative—to establish a new occupation whose members would be charged with both public and private responsibilities, concomitantly as agents of state purpose and commercial interests. The newly professionalized occupation—that of insolvency practitioners—was instituted to ensure that the professional workers who presided over companies in financial distress and in need of liquidation or reorganization would satisfy government purpose as they also satisfied interests of the workers themselves and the principals that hired them. As agents simultaneously of two sets of principals—the state and private commercial interests—insolvency practitioners sprung into being through a set of prelegislative and legislative maneuverings among four sets of actors.

▦ PROFESSIONALIZATION FROM BELOW: OCCUPATIONAL MOBILIZATION

From Corporate Undertakers to Company Doctors

Before 1985, the English market for services in the liquidation and reorganization of companies was substantially unregulated and open to any practitioners who could persuade clients of their merits. This market for the voluntary and compulsory liquidation of companies began to change rapidly over the two to three decades preceding the 1986 Insolvency Act, changes that precipitated adaptations in the social organization of insolvency practice and led to pressures for legal reforms. The rise of insolvency practitioners exemplified a double logic: (a) an expansionist logic to extend and consolidate control over a certain jurisdiction of work and (b) a logic of hierarchical closure, which itself contained a double move to detach the elites of the occupation from its proletariat and specialist insolvency accountants from generalist accountants (Dezalay, 1992). The press by professional elites for full professional validation stemmed not from material interests, which were already well satisfied, but from a complex of other motivations: (a) the desire to resolve a status inconsistency, insofar as the prestige of liquidators lagged the expanding responsibilities and powers of professionals in corporate reconstruction in a global economy; (b) an aspiration to expand the powers of practitioners beyond liquidation, or even reorganization of insolvent companies, to "save" and turn around companies short of insolvency; and (c) a drive to establish regulatory closure over a domain of work to enforce certain standards of admission and practice.

Bankruptcy work in the early 1960s was fragmented, marginal, and enormously variegated. Large accounting firms stayed away from insolvency because, according to a corporate lawyer closely involved with the insolvency reforms, "It was dirty work. . . . Only firms not at the top of the tree went in for insolvency work" (U.K. Interview, 91:20)[3]. In the rare case in which a major accounting firm such as Deloittes had an insolvency department, it was there less to make money than as a service function for auditing clients (U.K. Interview, 91:03:7). The high end of practice was dominated by "receivers" and corporate liquidators—qualified accountants who were appointed by banks and financial organizations to recover their loans from insolvent companies by selling off the assets of the company. Work at the low end of the bankruptcy and insolvency field was practiced by liquidators, a substantial proportion of whom had no formal professional qualifications. From time to time, a disproportionate number of these gained notoriety in adverse news articles and press notices when they were convicted of criminal offenses (Aris, 1985; *Sunday Times,* April 26, 1981, p. 62).

The economic and political changes of the 1960s and 1970s provided ample opportunity for expansion at both ends of the occupational prestige hierarchy. A succession of sensational collapses by well-known, good-sized companies caught the attention of accounting firms (Cork, 1988, pp. 71-78), the government, and the financial institutions of the City, including the Bank of England. The major "clearinghouse banks" developed "intensive care departments," which specialized in close supervision and expert advice to their troubled clients, and employed "teams of accountants" to provide independent appraisals and nurse businesses through difficult times (*London Times,* August 18, 1983, p. 15). A new profession of "company doctors" began to emerge in the management field. But most significantly for insolvency practice, the largest national and international accounting firms quickly established their internal insolvency departments, often by merging with the most successful and established insolvency firms (Aris, 1985; U.K. Interview, 90:14:1:4). In their turn, the major accounting professional societies acknowledged the reemergence of insolvency as a specialized field by forming specialist insolvency committees (*Sunday Times,* March 27, 1985; U.K., Interview 91:03:13).

Structural transformation, whether privatization at the national level, or practice concentration in the division of labor, requires cultural legitimization. Changes in the management of distressed corporations floated on an ideology of corporate reconstruction that championed "saving companies." Elite insolvency practitioners joined with management consultants to acclaim the value of reorganization when liquidation could be avoided. Cork's committee made company rehabilitation a priority from the beginning (Cork, 1988; U.K. Interviews, 90:04, 91:07, 90:20).

Demand for insolvency practitioners also grew at the lower end of the market. The secular trend in the rising volume of bankruptcies presented new demands for accountants and unqualified practitioners who were not previously experienced in liquidations and new opportunities for a tiny fraction of entrepreneurial pseudoprofessionals—styled by their detractors as "cowboy liquidators"—who used freewheeling strategies to exploit the pickings of financial distress.[4]

Establishing Collective Organization

These developments, at both the top and bottom of the market for liquidators, catalyzed the impulse of insolvency practitioners toward collegial organization. Because this field was substantially unregulated and because insolvency had marginal standing in the major English accounting associations, no collegial bodies for practitioners existed until 1961, when a small number of highly experienced practitioners formed a group that they called the Discussion Group of Accountants Specializing in Insolvency, which evolved into the Insolvency Practitioners Association (IPA). Members considered themselves an elite, because they were specialists with at least 5 years full-time work in the insolvency field.

After its contributions to a small piece of government insolvency legislation in 1976 and its regular consultations with the Insolvency Service of the Department of Trade and Industry, the government acknowledged the IPA as one of two major representative organizations of insolvency experts. The other group was a combined insolvency subcommittee of the Consultative Committee of Accountancy Bodies (CCAB), a consortium of the United Kingdom's leading accounting associations.

When the Labour government set up its Insolvency Law Review Committee in 1977 (Cork Committee), greater prominence for the IPA was ensured. The IPA and CCAB presented a series of submissions and representations that accompanied every step of the deliberative and parliamentary process through enactment of the statute and promulgation of insolvency rules. In sheer volume, IPA and CCAB submissions were matched only by the reports from the joint insolvency committee of the Law Society and Bar Council.[5]

Status and reputation propelled the drive toward professionalization from the professionals themselves. Even the elite of insolvency practice, who spearheaded legislative representations, was tainted by such epithets as "corporate undertakers" and sullied by the unsavory activities of cowboy liquidators. For the elite, professionalization of insolvency practice was intended to drive out incompetent, inexperienced, and occasionally unethical and criminal elements. Economics seemed marginal.

Given the ethos of saving companies, however, reputation was inseparable from responsibility for corporate reconstruction. The status project therefore intertwined with increased powers that Cork and others anticipated should be vested exclusively in licensed insolvency practitioners. The Cork Committee and the review of insolvency law, therefore, provided a singular moment in which a relatively low-prestige occupation, and a relatively peripheral accounting specialty, could obtain a distinctive identity and state legitimization.

▦ PROFESSIONALIZATION FROM BELOW: GUARANTEEING QUALITY FOR CLIENTS

Financial institutions and corporations, one set of principals in corporate reorganization, have compelling interests in the quality and availability of the practitioners with whom they would be compelled to deal.

Bankers insisted that there should be some minimal qualification for practice as a receiver, even if a standard would be difficult to apply, but it was chary of an entirely new occupational monopoly and advocated instead the appointment of receivers from several professions, including chartered surveyors and auctioneers. In practice, however, bankers could exercise control over practitioners through normal market mechanisms. Most of the major British clearinghouse banks had enduring patronage relations with particular established insolvency firms. And in case the power of appointment should be doubted, they maintained a black list of whom they would not appoint to act on their behalf (U.K. Interview, 91:06).

Some business groups supported the professionalization of liquidators, but it was not a high priority. The British Chambers of Commerce knew that they did not want a new monopoly, but then again, they wanted a uniform code of practice and ethics. The Institute of Directors supported professionalization not only because it would encourage corporate reconstruction by competent practitioners and, they hoped, "save" companies but also because a regulated profession could more reliably report on the business fraud that cast a pall over the reputation of company directors. A profession of insolvency practitioners charged with the obligation to report on delinquent directors would have the capacity to exercise a control function that the Institute of Directors could not. Moreover, the institute may have preferred to pass the washing of its dirty linen on to other parties so it could sidestep the need for expanded disciplinary apparatuses by the institute itself, a function that invariably creates conflict within a trade association (U.K. Interviews, 90:08, 91:12).

▓ PROFESSIONALIZATION FROM ABOVE: THE CIVIL SERVICE AND THE MERITS OF SELF-REGULATION

Civil service norms precluded departmental officials who were working on a legislative bill from openly dissenting with their minister. Other officials in the same department, however, could and did exercise their rights of expression through their civil service unions (U.K. Interview, 91:10). Neither the department nor the civil service union expressed expansionistic inclinations. Officials pressed for some level of expert qualifications, in substantial part because professionalized receivers and liquidators would permit tasks to be shifted from the public to the private sphere and because properly authenticated private professionals would no longer be required "to come dashing to the department for permission to do this, that, and the other anymore" (U.K. Interview, 91:10). Although they immediately agreed that there should be licensing of professionals in the field of insolvency, when given an option between direct state regulation by a specialized governmental unit (viz, themselves) or professional self-regulation by a private occupational entity, they categorically chose the latter. Administrative rationality and political sensitivities coupled to urge on the Cork Committee a classical English model of professional autonomy.

However, civil servants had a strong view about *what kind of work* they were prepared to let go into the private sector and what work they wanted to retain. Control mechanisms over company directors in the insolvency field had suffered from a central defect: They relied on overworked government officials in understaffed departments to bring actions against the tens of thousands of directors implicated in company failures. Furthermore, the Department of Trade and Industry had never managed to strengthen its legal powers to inspect company records or penetrate protective devices that surrounded company liens.[6] But if functions of the

Insolvency Service (DTI), the department responsible for bankruptcies and insolvencies, could only be passed to a private profession with the fiduciary guarantees of self-regulation, then the DTI itself resisted any responsibility for licensing those individuals or authorizing other bodies to license individuals. Given personnel constraints, the DTI much preferred self-regulation outside government, a wariness that presumably also stemmed from the vulnerabilities from discriminating among individuals and groups whose claims to professional status were reinforced by political pressures on the department.

However, the civil servants strongly preferred to retain work at the more sophisticated end of company liquidations and reorganizations, a view that coincided with the government's interest in a stronger measure of regulation—public and private—over business practice. Hence, the civil service fought a calculating game to divest itself of routine, uninteresting, individual cases, as well as contentious responsibilities for occupational licensing, in favor of expanding their capacity to regulate companies, their directors, and their practices (Halliday & Carruthers, 1993).

The Cork Committee and the Warrants of Professionalism

Nevertheless, the Cork Committee scarcely needed vigorous mobilization by interest groups to advocate some professional regulation of the insolvency field. Before any submissions from interest groups were solicited, an early consensus had emerged "that in the future administrators, liquidators, etc., would all be professional men." The principal issue was the form that professionalization would take and what occupations—accountants, lawyers, surveyors, civil servants—might be permitted to join and regulate the new profession.[7]

One key reason was pragmatic. Because the City (the financial district of London) had become increasingly aware of the need to save rather than dissolve companies, banks, insolvency practitioners, and even the government began to explore methods of corporate reconstruction. The Cork Committee hit on an innovation—which it labeled an administrative receivership—to do exactly this. Before a company became technically insolvent, it could apply to the court for a moratorium on the payment of its debts and ask the court to appoint an administrator, who would be an experienced insolvency practitioner capable of turning the company around before its financial circumstances became desperate. For this innovation to work, it required highly qualified practitioners to act as administrators. Because both management and creditors would have to be convinced that administratorships were in their ultimate financial interests, they too would need to have confidence in the capabilities of this new type of professional.

Professionalization, therefore, provided a means of ensuring that a minimum threshold of competence could be guaranteed courts, management, and creditors. In other words, the effective shift of corporate consciousness from a view of insolvency practitioners as "corporate undertakers" to "company doctors" could be smoothed by the guarantees implicit in professional status and self-regulation. Professionalization presented a conventional warrant of expert authority to prospective clients. Moreover, it increased the competitive advantage of qualified insolvency practitioners in their struggle with turnaround specialists, because access to the courts, and a court order for administratorships, provided more powerful, if not always so flexible, instruments to manage corporate reorganizations.[8]

In its final report, the Insolvency Review Committee recommended the formation of a new profession of insolvency practitioners. The report urged the adoption of some "minimum professional qualification and control" as a prerequisite for engaging in insolvency practice. An insolvency practitioner would need to have been in "general practice" for 5 years and to be a member of a professional body currently approved by the Department of Trade and Industry. The professional bodies, themselves, must satisfy the department of several prerequisites for approval: (a) that they have a code of ethical conduct; (b) that they have strict accounting rules for moneys belonging to third parties that pass through their hands; (c) that admission to the profession be by examination, including at least an optional paper on insolvency; (d) that the body have "an effective disciplinary body" with powers to deprive members of the right to practice; and not least, (e) that members be required to renew annually certificates to practice (Cork Report, 1982, chap. 15.).

▦ PROFESSIONALIZATION FROM ABOVE: STATE SPONSORSHIP OF PROFESSIONAL DISINTERESTEDNESS

Mrs. Thatcher's government committed itself to shifting public goods onto the private market. To accomplish this, at once the government needed to be assured that the market could bear the new demands placed on it and the public needed assurance that the market was a proper institution to handle matters previously thought to be the province of the state. Both required cleaning up what the government minister responsible for the insolvency legislation characterized as "the unacceptable face of capitalism." This in turn demanded not only a great improvement in the quality and efficiency of corporate management, but it also called for changes in "market morality"—the norms and sanctions that governed market behavior (Halliday & Carruthers, 1996). Thus, the insolvency legislation became embroiled in a much broader government set of initiatives, which did not always emerge through careful design and which sought to change public attitudes toward investment in markets and to change the ways company directors carried out their managerial responsibilities. Professionalization offered the government one way to devolve state functions onto the market and concomitantly to assure itself of market morality in corporate and professional practice.

The Green Discussion Paper issued by the government in 1980 laid out some ideas for insolvency legislation. The government proposed that a substantial proportion of bankruptcy and insolvency work be transferred from the government Insolvency Service to the private sector. But this move faced serious political difficulty if the government could not assure its constituents and the public that the functions previously carried out by civil servants, whose ethos presupposed disinterestedness, could be done so with equal or greater competence by no less disinterested private practitioners. The norms of the market—economic self-interest and the maximization of private gains—ostensibly subverted the government's purpose. Its preferred alternative, therefore, was to locate insolvency work in the only private market institution that also espoused disinterestedness— the professions. Moreover, because professionalization in its classical English form also included self-regulation, professionalization promised to relieve government departments of their intrusive presence in every phase of insolvency proceedings. According to a former president of the IPA and a member of the insolvency panel of the CCAB,

> the Department of Trade and Industry had their finger in everything any insolvency practitioner did, which was necessary when there were a lot of rogues carrying it on. But once you had established a proper separate profession that was properly regulated in its own right, you didn't need all this time-wasting at the DTI (U.K. Interview, 90:14:2; 11-12).

If virtue could be married to efficiency and produce a public good in a private market, then the Conservatives would vindicate their economic ideology in yet another realm of market activity, this time employing professionalization as its primary institutional mechanism.

According to a senior civil servant responsible for developing the government's insolvency policy, the ministerial view was that lack of controls over appointments of trustees or liquidators produced incompetence and dishonesty, so "there was a need for control," and that fitted comfortably with the government's policy on professions, which advocated "self-regulation within a statutory framework." Through the "Big Bang" in English financial services, the government held to the strength of its convictions in that arena of market activity most impermeable, it might be thought, to the virtues of self-policing.[9] The concept of statutorily governed self-regulation formed the centerpiece of the government's preferred mode of regulating services in the financial sector—a policy whose effectiveness, and controversiality, remains undimmed to the present (U.K. Interviews, 91:02:1:3; 91:17:2:9-10, 14-15; 90:02; 90:09:2:7-9).

The government's position on insolvency practice sprang from similar philosophical dispositions. In fact, however, political expediency did not permit, in the first instance, the wholesale removal of bankruptcy services from the Official Receiver's Office to the private sector. The opposition that developed to the government's 1980 Green Paper precluded privatization of an office that had been founded in the 1880s precisely to forestall the corruption that was rife in earlier market models of bankruptcy administration. Moreover, the private profession had no desire to be burdened with a raft of bankrupts with little or no capacity to pay. But resistance sprang not only from pecuniary motives. Insolvency practitioners espoused a concept of professionalization that located the search for bankruptcy fraud firmly in the public domain. For the Cork Committee, the IPA, the CCAB, and nonprofessional interest groups, the weight of government authority to police the margins of credit consumption was an irreducible public good that should not be alienated from the public sphere. That this argument served also to keep unremunerative bankruptcy work in the hands of government departments reinforced a public good with a private occupational interest.

The government's more considered views on insolvency practice were expressed in its White Paper released in mid-1984 and the draft bill introduced to Parliament late that year. The treatment of "professional standards for insolvency practitioners" in the very first chapter signaled the priority the government placed on insolvency practice as a key to the entire reforms. Essentially accepting the Cork Report in all respects, the White Paper reaffirmed the importance of professional competence and the creation of public trust in those who handled insolvencies.

The lord advocate, Lord Cameron, opened debate on the Insolvency Bill in the House of Lords with the observation that the legislation was drafted to ensure that "the public should have confidence" in insolvency practitioners (Lord Cameron, House of Lords, January 15, 1985, col. 877). The qualifications the government sought for insolvency practitioners fell into two classes—professional probity and professional competence—which in fact closely paralleled those that the government had also championed in the regulation of business. The Conservatives were determined to pursue in the insolvency field its more general philosophy of "self-regulation within a statutory framework." Lord Lucas, who led for the Insolvency Bill in the House of Lords, states that the government was frustrated with the degree of disorganization in the insolvency field, most particularly in the responsibility for regulation. The accounting professions were organized in at least four separate professional associations. The unqualified accountants had no professional regulatory apparatus. Lawyers and barristers engaged in insolvency work were monitored by yet other professional bodies. And the Department of Trade and Industry had long lost any chance of effective government regulation over professionals. Consequently, at a minimum, the government wished to consolidate divided professions and to unify the regulatory apparatus to provide uniformity of ethics, regulatory consistency, and a clear locus of professional responsibility. In other words, the government sought a comprehensive normative system, complete with policing powers, that operated within precise jurisdictions. Moreover, it wanted to hold somebody accountable for the quality of its regulatory controls. Concomitantly, of course, because the government's approach to lawmaking was to draft fairly general legislation and to fill in the details in secondary legislation and rules, it also needed private organizations that would cooperate in the design and implementation of the new legal and procedural order.[10]

Essentially, therefore, the government had a commitment to the imposition of what looked surprisingly like a cartel in a disorderly corner of the market for professional services. This apparent cartel seemed to conflict directly with the Conservatives' much-vaunted ideal of competitive markets and the steadfast opposition of Thatcherism to "closed shops" in other areas of professional services, such as law. The government sought its way out of this apparent contradiction with a complex form of professional regulation that spawned its own difficulties.

▦ CREATION OF A HYBRID PROFESSION

The government resolved its contradictory attitudes toward monopoly and competition by creating a multistructured or *hybrid* model of professionalization that, at once, sought a common framework to administer insolvency practice but that would also preserve diversity among occupations and professional associations. This deft step permitted the government to defend itself against accusations of creating a "closed shop."

The Insolvency Act created the new profession of insolvency practice. All the normal functions of professional associations—admissions, examinations, code of ethics, discipline, continuing education—were delegated to no less than *six* major professional associations: three major accounting bodies, the Insolvency Practitioners' Association, the Law Society, and the Bar. The two lawyers' organizations were included principally because the government was sensitive to criticisms that it was simply strengthening the accounting monopoly and because it conceded with Cork that there might be occasions when lawyers would be better qualified to act. Because the government was loath, for reasons of political expediency, to take away work from all insolvency practitioners who were not members of either the accounting or legal professions and because the IPA demanded minimum entrance requirements far higher than the government preferred, the act included a *seventh* organization that could also license practitioners—its own Department of Trade and Industry, which 4 years earlier had publicly expressed its desire not to have any such powers. Self-regulation therefore required the consensual regulation of the insolvency field by seven independent organizations that were required to reach agreement on common standards of admission, examinations, codes of ethics, and disciplinary procedures but that would apply them independently.

Why did the government adopt restrictive practices that directly abrogated its own first principles of economic freedom? Government sponsorship of professionalization turned on its readiness to tolerate some restrictive trade practices if that was a price that had to be paid for more efficient, stable, and "moral" markets.[11] The government did not consider the new profession of insolvency practice to be a complete monopoly, because a license to practice could be obtained through six professional bodies and through the Department of Trade and Industry itself, which permitted the government some control over the monopolistic instincts of other professional bodies. If, for instance, some of the professional licensing bodies sought to restrict entry to the practice of insolvency work, the government retained the power to maintain open entry through departmental licensing powers. But most important, the government tolerated restrictive practices because insolvency practitioners were charged with responsibilities to monitor directors in financially distressed companies.

Several members of the Cork Committee had been pessimistic about the implementation of the Cork Report. There were good reasons for low expectations. Insolvency legislation was not a great vote getter, and there were few highly organized interest groups in the insolvency area to exert pressure on the government.[12] And when the government seemed loath to move on Cork's Final Report—first to publish it, then to respond in a White Paper—these doubts seem to be confirmed.

Then, suddenly, in early 1984, some 3 years after the department had received the Cork Report, the government moved with surprising alacrity to present its policy proposals, draft a bill, and rush it through Parliament. Why the abrupt change in attitudes? The most compelling explanation comes from the government's recognition rather late in the day that the Insolvency Bill could be saddled to a much larger haul than liquidation and company reorganization.

In the first instance, the Insolvency Act institutionalized a classic liberal solution to the immediate presenting problems of liquidator competence and probity. Through professionalization, albeit in this strained and architectonic fashion, government could demarcate jurisdictions for insolvency practice (Abbott, 1988), legitimate a system of occupational governance, oversee development of an acceptable normative system, regulate admissions, and exert some control over the enforcement apparatuses of the respective licensing bodies. Moreover, the cost of regulation was almost entirely externalized to the professional bodies, thus attenuating government's responsibilities for the sometimes politically embarrassing lapses of failed professional responsibility. This solution was ideologically satisfying, too, because it married the values of efficiency and small government without appearing to erect a new private monopoly.

In the second instance, the government's sponsorship of professionalization inheres in its consistency with the ideology of privatization. In the government's view, the emergence of the new profession permitted simultaneously, a more efficient private solution to market failures and the correlative contraction of the state. We have shown that the two were contingent in the government's thinking and statutory design: Only a form of private institution that was culturally acceptable, with impeccable fiduciary bona fides, could be entrusted with responsibilities previously thought to be indissolubly wedded to the public sphere. The movement of work from the public to the private domains through professionalization yielded a double benefit for public servants. It married the status of their government department to a higher-status occupation charged with a higher mandate to reconstruct the leading institutions of capitalist society. Concurrently, it also shifted into the private sphere some of the more mundane and routine tasks that symbolically deprofessionalized civil servants, thus allowing them to adopt supervisory postures and more sophisticated methods of corporate surveillance.

The most notable outcomes of the legislation, however, were the structural innovations that converted professionalism into an agent of state regulation and moral reconstruction (Halliday & Carruthers, 1996). The Cork Committee handed the government two weapons with which to assault the failure of business to regulate itself: (a) director disqualification and (b) director vulnerability to civil suits through wrongful trading actions. On the initiative of insolvency practitioners, a director could be disqualified by the DTI from acting as a director in any company for up to 15 years. Moreover, the new provisions on "wrongful trading" permitted insolvency practitioners to identify directors who might be made personally liable for the debts of their company (Carruthers & Halliday, 1998).

These extraordinary legal innovations enacted professionalism on two additional counts. They pressured company directors to obtain expert advice more quickly and earlier in the downward spiral of financial distress, and thus, they activated more broadly and deeply the professional resources available to the business community. In addition, they pressed nonexecutive directors of companies—frequently the outside experts, who were not infrequently professionals themselves—to attend more closely to company affairs and to hold full-time managers more accountable. Business leaders and insolvency specialists concur that passage of the Insolvency Act, publicity through trade and professional associations, media attention, and the sharper teeth of court decisions have combined to alter the behavior of directors in large public and medium-sized companies in a way that beatifies professionalism (U.K. Interview, David Graham, Q.C.; U.K. Interviews, 91:20, 90:08, 91:12, 91:08).

But the serendipitous amendment to the bill as it wended through Parliament transported professional responsibilities onto a new plane of regulatory import. Faced with an amendment that charged every insolvency practitioner in a liquidation to write a report on every director, the government reluctantly accepted that newly minted insolvency practitioners offered a comprehensive means of overseeing directors of all insolvent companies.[13] It allowed the government to build a national database of directors engaged in more than one insolvency. And most important, it conveyed to directors the message that their decisions and activities were subject to observation and ex post facto examination. In short, the professionalization of insolvency practitioners intensified the pressure on business to "professionalize" its own activities through adoption of a code of behavior that would be defensible before the policing activities of insolvency practitioners. And to ensure that this chain of control remained unbroken, insolvency practitioners themselves might be personally liable for the debts of a failed company if they failed to fulfill their professional obligations to file reports, among other things.[14]

Professionalization of insolvency practice therefore presented the government with a brilliant alternative that at once unloaded costs of regulation onto the private market, essentially as a tax on insolvency practitioners (who resisted this added, unrecompensed, responsibility), and ensured saturation coverage of all defunct companies.[15]

If this extended empowerment of a market profession in its expansive definition of state-principal/profession-agent relations represents the most singular innovation of the Insolvency Act, its spawning of a hybrid profession represents an intriguing development in the organization and structure of professions.

▨ RECONCEIVING PROFESSIONAL REGULATION

The new profession in principle united at least two occupations; more accurately, it melded the insolvency segments of accounting, law, and surveying into a new second-order occupation. This "layering" of a secondary occupational label and monopoly over an already preexisting occupational title, most often also endowed with monopoly over a jurisdiction of work, created a new hybrid form of profession with few precedents. And although it was a primary qualification for some practitioners, it acted as a specialty qualification for others, essentially segmenting the internal market for accountancy services.

Despite its complexity, this hybrid form of professionalism suggests an alternative resolution of the incipient conflict that can arise when several occupations converge on a single domain of work. Under circumstances in which there is pressure for multidisciplinary partnerships (the partnership of different professions, such as accountants and lawyers, in one firm) and progressive specialization in the complexities of organization in the global economy, hybrid professionalism presents a new model. Professionals on the edge of their respective professional communities may share a stronger tie to a community of practice in an area such as insolvency than to law or accountancy. Put another way, lawyers, accountants, and surveyors who work on financially distressed companies may have more in common with each than with their original professions. This "transprofessional" community breaks out of conventional definitions of professional identity.

This structural analysis leads back to the theories of professions engaged at the outset. Contemporary theory on professions has focused too narrowly on professions' projects to establish exclusive control of markets for professional services. In Anglo-American formulations of professional projects, there is a derivative and limited view of the state. Professions co-opt public resources, including legal controls over markets, for their private interests. States are essentially captured and manipulated by greedy professions. And regulation in the literature on professions overwhelmingly means self-regulation. Professions seek state authority to govern their own affairs at arm's length from state interference.

When we juxtapose the classic Anglo-American model of professional co-optation of the state, or professionalization from below, with the Continental model of state sponsorship of professions, or professionalization from above, the insolvency legislation supports the proposition that state sponsorship can be a forceful agent for occupational development even in the seemingly unpropitious circumstances of a weak state in an Anglo-American country. The Conservative Party swept into power with a driving commitment to reduce state reliance and induce market vitality. As the warning salvo of the Green Paper (1980) abruptly announced, the government was prepared to entertain radical transformative measures and to push them forcefully through the legislature in which they had a massive majority. Consequently, the English state began partially to dismantle some of its traditional apparatuses and to externalize its established functions.

That this was not simply an ideological agenda pressed by an incumbent political party obtains some support from the DTI officials whose protestations that they were frustrated by excessive demands and inadequate powers cannot simply be dismissed out of hand. There is some verisimilitude to the official claims that they would rather retain supervisory powers and concentrate on serious matters in a diminished department than be swamped by trivial clerical work for which there was inadequate staffing. This assertion has added credence because it is consistent with a desire by civil servants to protect or enhance their own professional status within the state bureaucracy. Higher-level supervisory activities over more important individual and corporate bankruptcies carries much greater cachet and occupational satisfaction than the endless repetition of petty routines over minor cases, even at the cost of some jobs. This would also have been the case had officials been able to specialize in critical cases that would be presented to higher courts.

State activism was epitomized by the government's position on the disqualification of directors. Although some features of the notion were already on the lawbooks, and although Cork, too, was disposed to an expansion of disqualification provisions, the punitiveness of the government's proposals for automatic disqualifications betray its own distinctive interests in upgrading commercial morality. Similarly, the readiness of the state authorities to accept Cork's recommendations for the stripping of limited liability protections from miscreant directors signals the extraordinary measures to which the state would go to improve the quality and ethics of management.

Given these powerful ideological imperatives from the party in power, as well as the more limited interests of the civil service, the professionalization of insolvency practitioners represents an administrative convenience for government that coincidentally conformed with several of its guiding principles. In short, professions offered the state an economical, mostly privatized, broadly dispersed, self-regulating, quality-controlled means of implementing fundamental policy commitments to the rejuvenation of markets. The state openly sponsored both an enhancement of accountants' core practice and the creation of a new second-order specialist profession, complete with the standard elements of classic professions.

But this story cannot be told only in heroic measures of state triumphalism. State action did not occur in a vacuum of professional mobilization. The disturbances in the economic and legal environments of insolvency work altered the market and status positions of insolvency occupations. Insolvency practitioners of different stripes had interests that they pressed vigorously and, for the most part, successfully. The group with most to gain were the nonprofessional, nonqualified liquidators. Without academic credentials, licenses, and membership in one of the established professions, they stood on the margins of professional respectability.

Insolvency practitioners of all kinds, accountants and nonprofessional liquidators, had already begun to build an independent occupational standing before the insolvency reforms got under way. The Insolvency Practitioners Association and the CCAB insolvency committee were the associational expressions of an occupational transformation being spearheaded in global accounting firms and valorized in high-profile corporate rescues. The Cork Committee and the review of insolvency law, therefore, provided a singular moment in which a relatively low-prestige occupation and a relatively peripheral accounting specialty could obtain the distinctive identity and state legitimization that their heightened market profile seemed to warrant.

Yet the Cork Committee, and its satellite consultative groups, extended beyond the world of liquidators to a transprofessional community that embraced solicitors, barristers, legal academics, and bank legal departments. Closer to each other than most of their noninsolvency colleagues, the core of this loosely unified professional community had a history of collaboration on committees of inquiry, as well as a shared work experience in the higher reaches of corporate reorganization over countless major cases. The field of law it defined was not immune from powerful economic interests, as the mobilization of banks demonstrated on forms of security (Halliday, Carruthers, & Parrott, 1993). But it proceeded with relative autonomy and with a bravura performance of specialist, entrepreneurial boldness and political sagacity.

If there is a partiality of interests from both the state, in its sponsorship of professionalism for reasons of market morality, and from the insolvency practitioners, in their co-optation of state powers for reasons of power and repute, the aspirations of each were substantially satisfied by the other. The state's ideological commitment to smaller government coincided with the status interests of professions in an enlarged market. And the bid for professional status mobility of the insolvency practitioners coincided with the state's search for an effective regulatory instrument to improve the efficiency and morality of markets.

In historical sequence, however, the neatness of coincident interests becomes decidedly untidy as "streams" of solutions did not coincide precisely with "streams of problems" (Kingdon, 1984). The emerging momentum for professionalization from the civil servants, liquidators, and industry groups preceded by several years the awareness by government that the insolvency practitioner solution meshed with its project of market renovation. Conversely, the government's charge that the Cork Committee find ways to privatize bankruptcy gave the reformers an unexpected hook on which to hang their innovative proposals. Indeed, although the government eventually appropriated the reform proposals and expanded their import beyond the vision of the reformers, it did so belatedly, sometimes with initial reluctance, and for the most part fortuitously. In the politics of the moment, its growing awareness that insolvency reforms could aid privatization and that professionalization of insolvency practice could help reconstitute the moral economy of corporate governance, proceeded for the government by happenstance within a general ideological framework.

The dualism inherent in accounts of professionalism from above and below cannot adequately serve to characterize the complexity of interdependencies that arise between them. In fact, as the insolvency case vividly demonstrates, there is a very real sense in which professions and states can come to constitute each other (Johnson, 1990). For the state, the profession is a projection of regulatory mechanisms, of monitoring powers, of reconstructive capacities, of sociotechnical devices to order the central institution of the liberal state (Miller & Power, 1993). Constructing professions depoliticizes state functions and pushes state purposes into the realm of neutrality and, thereby, legitimacy. In this case, Johnson (1990) is right to conclude that "professionalism is a mechanism for incorporating independent expertise into the service of the state" (p. 61). Conversely, for the profession, the state is the embodiment of representative purpose, the institution that gives the profession not only its mandate but its meaning. The power and status of a profession, therefore, is inseparable from the value invested in it by state recognition of its expert and symbolic services.

Corporate decline, reconstruction, or failure, therefore, occurs in an institutional matrix shaped by the politics of professionalism, influenced by political ideology, and inscribed in law—statutes elaborated and qualified by case law. The "meta-bargaining" (Carruthers & Halliday, 1998) that occurs in legislative politics sets the parameters for everyday bargaining that occurs between creditors and debtors, managers and employees, professionals and their clients. Politics, in other words, frames everyday practice, and although it may be largely invisible in day-to-day activities, it nonetheless remains a looming if unseen presence. The law that expresses the political settlement among conflicting parties to meta-bargaining determines who will be the players in corporate reorganization, what resources they will have available to them, and as we have seen, what agents can exercise those resources.

Finally, it may be observed that the institution constructed to deal with corporate failure itself emanates in substantial part from cognitive theories that form the core of professional, political, and corporate ideologies. Mrs. Thatcher's government might not have had an entirely coherent political ideology, but it had a strong belief that markets delivered many goods better than states, and it had a set of supporting theories about what was wrong with current institutions, why corporate failure occurred at the rate it did, and how these should be corrected. In other words, behind its programmatic prescriptions stood theories of market behavior and business failure (Halliday & Carruthers, 1996). These were not the same theories as their American counterparts, and as a result, the policy prescriptions, professional incentive structures, and legal provisions that emerged from the 1978 U.S. Bankruptcy Code differed systematically, despite the commonality of each country's search for a more efficient way to rescue business (see Carruthers & Halliday, 1998). Indeed, whereas the English government sought to privatize areas of bankruptcy and insolvency practice, American reformers sought to nationalize work that previously had been carried out by private practitioners. In both cases, therefore, political ideology and the politics of professions were refracted through a political process of meta-bargaining. Both processes transformed the professions responsible for company liquidation and rehabilitation. Both processes spawned a new institutional framework for corporate failure. Changes in agency, in other words, were both the condition of institutional reconstruction and the expression of it.

NOTES

1. This distinction is well established in comparative studies of professions, although there is evidence that it is eliding or at least being renegotiated in a number of national situations, particularly as states seek to modify their relationships with private markets, and professions are reorganizing under pressures of national and global economic competition (cf. Brint, 1994; Freidson, 1986; Torstendahl & Burrage, 1990).

2. Although the passage of the Act represented the most wide-ranging reform of insolvency law in a century, there were two subsequent developments: (a) a consolidation of the Insolvency Act in the Companies Act to produce the Insolvency Act 1986 and (b) another consolidation and slight amendment of provisions on director disqualification from the Companies Act 1985 and the Insolvency Act 1985 in the Company Directors Disqualification Act 1986.

3. Numbers following interview citations refer to the authors' records of interviewer and page numbers of interviews.

4. 1970 was one of the worst years for bankruptcies since World War II (*London Times*, October 8, 1971, p. 22).

5. Written Submissions to the Cork Committee, Public Record Office, File BT 260, File BT 260, Kew (hereafter, PRO).

6. Oral testimony from the Institution of Professional Civil Servants, Insolvency Law Review Committee, June 13, 1978; PRO.

7. Minutes, Insolvency Law Review Committee (Cork Committee), March 1, 1977; March 24, 1977; June 14, 1978.

8. In theory, this argument could be reversed. Insolvency practitioners bent on upward mobility created a demand for their services by formulating the ideal of company reorganization and then offered themselves as the only experts capable of handling it. In other words, professionalization was a classic strategy of market creation and control (cf. Abel, 1989, on lawyers). But it is clear that the ideal of "saving companies," although politically convenient for insolvency practitioners, had a much broader well-spring from industry and government. Insolvency practitioners were opportunists—taking a rising complaint and swelling its tones.

9. Some insolvency practitioners suspected that the government had a subsidiary motive for keeping ethical regulation of practitioners away from a government department: the work of ethical oversight too readily embroils government in failures of regulation that create political problems for ministers.

10. Despite the fact that the Conservatives shifted deliberately away from Britain's well-established postwar politics of tripartite negotiations among government, labor, and business, the rejection of neocorporatist politics did not go

so far as to eschew government reliance on private bodies to effect public purpose. Indeed, Lord Lucas, government leader on the Insolvency Bill in the House of Lords, indicated privately that one motivation for professionalization was the need for government to deal with unified professional groups to better regulate them and their markets (U.K. Interview, 90:09).

11. A more conventional explanation was offered by Sir Gordon Borrie, Director of the Office of Fair Trading, who instanced insolvency practitioners as an example of "the activities of the uncontrolled professional operator who causes such public scandal that professionalization . . . is advocated in the public interest" ("The Professions: Expensive Monopolies of Guardians of the Public Interest?" 1984, *Journal of Business Law,* pp. 11-25).

12. In addition, Mrs. Thatcher did not appoint Royal Commissions or departmental inquiries because, said an Opposition M.P., if you already know the correct answer to an economic problem, there is little need to risk convening an independent body to tell you something different. Notable cases of shelved reports sprang readily to the minds of Cork Committee members.

13. Government resistance stemmed in large part because it was loath to weigh down the Insolvency Service with thousands of reports at exactly the time it was seeking to make government more efficient and to upgrade the seriousness of civil servant responsibilities.

14. See, for instance, the minister of state's comment that "at determined intervals practitioners will be required to submit a report on what they have done and what evidence of unfitness has been discovered about the directors of the company concerned during the period reported on. The secretary of state will thus receive reports on all directors who have been involved in insolvency proceedings. The reports will form part of a database that will gradually be built on all directors who have been involved in insolvency proceedings" (H.C. Vol. 83, St.Comm.E., July 18, 1985, col. 584.).

15. H.C. Vol. 458, St.Comm.E., May 16, 1985, cols. 55-68. Although the amendment was introduced by an Opposition member, it was strongly supported by Trotter, M.P., an insolvency practitioner, and other Conservatives.

▓ PRIMARY DOCUMENTARY SOURCES

Archives, Insolvency Practitioners' Association, London.

Department of Trade and Industry. (1984). *A revised framework for insolvency law* (Government Insolvency White Paper, Cmnd. 9175). London: Her Majesty's Stationery Office.

Parliamentary Debates, House of Commons. Standing Committee E. Session 1984-1985. Insolvency Bill (Lords). London: Her Majesty's Stationery Office.

Parliamentary Debates, House of Commons. Session 1984-1985. Insolvency Bill (Lords). London: Her Majesty's Stationery Office.

Parliamentary Debates, House of Lords. Session 1984-1985. Insolvency Bill (Lords). London: Her Majesty's Stationery Office.
Minutes of the Insolvency Law Review Committee. 1977-1982. Chicago: American Bar Foundation
Report of the Insolvency Law Review Committee. (1982). *Insolvency law and practice* (The Cork Report, Cmnd. 8558). London: Her Majesty's Stationery Office.
Papers, Insolvency Law Review Committee. File BT 260. Public Record Office. Kew, London.

▦ FURTHER READING

Badie, B., & Birnbaum, P. (1983). *The sociology of the state.* Chicago: University of Chicago Press.
Brint, S. (1990). Rethinking the policy influence of experts: From general characterizations to analysis of variation. *Sociological Forum, 5,* 361-385.
Burrage, M. (1990). Beyond a sub-set: The professional aspirations of manual workers in France, the United States and Britain. In M. Burrage & R. Torstendahl (Eds.), *Professions in theory and history: Rethinking the study of the professions* (pp. 151-176). London: Sage.
Burrage, M. (1990). Introduction: The professions in sociology and history. In M. Burrage & R. Torstendahl (Eds.), *Professions in theory and history: Rethinking the study of the professions.* London: Sage.
Burrage, M. (1992). *Professional self-government is the deep structure of English life.* Working Paper 92-11, Institute of Governmental Studies, Berkeley, CA.
Burrage, M., & Torstendahl, R. (Eds.). (1990). *Professions in theory and history: Rethinking the study of the professions.* London: Sage.
Campbell, J. L., & Lindberg, L. N. (1990). Property rights and the organization of economic activity by the state. *American Sociological Review, 55,* 634-647.
Delaney, K. J. (1996). Veiled politics: Bankruptcy as a structured organizational field. *American Behavioral Scientist, 39,* 1025-1039.
EEC Bankruptcy Report. (1976). *Report of the Advisory Committee on the terms of the draft EEC Bankruptcy Convention* (Cmnd. 6602). London: Her Majesty's Stationery Office.
Gilboy, J. (1992). *On government use of private resources in law enforcement.* Unpublished paper, American Bar Foundation.
Hall, P. A. (1986). *Governing the economy: The politics of state intervention in Britain and France.* New York: Oxford University Press.
Halliday, T. C. (1987). *Beyond monopoly: Lawyers, state crises, and professional empowerment.* Chicago: University of Chicago Press.
Halliday, T. C. (1989). Lawyers and the state: Neo-corporatist variations on the pluralist theme of liberal democracies. In R. Able & P. Lewis (Eds.), *Lawyers*

in society: A comparative approach: Vol. III. Comparative and theoretical studies. Berkeley: University of California Press.

Interim Cork Report. (1980). *Bankruptcy: Interim report of the Insolvency Law Review Committee* (Cmnd. 7968). London: Her Majesty's Stationery Office.

Justice report: A Report of the British Section of the International Commission of Jurists on Bankruptcy. (1975). London: Justice.

Karpik, L. (1988). Lawyers and politics in France, 1814-1950: The state, the market, and the public. *Law & Social Inquiry, 13,* 707-736.

Karpik, L. (1995). *Les avocats: Entre l'état, le public et le marché, XIIIth—XXth siècle.* Paris: Editions Gallimard.

Parry, N., & Parry, J. (1976). *The rise of the medical profession.* London: Croon Helm.

Siegrist, H. (1990). Professionalization as a process: Patterns, progression and discontinuity. In M. Burrage & R. Torstendahl (Eds.), *Professions in theory and history: Rethinking the study of the professions* (pp. 177-202). London: Sage.

PART IV

The Cognitive Construction of Failure

Prosaic Organizational Failure   10

LEE CLARKE
CHARLES PERROW

O rganizations fail often and they fail in important ways. Police departments become corrupt. Banks invest unwisely. Schools do not educate. Investment houses make bad bets. But large or powerful organizations rarely disappear, although one would think that failure would mean extinction. Only one work deals with this phenomenon in any systematic way, the sociological study by Marshall Meyer and Lynne Zucker (1989) with its evocative title, *Permanently Failing Organizations*. Even that remarkable work, however, is equivocal in that organizations may permanently fail in their official goals but not in their unofficial ones. Other than Meyer and Zucker's work, the social sciences offer little in the way of explaining either the sources of organizational failure or the meaning of organizational plans for responses to potential failure.

In what follows, we use a case study to suggest a theory of organizational failure that emphasizes the symbolism of organizational planning. The empirical material comes from the case of the Shoreham Nuclear Power Station on Long Island. Under pressure from regulatory agencies, in our case (or investment bankers or even unsatisfied customers or rambunctious competitors in other cases), the Long Island Lighting Company (LILCO) formulated the plans required for evacuating Long Island in the event of a nuclear accident and were in the process of obtaining approval for them.

There are two mainstays of our analysis: (a) organizations come to believe their own representations, and as a consequence, (b) they ignore the bulk of their experience that shows that these representations may be inaccurate. Clarke (in press) calls these plans "fantasy documents," and they are neither wholly believed nor disbelieved; certainty is impossible because fantasy documents cover extremely improbable events. They are tested against reality only rarely, in that, for example, none of the following disasters were believed to be credible events by the organizations involved: Three Mile Island, Chernobyl, Bhopal, the *Challenger,* and *Exxon Valdez.* In addition to being untested, the accident mitigation and/or evacuation plans—the "fantasy documents"—are likely to draw from a quite unrealistic view or model of organizations. The fantasy is that everything will work right the first time, that every contingency is known and prepared for. Thus, LILCO designed an emergency organization, the Local Emergency Response Organization, LERO, that was even more complex and bureaucratic than its own organization, and expected it to work. The plans, buttressed by many experts, including the Federal Emergency Management Agency (FEMA) and the Department of Energy (DOE), allowed leaders to make bold promises that their organizations could control a mass evacuation.

▨ THE SHOREHAM NUCLEAR POWER STATION

The Shoreham Nuclear Power Station used to live on the north shore of Long Island.[1] By the end of Shoreham's life, many people thought it utterly ridiculous to put a nuclear power plant on Long Island in the first place. But it was not always so. In fact it was not until the late 1970s that the notion arose that it might be dangerous to put a nuclear power station on Long Island. The "danger" people focused on, the conception of hazard that animated people to oppose the plant, was not the risk of meltdown or radiation release. The key danger, that is to say the key definition of unacceptable risk, was the risk of not being able to evacuate a large part of Long Island in the event of catastrophe.

LILCO promised that it could evacuate a 10-mile radius around Shoreham (known as the EPZ, or emergency planning zone). Some uncalculated but substantial reason for the decline and fall of Shoreham was LILCO's failure to demonstrate to others that its promise could be kept. Shoreham's fate depended on the evacuation plan because part of the fallout from Three Mile Island was that utilities were (and are) required to have such a plan; that plan, furthermore, must be approved by FEMA, the Nuclear Regulatory Commission (NRC), and local and state governments. These new requirements gave states and localities a warrant to insert themselves into decision processes that previously had been the exclusive province of federal agencies. It was this warrant that produced the documents we review here. If LILCO could not present a highly credible case that its evacuation plan would actually work, then Shoreham, and possibly even LILCO itself, would be at risk.

The main argument from Shoreham's proponents was that there was nothing special about nuclear accidents. A good deal of research on nonnuclear disasters, largely by sociologists at disaster research centers, which LILCO cited, tells us that people do *not* panic in emergencies and that most of the time emergency workers at least try to fulfill their responsibilities. To illustrate the reasoning, let us quote some testimony from LILCO consultants:

> The record is clear that emergency workers do their jobs when they understand that they have an emergency job to do, when they understand what that job requires of them, and when they have a sense of the importance of their job for overall community safety and to their work group. These understandings can be produced in different ways. For example, people who hold jobs that are in the routine of everyday life comparable to their emergency roles—for example, firemen—bring these understandings to the emergency setting. (NRC, 1983, p. 100)

Were a nuclear catastrophe akin to a flash flood, an earthquake, or commuting—all allusions asserted by LILCO—it would mean that large-scale evacuation was merely a big project, not an insurmountable obstacle. More, it would mean that an organization could overcome the considerable uncertainties that would attend a very serious worst-case event.

For their part, Shoreham's opponents argued that the station was such an exceptional case that there were good reasons to think that officials and organizations would not be able to control an evacuation. They pointed out that denizens of Long Island evinced considerable distrust of LILCO and so wouldn't believe expert proclamations or follow official orders in an emergency. Worse, the same research that shows that most emergency workers in most disasters do what they are supposed to do also shows that when disaster comes, what is highest on people's priority list is their families. Not only would people fail to follow the plan in the event of a severe radiological emergency, Shoreham's opponents reasoned, but those asked to function as evacuation workers would likely try to protect their families first. If the whistle blew and people did not take their posts, massive unpredictability—not controlled evacuation—would ensue. Were that the case, then Shoreham would not pass a pivotal test for ensuring public safety. LILCO, in other words, needed people, and the courts and federal agencies, to believe their promises. The fantasy documents were crucial representations of those promises.

▨ AN EVACUATION EXERCISE

LILCO's credibility problem was large indeed. Surveys consistently showed that people did not even trust LILCO executives' explanations for high electricity rates, so it would be hard to persuade them that those same executives would have the public interest in mind when making decisions about a multibillion-dollar nuclear investment. LILCO used several devices to remedy the credibility gap. Those devices were designed to convince the public and other organizations that they had planned well for catastrophe at Shoreham. Computer simulations, used throughout industry, were one such device:

> LILCO's analysis . . . shows a normal evacuation time of 4 hours and 55 minutes for the entire EPZ in normal weather and with traffic guides. These times compare favorably to other plants located in and supported by New York State. . . . A comprehensive 1982 [NRC] study evaluating 52 nuclear plant sites on a consistent basis showed that half the plants studied had evacuation times in excess of that expected for Shoreham. (quoted in McCaffrey, 1991, p. 134)

But the value of simulations would be mainly internal, useful to nuclear experts and technical decision makers for bringing problems to the fore that they may not have conceived or for ratifying presumably resolved dilemmas. Simulations would do nothing for the public relations and credibility problems because they were too technical and too unreal.

So LILCO conducted a series of real-time exercises. Important parts of the evacuation plan would not, for various reasons, be tested. The sirens would not actually cry out, and the public would not actually be moved. The radio and television stations would only pretend to announce disaster. The plant would not be SCRAMMED (shut down), because it was not even on line. One of the most significant parts of the plan that could not be tested concerned state and local governments. New York State, Nassau and Suffolk counties, and most local governments (including the police, who we gather were skeptical if not incredulous) had proclaimed their opposition to the Shoreham plant, in accordance with the preferences of most Long Islanders (who, incidentally, were unaware the exercises were going on), and refused to participate in any of the planning process. That was a problem because the federal licensing rules required just that sort of participation. LILCO's short-term solution to this problem was to convince federal regulators to act *as if* state and local governments participated. Even with these limitations, however, there was considerable realism to the exercises.

A methodological note: We have searched far and wide for training simulations of similar magnitude, to no avail. There *do* exist cases of emergency exercises involving local police and fire departments in other states simulating events such as airplane crashes and propane explosions at local airports and the like. Although interesting, the emergency organizations in those cases had considerable prior and even relatively frequent experience with the routines they would activate in an emergency. Thus, the relevance of those cases for Shoreham is extremely limited. Another source of comparative data is the military where such exercises are commonplace, but detailed documents on those exercises are not available.

There were a series of LILCO exercises, but we focus here on one that took place on February 13, 1986. The exercise involved, among other things, sending evacuation workers on their missions, setting up media centers with pretend reporters, arranging command posts, telephone calling, and sending emergency vehicles to mock emergencies (FEMA, 1986). LILCO's main agent for organizing emergency planning was LERO. LERO's plan used utility employees, contractors, private organizations, and the DOE in both its plan and the exercises. Thirty-eight evaluators from federal agencies (e.g., FEMA, the DOE, the NRC) were on hand to judge 17 key pieces of the plan, including emergency operations, emergency staging areas, medical drills, decontamination facilities, traffic control, bus evacuation routes, and radiological monitoring, among others. The main point, said FEMA, was that "LERO was to be responsible for ensuring that its resources actually deployed in adequate numbers to reasonably test its notification, mobilization, command, coordination, and communications capabilities" (FEMA, 1986, p. 19).

Following is a skeletal chronology that frames our subsequent discussion (all page numbers to the end of this section refer to NRC, 1986):

6:52 a.m.   Emergency Broadcast System (EBS) announcement that schools would close because of problems then developing at Shoreham. In LILCO's estimation this would not be sufficiently alarming to people that they would begin to evacuate, so no provision was made, in either the exercise or the actual plan, for such potential evacuees.

8:19 a.m.   Site Area Emergency. The Shoreham Nuclear Power Station suffers a break in the high-pressure coolant injection steam line. Core melt becomes highly probable.

8:41 a.m.   Starting here, and continuing for every 15 minutes, the plan calls for the issuance of messages that there was a radiation release at 8:19 a.m. An advisory is issued that dairy animals should eat only stored feed.

9:39 a.m.   General emergency declared. There has been a total loss of the emergency core cooling system and two of the three fission product barriers have failed. In other words, Shoreham is melting down and the radiation is going to be released to the environment. Forty percent of LERO traffic guides have been contacted; none are at their field posts to perform their duties (p. 112). Traffic guides were dispatched only *after* the evacuation recommendation in the general emergency EBS message.

10:24 a.m. Several EBS messages recommend that evacuations begin.

10:30 a.m. A request is issued for a bus to be dispatched to Ridge Elementary School, which is not far from Shoreham; bus arrives 3 hours later at 1:23 p.m. The bus driver was not dispatched to pick up a bus for 40 minutes and then, apparently, got lost (p. 140). The bus still had not arrived at the Nassau County Coliseum, the terminus of the evacuation efforts, with its pretend 40 children, by 4:23 p.m. The implication is the bus and the children never made it out of the EPZ.

10:40 a.m. Gravel truck freeplay impediment is injected; discussed below.

11:00 a.m. Fuel truck accident injected (p. 120); discussed below.

11:46 a.m. EBS message recommending that entire EPZ evacuate.

Overall, FEMA (1986) judged the exercise a success. LERO demonstrated "that it has adequate access control and that security can be maintained" (p. 29), that it "can establish appropriate communications links" (p. 29), that the operations centers worked well. FEMA would reckon that communications were acceptable at the emergency operations center and note that "evacuation personnel were well trained" (p. xii). FEMA did, however, admit "a need for greater communication and more efficient sharing of information" (p. xii) and admitted that in one of the two surprise events, to which we return below, "all pertinent information was not transferred from the freeplay impediment message forms introduced by the exercise controller to the LERO message forms" (p. 3). The missing information was, incidentally, critical. For the other surprise event, FEMA pointed out that the "message concerning the 'visual check' of the fuel truck impediment from the Bus Dispatcher at the Patchogue Staging Area to the Transportation Support Coordinator was partially illegible and was not written on a standard LERO message form" (p. 30). According to FEMA, however, most communications, for instance, involving radio and telephones, "were established rapidly and maintained throughout the exercise" (p. 32). By FEMA's lights, nearly all the objectives of the exercises were met, including the most demanding, about which FEMA concluded, "The LERO [Emergency Operations Center] met the exercise objective of demonstrating the organizational ability to manage an orderly evacuation of all or part of the 10-mile EPZ including the water portion" (p. 34).

One might conclude, judging only from FEMA's assessment, that there were but minor problems in the exercise and that the problem of planning for a meltdown of a nuclear power plant in the middle of Long Island had been solved. The discussion of the surprise events, from which we quote above, sounds as if the most important failures in the exercise were simply a partially illegible message and another message not being written on the standard form. Were that true, were the only failures in fact writing problems, opening Shoreham should proceed directly.

▨ A FEW PROBLEMS

Natural and technological disasters, and those who write about them, provide plenty of data on organizational breakdown.[2] Organizations lose their mandates, personnel sabotage procedures, internal politics compromises vigilance, production pressures foster myopia in leaders, small failures cascade into catastrophe, systems are overwhelmed, and so on. Although that research has been invaluable for many purposes, it is limited to systems that were operating under difficult—sometimes impossible—conditions.[3] In such cases we often must attribute failure to the overwhelming influence of external factors.

But on Long Island we had an instance of organizations working under nearly *best-case conditions:* It was a sunny day and traffic was innocently and unconcernedly moving well. It was not rush hour; the precise time and sequence of events was set weeks before. There had also been previous exercises. Reading through the volumes of description available on the Shoreham case, it is clear that much of the behavior in the exercise was highly scripted. Like the acts in a high school play, little was left to chance. We might have expected that even the responses to the two surprise ("freeplay") messages would have been scripted. Accidents resembling the freeplay ones are not rare on busy Long Island roads.

There were other reasons to expect that success, not failure, would characterize the exercise. Significant amounts of organizational, political, economic, and even individuals' energy were spent on LILCO's exercise. Evacuation workers had 3 to 5 years of training; they took classes, received instruction, engaged in tabletop exercises and drills, and even participated in full-scale exercises. Federal regulators, especially FEMA and the DOE, as well as private consultants, worked closely with LILCO to develop the plan for the exercise as well as the plan for the exercise's evaluation. Workers spent untold hours in classes, learning about dosimeters, the EPZ, and radioactivity. Executives spent untold hours working with the press and leaders in the business community. Let us not forget that much of the planning was quite public, LILCO's actions open to outside scrutiny. The exercise, too, would become very public because extensive litigation was in process with much more to come. A great deal was at stake.

Despite all the oversight, despite all the incentive and opportunity to make the exercise work well, there was instead massive organizational failure. A good deal more went wrong than the failure to fill out a form correctly. Many of the personnel at the staging areas were new and, without previous training, had to have their responsibilities explained *during the exercise* (NRC, 1987a, p. 50). Recall from the chronology that the "site area emergency" was declared at 8:19 a.m., yet none of the road crews—who were on official notice that they would be called—arrived at the three staging areas until after 10:00 a.m. A few never reported at all. By 9:39 a.m. when a "general emergency" had to be declared because all the plant's safety systems had failed, only 11% of the road crew—again, aware that they would be used—deemed essential by LILCO's plan were available.

Neither the Long Island Railroad (LIRR) nor the Federal Aviation Administration were notified of the emergency because no procedures were in place for it (FEMA, 1986, p. 29); apparently no one thought of that. Note that the LIRR runs many trains through and around the EPZ and there is a large airport in the middle of Long Island (Islip); nearby is the site of the major traffic control center in the region, and planes bound for LaGuardia and Kennedy routinely fly over the area.

A large part of LILCO's evacuation plan depended on bus drivers. Those drivers would be especially important for people who needed extra help getting out of harm's way, chiefly children and the mentally and physically incapacitated. The children were perhaps the linchpin in the machine, for both symbolic and practical reasons. If the problem of evacuating the children could not be resolved, the exercise would likely be seen as absurd. Symbolically, children are the pure, the pristine, the most innocent of victims. They could have had no say in whether Shoreham would be built, and it would be difficult for anyone to argue any fine points about risk/benefit trade-offs in the face of cancer-ridden innocence. Practically, if the buses could not be counted on to evacuate the children and if people did not believe the buses could be counted on to evacuate their children, the plan could never succeed. Instead of everyone moving toward the presumed safety of the Nassau County Coliseum, some nonnegligible proportion of Long Island would be moving in the direction of nuclear danger to get their children. LILCO needed the buses to work.

Although the bus drivers, as one might expect, were drilled extensively before the exercises, the buses in large measure did not work. Bus drivers did not take time to read dosimeters (some apparently did not know how to; it had been a problem on previous exercises and the same happened with some ambulance crews), a task required by the plan. One driver, asked by a FEMA evaluator to participate in the exercise, responded that he did not "wish to drive as he had trouble reading signs. This driver even threatened to quit LERO" (FEMA, 1986, p. 105). Postexercise assessment made clear that many bus drivers did not know the boundaries of the EPZ, which meant they did not know when they were or were not "safe" (FEMA, 1986, p. 111). Nearly one third of the bus drivers failed to follow preassigned routes (NRC, 1989, p. 101), which means they either went their own way or they got lost; many did not contact the people they were supposed to contact. They were not alone, however, as some of LILCO's official "traffic guides" did not know the proper routes the buses were supposed to travel, nor did they know the organizational structure of LERO or the plan's procedures (FEMA, 1986, p. 116).

Another important part of the plan, and the exercise of course, concerned the procedures for communicating with the public. Here, we might have predicted, would be an area ripe for organizational perfection. Knowing well ahead of time just what the emergency would be, the announcements would be carefully prepared, and we might reasonably have expected the responses to those messages, with minor variations perhaps, to be carefully crafted and accurate. Such was not the case. EBS messages were sometimes four single-spaced pages long (FEMA, 1986, p. 136), which, read over television and radio, would surely have been too long for people to follow carefully, even if they had been constructed in a crystal clear fashion. In fact, the EBS messages were crafted poorly. Sometimes, there was conflicting information in the same message. One such message advised people outside the 10-mile EPZ that "no protective action was necessary," immediately followed by a paragraph advising that they take blankets, pillows, and medications as they "could be away for days" (FEMA, 1986, p. 139). Sometimes *new* information was presented at the end of the message, which would likely raise questions just at the time people would be expecting answers. As but one example, in a series of three EBS messages, the first two told people that children from a local school district would be taken to the Nassau Coliseum; in the last, they were told the children were not in fact at the Coliseum but at a different place (Hicksville) "for monitoring and decontamination" (FEMA, 1986, p. 138). Such a sequence of messages could have produced only anxiety and possibly panic among worried parents, parents likely to stop at nearly nothing to ensure the safety of their loved ones.

This obvious anxiety was consistently downplayed by LILCO, which had every confidence that its instructions would be obeyed. Yet even this conceit was not scripted. LILCO retained a world expert on radiation hazards from nearby Brookhaven National Laboratories—a government organization that took public positions supporting LILCO and its nuclear plant. He was to be the expert on hand in the EBS station, available to answer questions by FEMA workers posing as reporters. The reporters exhibited none of the ruthless questioning that might be expected under the circumstances, but one of them asked Dr. Brill, the expert, if he expected the population would evacuate the EPZ when they were asked to. Dr. Brill replied that they would but that he would not! He explained, certainly to everyone's surprise, that although he lived within 2 miles of the plant, he would probably be one of the "diehards" who would not leave his home. This was at a time when LILCO had suggested the complete evacuation of the 10-mile EPZ and when the reactor core was two-thirds uncovered. Alarmed by this violation of the order, the FEMA workers asked "why?" Dr. Brill's view was that the traffic jam would be so enormous that people evacuating would be exposed to more radiation in their autos than if they hid in their basements. LILCO's expert would thus have made matters much worse. A key argument of those who opposed the plant and doubted LILCO's ability to evacuate Long Island in a few hours was that the traffic jam would be so enormous that only a minority would escape. (On Dr. Brill, see NRC, 1989, pp. 161-169.)

Rumor response and press conferences evinced other failures. One prevalent failure in rumor response was a long lag between the time of a request and a response to the request. Examples included "people"— FEMA workers calling in pretending to be citizens—hearing fire trucks and calling the command center to ask about them. They usually received a very late response or no response at all. Others, preparing to evacuate and calling to ask what ought to be done with their pets, also received delayed responses or no response at all. Sometimes "residents" asking the experts for advice were told both to evacuate and take shelter. A pretend woman who was 4½ months pregnant was allowed to drive through the EPZ without being reminded of the risk to her fetus. The simulated press conferences were full of evasive-sounding answers and dismissals of people's worries.

Although FEMA judged the behavior of the traffic guides at the three staging areas—in Patchogue, Port Jefferson, and Riverhead—largely a success, in fact the earliest that any traffic guides were dispatched was 10:25 a.m. and the latest completion was at 12:49 p.m. (NRC, 1986, p. 113), which were, respectively, 3.5 hours and 6 hours after local schools had been closed. Yet LILCO's plan held that emergency information would be disseminated to the public every 15 minutes telling people that LILCO personnel would be guiding traffic. Thus, the exercise would leave people with the impression that LILCO could not be counted on to help people evacuate should the need arise.

Much of this would be standard in a real worst case. Had Shoreham turned itself into a molten radiating mass, we certainly would have seen—we invariably do—confusion in rumor control, conflicting advice, contradictory statements, and evasion or even dissembling at press conferences. But when we see these kinds of failures in an important exercise with prior planning and training, and plenty of warning, we must begin to wonder, What are the possibilities and limits of organizational learning? Or more specifically, What could make organizations fail so? Truthfully, social science is at a loss to answer these fundamental questions.

■ A TALE OF TWO TRUCKS

Some parts of the exercise were not entirely known in advance and so could not have been fully scripted even had the participants tried. FEMA called these "freeplay messages," and the idea was to introduce surprise problems to which LERO personnel could respond. If LERO were organized properly and its personnel trained well, as LILCO believed, the responses would be prompt and appropriate. Of course, emergencies are by definition not routine events and will contain surprises. No one ever expects such responses to be perfect—it is probably sheer accident when responses in times of crisis are perfect—but it was entirely reasonable to expect they would be sufficiently appropriate to permit the conclusion that LERO was more or less prepared. That, indeed, had been LILCO's promise.

The first freeplay involved a gravel truck turned sideways in the road with a broken driveshaft, and the second an overturned fuel truck (both "accidents" were simulated). According to LILCO's plan, if a traffic impediment cropped up during the evacuation, a clear and set channel would route the information from the field, through various officers, to the road logistics coordinator at the Emergency Operations Center (EOC). During both the fuel truck and the gravel truck impediments, this channel was entirely subverted. Rather than field personnel routing the information through those channels, FEMA observers noticed the failure and on their own stepped in and informed the EOC directly that there were traffic impediments (NRC, 1987b). The messages that were given to the EOC were mostly clear and appropriate, portraying accurately the information necessary for a timely resolution of the problems. Not everything goes wrong that can, Mr. Murphy to the contrary.

But there was a failure to properly inform the chain of command. In practice this could easily have meant that key but lower-level personnel would not know that roadways were blocked. Two hours after the gravel truck impediment, the transportation support coordinator did not know that a bus evacuation route was potentially blocked (NRC, 1987b, p. 36), and there was no public dissemination of information about the impediments (e.g., an EBS message) until 1:45 p.m. So it was more than a failure of a formal plan; it was also potentially a failure of organization. It turned out that for the gravel truck accident, which was "injected" into the exercise at 10:40 a.m., the FEMA observer informed the evacuation coordinator at about 12:13 p.m.; had that not been the case, it would have taken even longer for LERO to respond. Traffic was not then rerouted, nor had any equipment been dispatched to remove the gravel. Once LERO finally did send equipment to the gravel truck, it sent only one tow truck and no scraper or other equipment that could move a large pile of rock from the road. That one tow truck, even FEMA agreed, would not have been adequate to move a gravel-laden dump truck with a broken driveshaft and three disabled cars.

The FEMA fuel truck freeplay was introduced at 11:00 a.m. The notice read that the fuel tanker jackknifed and overturned on a busy, main evacuation route (Route 25a), blocking both east- and westbound traffic as well as both shoulders. The fuel was leaking from the ruptured tank, although there was no fire yet. The message gave the exact location of the accident and all the key conditions surrounding it. No equipment was dispatched to the scene for 2 hours and 48 minutes by the road logistics coordinator (NRC, 1987b, p. 41). There were no efforts to inform the public, many of whom might be expected to use the road to flee the area, for 2 hours and 43 minutes. As with the gravel truck accident, LILCO finally sent one tow truck, but of a size (10,000 pounds) appropriate for passenger cars and small commercial vehicles. Some road crews were dispatched by 11:50 a.m. but did not get to the scene until about 2:00 p.m. Even the FEMA evaluator had left the scene by then.

In a better execution of the plan, the traffic would have been rerouted within 10 or 20 minutes of the freeplay injections and, in the opinion of local police officers, could have been done easily (NRC, 1987b, pp. 52-57). Instead, the reroutes were longer than necessary and in the case of the fuel truck, the reroute was to an area "among the most congested in the entire EPZ," according to local police officers (NRC, 1987b, p. 56). One of the reroutes for the fuel truck freeplay would have led people into a cul-de-sac and other dead-end roads. LILCO lives on Long Island but was unaware of the myriad roadway and traffic problems it would face should massive evacuation be necessary.

LILCO's response to criticism after the exercise was instructive. When LERO officials were asked about the deficiencies in planning alleged by Shoreham's opponents, they responded that there were no problems for two reasons. First, the information would have gotten to the necessary people "in a timely manner by other paths," although none of those paths were specified (NRC, 1987b, p. 4). Second, "following the Exercise, steps have been taken to improve further both the Plan and Procedures and LILCO's training program as they relate to dealing with road impediments" (NRC, 1987b, p. 4). The steps are not detailed, but as we shall see, it would be quite predictable if they consisted primarily of adding more levels of authority, more units, and more personnel. The emergency organization, LERO, was a striking example of believing in the document that promises to surmount all problems. Believing the fantasy, LERO would then work from rational bureaucratic prescriptions that were likely never to work the first time and that could not have been modified by continued use. Belief in the evacuation of Long Island in a few hours time went hand in glove with belief in the faultless operation of endless bureaucratic layers and channels.

LILCO judged its response to the impediments a success. "It is apparent," LILCO officials said,

> that in large measure LERO demonstrated its ability to respond to roadway impediments during an evacuation of the Shoreham EPZ. This is true even though the LERO organization had never practiced responding to such *extremely severe* [italics added] accidents that blocked entire roadways and thus required not only actions to remove the impediment but also actions to ensure that evacuating traffic was not unnecessarily impeded. (NRC, 1987b, p. 19)

Severe accidents of this sort, of course, are uncommon but far from rare on crowded Long Island roads even in such beautiful weather and low traffic volume as they enjoyed on the day of the exercise. (A summer day, with thousands of tourists near the beaches, or a winter storm day, would be something else.) Had there also been a nuclear accident and hundreds of thousands of vehicles on the roads, "extremely severe" accidents would possibly be commonplace.

Another, less ambitious, exercise was carried out in June of 1986, about 4 months later. We haven't the space to detail the problems and successes of that exercise, except to note that there were still substantial problems in responding to the road impediments. "Overall response," said one evaluating organization, "by the participants can be classified as poor; however, due to the nature of the drill and the participants, this was not totally unexpected" (Impell Corporation, 1986). What the evaluator means by "the nature of the drill and the participants" is that many of the personnel were new and so had not been involved in previous exercises. LERO's problems would never be solved and its fantastic promises would never be believed.

It is important to note that we have hardly exhausted the failures exhibited in the exercise. In fact, there were many, many more failures and there were many, many more types of failures. It is also important to note that most of those failures could easily have made a huge difference in a real emergency. Our high-technology systems, because of their highly interactive and tightly coupled nature, are fraught with potential for small failures to cascade into or combine with other failures and bring down the whole system (Perrow, 1984).

ORGANIZATIONAL FAILURE AND
FANTASY DOCUMENTS

Although FEMA resolutely judged the exercise a success, a three-judge panel ruled otherwise and threw the quality of LERO's preparation into doubt. The question became moot when the plant was shut down and the reactor turned off. No one can be sure how much LILCO's poor performance in the exercise contributed to the final judgment, but we think it was considerable. The three judges in no way could be considered enemies of nuclear power, and their finding that the company was unprepared after years of preparation for a test that can only be called a very low hurdle must have counted for a lot. Why did LILCO fail when so much was at stake?

Opponents of Shoreham concluded that LILCO could not follow its own plan and that the reason it could not was that the organization itself, in myriad ways, was incompetent. It is tempting to come to a similar conclusion for there *is* evidence of poor training, thoughtless response, and ill-conceived procedure. Yet the "incompetent organization" theory rests, finally, on the premise that LILCO was exceptional, that it was singularly without good leaders, smart workers, and acceptable procedures for learning from its mistakes. We do not think LILCO was a particularly incompetent organization, off our organizational theory and performance map, so to speak. Our research and experience (we both lived on Long Island for some time) confirm that LILCO has made its share of mistakes, even disregarding the Shoreham station. But those mistakes were not extraordinary in either their frequency or severity. Nor can lack of preparation or expertise explain LILCO's failure. Indeed, quite the opposite. The question is how could it have failed given its preparation and expertise? The utility had been involved in the Shoreham project for more than 20 years, which is certainly sufficient time to learn some technical lessons about nuclear design and disaster preparation, to learn some political lessons about risk communication, and to learn some coordination lessons about organization. And as noted, the exercise we spent the most time analyzing was only one in a series of exercises, albeit an important one, so that there were opportunities for organizational learning. In addition, FEMA, the DOE, and the NRC were highly committed to seeing Shoreham open (keep in mind that *no* nuclear plant had been blocked by local opposition) and so lent their own extensive expertise to the project. Not only was LILCO itself a competent organization, but it was surrounded by competent organizations that supported the opening of Shoreham.

Nor can we attribute the failures to lack of commitment. Although we concede the possibility that LILCO failed because the exercise was not "the real thing," we think there is overwhelming reason to think otherwise. The plant cost $5.5 billion to construct, and though it is certainly true that the utility could, indeed did, pass that cost on to consumers, utility executives were not so powerful that they could simply ignore such a huge investment. Moreover, LILCO decision makers, like everyone else, knew that Shoreham's opening would be much more likely if the exercises were a big success. Were the exercises to fail, as we have seen they did in important ways, Shoreham's opponents would argue that LILCO could not control a large evacuation and if that could not be demonstrated, then it would be very difficult to grant the plant a full-power license. Perhaps the best reason to think that LILCO took the exercises seriously was the simple fact that everyone was watching: courts, lawyers, social protest groups, the media, local governments, banks, and the general public. It was not only in LILCO's best interest to do well under such conditions, it was LILCO's *only* interest.

We think that the repeated failures in all areas of the exercise were due to a logic required of our risky systems. It runs as follows: We increasingly depend on systems that have catastrophic potential. A few actively oppose those systems, and a common response to that opposition is to produce plans that promise personnel, equipment, and organization that will respond effectively to severe emergencies. The plans are "fantasy documents," and they have some interesting characteristics. They emanate from systems that are either new (such as nuclear power) or newly scaled up (oil shipments from the Alaskan slope), and thus, the historical record is absent or unrepresentative. This absence removes what might otherwise function as a reality check, because we do not know how such a system will behave under stress. Moreover, even if we had some experience with the behavior of comparably risky systems, the plans must be designed to cover a wide range of particular accidents, and each accident may be different enough to be off the plan's map. This leads to the absence of a second reality check: Each accident is unique, and plans cannot cover everything.

Next, fantasy documents are designed to be maximally persuasive, because regulators, lawmakers, and the opponents of the system must be assuaged as much as possible. Thus, do the plans make the most benign assumptions about the environment. Fantasy documents such as the exercise plan for evacuating Long Island specify relevant actors and the story lines those actors are supposed to pursue. Fantasy documents describe the scenery, necessarily neglecting much as they construct the organizational stage on which the fantasy will presumably work itself out. Fantasy documents detail the timing of assault, of reaction, and of recovery: when the disaster will strike, and how, and when—never if—the all clear will sound.

One important consequence of fantasy documents is that they license persuasion of employees. The employees, of course, want to believe that it is impossible for their Russian reactor to explode, for the booster rocket joints to fail, and so on. The organization encourages them to believe so with the fantasy documents. Thus, the people with the most experience with the organization they give their lives over to are not encouraged to bring that experience to bear on the credibility of the fantasy document.

One of the best pieces of evidence for the self-deceiving character of fantasy documents was the organizational structure of LERO. In the organizations literature, "span of control" refers to the number of subordinates that a superior is responsible for and encompasses the variety of functions those subordinates must fulfill. There is no optimal span of control, chiefly because whether an organization functions well or poorly with a certain span depends on the nature of the task. If the jobs of subordinates are routine, easily monitored, of a similar function, and not interdependent, a fairly large span of control, between 10 and 30 even, can be quite acceptable. But when the tasks are nonroutine, when performance checks are difficult to execute, when there is variation in the tasks, and most especially if there is a high degree of interdependence between the tasks, then a very small span of control, between 2 and 5 perhaps, is appropriate. The director of local response, the head position in LERO, had only two positions directly reporting. But the lead communicator, which was an important node of information coordination, was responsible for 13 people in five separate departments. There was substantial variation in the tasks of the departments. The span of control in that case was clearly inappropriate and helps explain why there was a delay of $4\frac{1}{2}$ hours before the state of Connecticut was notified of the "disaster." Similarly, the ambulance coordinator would have been responsible for 256 emergency response personnel; the radiation health coordinator had responsibility for 200 positions with a variety of functions attached to them (NRC, 1987a, pp. 192-198).

LERO's organizational structure was that of a conventional, centralized bureaucracy, which we know is appropriate only when operations are continuous, tasks are routine, social environments are stable, and technologies are clear. Bureaucratic organizations such as LILCO are structured to accomplish some tasks efficiently and effectively but not others. Routine, predictable demands provide organizations opportunities to learn because they happen in similar ways over time. Because the tasks and even problems with the tasks recur, organizations can write procedures, even manuals, for how best to respond. Recall LILCO's demurral that it had not prepared for an accident involving a truck that completely blocked traffic. Such an accident was "extremely severe" to LILCO, yet it was not to fire and police departments or to a wrecker service with large tow trucks. To create highly successful plans, organizations require that the problems for which they are planning recur on a more or less regular basis. Absent such recurrence, they cannot build the structural mechanisms that permit successful response. It is easy to see that LERO, and the problems LERO would face, bore no resemblance to such conditions. It would operate rarely (indeed probably only once), the emergencies to which it would respond would be anything but routine, the social environment would be like nothing LERO had known, and the technologies for responding to a nuclear meltdown, although intelligible in the abstract and beforehand, would likely become confusing and ambiguous as a nuclear disaster proceeded (Erikson, 1994).

It is unlikely that an organization with the experience of the Long Island Lighting Company would establish a profit-making subsidiary with anything like this unwieldy structure. What the long lines of communication and the gigantic spans of control and the unspecified terms of interactions between groups represent is a pledge, a promise, a paper demonstration that every effort is being made to ensure proper communication, rapid response, traffic route awareness, dosimetry skills, and more.

When fantasies are proffered as accurate representations of organizational capabilities, then we have the recipe not only for organizational failure but also for massive failure of the publics those organizations are supposed to serve. Fantasy documents normalize danger by allowing organizations and experts to claim that the problems are under control. Complex, highly interactive systems increasingly insinuate themselves into society. The justifications that attend those systems often mask the failures we need to see more clearly.

▦ NOTES

1. Actually, it is still dying. The Nuclear Regulatory Commission allowed the Long Island Lighting Company to power up the plant to 5% of its capacity, contaminating the core and creating a huge amount of radioactive waste.

2. On natural disasters, see Kreps (1984) and Quarantelli and Dynes (1977). On technological disasters, see Perrow (1984) and Sagan (1993).

3. It also often suffers from the problem of sampling on the dependent variable, a methodological problem that has not received the attention it deserves.

Permanent Failure and the Failure of Organizational Performance

11

MARSHALL W. MEYER

Permanently Failing Organizations (PFO) (Meyer & Zucker, 1989) observed that many organizations persist despite unsatisfactory performance—in other words, the organizational landscape is littered with chronic underperformers. This observation is not altogether startling. After all, performance differences exist, even among organizations that have survived for many years. What was unique to *PFO* was the argument that persistent low performance arises from people's motivation to maintain organizations. Basically, *PFO* argued that the motivation to maintain organizations does not necessarily decline with performance and under some circumstances increases as performance declines. Although owners and shareholders may seek to exit from underperforming firms, employees, customers, and suppliers dependent on such firms generally do not. In fact, the attachment of dependent actors to a firm often grows as performance deteriorates and more is sacrificed to sustain the organization. The upshot of *PFO* is this: Organizations become frozen in patterns of low performance when owners seeking to exit are frustrated by dependent actors seeking to delay or block exit. *PFO* in this sense describes the failure of organizational failure. Organizations do not fail when they should because intramural politics displaces economics. The consequence is that organizational failure is a poor index of organizational performance.

197

This chapter extends the argument put forward in *PFO*, although in a way that could not have been anticipated from the original text. *PFO* was written as if the measurement of organizational performance were not problematic, even though the text acknowledges that performance constraints facing organizations may be complicated or inconsistent (Meyer & Zucker, p. 19). Here, this position is revised substantially. I argue that virtually all measures are poor indexes of performance because organizational performance, unlike other types of performance, lies largely ahead and beyond the reach of measurement. The consequence of flawed measurement is the failure of organizational performance, a failure that managers have begun to experience but that has not yet been noticed in academic discourse. The failure of organizational performance poses some profound research questions, among them how organizations measure, reward, and report performance in a world where all performance measures are second-best.

I begin with the performance measurement problem many managers experience, the problem of making sense of the myriad performance measures the world makes available to them. This problem is endemic in firms today. Performance measures, or, better, measures suspected of measuring performance, are generated far more rapidly than people are able to digest them. The difficulty is not a matter of knowing how to measure. The difficulty, rather, is knowing what requires attention and what does not. I then turn to the causes of this problem. One cause lies in the peculiar nature of the performance of the firm: It is different from the dictionary definition of performance and all but beyond the reach of measurement. The peculiar nature of the performance of the firm means that first-best measures are generally not available and that firms must settle for second-best measures. Another cause lies in the tendency of the measures we use to gauge performance to run down, to lose variance and hence their capacity to discriminate good from bad performance. This means that the supply of performance measures must be replenished constantly and is always in turmoil. Still another cause of the problem lies in the ease with which new measures can be invented. At the beginning of the 20th century, it was impossible to construct performance measures because firms disclosed almost nothing about their performance. Today, as a result of disclosure requirements and other pressures, measures can be constructed easily. Basic financial data for publicly traded companies are readily available. Customer data are collected routinely by market researchers, sometimes bypassing firms altogether. Because there are powerful incentives to invent new performance measures and ample data from which to construct measures, there is a continuous stream of new measures that may or may not predict performance outcomes better than established measures. In the concluding section, I trace the implications of the failure of organizational performance for managers and researchers. For managers, the challenge is to act more like researchers by examining measures carefully and rejecting those not likely to contain information about long-term performance. For researchers, the challenge is to understand why managers choose some measures and reject others or why, in many instances, managers avoid such choices and measure everything. The issue for researchers is not explaining why organizations differ on a particular performance measure. It is, rather, explaining why organizations choose particular measures but, with few exceptions, later find these choices unsatisfactory.

▦ THE PROBLEM OF TOO MANY MEASURES: THE HANK MOLES PROBLEM

Many corporate scorecards, even "balanced scorecards," contain 50 or 60 measures, a number far too large because neither relationships among measures nor the impact of measures on business results can be grasped by most people. I call the problem of too many measures the Hank Moles problem. Hank Moles was the newly designated head of Phillips Petroleum's Borger refinery strategic business unit in 1992. The Borger refinery needed to achieve dramatic cost savings because industry overcapacity had eroded its profitability and threatened its survival. Hank Moles sought to save the business by identifying a set of key performance indicators (KPIs), process measures predictive of profitability:

> Within the Borger refinery, the area and functional teams were managed as performance centers, and every employee was asked to identify [KPIs] that would be used to evaluate their individual and team performance. "We use KPIs to ensure that efforts are focused on key performance areas of the business," Moles explained, "and to avoid sub-optimizing. The P&L is not the only way to understand the business. It helps us understand end results, but more specific information is needed to understand the process that created these results. We need to measure process performance directly. We have begun to link process performance back to the P&L, but we still have a ways to go before we really understand these critical linkages . . ."

Moles considered this to be "the greatest challenge I've faced in attempting to transform our organization. How do you choose the right KPIs? How do you define a set of measures and get access to information that allows you to manage those KPIs." (Phillips 66, 1994, p. 15)

The problem facing Moles was a special case of a general problem: There are many plausible causes of profitability and hence many plausible performance measures. These plausible causes of performance range from the design features of a product or service to the conformance of the product or service to design specifications, the channels through which the product or service is sold, the speed with which it is delivered, the fit of the product or service to customers' requirements, the cost of developing and producing the product or service, the price to the customer, the customer's satisfaction, the customer's propensity to become a repeat customer, and so forth. Cost, another source of performance, is almost always a complex calculation involving many factors. And people and their predilections are involved at every step. Knowing which of these potential causes of performance actually contribute to performance and how they contribute to performance—some have an immediate impact, whereas the impact of others is delayed—is essential when deciding which to measure and monitor and which to ignore. But knowledge of this sort often proves elusive. An irreducible endogeneity, a chicken-and-egg problem, a catch-22 bedevils almost all efforts to choose performance measures. Only those processes contributing to performance should be measured and monitored. But processes must be measured and monitored before their contribution to performance can be known. To know what you should measure, you must first measure everything. Hank Moles tried to solve the chicken-and-egg problem by measuring everything at the Borger refinery and then determining which of the many measures describing the refinery's processes gauged its performance:

We've asked everyone to define KPIs that are to be used to measure performance. Area team managers and supervisors are working with their teams to help each individual to define his or her personal KPIs and to help the team develop their collective KPIs. By the end of the year, we want to see the KPIs posted on the walls throughout the refinery. Over time, we want to see charts that show our performance against KPIs over a three-year time horizon that link back to our strategic goals and objectives and link forward to our performance and profitability in the marketplace. Only then will we understand the dynamics of this business. (Phillips 66, 1994, p. 15)

Moles's method of choosing measures was unusual only because it was transparent. Usually, measures are chosen behind closed doors. In other respects, what Moles did was not unusual—measure everything, or nearly everything, consistent with the firm's strategy and then hope that the right measures will surface somehow. But what Hank Moles did is also an unpromising approach to measurement. Plastering the walls or filling scorecards with performance indicators and then waiting several years for patterns to emerge is a luxury that few firms can afford. Most bosses need performance measures in a hurry. And even if bosses are not in a hurry, it is far from certain that any key measures will surface with time. Few social scientists have been able to parse performance data such as those available to Hank Moles, and even fewer managers are equipped to analyze data of this complexity.

▨ IS PERFORMANCE BEYOND THE REACH OF MEASUREMENT?

Choosing performance measures involves much more than manipulating data. It also requires recognizing that many of the performance outcomes investors and managers seek are beyond the reach of measurement because these outcomes are realized in future rather than today. Consider the difference between the dictionary definition of performance and the economic performance of the firm. The dictionary gives several definitions of performance,—for example, what has been accomplished and the functioning of an object or system. What has been accomplished can be measured readily—for example, last year's growth and earnings. The functioning of a system can also be measured in most instances—for example, the cruising speed and range of an airplane. But the economic performance of the firm is neither its past accomplishments nor its current functioning, although accomplishments and functioning can contribute to firm performance. Following Franklin Fisher (1988, p. 256), the economic performance of the firm is "the magnitude of cash flow still to come," discounted, of course, to present value. The crucial phrase is "still to come." So long as the economic performance of the firm is understood as future cash flows, performance is realized in the future, not the present and not the past. The future realization of performance has profound consequences for measurement. Simply put, although we can measure current cash flows, we cannot measure cash flows still to come because they have not yet been realized. Cash flows still to come will always remain beyond the reach of measurement. They can be projected or predicted, to be sure, but they cannot be measured directly. Firms, as a consequence, are forced

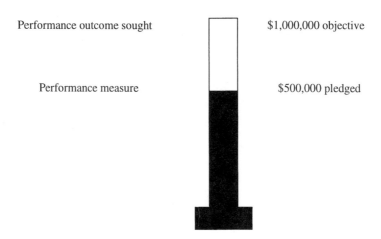

Performance outcome sought $1,000,000 objective

Performance measure $500,000 pledged

Figure 11.1. United Way Thermometer

to settle for second-best measures, measures they believe to predict future cash flows, rather than the first-best measures they would prefer.

Some second-best measures are good proxies for actual performance. Take the simplest case, the United Way thermometer that stands in your lobby toward the end of the year. It looks much like the thermometer in Figure 11.1. At the top of the thermometer is a goal—say, $1 million. (In some cases, extra space will be left above the $1 million mark should the goal be exceeded.) At the beginning of the United Way drive, the thermometer reads zero. During the course of the campaign, it rises. Should the thermometer reach the $500,000 mark toward the middle of the campaign and approach the $1 million toward the end, the United Way campaign will be said to be "on target." Should pledges fall signifi-cantly below these levels, there will be calls for greater effort. The performance of the United Way campaign, in other words, is gauged by its progress toward the $1-million goal, and the thermometer is a device allowing people to measure its performance. Note that the performance of the United Way campaign is judged by the comparison of two elements in the thermometer, a performance *measure* (the height of the column indicating pledges) and a performance *outcome* that is sought (the $1-million goal), the former gauging progress toward the latter. The performance measure, moreover, supplies two pieces of information— (a) accomplishments—in this instance, pledges to date (e.g., $500,000 at the midpoint of the campaign)—and (b) the likelihood of achieving the $1 million objective based on past experience.

TABLE 11.1 Past Performance Versus Current Performance

	Past Performance	*Current Performance*
Information sought from measures	Did we meet objectives?	Will we meet objectives?
Number and variety of measures	Few measures, mainly financial	Several measures, both nonfinancial and financial
Comparability of measures to outcomes sought	Measures comparable to outcomes sought	Measures generally not comparable to outcomes sought
Use of measures	Reporting results, compensating people	Managing the business

Finding second-best measures for firms is far more complicated than finding measures for the United Way drive. The performance measure used by the United Way drive, pledges to date, can be easily compared with the performance outcome ultimately sought, pledges at the end of the drive, allowing people to assess intuitively the distance between the objective and accomplishments to date. In contrast to the United Way drive, most of the performance measures used by firms are not comparable to the performance outcomes they seek: How does one judge, for example, the distance between customer satisfaction and the objective of 20% return on equity (ROE)? The performance measure used by the United Way fund drive, moreover, is known from experience to predict the likelihood of a successful drive. Current pledges are highly correlated with total pledges. The performance measures used by firms, nonfinancial measures especially, may or may not predict long-term financial performance. Customer satisfaction, for example, may or may not predict subsequent financial performance—the jury is still out (Anderson, Fornell, & Lehman, 1994). And current financial performance does not necessarily ensure subsequent financial performance either. All mutual fund advertising contains disclaimers such as "Please remember that past performance is not a guide to future returns" (advertisement, *Financial Times,* August 10/11, 1996, p. 24). Firms should consider the same disclaimer.

Because all performance measures are inherently imperfect, although the degree of imperfection varies, many businesses prefer to measure past performance perfectly rather than current performance imperfectly. In other words, they prefer to look backward rather than forward. Table 11.1, which compares past performance with current performance, helps explain why the predilection to look backward is so strong.

Consider past performance. We measure past performance to answer the question, "Did we meet objectives?" This question can be answered easily. Financial objectives are paramount for most firms, financial results can be ascertained readily, and results are comparable with objectives—the target was 20% ROE, and the result was 21%. Consider now current performance. We measure current performance to answer the question, "*Will* we meet objectives?" This question is much more difficult to answer because projection or prediction is involved. Both financial and nonfinancial measures may predict the attainment of financial objectives, but there are many more nonfinancial than financial measures, none of which is comparable to the financial outcomes sought. Past performance must be measured for purposes of financial reporting and is often measured for purposes of compensation. But past performance measures usually contain little information useful in managing the business. Like sunk costs, measures of past performance should be ignored unless they can be extrapolated to future performance outcomes. Current performance, rather, must be measured to manage the business. The United Way thermometer illustrates this principle nicely. Last year's results may be used to set targets for this year's United Way campaign but otherwise have no bearing on whether this year's targets will be met. Only current pledges can predict the likelihood of meeting targets, and actions taken by campaign coordinators will be based on current pledges.

▦ THE RUNNING DOWN OF PERFORMANCE MEASURES[1]

Not only is it difficult to find satisfactory second-best measures, but once found, measures tend to lose their usefulness because their variance collapses, making it difficult to discriminate good from bad performance. Sometimes, declining variance signals improvement even though mean values of performance measures remain unchanged. Stephen Jay Gould, for example, has shown that mean batting averages in major league baseball have remained in the range of .260 for the last 115 years, but their variance has collapsed dramatically; not only have .400 hitters disappeared, but very few .200 hitters (other than pitchers) remain as well. Gould (1988, p. 326) attributes the collapse of variance in batting averages to "an excellence of play" on both sides of the plate. Even though there is no improvement in batting averages, both batters and pitchers improve over time and are now approaching a "right wall" of human limitations that constrains variance in their performance (Gould, 1996, p. 119). Sometimes, variance declines as mean values of performance measures improve. The overall safety records of power plants monitored by the U.S. Nuclear Regulatory Commission has improved dramatically since the mid-1980s, causing variance in individual safety measures to decline. A consistent pattern has occurred across five measures, SCRAMs (automatic reactor shutdowns), safety system actuations, occurrences classified as "significant events," safety system failures, and radiation exposure. Without exception, the plants that were in 1985 the worst performers on these dimensions have improved over time, whereas the best performers in 1985 have changed little or not at all, leaving only minor differences across plants. Sometimes, variance declines because organizations imitate one another in structure and performance, even though performance improves in some dimensions, remains flat in some dimensions, and deteriorates in still over dimensions. Three measures that were key indicators of hospital performance from the mid-1930s through 1980 exhibited different trends in this interval. Average length of stay moved downward (indicating improvement), cost per in-patient day moved sharply upward (indication deterioration), and occupancy rates remained essentially flat (indicating neither improvement nor deterioration). Despite these divergent trends, differences in all three measures of hospital performance across the three principal types of hospitals, voluntary, for-profit, and government, diminished substantially from the 1930s through 1980.

Performance measures lose variance for reasons other than improvement or imitation. In some instances, variance in measured performance collapses because people learn how to manipulate measures without improving actual performance. Illustrations of manipulation abound. Teachers "teach to test" to improve and hence diminish variation in test outcomes. Police investigators elicit multiple confessions from suspects to maintain clearance rates, which may bear little relation to the actual number of crimes solved. Variation in quarterly earnings may be deliberately smoothed so as to give the appearance of consistent performance. In other instances, variance collapses due to selection: New firms enter the market closer to the mean than existing firms, and firms whose performance is substantially below the mean leave. The impact of selection on variation in performance measures is illustrated by the history of money market mutual funds. From September 1975 to December 1991, the period for which comparable data are available, the number of money market funds grew from 29 to 543; many new entrants were attracted to the market, but some funds folded or merged. During this interval, the variability in yields—measured by standard deviations of dividends paid to shareholders—of money market funds declined dramatically.

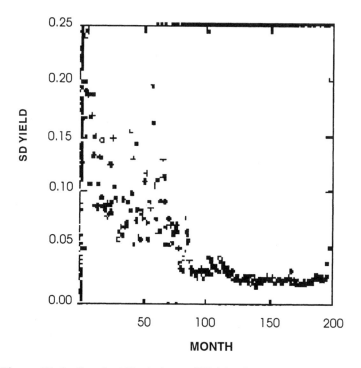

Figure 11.2. Standard Deviations of Yields of Money Market Funds, September 1975 Through December 1991

Figure 11.2 displays the standard deviations of yields for all money markets funds over time. The pattern of declining variability from 1975 through 1983 (Month 100 in Figure 11.2) is unmistakable. A similar pattern of declining variability in yields holds for all types of money market funds—for example, funds investing in U.S. government debt, funds investing in state and local government bonds, and funds investing in prime corporate debt. The experience of money market funds investing in high-yield corporate bonds ("junk bonds") is especially interesting. Junk bond money market funds did not appear until 1980, and standard deviations of their yields, although consistently higher than other types of funds, declined steadily through 1988, after which there were year-to-year fluctuations but no consistent trends in variability (Makadok & Walker, 1996).

Declining variability usually forces firms to seek new measures that differ, sometimes dramatically, from existing measures. Batting averages no longer figure significantly in contract negotiations in professional baseball, and differences in batting averages between players receiving minimum salaries and players receiving star salaries are minuscule.[2] The functional performance measures used by hospitals from the mid-1930s through 1980 have been displaced by procedure-specific mortality rates. The Nuclear Regulatory Commission searches continually for new safety measures to replace measures for which variance has vanished. Today, money market funds appeal to investors more on convenience (e.g., cash management accounts offered by brokerage houses) or customer service than on yields. Although these new measures generally have greater variance and are better able to discriminate good from bad performance than measures that have run down with use, they are also weakly correlated with existing measures. Continual replenishment of measures means that performance measures will tend to be uncorrelated with one another, a phenomenon that has vexed both social scientists and business people who have failed to understand that measures gauging progress toward an objective that lies ahead need not be strongly correlated.

▦ THE INVENTION OF NEW MEASURES

The ready availability of information about firms has changed the way new performance measures are invented. The invention of measures has shifted from firms to outsiders, the latter being mainly consultants and journalists. The motivation to invent measures has shifted correspondingly. In the past, firms designed measures for purposes of internal control, and what results firms did disclose were limited and self-serving. Today, consultants and journalists design measures to draw clients and readers. Measures are constructed from publicly available data, and ratings and rankings based on these measures are then called performance. A torrent of new measures has resulted.

The shift in the origins and motivations of measures is best illuminated by comparing measurement practices a century ago with practices today. Nineteenth-century firms measured their costs and revenues meticulously, often inventing new measures in the process. But they were careful to disclose very little information and often told their shareholders nothing whatever about their performance. Railroads routinely understated their profits to justify high rates to regulatory authorities. Well into the 20th century, many manufacturing firms disclosed nothing other than their capitalization and dividend record. Operating results were released only when firms found it in their interest to do so. U.S. Steel, for example, was incorporated in 1901 and was thereafter under continuous investigation for antitrust violations until it was exonerated by the Supreme Court in 1920. U.S. Steel waged its legal battle in the arena of public opinion as well as in the courts by reporting profits and other information germane to performance at the end of every quarter. The strategy of "publicity" departed from accepted corporate practice and was aimed at portraying the company as socially responsible rather than anticompetitive. What is important is that U.S. Steel could have chosen to disclose nothing about its performance. No outside agent could have assembled the information needed to estimate U.S. Steel's revenues or profitability.

Today, a large pool of financial data that can be readily transformed into performance measures has been created in response to stringent disclosure requirements, the growing influence of equity analysts and fund managers, and the demands of activist shareholders. Consultants and journalists use these data to measure and rank firms, and their rankings are then published, just as *Consumer Reports* publishes its rankings of toasters. One illustration of how financial data are used to create new measures is economic value added or EVA. EVA was invented by Stern, Stewart and Company and has been trademarked by Stern, Stewart. EVA measures residual income, earnings (with some adjustments) less the market cost of capital. Both components of EVA are publicly available. Unique to EVA are the adjustments to earnings. Stern, Stewart ranks firms on EVA in its "Performance 1000," and these rankings have drawn the attention of the investment community because the EVA appears to measure performance relative to the market. Encomiums for EVA appear regularly in the business press. In the fall of 1993, for example, *Fortune,* proclaimed EVA as "the real key to creating wealth" (Tully, 1993). Recently, *Fortune* reported that EVA has displaced EPS as the critical performance metric for firms such as AT&T and CS First Boston (Topkis, 1996). But academic studies suggest that EVA does not necessarily measure what the investors are looking for. Using the Stern, Stewart's data, Gary Biddle, Robert Bowen, and James Wallace (1996) find, for example, that earnings are better predictors of share values than EVA: "All of the evidence points to earnings having at least equal (and often higher) relative information content [than EVA]." James L. Dodd and Shimin Chen (1996), also using the Stern, Stewart data, report that while EVA is somewhat predictive of share prices. Return on assets is a much better predictor.[3]

Nonfinancial data that can be transformed into performance measures are routinely gathered by market researchers, who are often able to reach customers without seeking the permission of firms whose performance they are rating. *Business Week*'s biennial rankings of business schools illustrate the use of market research methods to construct new measures.

The 1988 *Business Week* ranking of business schools was based on measures that were unconventional at the time. *Business Week* explicitly rejected traditional academic standards based on peer evaluation of faculty quality and overall reputation in favor of rankings based on assessments made by students and recruiters:

> Until now, rankings have been based largely on the reputation of the schools' professors and their published work in academic journals. Typically, B-school deans or faculty are asked to list the top schools in order of personal preference. A school's prestige usually looms large in such ratings, and the deans and faculty members tend to give lots of weight to a school's reputation for academic research. . . . *Business Week* took a strikingly different approach, surveying both the Class of 1988 and corporate recruiters to determine the best business schools. In effect, the survey measures how well the schools are serving their two markets: students and their ultimate employers. ("Best B Schools," 1988, p. 76)

Business Week, in fact, did more than survey students and employers. It invented a new performance measure for business schools based on input from students and recruiters rather than from deans and professors, ranked business schools on this measure, and then published its rankings—again, like *Consumer Reports* publishes rankings of toasters. Whether *Business Week*'s rankings gauge business school performance better than traditional measures cannot be determined with certainty. The ultimate performance criterion for business schools, according to *Business Week,* is how well schools serve students and employers. This would best be measured by the career trajectories of graduates, but such a measure is not available because career trajectories lie ahead. *Business Week*'s rankings have nonetheless been consequential for business schools, mainly because of the publicity they have received. Teaching has become more important at almost all business schools, applications to top-ranked schools have increased substantially, and as Kim Elsbach and Roderick Kramer (1996) have shown, established perceptions of organizational identities at many business schools have been shaken.

All of this recent measurement activity has overlooked the difference between rankings of business or business schools and rankings of toasters. The performance of a toaster can be evaluated by criteria of functionality, features, and reliability that can be readily observed. The performance of a business is revealed only over time as cash flows accrue, just as the performance of a business school is revealed only as the careers of its graduates unfold. EVA and *Business Week*'s rankings of business schools, thus, are second-best measures. Whether they contain more information about performance than other second-best measures remains to be determined.

▓ IMPLICATIONS FOR MANAGERS AND RESEARCHERS

There is no elegant solution to the Hank Moles problem, the problem of sorting through the large and growing supply of second-best measures. Even approximating a solution is awkward. To look forward, which good performance measures must do, the time frame must be shifted backward to ask the following questions: Did the measures now believed to predict performance outcomes predict results in the past? and Will we able to improve these measures further? Hank Moles was trying to answer these questions, although he never stated them as such.

An example will help. Suppose it is believed that customer satisfaction should be measured, rewarded, and perhaps reported because it drives financial performance. To establish whether a relationship between satisfaction and subsequent financial performance existed, the impact of last year's customer satisfaction on this year's financial results must be ascertained. If no relationship between satisfaction and financial performance existed, it is unlikely that such a relationship now exists, although this is by no means certain because satisfaction may have been measured poorly. If a relationship between the satisfaction and financial performance existed last year, the likelihood that the relationship exists this year is greater. If it appears that a relationship between satisfaction and financial performance now exists, it also must be demonstrated that customer satisfaction can be improved. If customer satisfaction did not respond to incentives in the past, there is little likelihood that satisfaction will respond to incentives today. If customer satisfaction responded to incentives in the past, there is a greater likelihood that it will respond to incentives today, provided, however, that satisfaction has not reached an asymptote and cannot be improved further. There are, then, two tests of any measure, tests that are simple in principle but difficult in application: (a) Did a relationship exist between the measure and business results, and (b) can the measure and hence business results be improved further? These tests are imperfect because they make use of data describing the past performance of the firm. And the reliance on past performance data means that there are no tests for measures not previously used.

These tests were, in fact, applied to the metrics used in the retail operations of a large financial services firm. The firm, called Global Financial Services (GFS), had two customer satisfaction metrics—one measuring overall satisfaction with GFS, another measuring satisfaction with specific aspects of branch operations. The management of GFS believed the overall satisfaction measure to be the more important of the two, set aggressive targets for improving overall satisfaction, and rewarded improvements in overall satisfaction with GFS. More modest targets were set for improving satisfaction with branch operations, and improvements in branch operations were not rewarded. The researchers' findings were inconsistent with the expectations of management. The rate of improvement in overall GFS satisfaction was significantly slower than the rate of improvement in satisfaction with branch operations. Moreover, overall GFS satisfaction had no impact on the subsequent financial performance of branches, whereas satisfaction with branch operations affected the subsequent financial performance of branches dramatically—a 1% increase in satisfaction with branch operations resulted in a .9 of 1% increase in branch profitability 6 months later (Ittner, Larcker, & Meyer, 1997). The results of these tests suggest that satisfaction with branch operations is a far better performance measure than overall GFS satisfaction; the correct inference, of course, is that satisfaction with branch operations *was* a better performance measure than overall GFS satisfaction. Whether satisfaction with branch operations will remain the better performance cannot be ascertained with certainty, of course.

Most managers have neither the time nor the inclination to sort through second-best measures as thoroughly as academic researchers. This raises the question of how managers actually choose performance measures. Usually, one or another ad hoc method is used. Sometimes, managers seek consensus by rating measures on criteria such as relevance to objectives, quality, and availability and then choose the measures receiving the highest ratings. Sometimes, managers choose measures by inspiration—by drawing charts connecting strategic objectives to measures and then assuming these connections to represent actual causal linkages. A typical case study reads, "In addition to aligning the scorecard measures to the three strategic themes, the team developed causal links across the objectives and measures . . ." The case makes it clear that these links were not established statistically. And sometimes top managers drive measures from the top to the bottom of the organization by fiat. The problem with using consensus, inspiration, or fiat is that they limit communication about measures and ensure that the impact of measures on business results will remain unexamined. What follows is an accumulation of measures because no one knows how to make any of them go away—no one has the tools with which to ask whether a measure actually drives business results, and no one is brave enough to raise this question. Ultimately, there is loss of focus and business direction or, worse, the business goes in the wrong direction because the wrong measures were chosen.

Some managers, the minority, pursue measures more systematically, usually by observing customers' behavior. To illustrate: A distribution organization developed a set of supply chain metrics. The three initial metrics included the direct cost of distribution, inventory costs, and the on-time delivery rate. Later, a fourth measure capturing price deterioration of products in the supply chain was added. Together, the four metrics captured the costs of distribution quite well but the revenue consequences of distribution poorly because the impact of stock outages, caused by late deliveries, on sales was not known. To determine whether stock outages affected sales, the behavior of customers in retail outlets was observed directly. Little impact of stock outages on customers' propensity to switch brands was detected, and a cost-minimizing strategy that ignored on-time delivery was pursued. Even so, the distribution organization will continue to monitor customers and is prepared to improve the on-time delivery rate (and incur higher distribution costs, because larger inventories will be required) should brand loyalty deteriorate.

The critical issue for researchers and managers, then, is not how organizations perform but, rather, how organizations choose their performance measures. The hypothesis I wish to suggest is that the more systematic the search for measures—in other words, the more vigorously relationships between measures and long-term business results are pursued—the better the measures that result and the fewer the failures of performance, Having said this, it should be emphasized that all measures are second-best, that the choice is between better and worse second-best measures rather than between first-best and second-best measures. The difference between this hypothesis and the central hypothesis of *PFO* is subtle but significant. *PFO* argued that sustained low performance is the normal and natural state for many organizations. Here, I have argued that most organizations fail to understand their performance because their measures and their methods for finding measures are primitive. Rather than permanent failure, this is the failure of performance itself.

▨ NOTES

1. This section is largely a summary of Marshall W. Meyer and Vipin Gupta (1994).

2. In 1991, for example, the difference in batting average between the lowest paid (average salary $110,000) and the most highly paid baseball players (average salary $3.5 million) was only .005.

3. Dodd and Chen (1996) also suggest that when calculating EVA it is inefficient to make adjustments to earnings as suggested by Stern, Stewart.

PART V

Structural Failures

Success and Failure in Institutional Development

A Network Approach

FRANK P. ROMO
HELMUT K. ANHEIER

In his famous formulation of the iron law of oligarchy, Robert Michels (1962) proclaims that "it is organization which gives birth to the domination of the elected over the electors, of the mandataries over the mandators, of the delegates over the delegators. Who says organization says oligarchy" (p. 15). In this article, we revisit the problem of oligarchy in organizational development and consider two rival theories: (a) Michels's (1962) power perspective, which posits that as a consequence of formally organizing, elites will always emerge and come to dominate the relatively powerless and marginally participating majority, and (b) Olson's (1971) "free rider" model, which suggests that nonparticipation—and therefore submission to oligarchic rule—is likely to be a function of the public (i.e., the "free") nature of the goods and services that organizations offer their members. In an apparent reversal of Michels's logic, Olson sees a free-riding majority inevitably exploiting a small number of active members (i.e., Michels's elite) in the provision and consumption of organizational goods and services.

According to Michels (1962), as an organization develops, it tends to adopt a hierarchical system of rational administration that imposes predictability on its operations. Such developments, however, create oligarchic tendencies: Leaders, due to their positions in the organization, have access to resources that give them an advantage over other members who attempt to change organizational policy. These resources include (a) exclusive access to information that can be selectively used and manipulated to define the operational reality of organizational life and (b) control over the formal means of communication with membership, which allows them to present their case at the organization's expense.

Although these resources at once generate and enhance the leader's ability to control the organization, other factors increase oligarchic tendencies through what Michels (1962) calls "the incompetence of the masses." Although the rank-and-file member may be highly motivated to participate, the average member's structural position in the organization constrains participation and promotes oligarchic domination.

Mancur Olson (1971), in his *The Logic of Collective Action,* concentrates on Michels's "incompetent masses" theme and develops a contending approach. For Olson, the average member's motivation to participate is greatly influenced by the kinds of goods and services that organizations provide. Of particular concern are "public goods"—that is, products and service that, once provided, cannot be withheld from consumers who do not wish to pay for them. For Olson, public goods encourage the free rider phenomenon, in that it is not rational for recipients of public goods to pay for them if they do not have to. Assuming that members of organizations are rational actors, they will be motivated to limit their participation and other contributions to the lowest possible level. With this logic, Olson flips Michels's perspective on its head. Instead of the exploitation of the many by the few, Olson suggests that nonparticipation is a result of free riding, and it is better understood as the exploitation of the few by the many.

We apply both perspectives to the study of formal interorganizational networks and institution building in two African countries, Nigeria and Senegal. In both cases, there were clear and obvious reasons for private voluntary development organizations (hereafter referred to as PVOs) to band together and develop formal consortia. Among these reasons, the two most important for our purposes were (a) to attract funds from large international donors (the Nigerian case) and (b) to create a formal negotiating body and thereby strengthen the bargaining positions of member PVOs in dealings with the national government and international donor agencies, both of which threatened PVO autonomy (the Senegal case).

Whether it is, as Michels claims, the incompetence of the masses, or as Olson proposes, the tyranny of the masses, our view is that the provision of public goods, at least theoretically, reinforces oligarchic tendencies in organizations. In both the Nigerian and Senegalese case studies, the consortia were to offer participating PVOs quasi-public goods. In this study, then, we shall be concerned with both the degree to which each consortium developed oligopolistic governance structures and whether these tendencies were primarily supported by the incompetence of the masses or by the sum of individual decision to free ride.

TWO CASE STUDIES

Our two case studies are strikingly similar (see Anheier, 1986, 1987). In both, the leadership of a local PVO sought to develop a democratic umbrella organization with a permanent administrative apparatus that would offer quasi-public goods and services to a geographically dispersed membership. The services offered by each consortium were substantial and could greatly benefit each participating PVO. In each case, potential members of the two consortia faced equivalent opportunity costs: they had to send a representative to an inaugural meeting; all other participation was voluntary. Indeed, the inaugural meetings in each country were well attended by PVOs representing the wide array of regions and operating in a broad spectrum of social, cultural, and economic programs and activities.

In the Nigerian case, the formal establishment of the consortium—called NADA—would have essentially guaranteed large, long-term grants from an international funding agency (the Foundation). This money was to be funneled through the consortium's permanent administrative apparatus to member PVOs. Potentially, such a steady funding source could improve the financial situation of all NADA members. But before the flow of money would begin, the Foundation required that NADA develop a formal constitution and enlist a sufficiently large membership that was both regionally and programmatically representative of Nigeria's PVOs. A crucial issue in the development of the consortium was which of the many PVO representatives interested in NADA should be offered posts in the administration and therefore gain (at least some) control over the distribution of Foundation grants.

In the Senegal case, the consortium—called SADA—was charged with the responsibility to protect the autonomy of local PVOs. This involved securing pertinent information about government and international donor activities and developing strategies for insuring PVO autonomy. Like NADA's management, SADA's was to seek and distribute funds from external donors. It had, however, a more contentious ambition. In Senegal, the largest PVOs maintained long-term ties to international donors and acted as intermediaries by "subcontracting" for required services, programs, and activities from smaller, local PVOs. To secure the support of several small regional PVOs critical of the subcontracting practice, SADA offered to take over this responsibility traditionally held by its largest members. Obviously, this threatened the power of larger and better off PVOs sin SADA.

The similarities in intraorganizational contingencies suggest that both NADA and SADA would exhibit equivalent developmental trajectories. There was, however, a significant difference between the two consortia. In contrast to SADA, the leader of a local Nigerian PVO (called ERA) received a substantial start-up grant form the Foundation to establish NADA. This money gave ERA a significant economic advantage in becoming the leader of the consortium. In theoretical terms, ERA's privileged ties to the Foundation and access to crucial information about funding opportunities should be seen as a means for further consolidating its power in NADA.

The organizer of SADA (the leader of a PVO called NCNW) did not have this luxury. SADA sought, and received, start-up and operational funds from a broad base of its members. (Later in its development, the administration did secure an external grant to support continued operations.) In contrast to NADA—where, according to Michels's perspective, many organizational factors favored oligopolistic tendencies—SADA's reliance on membership donations indicates the possibility that donor-members would seek some sort of return on their investments, which could enlarge participation and push the organization in the direction of democratic governance.

This difference in initial funding suggests that NADA would realize oligarchic tendencies much sooner and more dramatically than SADA. In reality, the opposite happened. SADA, from its inaugural meeting and throughout the 3-year observation period, displayed much stronger oligarchic tendencies in its governance structure than NADA. SADA was characterized by a powerful elite and a larger group of marginally involved PVOs. Whether marginal members were principled nonparticipants (i.e., Olson's free riders) or lacked the resources to fully participate (Michels's incompetent masses) is still at issue. In either case, SADA was a successful organization and accomplished a number of the goals it initially set for itself.

In contrast, NADA began with much more intense and widespread involvement by participating PVOs in governing the organization. It too had a large group of marginally involved members, indicating either free riding or the incompetence of the masses. Nonetheless, when compared with SADA, the NADA membership displayed a greater breadth and depth of participation. The intensity of initial participation was marked by a broader array of conflicting interests stoked by a balance of power among competing PVOs. Moreover, support relationships in NADA were more sparse than in SADA. However, no one legitimate authority emerged in the end, and NADA consequently became a stillborn organization, never to accomplish any of its goals.

This paradoxical development outcome suggests that intraorganizational factors alone may not account for the differential development trajectories of NADA and SADA. For example, ERA's initial ties with the Foundation (which included exclusive financial arrangements and access to crucial information) or its expertise in international grant making did not, as Michels's perspective would suggest, lead to its political domination of NADA. Why was this the case? And why did SADA develop oligarchic structural tendencies sooner and more completely than NADA?

Our central strategy is to concentrate on the marginal members of both consortia. Are these marginal members, as Olson suggests, free riders? Or are they, as Michels claims, the incompetent masses whose participation was encumbered by limited resources and inadequate information? The answer to this question is the linchpin in our efforts to join the macro- and microlevels of analysis we use to explain the different development of these two organizations.

ANALYSIS

We begin with a blockmodeling analysis of social networks (see Anheier, Gerhards, & Romo, 1995; Romo & Anheier, 1996; White, Boorman, & Breiger, 1976, for methodological details). Our intent is to delineate the social structural arrangements of both NADA at the time of its inaugural meeting and its failure shortly after and SADA about 1 year after its inauguration and initial formation. The network data for each consortium were collected in the course of 18 months of field research in Nigeria and Senegal with the help of personally administered questionnaires addressed to PVO representatives at meetings during the formation period of each consortium (Anheier, 1987). In addition to network items, it included questions about organizational activities and funding as well as questions about opinions and attitudes about the consortium's objectives. We managed to conduct interviews with 59 of NADA's 60 members (one organization had become defunct) and 37 of the 42 PVOs in SADA. The five missing organizations are smaller PVOs, three of which are international organizations that maintained either a temporary presence in Senegal or had their West African headquarters elsewhere.

The network questions included in the questionnaire can be classified into two broad categories: *support relations* and *conflict relations*. Support relations include directed network ties pertaining to (a) whether PVO representatives intend to *initiate, intensify,* or *continue* cooperation with particular (i.e., self-selected) members of their respective consortia; (b) whether they would work to further *include* or *incorporate* selected members in the governance and operations of their respective consortia; and (c) whether they *concur* with the opinions and intentions that particular others have about their respective consortia. Conflict relations include directed network ties pertaining to (a) whether PVO representatives intend to *withdraw* or *end* cooperation with selected members, (b) whether they would work to *exclude* or *prevent* particular members from participating in their respective consortia, and (c) whether they *dispute* the opinions and intentions that some members have about their respective consortia. In answering these network questions, PVO representatives had complete lists of member organizations in front of them, and for each question, they were asked to either name or check off the relevant organizations.

Attitudes About Free Riding. In particular, members indicated (a) their level of commitment to either NADA or SADA (i.e., the level of importance that they attach to the existence of the consortium irrespective of the personal advantages that they or their own PVO might accrue) and (b) their pecuniary motives for joining the consortium (i.e., level of importance that they attach to the financial benefits or funding that might come from membership in NADA or SADA). These two indicators, taken together, form a four-category variable in which the first two categories denote a low commitment to the consortium coupled with a high demand for pecuniary returns. These two categories are grouped together and taken to indicate an inclination for, or favorable attitude toward, free riding. The last two categories of this composite indicator signify a high commitment to the consortium coupled with a low demand for pecuniary returns. These last two categories are grouped and taken to indicate a disinclination for, or an unfavorable attitude toward, free riding.

Attitudes About Oligarchy. Members of the NADA and SADA consortia were also asked to assess organizational services that might be furnished by a permanent administrative staff if one were appointed to direct the consortium. Specifically, they indicated whether the provision of managerial direction and advice concerning the operations of the consortium was an important function of consortium directors. We take a response of "important" to this question as indicative of a favorable attitude toward oligarchy and a response of "unimportant" as evidence of an unfavorable attitude toward oligarchy. Although not a perfect measure of oligarchic attitudes, the question on which it is based takes on special significance in the organizational culture common among PVOs in developing countries—an "antibureaucratic" culture that stresses self-help and voluntary initiatives.

In reference to Michels's ideas, we should expect that any attempt at formally organizing will be accompanied by a bipolarization of members into organizational elite and rank and file. The blockmodel analysis will allow us to assess the degree to which the network structure in each consortia is divided into a group of small but of highly interconnected active blocks (Alpha Blocks), on one hand, and a set of large, isolated, and marginal blocks (Omega Blocks), on the other hand. We will test this bipolarization by dichotomizing block assignment into such Alpha and Omega blocks according to the scheme suggested by Romo and Anheier (1991). Specifically, we are interested in a set of competing hypotheses about the ways that network bipolarization is reflected in the distribution of individual attitudes in terms of oligarchic constraints and free riding.

Michels's Organizational Elitism Hypotheses. The first hypothesis from Michels's perspective can be stated as follows: Members of the Alpha blocks will be more likely to express favorable attitudes about centralized administrative dominance (oligarchy) than will members of the marginal Omega blocks. The logic on which this assertion is based presumes that those who view themselves as the potential leaders of the consortium are also more likely to express favorable attitudes about the need for centralized control over the activities of the consortium. Here, it is assumed that one's view of his or her potential to become a leader of the group is rooted in one's structural position in the consortium's network. Specifically, members of the relationally active and highly integrated Alpha blocks are more likely than members of the relationally marginal Omega blocks to view themselves as more politically powerful and therefore as potential leaders. This logic, then, links the expression of favorable attitudes about oligarchy to relational centrality and, by inference, political elitism in the consortium. This is consistent with Michels's ideas about the exploitation of the many by the few.

The second hypothesis deals with attitudes about free riding. It is a null hypothesis about the relationship between free riding attitudes and structural position. It states that members of the Omega block and members of the Alpha block are equally as likely to express favorable and unfavorable attitudes about free riding. In Michels's model, lack of participation in the organization is a social structural phenomenon and not a matter of personal choice. The underlying assumption is that all members are equally inclined (or disinclined) to participate, but due to the unequal distribution of power and the ability to control crucial information, large portions of the membership are forced into marginality. This logic leads to the expectation that marginal members—who are judged to be such by virtue of their positions in the social network— should not be any different than central members in terms of their expressed level of commitment and demands for pecuniary returns.

Olson's Free Rider Hypotheses. A competing set of hypotheses can be constructed from Olson's logic of collective action. As in the case of Michels's approach, structural bipolarization of the network into Alpha and Omega blocks is consistent with Olson's ideas. However, attitudes about oligarchy are of little concern in this approach. Nonetheless, Olson's logic would lead one to anticipate an outcome that invalidates Michels's elitism hypothesis about distribution of attitudes in support of centralized management. But before developing this implication any further, it is first necessary to concentrate on Olson's principal concern: free riding. From the perspective of his model, it is perfectly rational for most members of the organization to participate as little as possible and take from the organization as much as they can get, especially when the organization is providing public goods, as was the case in both NADA and SADA. This logic leads to the following hypothesis concerning the relationship between free rider attitudes and structural position in the consortium's network: Members of the Omega blocks are more likely to express favorable attitudes toward free riding than are members of the Alpha blocks. From Olson's point of view, the structural marginality of the Omega blocks is a result of members' prudential decisions to limit participation in the organization. As such, limited involvement in the consortium's network should be correlated with a lack of commitment to the formal consortium as well as excessive demands for pecuniary returns; in short, favorable attitudes toward free riding. Members of the Alpha blocks, on the other hand, have demonstrated a high degree of involvement in the consortium with their comparatively intense-level network activity. In Olson's model, energetic involvement in organizational affairs is concentrated among the moral entrepreneurs of the organization, who are also likely to express and evangelize attitudes of commitment to the formal organization irrespective of the possible returns. In other words, such moral entrepreneurs are likely to be opposed to free riding.

Although attitudes about oligarchy are not directly addressed, Olson's free rider model implies that most members of the formal consortium, if concerned at all about oligarchic domination, might even welcome it. After all, it is the leaders and other central members of the organization who provide the necessary labor to guarantee the provision of public goods. Thus, Olson's perspective predicts no differences in the distribution of attitudes about oligarchy across different hierarchical positions. If this view is correct, then we expect that members of the Alpha blocks are no more likely to have favorable attitudes toward oligarchy than are members of the Omega blocks. This expectation is the null hypothesis of prediction based on Michels's ideas.

▓ THE NADA AND SADA BLOCKMODELS

Tables 12.1 and 12.2 show the inaugural social structures of NADA and SADA. In comparing the two network structures, first note that both organizations are characterized by a large Omega block of marginally participating members. To see this, notice that Block 1 in both Tables 12.1 and 12.2 has the largest absolute and relative frequencies (respectively labeled SIZE and PCT). In both organizations, Block 1 represents more than 40% of each population. Concentrating on the image matrices (i.e., Tables 12.1c, 12.1d, 12.2c, and 12.2d), notice that the tie sending behavior of Block 1 in both organizations indicates that they have very few conflictive or supportive responses to other members of their respective populations. Turning to the density matrices, it becomes clear that this condition is far more exaggerated in the SADA case (Tables 12.2a, 12.2b) than it is in the NADA case (Tables 12.1a, 12.1b), indicating that SADA's Block 1 is far more marginal than NADA's Block 1. This is especially apparent when comparing NADA and SADA support networks (i.e., Tables 12.1b, 12.2b). NADA's Block 1 is far more active than SADA's Block 1.

Next, consider the striking differences between NADA and SADA in conflict relations. In SADA (Table 12.2c), the conflict relations are highly localized, largely restricted to Block 4, whose members appear to harbor antagonism for all other blocks. (Block 6 also displays some opposition to members of Block 3 and 1.) In contrast, conflict relations in NADA (Table 12.1c) are more widespread: four of the six blocks in this network display a substantial amount of antagonism. Whereas Block 1 appears to be the target of most of the conflict relations, all others but Block 2 receive at least one conflict tie. The conflict density matrices (Tables 12.1a and

TABLE 12.1 The NADA Network

Table 1a: Conflict Density Matrix: NADA

	Blk 1	Blk 2	Blk 3	Blk 4	Blk 5	Blk 6
Blk 1	0,20	0,08	0,13	0,15	0,06	0,11
Blk 2	0,29	0,03	0,11	0,06	0,02	0,03
Blk 3	0,42	0,44	0,15	0,41	0,36	0,56
Blk 4	0,38	0,06	0,04	0	0	0,08
Blk 5	0,68	0,34	0,83	0,83	0	0,25
Blk 6	0,53	0,23	0,47	0,08	0,25	0,08

Median Density = 0,15

Table 1b: Support Density Matrix: NADA

	Blk 1	Blk 2	Blk 3	Blk 4	Blk 5	Blk 6	SIZE
Blk 1	0,17	0,15	0,25	0,29	0,28	0,18	24
Blk 2	0,13	0,30	0,17	0,42	0,50	0,63	16
Blk 3	0,22	0,18	0,74	0,19	0,17	0,31	9
Blk 4	0,38	0,77	0,78	0,67	0,92	0,75	3
Blk 5	0	0,25	0,03	0,17	0,67	0,56	4
Blk 6	0,20	0,77	0,50	0,83	0,69	0,83	4

Median Density = 0,31

Table 1c: Conflict Image Matrix: NADA

	Blk 1	Blk 2	Blk 3	Blk 4	Blk 5	Blk 6
Blk 1	—	—	—	—	—	—
Blk 2	—	—	—	—	—	1
Blk 3	1	1	—	1	1	—
Blk 4	1	—	—	1	—	—
Blk 5	1	—	1	1	—	—
Blk 6	1	—	—	—	—	—

Table 1d: Support Image Matrix: NADA

	Blk 1	Blk 2	Blk 3	Blk 4	Blk 5	Blk 6	PCT
Blk 1	—	—	—	—	—	—	40%
Blk 2	—	—	—	1	1	1	27%
Blk 3	—	—	1	—	—	1	15%
Blk 4	1	1	1	1	1	1	5%
Blk 5	—	—	—	—	1	1	7%
Blk 6	—	1	1	1	1	1	7%

TABLE 12.2 The SADA Network

Table 2a: Conflict Density Matrix: SADA

	Blk 1	Blk 2	Blk 3	Blk 4	Blk 5	Blk 6
Blk 1	0,09	0,09	0,06	0,06	0,08	0,07
Blk 2	0,03	0	0,17	0,17	0,14	0,17
Blk 3	0,10	0	0	0	0	0
Blk 4	0,73	0,50	0,44	0,50	0,48	0,39
Blk 5	0,03	0	0	0	0,02	0,05
Blk 6	0,44	0,33	0,39	0,33	0,29	0,30

Median Density = 0,09

Table 2b: Support Density Matrix: SADA

	Blk 1	Blk 2	Blk 3	Blk 4	Blk 5	Blk 6	SIZE
Blk 1	0,02	0,06	0	0,10	0,07	0,09	16
Blk 2	0,72	1,00	0,50	0,67	0,71	0,75	2
Blk 3	1,00	1,00	1,00	1,00	1,00	1,00	3
Blk 4	0,88	1,00	1,00	1,00	1,00	1,00	3
Blk 5	0,55	0,79	0,48	0,67	0,57	0,55	7
Blk 6	0,30	0,67	0,28	0,50	0,55	0,63	6

Median Density = 0,67

Table 2c: Conflict Image Matrix: SADA

	Blk 1	Blk 2	Blk 3	Blk 4	Blk 5	Blk 6
Blk 1	—	—	—	—	—	—
Blk 2	—	—	1	1	1	1
Blk 3	1	—	—	—	—	—
Blk 4	1	1	1	1	1	1
Blk 5	—	—	—	—	—	—
Blk 6	1	1	1	1	1	1

Table 2d: Support Image Matrix: SADA

	Blk 1	Blk 2	Blk 3	Blk 4	Blk 5	Blk 6	PCT
Blk 1	1	1	1	1	1	1	43%
Blk 2	1	1	1	1	1	1	5%
Blk 3	1	1	1	1	1	1	8%
Blk 4	1	1	1	1	1	1	8%
Blk 5	1	1	1	1	1	1	19%
Blk 6	—	1	—	1	1	1	16%

12.2a) reveal that the intensity of antagonism in NADA is much higher than in SADA. In NADA, the median conflict density is 0.15, compared with 0.09 for SADA.

Conflict ties indicate perceived differences in opinion, members' intentions to reduce cooperation with one another, and their desires to exclude one another from participation in their respective consortia. NADA members, as an aggregate, harbored much more dissatisfaction with the constitution of their consortium than did SADA members. This pattern is further reinforced by the support networks, as shown in Tables 12.1d and 12.2d. NADA's support image matrix is more sparse, more partitioned, and more selective than SADA's. The median support density for NADA network is 0.31, whereas in SADA it is 0.67, twice the size of NADA's median.

What do these two structures suggest about the emergence of oligarchic structures? Let us begin with the large blocks of relational marginals, specifically, Blocks 1 and 2 in NADA and Block 1 in SADA. As pointed out earlier, Romo and Anheier (1991) suggest that such marginal Omega blocks are characteristic of social networks measured in hierarchical organizations. Also discussed earlier, the emergence of Omega blocks in organization is consistent with both Michels's and Olson's models.

In addition, the degree and extent of conflict in NADA coupled with the exclusionary nature of its support network further reduces oligarchic tendencies. NADA's structural features make it unlikely that a coalition of members who are capable of usurping oligopolistic power will emerge. In NADA, Blocks 4, 5, and 6 (constituting more than 18% of the population) are in an uneasy coalition (i.e., there is some internal discord), united against Block 3 (about 15% of the population), whereas the majority of bystanders (Blocks 1 and 2, with about 67% of the population)[1] are splitting their support among Blocks 3, 4, 5, and 6. This all indicates that NADA is characterized by a tournament structure in which small contestant blocks align, realign, and struggle with each other for the support of a large enough constituency (usually from the Omega blocks) to legitimate their control over the organization. It is the structural manifestation of Schumpeterian pluralism, which proffers that elites are fragmented and set in competitive relationships by the need for democratic legitimation and self-defense (Schumpeter, 1976). Conceivably, one outcome is democratic governance, insofar as the tournament results in a system of free competition between rival elites for popular endorsement. However, if no elite or coalition of elites achieves popular endorsement, the organization may enter the state of structural stalemate and finally fail (Anheier & Romo, 1992).

In contrast to NADA's tournament structure, SADA displays a congruence structure with hierarchical tendencies. First, SADA's Omega block is less linked to other parts of the network than NADA's Omega block. This indicates that members of this block will be less likely than members of NADA's Omega block to become involved in organizational affairs. This feature gives SADA's structure additional hierarchical tendencies. The localized nature and comparatively lower levels of antagonism, coupled with the inclusiveness of SADA's support network, suggest high levels of cooperation and consensus among relationally active blocks. SADA's congruence structure is more susceptible to oligarchic tendencies than is NADA's tournament structure. The general state of mutual support without a significant presence of contentious or assertive watchdogs can breed complacency—a fertile soil for the growth of oligarchic domination.[2]

ATTITUDES ABOUT OLIGARCHY AND FREE RIDING

Although the blockmodeling analysis is highly suggestive, it leaves a number of questions unanswered. For instance, are members of the Omega blocks relationally inactive by choice, as Olson contends, or are they structurally inhibited by their social structural circumstances, as Michels suggests? This question pits motivation against social constraints; a lack of will to be involved as opposed to a lack of sufficient information needed for participation. To be sure, this is a classical sociological question. One way to garner some insight into this problem is to go straight to the heart of the matter and assess individual attitudes toward involvement. Specifically, we shall look at what members of NADA and SADA think about free riding. Are, as Olson contends, the members of the relationally marginal Omega blocks more likely to display low commitment and high expectations for returns than are the more connected members of the Alpha blocks, or are they, as Michels posits, no different from Alpha block members in their desire to free ride? Do members of the Alpha block envision a more prominent role for centralized authority than do members of the Omega Blocks? That is, are favorable attitudes about oligarchy an elitist orientation, as Michels's model suggests, or are such attitudes randomly distributed in the population, as Olson's approach implies? Moreover, is the bipolarized organizational structure envisioned by both Michels's and Olson's perspectives an adequate depiction of the facts, or is the distribution of attitudes with respect to the full relational structure more complex? Finally and with respect to all of the questions posed above, are there any differences between the two consortia?

TABLE 12.3 Logit Models of Attitudes About Oligarchy

Table 12.3a: Main-Effects Model

Variable	Estimate	Standard Error	Chi-Square	Probability
Intercept	−0.212	0.239	0.79	0.374
Consortium	0.179	0.260	0.47	0.492
Structural position	0.667	0.245	7.38	0.007
Likelihood ratio test 1: Dichotomized blocks $df = 1$			0.01	0.946
Likelihood ratio test 2: Two versus six blocks $df = 9$			12.49	0.187

Predicted Data From the Main-Effects Model

	Consortium		Structural Position	
Attitude About Oligarchy	NADA	SADA	Alpha	Omega
Favorable	48.0%	39.3%	62.6%	30.6%
Not favorable	52.0%	60.7%	37.4%	69.4%

Table 12.3b: Reduced-Effects Model

Variable	Estimate	Standard Error	Chi-Square	Probability
Intercept	−0.156	0.224	0.48	0.487
Structural position	0.602	0.224	7.23	0.007
Likelihood ratio test 1: Dichotomized blocks $df = 1$			0.49	0.784
Likelihood ratio test 2: Two versus six blocks $df = 10$			12.97	0.226

Predicted Data From the Main-Effects Model

	Consortium		Structural Position	
Attitude About Oligarchy	NADA	SADA	Alpha	Omega
Favorable	45.1%	45.1%	61.0%	31.9%
Not favorable	54.9%	54.9%	39.0%	68.1%

Tables 12.3 and 12.4 present the results of a logistic regression analysis of response probabilities designed to answer these questions. Turning to the individual estimates in Table 12.3a, we observe that the members of NADA and SADA differ little in their attitudes about oligarchy. This is indicated by the relatively small and statistically insignificant estimate for consortium. In Table 12.3b, the model is evaluated, showing the predicted

probabilities of favorable and unfavorable attitudes about oligarchy. The second part of Table 12.3a (under the column heading "Consortium") shows that 48% of members of NADA are favorable toward oligarchy compared with 39.3% of SADA's membership. In other words, NADA's members are just more than 8% more likely to express favorable attitudes about oligarchy than are members of SADA. However, this moderate effect—as the chi-square statistic for the estimate demonstrates—is very likely to have happened by chance. The real difference in the way PVO leaders express attitudes about oligarchy is observed in the effect of structural position, which is relatively large and statistically significant. The predicted data show that 62.6% of the Alpha block support oligarchy, whereas only 30.6% of the Omega block are favorable—that is, a 29% difference. It would appear that attitudes about oligarchy are primarily determined by structural position.

Finally, we test the bipolarization hypothesis suggested by both Michels's and Olson's perspectives on the reduced-effect model in Table 12.3b. The chi-square statistic associated with the Likelihood Ratio Test 2 is statistically insignificant, indicating that, at least for attitudes about oligarchy, the bipolarization hypothesis holds under the restrictions imposed by the main-effects model.

In summary, the logit analysis of attitudes about oligarchy in Table 12.3 supports Michels's elitism hypothesis. In both consortia, members of the Alpha block are much more likely to favor centralized authority than are members of the Omega blocks. Consortium did not contribute significantly to the explanation of individual attitudes.

Next, we turn to the analysis of attitudes about free riding (Table 12.4). Here we encounter a more complex situation. In examining the main-effect model, we observed a poor fit, indicating the necessity of including the two-way interaction between consortium and structural position. Moreover, in fitting the saturated model to the data, we found that in estimating the interaction, the nested-effects specification provided better results than the straight multiplicative term. In this case, the two nested effects are to be interpreted as the effect of structural position within NADA, and the effect of structural position within SADA.

Table 12.4a presents the individual estimates and attendant statistics, and the modeled response probabilities for attitudes about free riding are evaluated in Table 12.4b. This table records almost no difference between the Alpha and Omega blocks in the NADA consortium. For both blocks, the probability that a member will favor free riding is only 15% (Table 12.4b). Clearly, the vast majority of NADA's members have expressed high commitment to the consortium while expecting little in the way of

TABLE 12.4 Logit Models of Attitudes About Free Riding

Table 12.4a: Main-Effects Model

Variable	Estimate	Standard Error	Chi-Square	Probability
Intercept	−1.274	0.277	21.07	0.000
Consortium	−0.653	0.310	4.44	0.035
Structural position	−0.461	0.313	2.17	0.141
Likelihood ratio test 1: Dichotomized blocks $df = 1$			2.81	0.094
Likelihood ratio test 2: Two versus six blocks $df = 9$			10.55	0.308

Predicted Data From the Main-Effects Model

	Consortium		Structural Position	
Attitude About Oligarchy	NADA	SADA	Alpha	Omega
Favorable	13.1%	35.7%	12.4%	26.2%
Not favorable	86.9%	64.3%	87.6%	73.8%

Table 12.4b: Nested-Effects Model

Variable	Estimate	Standard Error	Chi-Square	Probability
Intercept	−1.094	0.299	13.38	0.000
Consortium	−0.626	0.299	4.38	0.036
Structural position	−0.979	0.459	4.55	0.033
Structural position in NADA	0.964	0.598	2.60	0.107
Likelihood ratio test 1: Dichotomized blocks $df = 1$			0.00	1.000
Likelihood ratio test 2: Two versus six blocks $df = 8$			7.97	0.436

Predicted Data From the Main-Effects Model

	NADA		SADA	
Attitude About Free Riding	Alpha Block	Mega Block	Alpha Block	Mega Block
Favorable	15.0%	15.4%	19.0%	62.5%
Not favorable	85.0%	84.6%	81.0%	37.5%
Main-effect consortium				
Favorable	15.2%		40.1%	
Not favorable	84.8%		59.9%	

returns. SADA members, on the other hand, show a considerable differ-ence in free rider attitudes across structural position. Only 19% of the members of the Alpha block in SADA express favorable attitudes, com-pared with almost 63% for the Omega block. This difference in the distribution of favorable attitudes across structural position extends to a considerable difference in the level of support for free riding between the two consortia. The main effects of consortium are evaluated in the bottom half of Table 12.4b. Whereas, on average, only 15.2% of all NADA members favor free riding, more than 40% of the SADA members support free riding.

Finally, we test the bipolarization hypothesis suggested by both Michels's and Olson's perspectives on the nested-effects model for atti-tudes about free riding. The chi-square statistic associated with the Likelihood Ratio Test 2 is statistically insignificant, indicating that the two-block transformation of structural position fits observed data gener-ated by the original six-block solution. We conclude that the bipolarization hypothesis holds for attitudes about free riding.

In summary, the logit analysis of free rider attitudes only partially supports Olson's perspective. Our analysis of the NADA consortium produced evidence in support of the null hypothesis: Omega block members were no more likely to express support for free riding than were members of the Alpha block. Indeed, the vast majority of all members of the NADA consortium (almost 85%) disapproved. This finding endorses the notion that marginal members of the NADA consortium did not come into this status by choice. Relational inactivity and isolation are not correlated with the lack of expressed commitment to the organization. Nor were the marginal members more likely to make excessive demands on the organization. To be sure, the only explanation left is provided by Michels's perspective: Marginal members of the NADA consortium, although possessing a high level of commitment, are nonetheless dis-patched into relational inactivity by social conditions that limit their access to the kind of information required to make network choices. The nature of these social conditions remains shrouded, and we shall have more to say about them later.

The SADA case, however, corresponds to Olson's free rider hypothe-sis. The members of the Omega block were far more likely to embrace a free rider orientation than were members of the Alpha block. Moreover, when compared with NADA, a much larger segment of the SADA membership accepted a free rider stance (15% in NADA and 40% in SADA). Finally, the analysis of free-riding attitudes also provided support for the bipolarization hypothesis implied by both Michels's and Olson's models.

Beyond testing competing hypotheses, the most important result of this analysis is to be found in the way that it uncovered key constitutional differences between the NADA and SADA organizations. At a social structural level, NADA manifests a tournament network structure. This sort of structure, coupled with a highly committed membership that is extremely opposed to free riding, is likely to foster intense and widespread political maneuvering and competition. The chance that a leadership coalition with general support from the membership will emerge in such situations is very low. Although the informal structure was bipolarized at the network level and with respect to the distribution of elitist attitudes about oligarchy, the informal structure never changed to a formal oligarchy. Indeed, NADA appeared to be an organization that was largely composed of recalcitrant leaders unwilling to submit to the necessary organizational role of follower.

Like NADA, SADA had a bipolarized informal structure both at the level of the network and in the distribution of elitist attitudes about oligarchy. In contrast to NADA, SADA displays a congruence network structure, with comparatively low levels of antagonism and very localized conflict. Moreover, support relations in SADA were very inclusive, suggesting high levels of cooperation and consensus. SADA was also characterized by a membership whose relational activity did correlate with commitment. The marginal members of the Omega block were more likely to embrace free rider attitudes than were members of the Alpha block. Although at first blush, a large proportion of free riders may seem deleterious to the operations and ultimate survival of any organization, on further analysis it becomes clear that such a condition guarantees one important thing to all organizations: There will be a sufficient number of members willing to occupy the role of follower.

▨ SOCIAL INFRASTRUCTURE AND ORGANIZATIONAL DEVELOPMENT[3]

Both Michels's and Olson's intraorganizational perspectives have been helpful in identifying the seeds of the differential development of NADA and SADA. But from where did these seeds come? The intraorganizational factors emphasized by both of these perspectives cannot provide adequate insight to this problem. To answer this question, we must situate NADA and SADA in a broader social, cultural, and political context and address several questions: Do members of a particular block represent PVOs with similar social, political, and cultural attributes? Are there variations in these infrastructural characteristics across different blocks? Finally, how do differences and similarities relate to NADA's tournament structure and to SADA's congruence structure?

Nigeria

Modern Nigeria is characterized by numerous disputes about the distribution of political power among its major ethnic groups and among the educated southern elite and northern religious hierarchy (see Zartman, 1983). The formation of political parties developed along ethnic and regional lines and became forums of ethnic and regional interests rather than national politics. From its postcolonial inception, the Nigerian state has been dominated by interethnic and interregional struggles for power over budget allocations and federal resources, fueled equally by the large oil revenues of the 1970s and the austerity measures of the 1980s.

The deep ethnic and regional cleavages, as well as a general atmosphere of distrust has also infected Nigeria's religious community as well as its nonprofit sector (Kalu, 1978). Despite the relative Moslem majority, no one religion dominates the society. Islam, the Roman Catholic Church, several Protestant denominations, a growing number of African churches, and an expanding secular movement among the southern elites have been engaged in an ongoing struggle for religious and political influence at the federal and regional levels. There have been persistent conflicts between proponents of a secular society and those who want a religious society.

Nigeria's fractured social infrastructure is vividly reproduced in the blockmodel of NADA's membership (see Table 12.1). The categorical and ideological purity of block membership is striking. Block 6 contains the representatives of Nigeria's four largest conservative Protestant churches. As a unit, they are one of the contestants for the power in the NADA organization. The four members of Block 5 are representatives of large secular rural development agencies. Thought to be the most "professional" and "Western" organizations in NADA, and supported by international funds, they are exclusively run by U.S. personnel. As the block with the most financial resources, it is another contestant for power in NADA. Block 4, yet another contestant, contains the liberal Protestant organizations (advocating theology of liberation) and includes ERA, the recipient of the start-up grant from the Foundation.

The three contender blocks, although showing some internal turmoil, appear to have formed a shaky coalition against the last contender, Block 3. With nine members, Block 3 incorporates larger regional and national women's associations in Nigeria. They are poor in resources, and they are hostile to everyone but themselves; that is, they support no one but themselves. Block 2 is a quasi-Omega block. Its 16 members are small and poor Protestant development organizations and small Protestant churches spread throughout Nigeria. Although they send support ties to three of the top four contenders in Blocks 4, 5, and 6, they show no sign of mutual orientation. Block 2 shares the quality of poverty with the 24 members of Block 1. Block 1—NADA's Omega block—contains backwater secular development organizations and all Catholic member organizations.

NADA's Omega block was often precluded from participating by the other four blocks. During its 3-year history, NADA had several "inaugural" conferences and a number of "interim task force" meetings, each one called by members of different contender blocks. These meetings were often attended by a different set of PVOs, depending on who organized the conference and constructed the invitation list. These circumstances support the conclusions of the previous analysis that the members of the Omega blocks in NADA were more like Michels's incompetent masses than Olson's free riders.

NADA was a mirror image of the fractured state of the social infrastructure within which it emerged. As Table 12.1 portends, NADA remained in a perpetual state of structural stalemate for its entire 3-year history from 1981 to 1984. No PVO in the four contestant blocks was able to establish itself as a legitimate authority and convert the tournament structure into an organization capable of eliciting compromise. In the last analysis, NADA's life was full of misunderstandings, communication problems, confusion, and disturbances. In 1984, NADA, in a most unspectacular manner, was put to rest, and the process of creating a national consortium came to a halt.

Senegal

Just as NADA's tournament structure and its ultimate demise could be located in the Nigerian social infrastructure, so too can SADA's congruence structure, its slide to oligarchic domination, and its success be attributed to the broad social, cultural, and political traditions of Senegalese society (see Waterbury & Gersovitz, 1987). Despite a relative ethnic diversity, postcolonial Senegal presents one of the few examples in recent African history where the ethnic factor has played a negligible role. The major reason for the absence of ethnic conflict is Islamic hegemony.

The social infrastructure of Senegalese society is characterized by a long tradition of oligarchic domination, including the traditional castelike societies with their provider-client systems, the Islamic brotherhoods, and a postcolonial government with its long periods of single-party rule. In many ways, the structure of the PVO sector parallels aspects of both the provider-client systems common in the traditional Senegalese societies and the role of Islamic leaders, the marabouts, as middlemen between government and populace: Large urban-based development organizations have established long-term relations with international donor agencies. They solicit funds from donors and subcontract with smaller urban and rural PVOs for development services. Thus, there exists an extensive informal transactional structure among Senegalese PVOs centered around large, urban-based core PVOs. Similar to the marabouts' role in the country's political system, these core organizations act as brokers, linking small, backwater PVOs with the international community of donors. In a fashion similar to the traditional provider-client system, the core serves as providers to a large clientele of small and remote PVOs, providing them with the gift of funding. As a result, the large urban-based development agencies have accrued a tremendous amount of prestige with rural PVOs, and they have a great degree of influence over these organizations.

The SADA network (Table 12.2) does not reflect the ideological and ethnic divisions that characterize NADA's structure. Rather, the block-model partitions reflect Senegal's provider-client infrastructure. Block 6, for example, contains the large urban-based provider organizations. Each of the six members has long-term ties with international funding agencies, and they all subcontract with smaller rural and urban PVOs for developmental services. They are among the "progressive" PVOs in Senegal, advocating vocational education, self-help and food-for-work programs, and environmentalism. Members of Block 6 were among the initial organizers of SADA, in that they had the most to lose from governmental intervention in PVO affairs.

The seven members of Block 5 were also among the movers and shakers of SADA. In contrast to Block 6, they operated traditional nonprofit programs (e.g., family welfare, Catholic relief agencies) and were less wealthy and less influential than members of Block 6. Like members of Block 6, however, Block 5 was urban based and had much to loose from government intervention.

The three members of Block 4, at odds with Block 5 and Block 6, were active but were small local village associations and missions. Located far from the Dakar headquarters of Block 5 and Block 6 organizations, they were less interested in PVO autonomy than in altering the provider-client funding relationships. They wanted SADA to supervise funding arrangements and to shift some of the responsibilities from Blocks 5 and 6 to SADA.

The relational behavior of Blocks 2 and 3 is very similar, and they can be considered together. Although they were active in the blockmodel of SADA's network, they had little to do with the establishment SADA and did not participate in its continued operation. The two members of Block 2 were French organizations operated by French nationals, and neither autonomy nor funding were pressing issues for them. Block 3 was a mixture of small rural Senegalese associations. For both blocks, the lack of participation was the result of neither financial hardship nor that of exclusion by more powerful members of SADA. All evidence suggests that they voluntarily stayed out of SADA's affairs. Indeed, their behavior appears to resemble Olson's free riders.

The 16 members of Block 1—SADA's Omega block—were basically composed of small urban and rural organizations. Many were new and not fully functioning, and some were financially troubled. The latter, however, constituted only about 20% of block membership. The other 80% voluntarily stayed out of subsequent SADA activities. In this regard, SADA's Omega block tends to exhibit behavior characteristic of Olson's free riders.

In contrast to NADA's retarded formation, SADA's formation was swift and complete. In February 1982, when the inaugural assembly met, preparatory committees (consisting of members from Blocks 5 and 6) had not only drafted a constitution and a set of bylaws, it had already prepared a budget and scheduled activities for the first year of SADA's operation. The assembly quickly elected an executive committee (primarily populated by Block 5 and 6 members), and SADA was in business. SADA's executive committee, selected largely from the core providers in Blocks 5 and 6, singled out the government threat as the primary problem. The committee unilaterally decided to hire a former cabinet officer to follow up on all dealings with government. Their newly acquired expertise in governmental affairs allowed SADA to use long and complicated legal procedures to stall government intervention. In the meantime, SADA used its informal access (via the former cabinet officer) to cajole and co-opt decision makers in important central government institutions. The executive committee also included one of Senegal's most powerful marabouts in SADA's governance structure. This gave SADA maraboutic support in responding to the governmental threat, and attempts by government to intervene in PVO affairs were successfully naturalized.

▦ CONCLUSION

In our analysis of organizational development, we observed that incipient intraorganizational issues implied that both NADA and SADA would quickly develop hierarchical governing structures. Moreover, NADA should have propagated this structure sooner and more completely than SADA. In fact, the opposite happened. How can we explain this result?

To do this, we follow Weber (1978), who, like Michels and Olson, approached organizations as political entities and emphasized the infrastructural conditions involved in sustaining their development. In contemporary organizational theory, interest in the social infrastructure initially focused on resource dependencies and the constraints and opportunities offered by the external environment (see e.g., Aldrich & Pfeffer, 1976; Pfeffer & Salancik, 1978). This perspective has been expanded by such neoinstitutional theorists as DiMaggio and Powell (1983; Powell & DiMaggio, 1991) to incorporate a much wider array of institutional, cultural, and political forces shaping organizations. According to this view, organizational structures are affected by (a) institutional and economic relations with the state and other external organizations, (b) the social and cultural characteristics of the pool of available personnel, and (c) the visibility of the way that other proximate organizations operate. In short, an organization acquires a structure that, in tendency, is "isomorphic" to the social infrastructure in which its development is embedded. Similarly, Meyer and Scott (1983) argue that societies develop specific types of organizing, or "blueprints," that may lead to characteristic institutional outcomes, such as NADA's tournament structure or SADA's congruence structure.

Thus, NADA's and SADA's organizational development—as reflected in the blockmodel analysis and their histories—was very consistent with key features of the social infrastructure in each society. Nigeria, whose social infrastructure is characterized by interminable ethnic, territorial, and religious rivalries, spawned NADA. This organization displayed highly conflictive and disjunctive interrelations among its membership—demarcated by ideological and regional differences—which immediately congealed into a "tournament" structure. In its short history, NADA was unable to resolve conflicts and reduce suspicions. Thus, potential leaders could not generate sufficient political support from members, and oligopolistic tendencies never completely evolved. Like many other planned development efforts in Nigeria, NADA collapsed in a cloud of misunderstandings, communication problems, suspicions, and confusion, which mirrored the prevailing acrimonious diverseness that characterized Nigerian society.

Senegal, on the other hand, has a social infrastructure distinguished by a traditional provider-client system, which stimulates and reinforces oligarchic domination in institutions. In accordance with the provider-client system, Senegalese PVOs informally organized networks in which a few large, urban-based core organizations seek monetary support (from international aid agencies and local donors) and "provide" funding to the multitude of small, backwater "client" PVOs. It was on the switch tracks of these informal but highly institutionalized transaction networks that the oligopolistic governance structure of SADA developed.

Finally, what is the relationship between the establishment of an oligarchic governance structure and organizational success and failure? The most complete oligarchic development occurred in the organization with the highest proportion of free riders. Although we see free riding as a necessary condition of oligarchy, we also contend that it is a product of the social infrastructure of organizational development. Apparently, free riding has more to do with attitudes and traditions about authority relations—that is, the Weberian notion of legitimacy—than it does with, as Olson suggests, purely selfish (i.e., rational) considerations about the nature of the goods and services offered. This is not to say that the free riders in the SADA consortium did not individually experience themselves as making self-serving decisions when they chose to limit their participation. Rather, their decisions to limit participation were first predicated on a preorganizational trust in the legitimacy of prevailing leaders—in this case, leaders in the traditional provider-client system.

The hedonistic calculus of economic rationalism is inadequate in accounting for the difference in free riding in these two African organizations. Otherwise NADA would have exhibited more free-riding behavior, for they had much to gain by simply letting NADA exist. NADA members could not do this. Was this irrational? We think not. In obstructing NADA's organizational development, PVO representatives may well have experienced themselves as self-interested. And like SADA members, these ideas were ultimately embedded in the general traditions of their society. In NADA's case, the social infrastructure was characterized by a long tradition of ethnic, regional, and religious distrust and unresolved antagonisms. In this context, the conflictive orientations of NADA's members may have been self-preserving and therefore rational.

The noncoercive establishment of oligarchic governance structures depends on a sizable majority of members who contentedly volunteer to limit their participation in organizational affairs. Although part of their contentment may result from the opportunity to obtain something for free (i.e., free riding), members must first recognize and acquiesce to a leader's right to rule (i.e., legitimacy). We found evidence that the forms of political legitimacy imprinted on the social infrastructure help clarify the differential development trajectories of NADA and SADA. Thus, we conclude that theoretical attempts to explain social organization with universalistic assumptions about human orientations (e.g., rationality) may be misleading unless grounded in the prevailing social and cultural institutions within which human activities are performed.

▨ NOTES

1. We have labeled Blocks 1 and 2 as bystanders because they show insubstantial evidence of self-reference or mutual orientation. The diagonal entries of the support density matrix (see Table 12.1b) indicate the degree to which members of each block cooperate, share opinions, or support one another. More generally, diagonal entries demonstrate the extent of mutual orientation within a block, which is the necessary basis of coalition formation and mutually oriented activity. Blocks 3 through 6 have very high diagonal entries, ranging between 0.67 and 0.83, whereas Blocks 1 and 2 have very low entries (i.e., 0.17 and 0.30, respectively). Even though the members of Block 2 are somewhat more connected than members of Block 1 (they send some support ties to Blocks 4, 5, and 6), their lack of mutual orientation indicates that this set of actors, like Block 1, can be considered an Omega block.

2. The exceptions to this interpretation are the three members of Block 4. They bare antagonism for everyone, including themselves. They appear likely candidates to fill the role of contentious watchdog. But as we shall see, they were small PVOs with little or no influence in SADA, thereby reducing the impact of their antagonisms on organizational affairs.

3. The following discussion is primarily drawn from Anheier (1986, 1987, 1994b). Materials refer to the period between 1982 and 1985 and do not necessarily indicate current conditions.

Stalemate
13

A Structural Analysis of Organizational Failure

HELMUT K. ANHEIER
FRANK P. ROMO

In the early 1970s, the sociologist Michel Crozier (1974) wrote a passionate and insightful book on the French political and adminis- trative system: *The Stalled Society*. French public administration, he argues, represents an overregulated social system with anarchic tendencies in which stability combines with predictable inefficiency to produce a situ- ation in which its victims become accomplices and its accomplices victims (p. 77-80). Crozier labeled such phenomena *structures bloquées,* or stalled social structures.

Crozier's most striking example of a stalled social structure is the conflict between two occupational groups in state-owned corporations. The higher-status *polytechnicien* engineers control rewards, whereas the lower-status mechanical engineers control everyday work operations, the major source of uncertainty in the organization. In the absence of status mobility—that is, *polytechniciens* cannot move down in rank below a certain threshold, and mechanical engineers cannot move beyond it—they can only block each other in changing what both regard as an unsatisfac- tory situation: for cooperation means that one group has to give up what it uses to keep the other at bay. Thus, the *polytechniciens* adjust themselves to irrelevance in day-to-day operations, and the mechanical engineers are content with improvisation and preservation of outdated technology.

"Each of the two groups possesses half of what is needed to transform an anachronistic situation," Crozier (1974, p. 85) writes. As a result, efficiency, job satisfaction, and other performance indicators remain low.

Stalemate is not restricted to formal organizational structures and organizational fields. A prominent example of political stalemate is described in O'Donnell's (1973) study of party competition and alliances in Argentina between 1955 and 1965. O'Donnell called the Argentinean political party system of that period the "impossible game," in which "both winners and losers must lose" (p. 175). Similarly, the party system in the Weimar Republic showed elements of stalemate that facilitated its ultimate breakdown (Linz & Stepan, 1978). The fragmentary party system institutionalized basic cleavages of the political order (democratic, communist, authoritarian) that overlapped with regional, religious, and economic interests on the one side and complex interpersonal social structures among elite factions and opposition groups on the other (Broszat, 1984; Linz & Stepan, 1978; Neumann, 1932/1986).

As the examples have already illustrated, the failures discussed here occur in the social fabric of organizations and institutions. The inefficiency of French state-owned enterprises, as Crozier shows, is the primary result of a seemingly intractable conflict between the *polytechnicien* and the mechanical engineers. In this respect, the analysis of stalemate goes beyond the economic calculus of performance and efficiency. Indeed, as we will see later, stalemate may, at least in the short and medium term, not necessarily coincide with situations of economic distress, as would be the case for large-scale corporate failures and bankruptcies.

The following analysis follows a Simmelian approach (Simmel, 1968, p. 186) and tries to explore stalemate as a distinct *form* of failure. As we will see throughout the various case studies in this chapter, the identifying characteristic and necessary condition of stalemate is a significant overlap between conflict and support relations among participants. Such situations can produce stalemate because parties may have to establish or maintain cooperative relations with those they oppose, and vice versa. Organizations allied on some issues may find themselves set up against each other in different areas. Thus, stalled social structures are characterized by ambivalent relations, in which conflict and support converge, "enemies" become "friends" in some areas, and "friends" become "enemies" in others.

▦ TYPES OF FAILURES

Recent work on organizational failures shows that failures can be the result of various simple and complex structural processes and sometimes counterveiling tendencies (see Brüderl, Preisendörfer, & Ziegler, 1992; Brüderl & Schüssler, 1990; Caroll & Hannan, 1995; Ross & Staw, 1993; Valentin, 1994; Whetten, 1987; Wholey, Christianson, & Sanchez, 1992). Against the numerous classifications and types of failure suggested in the literature, it is useful to think of failure as the outcome of various individual decisions that participants make in terms of what Hirschman (1970) called "exit," "voice," and "loyalty." In other words, members of organizations can either leave the organization, try to change it, or remain loyal to the way things are. Thus, if all members of an organization exit, the entity will begin to disintegrate and sooner or later cease to exist. Conversely, if all members express voice, the organization may resemble a highly active and potentially anarchic arena of different views, options, and actions taken by participants. This is close to the image of organizations projected in what has been called the "garbage can" model (Cohen, March, & Olsen, 1972) of organizational behavior. Finally, if all members remain loyal, irrespective of performance criteria, the organization may continue to exist unhindered by efficiency and other economic considerations.

However, what happens if those who prefer to exit cannot, being captive to cross-cutting interests and those who express voice cannot do so because of cross-cutting conflicts? The result is that participants or members remain part of the institution, but not because of loyalty; rather, they stay because they have no other viable option available to them. This is the breeding ground for stalemate, as the following example will demonstrate:

Illustrating Stalemate: The Industry Financing Project

In 1983-84 a European and U.S.-based donor organization jointly allocated 165 million ECU (European currency units or $300 million at that time) for small-scale industrial development in Nigeria. The funds were to be distributed and administered by a state-owned Nigerian industrial development bank in the form of soft loans. The prime objective was to improve small-scale industrial production to reduce Nigeria's extreme reliance on imported inputs and goods.

By 1985, only 25 million ECUs had been spent; the average loan amounted to 2 million ECUs, and the 20 loans issued created a total of 165 new jobs in a country of 90 million people. To put the average loan size of 2 million ECU into perspective, it has to be considered that the great majority of small-scale industries would require little more than 20,000 ECUs to improve production. It becomes clear that the loans, originally earmarked for small-scale industries, went almost exclusively to larger businesses when we consider that small-scale industries in Nigeria are officially defined as firms with less than an equivalent of about 300,000 ECUs in total assets.

One would expect the two donor organizations to refrain from further involvement in small-scale industry financing in Nigeria unless measures were taken by the Nigerian partner bank to secure greater goal achievement. But on the contrary, in early 1985 both donors were negotiating an additional small-scale industry grant of 40 million ECUs with the Nigerian authorities under basically the same conditions. To understand how a program can fail to meet its objectives and still succeed in obtaining continued financial support, we have to analyze prevailing interest configurations among the key stakeholders involved.

The European donor organization took the grant as an opportunity to move beyond its hitherto somewhat marginal involvement and relevance in Nigeria and wanted to establish a "visible" presence in the country. Moreover, the grant was viewed as a vehicle to initiate increased cooperation with the U.S.-based donor organization, not only in Nigeria but also in other parts of Africa.

The state-owned Nigerian partner bank had been under much criticism by outside donor organizations for its organizational weakness, operational difficulties, and general inefficiency, as well as for its preference to issue only low-risk loans to well-established enterprises in often peripheral markets. At the same time, the new military government advised state-owned development banks to follow the strictest loan-screening procedures possible to avoid high default rates and to counteract the many allegations of past fraudulent practices. In addition, fearing a slowdown in industrial output at that time, the Nigerian Central Bank required all commercial and merchants banks to reserve not less than 16% of their total loans and advances exclusively for small-scale businesses wholly owned by Nigerians.

Suddenly, considerable amounts of funds were available to small-scale industrialists. A representative of the European donor agency acknowledged that the entire program faced severe difficulties in receiving sufficient numbers of innovative and promising grant applications.[1] Rather than risking to disburse smaller amounts of funds, and thereby jeopardizing a potentially larger role in Nigeria, the European donor decided to approve loans to larger companies—for example, to a nail manufacturing plant or a baby diaper production facility. However, the almost exclusive reliance of these industries on imported inputs hardly promoted the original goal of a greater use of indigenous raw materials. The American-based donor organization, together with its European partner, decided to withhold criticism of the Nigerian development bank's overly restrictive loan policy. Their decision was influenced by difficulties with the Nigerian government concerning other development projects and a highly politicized atmosphere of debt negotiation with a multitude of other donors and foreign private banks.

This case study illustrates how organizations initially shared a common goal that became distorted over time. The maintenance rather than the achievement of the program emerged as the primary interest among the various stakeholders involved; the prevailing interest configuration became a life support system of the very program it had stifled. The Nigerian industrial development bank had to operate under two conflicting directives. On one hand, there was the interest of the donor agencies demanding flexible and efficient loan processing; on the other, there were the strict requirements of the military government. Given the political realities in Nigeria, the bank had to follow the government's path. By doing so, the bank became almost immune against donor criticism, unless the latter were to risk criticizing the new military government. This, however, ran counter to their interest in continued and increased involvement in Nigeria. Thus, the emerging stalemate among key stakeholders was responsible not only for the failure of the program but also for its continued support.

Voice, Exit, and False Loyalty

When exploring voice options in organizational settings, we are reminded of Zald and Berger's (1978) theoretical analogy between social movement theory and failures in organizational sociology. For Zald and Berger, a *coup* involves a small conspiratorial group whose succession to power may lead to profound political and structural changes. For example, a group of managers of the Nigerian Central Bank fiercely loyal to the military regime could have openly declared how and under what conditions loans of what amount were to be made to small-scale industries or any other recipient. By contrast, an *insurgency* tends to involve larger groups trying to infiltrate the power structure to challenge the organization. One could imagine a group of midlevel managers in some of the key institutions involved making a concerted effort to influence and change the prevailing loan policy toward more optimal usage of funds. Finally, Zald and Berger (1978) talk about *mass movements,* which involves a broad-based opposition that aims to redirect the group's power and resources. For example, a broad coalition of representatives from the various institutions involved, including perhaps the associations of small-scale industrialists that existed in Nigeria at that time, could have put forward their claims for more rational and efficient uses of the funds available.

However, as the Nigerian example shows, stalled social structures limit such voice options available to participants and therefore make coups, insurgency, and mass movements more difficult to organize. Yet it is also difficult for parties to dissociate themselves—that is, to exit from the organization. In essence, we can distinguish between three exit phenomena:

▪ *Breakdown* involves substantial and widespread antagonism among groups, and intergroup conflict can result in the dissolution of the organization; for example, conflicts between the donor agencies on one side and the Nigerian banks on the other could have reached such high proportion that parties would be compelled to withdraw from the loan scheme altogether. The counteracting interest configuration, however, prevented this, as well as the other exit options, from taking place.

▪ *Disintegration* is a more extreme form of breakdown and contains the additional element of pronounced internal conflict among feuding groups; for example, if in the Nigerian small-scale industry financing project, internal disputes within the Central Bank or among the staff of the two donor agencies had gained momentum, the scheme could have fallen apart sooner and more easily.

▪ *Factionalism* is a less dramatic version of breakdown whereby bilateral support alliances disproportionately direct "blame" and conflict to third parties. This would have been the case in our Nigerian example, if the donor agency and the Central Bank had formed a coalition to blame the industrial development bank for the low performance of loan disbursements.

Although some failure processes are associated with voice and some with exit, others are the result of loyalty. This is the case in what Meyer and Zucker (1989) diagnose as *permanent failure,* the combination of low performance and high persistence. In other words, groups and coalitions within the organization keep the entity alive, independent of its goals, achievements, or performance. Meyer and Zucker (1989) suggest that permanent failure tends to occur when the motivations to maintain an organization become divorced and attached to different groups within the organization. Examples of permanently failing organizations are (a) loss-making corporations in which unions nonetheless demand higher wages, while management seeks government support to make up current and anticipated operating deficits, or (b) public agencies that continue to exist even though their rationale for operating has long ceased. In such cases, neither exit nor voice represents the critical options for organizational behavior; rather, permanent failure represents loyalty in Hirschman's (1970) conceptual scheme.

How, then, does *stalemate* differ from other failures in structural terms? Clearly, stalled social structures are akin to permanent failures. The difference, however, lies in the notion or type of loyalty involved. Although in permanently failing organizations all participants can be quite content with the prevailing situation and, indeed, express loyalty to the organization in view of its continued persistence, stalemate implies a somewhat more complex relationship among stakeholders. To appreciate this difference, let us first compare stalemate with factionalism and assume a simple organization with groups A, B, and C, in which relations can be supportive, conflictual, or absent (see Figure 13.1, shown later). In the case of factionalism, A and B unite against C. In turn, C can either accept that condition (loyalty) or attempt to change it through voice, or C can exit in Hirschman's (1970) terminology. In stalemate, however, neither exit nor voice is a clear alternative because significant overlap exists between support and conflict ties. For example, while A and B are in conflict with each other, both are in conflict with C. However, in terms of support, A and B are allies and both receive support from C. A is in conflict with group B, which is in conflict with group C that A is in conflict with, while A gives support to B and receives support from both B and C. In stalled social structures, groups tend to support those who oppose them and to contend with those who give support.

Thus, neither exit nor voice becomes clear and unambiguous alternatives. In contrast to permanent failure, stalemate involves false loyalty kept together by what makes it fail. Indeed, with both exit and voice options limited, we find two forms of false loyalty: *passive compliance,* as shown by the donor organizations who did not want to challenge the Nigerian Central Bank, and *preventive stalling,* exercised by the development bank, which implies organizational behavior aimed at avoiding what is perceived as worse case scenarios—for example, the discontinuation of the loan program. In settings involving larger numbers of stakeholders, the behavior and "anatomy" of stalemate can be quite complex in its structure and not obvious in terms of organizational theory, as the following example will demonstrate.

▓ NADA: A STUDY OF STALEMATE

The case study of NADA[2] (Nigerian Association of Development Agencies; see also Chapter 12, this volume) deals with the emergence, initial development, and final collapse of a consortium of private voluntary organizations (PVOs). In recent years, PVOs have become increasingly important agents of local development in the Third World (Anheier & Salamon, 1998). Their macroeconomic impact, however, has been minimal. To increase the effectiveness of PVOs in Nigeria, policymakers and funding agencies have long sought to integrate the numerous, small PVO projects into larger federations such as NADA (see Anheier, 1994a).

Nigeria, Africa's most populous and perhaps most complex and heterogeneous country, is characterized by a fragmented elite and overlapping regional, religious, and ethnic cleavages (see Zartman, 1983, for the situation in the 1980s). Many PVOs are religious organizations, either Christian or Moslem, whereas others are secular. It is therefore not surprising to see conflict between secular and religious PVOs as well as between religious and regional forces (Anheier, 1989). What is surprising, however, is that NADA's emergence and short duration produced a stalled social structure among its 60 member organizations, causing its ultimate if slow dissolution. In NADA's case, the stalled social structure created severe discontinuities in organizational development and seemingly accidental occurrences that projected an interorganizational image of anomie. In the case of NADA, we are faced with an emerging organizational field in which traditional Nigerian cultural values, various Protestant denominations, Catholicism, liberation theology, feminism, social democratic ideas, and Islam come together to produce a most "fluid" and extremely heterogeneous ideological background. In other words, the fundamental value conflicts of Nigerian society surfaced in the creation of NADA.

A Brief History of NADA

NADA's short organizational history is not only a history of the complicated interaction among Nigerian PVOs; it is also the history of a grant. This grant was made available to a small Nigerian PVO, called ERA, by an overseas donor organization, the Foundation, to support the creation of NADA. ERA, a recently established ecumenical PVO, is located at the periphery of established church organizations in Nigeria. ERA, an advocate of liberation theology, is not a powerful organization in terms of budget, size, number of staff, or volunteers. ERA's strength lies in its elaborate links to the international donor community. Network analysis has long emphasized the importance of weak ties (Granovetter, 1973) in the area of resource allocation and information transfer, and it was just such a weak tie that brought about the first contact between ERA and the Foundation in 1979: The NADA grant was first discussed at a social gathering with an informal discussion on the possibility of creating a common forum for Nigerian PVOs.

In 1980 and early 1981, ERA sent out letters to a number of Nigerian and international PVOs discussing the need for a national federation and requesting opinions on policy and how to proceed. Excerpts from replies to this letter formed an integral part of ERA's grant application. In its proposal, NADA's membership target group consisted of local Nigerian PVOs, in particular recently established grassroots organizations. The grant application stated the three objectives to be served by NADA: (a) to provide technical and managerial training facilities to member organizations, (b) to serve as an information center and clearing house, and (c) to offer a common forum in the formulation of policies concerning social and economic development.

In early 1982, a first national consultation was held. This conference, attended by most of NADA's prospective member organizations (with the exception of Moslem groups), elected an organizing committee. The committee received a mandate to prepare a constitution, compose a set of bylaws, and plan and schedule NADA's official inauguration. The 1982 conference and following meetings attracted a total of 60 PVOs; 17 were national organizations and 43 operated at a regional or local level; 37 were churches or church-related organizations, either linked to the Catholic Church of Nigeria or to various Protestant denominations, and 23 represented secular organizations. At that time, they carried out a total of 478 projects, mainly in the areas of agriculture (15.7% of all projects), community development (7.8%), education (22.2%) health services (13.8%), general welfare and relief (18%), and family and population (7.9%), among others (Anheier, 1989).

Although in the fall of 1982 only a few minor administrative glitches disturbed the flow of activity by the organizing committee, confusion intensified as parties competed to prepare conferences and consultations. The organizing committee scheduled NADA's official inauguration in February 1983. Unexpectedly, only 12 PVOs attended. The conference decided to reschedule NADA's inauguration for October 1983. Despite difficulties in locating a venue acceptable to all prospective members (secular, Christian, and Moslem) and members' growing hostility and indifference, NADA's inauguration was then rescheduled to April 1984.

This second inauguration disappointed all parties by the low turnout of 17 PVOs. After a third failed attempt in late 1984, the process of creating a federation halted, to be replaced by accusations and counteraccusations between ERA, the Foundation, and other major organizations concerned. After over 4 years of misunderstandings, communications problems, confusion and disturbances, and three canceled inaugurations, NADA, without members or budget but with an elaborate constitution and a formidable set of bylaws, was ultimately abandoned.

The process of goal displacement paralleled NADA's increasing organizational difficulties. The original grant proposal did not include fundraising as one of NADA's goals. However, the organizing committee spent most of its time discussing whether or not NADA should engage in active fund-raising for its members. Eventually, it was decided to introduce a bylaw specifying that "unless requested, NADA shall not undertake to raise money on behalf of member organizations"—a provision that, according to a member of the organizing committee, should be "communicated very carefully." The initial proposal planned only one paid position, with other tasks to be performed on a voluntary basis by members. NADA, in its short history, accumulated, at the national level alone, 25 paid offices, including a president, three vice presidents, and a public relations officer. Furthermore, NADA's membership diverged radically from its original target group. The original target membership of "numerous local organizations springing into existence" was soon barred by a clause in the constitution that restricted membership to organizations that "have actively existed for at least five years."

Why Did NADA Fail?

What accounted for NADA's failure? Organizational theory suggests a number of explanatory variables for interorganizational failures of cooperation and coordination. These variables, however, which do not consider social structure explicitly, are inadequate to explain stalemate:[3]

Lack of Commitment and Incentives (Coleman, 1990; Knoke, 1981; Olson, 1971; Williamson, 1975). Of NADA members, however, 63% felt that NADA was of potentially great importance to their organization, and only 25% regarded NADA as unimportant.[4] NADA would have greatly enhanced the grant worthiness of Nigerian PVOs, because international donor organizations were then in a position to channel funds to local organizations through NADA. NADA, in turn, would have been responsible and accountable for allocated funds, thereby reducing trans-action costs for donors and recipients. Consequently, NADA would have widened its members' funding arena and reduced funding instabilities, a problem confronting nearly half (44%) of its members.

Efficacy (Linz & Stepan, 1978; Hall, Clark, Giordano, Johnson, & Van Roekel, 1977; Suchman, 1995). If we use the degree to which NADA was able to meet original expectations among members as an indicator of efficacy, we find that 58% were fully satisfied with results of the major 1982 conference, and only three members expressed the opposite opinion. In June 1983, 66% of the organizations had decided to join NADA as full members, 10% opted for associate membership status, 22% were still undecided, and only one organization was firm in its decision not to join the consortium.

Lack of Leadership Formation (Cameron, Kim, & Whetten, 1987; Olson, 1971). The 1982 consultation resulted in the creation of an organizing committee, which, well-balanced in terms of secular and religious representation, drew from organizationally "weak" as well as "powerful" parts of NADA's potential membership. NADA did not suffer from a restricted pool of members willing to assume management posi-tions: 60% expressed interest in working in NADA's future executive committee.

Pronounced Resource Dependencies (Aldrich & Pfeffer, 1976; Hager, Galaskiewicz, Bielefeld, & Pins, 1996; Schmidt & Kochan, 1977). Exter-nal resource dependencies vis-à-vis other organizations were not pro-nounced: Although 56% of NADA members received funds from inter-national donor organizations, only six (12%) depended on inputs by a single donor for more than 50% of their budget. Resource dependencies, affecting 50% of NADA's members, were mainly internal and in the area of personal donations and membership dues (37%). Participation in NADA would have meant a relief from restrictive resource arenas.

Extreme Environmental Turbulence and Jolts (Aldrich & Pfeffer, 1976; Meyer, 1982; Whetten, 1987). Two indicators of the larger organizational environment, the political climate in Nigeria and the general interest in PVO federation, speak in favor of NADA. Except for the last 4 months of the 4-year formation process, NADA grew in a majoritarian democracy. Religious-secular as well as Christian-Moslem frictions were lower than in the periods that preceded NADA. Moreover, in a comparative study of

PVO consortia in West Africa (Anheier, 1994a), we found that NADA began under the most favorable conditions of auspices, funding, political context, incentives, and member commitment. Yet of the consortia studied, only NADA failed.

Thus, we find that conventional explanations for NADA's demise remain unsatisfactory. Indeed, with so much speaking in favor of NADA's success, its failure is not obvious in the light of current organizational theory. As we will show in the following section, NADA failed because it developed a stalled social structure. What, then, are the characteristics of stalemate, and what underlying factors help account for its development?

▦ STALEMATE

NADA showed several characteristics that seem indicative of stalled social structures. Each indicator taken for itself may not be unique to stalemate and, by implication, to other types of failures. Together, however, they signify stalemate. First, goal displacements and distortions are complex. For example, the original objectives in the areas of training, information, and policy formulation were soon replaced by fund-raising as one of the consortium's main yet "covert" objective. Moreover, NADA's target constituency, local grassroots organizations, was excluded from membership even before its formal creation. A "minimalist" organizational design based on voluntary labor inputs and contributions inflated into a top-heavy structure of 25 paid professional posts at the national secretariat level alone.

Second, bargaining processes, although difficult to initiate, are even more difficult to maintain. At one stage in NADA, for instance, a special subcommittee of three members was created to solve a central logistical problem of finding a conference facility acceptable to all prospective members. Soon, however, the committee dissolved after having run into such communication and coordination difficulties that two of its members declined further participation.

Third, and related to the second characteristic, there were high constraints on coalition formation. The attempts by potential member organizations to form coalitions were short-lived and torn by conflicts. In each of these instances, conflicts and interests cross-cut each other. For example, potential regional coalitions among northern and eastern Nigerian PVOs soon encountered either religious, ethnic, or political difficulties or some combination thereof. Likewise, special-industry coalitions such as agriculture or social welfare soon faced regional tensions.

Fourth, and related to the constraint on coalition formation, stalled social structures inhibit the emergence of mediator roles. Such positions acceptable to the major conflicting parties are absent as are "middlemen" and "local bridges" (Granovetter, 1973) that could bypass blockages and allow coalition formation and a freer flow of information. ERA, the grantee, was perhaps the only organization positioned to mediate among the Protestant churches, the Catholic Church, the secular associations, and potential Islamic groups. However, when NADA began to experience increasing difficulties, so did ERA; and when the Foundation assumed a more critical opinion on ERA's "implementation capacity," ERA itself became subject of debate among NADA members, with accusations ranging from "well-meaning but incompetent" to having "fraudulent practices."

Fifth, stalled structures are subject neither to sudden breakdowns nor to explosive conflict situations; rather, they tend to induce inactivity and slow decline. Sudden breakdown and rapid changes (see Useem, 1985) rarely occur. What makes the social structure fail also keeps it from rapid dissolution. Conflict ties between organizations are slow and difficult to change because—to employ Simmel's (1968) distinction—ties are frequently rooted in deep-seated value conflicts rather than means-rational conflicts of interest. These value conflicts overshadow situations that seem to dictate collective action.

Relational Properties

Underlying these characteristics of goal displacement, restraints in collective action and coalition formation, and the slow process of decline is the signature element of stalemate—that is, the overlap between conflict and support. Being friend and enemy at the same time becomes the necessary condition of stalemate. In measuring the signature element of stalemate, we make use of the triad approach (see Figure 13.1) in network analysis (Davis & Leinhardt, 1971; Holland, 1971, 1977; Holland & Leinhardt, 1970; Wasserman & Faust, 1994). Triads are the "molecules" of social structure. As employed here, the concept of ambivalent triads is an extension of the Davis-Holland-Leinhardt (DHL) model (Davis, 1979; Hallinan, 1974) as developed by Noma and Smith (1978).

In the original DHL model, dyads between network members are either mutual ($A \leftrightarrow B$), asymmetric ($A \rightarrow B$), or absent (A B). This leads to the well-known 16 triad types that have been extensively applied in structural analysis (see Davis, 1979; Johnsen, 1985).

A restriction to only three dyad types is a major limitation of the original DHL. The model assumes a world perhaps somewhat too neat and tidy for organizations in decline. In the combinatorial complexity of failing social structures, members may be in a structural position where they support opponents and oppose their allies. Sometimes, organizations

C
A
B
Factionalism
C
A
B
Stalemate
legend: ------- conflict
_____ support

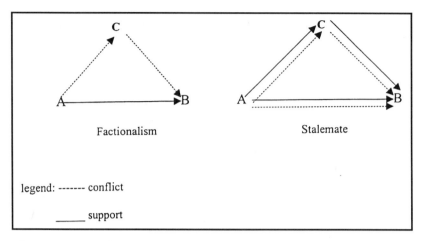

Figure 13.1. Factionalism and Stalemate

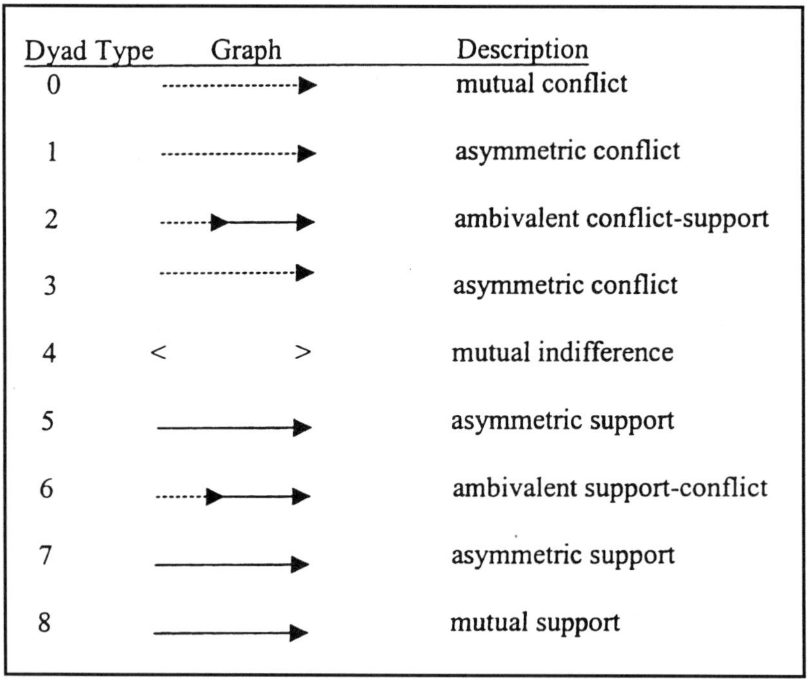

Dyad Type
Graph
Description
0
mutual conflict
1
asymmetric conflict
2
ambivalent conflict-support
3
asymmetric conflict
4
mutual indifference
5
asymmetric support
6
ambivalent support-conflict
7
asymmetric support
8
mutual support

Figure 13.2. Dyad and Triad Notation

NOTE: The notation follows the coding scheme introduced by Noma and Smith (1978). In the triad census, Dyads 1 and 3, Dyads 2 and 6, and Dyads 5 and 7 are treated as isomorph.

find it difficult to identify "who is friend and who is foe." Thus, we may find situations in which the strictly balanced theoretical postulates of the DHL model may no longer apply: The friends of friends may no longer be friends but enemies, and the enemies of enemies may be enemies rather than friends.

Thus, based on the three dyad types, the DHL model does not allow for ambivalent relations, which typically occur when support and conflict overlap in social networks. However, if we allow for ambivalence, where A, for example, sends an asymmetric support tie to B (A → B) and receives an asymmetric conflict tie from B in turn (A ← B), we may be in a better position to capture some of the structural complexity of failures. Allowing for ambivalence, we obtain the nine possible dyad types displayed in Figure 13.2 (mutual conflict, two types of asymmetric conflict, asymmetric conflict-support, asymmetric support-conflict, mutual indifference, two types of asymmetric support, and mutual support), which result in 138 nonisomorphic, unique triads (Noma & Smith 1978).[5]

In successive articles, Davis, Holland, and Leinhardt (Davis, 1979; Davis & Leinhardt, 1971; Holland, 1971, 1977; Holland & Leinhardt, 1970; see also Johnsen, 1985) have demonstrated that specific triad types can be associated with, indeed lead to, different outcomes at the group level. Accordingly, if we assume that social structures can be measured by the 138 triads ("molecules") in terms of support, conflict, and indifference relations, then it must be possible (as Davis, Holland, and Leinhardt did) to identify different types of group structures by their specific triad distributions. If we further assume that failures are related to the occurrence of characteristic triad types, then triad distributions can help identify different types of decline patterns in organizational settings.

The 138 triads can be grouped into six triad domains (Noma & Smith, 1978). First, *rank triads* lead to an ordered arrangement of network members in terms of hierarchy. For instance, if all relations in a social structure consist of asymmetric support dyads and form 5-5-5 triads, where A supports B and C, and B supports C, the result is a perfect support hierarchy of members (Figure 13.3a).

The second triad domain, *cluster triads,* leads to cliques—that is, densely connected groups within the organization. For example, when all k relations in a social structure are mutual support dyads (Type 8), they form k^3 8-8-8 triads (Figure 13.3b), and the social structure forms a common clique of size k.

In the third domain of triads, *rank-cluster triads,* cliques are hierarchically arranged. Davis and Leinhardt (1971) suggest that low-status clique members tend to choose members of higher-status cliques. Because such

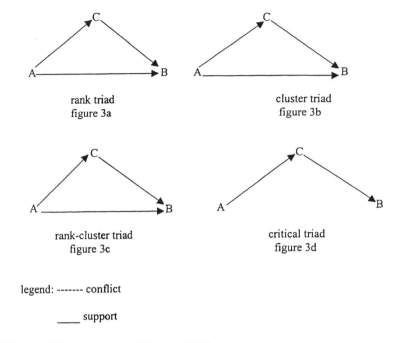

rank triad
figure 3a

cluster triad
figure 3b

rank-cluster triad
figure 3c

critical triad
figure 3d

legend: ------- conflict

_____ support

Figure 13.3. Examples of Types of Triads

choices, or support relations, tend not to be reciprocated by the higher-status clique, hierarchical elements, in addition to cluster tendencies, are introduced into the social structure. An example of a rank-cluster triad is the 5-8-7 triads in Figure 13.3c, where A and C support each other (i.e., the cluster element, Dyad Type 8), and both send a nonreciprocated support tie to B (the rank element, Dyad Types 5 and 7).

The fourth type, *critical triads,* lacks the qualities of rank, cluster, and rank-cluster and does not lead to structural elements in terms of cliques and hierarchy. It is useful to think of critical triads as "noise" and "random elements" in the social structure. Figure 13.3d presents an example of a critical triad.

The fifth and sixth triad class involve ambivalent dyads. Ambivalent triads indicate overlaps between support and conflict relations. At the dyad level, this support-conflict overlap is operationalized by dyads of Types 2 and 6, the ambivalent conflict-support relation and the ambivalent support-conflict relation. Thus, we are interested in triads that contain support-conflict dyads *and* lead to hierarchical and cliquing tendencies. These are the *ambivalent rank cluster triads,* which, when significantly

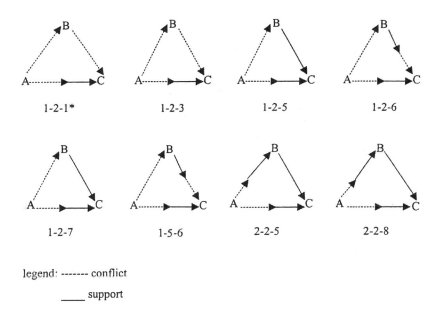

legend: ------- conflict

_____ support

Figure 13.4. Some Ambivalent Triads of the Rank-Cluster Type
*Triad identification numbers are according to Noma and Smith (1978); see Figure 13.2.

accumulated, become the building blocks of stalemate. Of the 138 triads, 39 are ambivalent rank-cluster triads and combine the qualities of ambivalence and rank-cluster. For example, the 1-2-1, 1-2-3, 1-2-5, 1-2-6, and 1-2-7 triads in Figure 13.4 are all variations of a "basic theme"; the asymmetric conflict dyad between A and B combines with the ambivalent support-conflict dyad between A and C, in which A is the opponent of his friend, C. The "variation" is introduced by the different B-C dyads. The significant and systematic overlap between conflict and support relations is expressed in the greater than chance frequencies of the 39 ambivalent rank-cluster triads in a social structure. Thus, in the case of stalled organizations, we expect a significant surplus of ambivalent rank-cluster triads—the structural signature elements of stalemate.

Conversely, we expect that ambivalent triads that do not lead to structured (rank-cluster) overlaps between support and conflict to occur significantly less frequently than chance in stalled social structures. The sixth triad domain is called *critical ambivalent triads*. Of the 138 triads, 29 are critical ambivalent triads whose accumulation does not lead to structured and systematic support-conflict overlaps. If they occur at chance

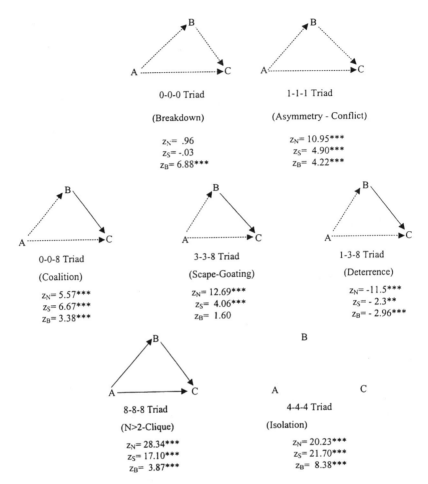

Figure 13.5. Characteristic Triads Required for Different Types of Structural Failures and States[a]

a. z_N = z-score for NADA; z_S = z-score for SADA; z_B = z-score for STRATFIELD.
**Significant at .01 level; ***significant at .001 level.

level or less we can think of critical ambivalent triads as "ambivalent noise" in the social structure, similar to the critical triads. In social structures not in stalemate, Dyads 2 and 6 form ambivalent triads in "unsystematic" ways that do not lead to structured arrangements in terms of rank-clusters.

Although we hypothesize that the surplus of ambivalent rank-cluster triads is associated with stalemate, ceteris paribus, other triads characterize different types of failures (see Figure 13.5).

▓ The following triads are associated with breakdown: the 0-0-0 triad, in which mutual conflict exists between A, B, and C, and the 1-1-1 triad, in which conflict is asymmetric. Thus, a higher than chance frequency of both the 0-0-0 triad and the 1-1-1 conflict triad indicates the degree of structural breakdown.

▓ The degree of "cliquishness" of a social structure is measured by the prevalence of 8-8-8 triads, which is required for all cliques with more than two members. The less than chance frequency of the 8-8-8 triad combined with the triads required for breakdown indicates structural disintegration. In such structures, we also expect a higher than chance frequency of the isolation triad, 4-4-4, which is required for completely disconnected triplets.

▓ Three triads are characteristic of factionalism: in particular the scapegoating triad (3-3-8) and the 0-0-8 triad (coalition) but also the 1-3-8 triad (deterrence), in which C sends a conflict tie to A who, in turn, is in conflict with C's support relation, B.

Three hypotheses summarize our argument:

H1: *Surplus hypothesis*: In stalled social structures, ambivalent triads in the cluster and rank domain are significantly more frequent than in other comparable social structures and random graphs.

H2: *Deficit hypothesis*: In stalled social structures, critical ambivalent triads are significantly less frequent than in other comparable social structures and random graphs.

H3: *Comparative hypothesis*: Triads required for other types of structural failures and states are unable to identify stalled social structures from other types of failures and comparable social structures.

▓ DATA AND ANALYSIS

We use three case studies to explore the empirical implications of stalemate and other types of failures.

NADA presents the central case study for this analysis. In the statistical sense, no sample was taken; rather, the universe of all relevant member organizations constituted the network population. We included all organizations attending the 1982 national conference, in addition to a number of organizations that expressed keen interest in NADA before its collapse in 1984. This produced a total network population of 60 organizations. In the course of 15 months of field research (see Anheier, 1987), a variety of relational and nonrelational data were collected, using a variety of sources and field methods.[6] These diverse data sources laid the foundation for the reconstruction of the existing multiple interorganizational relations in the form of matrices of size 60 × 60 for 10 types of ties (see the appendix). All matrices are chosen to be binary, where a nonzero entry indicates the presence of a given type of tie, and a zero entry indicates the absence of that relation.

To increase the scope of the test conditions for the hypotheses, we introduce comparative components. The first contrasting yet comparable case is offered by the federation of Senegalese PVOs, SADA (see Chapter 12, this volume).[7] Fortunately, SADA, although far from being a trouble-free organization, experienced neither stalemate nor any other type of failure. Data on SADA are based on a questionnaire distributed to all SADA members during 4 months of field research in Senegal. Data collection and analysis of SADA for seven types of ties was designed and carried out parallel to NADA.

Finally, *STRATFIELD*[8] presents a social structure in breakdown. In contrast to both NADA and SADA, STRATFIELD stands for an inter-personal network (Romo, 1986; Romo & Anheier, 1991). Data on 16 "positive" and "negative" affect-choice relations were obtained in a 2-year participant observation of conflict resolution in a mental institution. During that time, STRATFIELD underwent severe interpersonal conflicts that led to eventual breakdown and subsequent contraction through the expulsion of several staff members.

Analysis

A coincidence analysis (Burt & Schott, 1985) revealed that the 10 input relations for NADA and SADA can be conveniently collapsed into three distinct relational contents (Burt, 1983b).[9] What has been labeled support in the analysis so far, in fact, consists of two components (Table 13.1): The first content measures a mixture of loyalty and deference (membership, funding, leading role)—that is, "weak support." The second content seems to indicate "stronger," active support relations (acquaintance, cooperation, intended cooperation, voting). In all three cases, content reliabilities are high and well above critical levels (see Table 13.1). Because the first content turned out to be a subset of the second component, we restrict further analysis to strong support and conflict relations only.

TABLE 13.1 Types of Ties, Short Tie Description, and Density of Input Matrices (M^1) for NADA[a]

M^1	Short Description	N	d	r
Content 1: Weak Support Relations				
M^1	Personal, organizational membership	89	2.5	.972
M^2	Funding	239	6.8	.941
M^3	Leading role	542	15.3	.917
Content 2: Strong Support Relations				
M^4	Acquaintance	833	23.5	.978
M^5	Existing cooperation	373	10.5	.930
M^6	Intend to cooperate	551	15.6	.920
M^7	Vote for	239	6.8	.998
Content 3: Conflict Relations				
M^8	Exclude	268	7.6	.997
M^9	Insignificant role	413	11.7	.996
M^{10}	Decline cooperation	420	11.9	.997

NOTE: N = number of observed ties in M^1; d = density of M^1 (relational densities were multiplied by 100 to range between 0 and 100; r = reliability indicators obtained by using STRUCTURE (Burt, 1987). Reliability indicators can be interpreted like item-scale reliabilities. The percentage of variance in distances among ties accounted for by a single-principle component is 88.34% for Content 1, 88.13% for Content 2, and 98.68% for Content 3.
a. See the appendix for a description of ties.

The triad census uses SHED (Noma & Smith, 1978).[10] The program requires trichotomous data as input (conflict—indifference/absence—support) coded 0, 1, and 2, respectively. Input data were provided by the Boolean unions of strong support and conflict contents each, as based on the results of the coincidence analysis. The triad census in SHED also provides a test of statistical significance based on z scores for the deviations of triad frequencies from chance levels given the dyad distribution summarized in Table 13.2. As in the case of NADA, the SADA and STRATFIELD data were subjected to SHED.

RESULTS AND DISCUSSION

Table 13.3 presents a summary of the results, whereby NADA serves as the focal social structure. "Surplus" indicates the number of times triad types in the various domains occur at above-chance levels (level of

TABLE 13.2 Distribution of Dyads (in percentages)[a]

Type of Dyad	Description	SADA	NADA	STRATFIELD
8	Mutual support	25.16	15.88	5.92
5, 7	Asymmetric support	32.90	25.37	16.84
4	Null relation	24.30	26.60	43.55
1, 3	Asymmetric conflict	9.68	19.89	18.94
0	Mutual conflict	.86	3.16	8.25
2, 6	Ambivalence	7.10	9.10	6.50
Number of dyads		465	1,770	810
		(100%)	(100%)	(100%)

a. For dyad notation and coding, see Figure 13.3.

significance .05) given the dyad distribution in Table 13.2. Likewise, *deficit* refers to the number of times triads occur significantly at below-chance level. *Comparative surplus* means the number of times that NADA has a significant surplus of a specific triad compared with SADA or STRATFIELD where this triad occurs either at or below-chance level. *Comparative deficit* implies that NADA has a significant deficit of a triad type in comparison with the other two cases respectively, in which the triad is observed at or above-chance level.

The results in Table 13.3 confirm that for the surplus hypothesis in stalled social structures, ambivalent triads in the cluster and rank domain are significantly more frequent than in both random graphs and other social structures. NADA shows a surplus in 22 of the 39 triads of this type, compared with 10 in the case of SADA, and 15 in the case of STRATFIELD. Moreover, compared with SADA, NADA has a comparative surplus of 13 (among them are the eight triads displayed in Figure 13.5) and a comparative deficit in only two triads. Within this triad domain, NADA and SADA differ substantially in 16 of 39 triads. Compared with STRATFIELD, NADA shows a comparative surplus in 14 and a comparative deficit in 8 triads. NADA and STRATFIELD differ significantly in 22 of the 39 ambivalent rank-cluster triads.

The deficit hypothesis states that in stalled social structures, critical ambivalent triads are significantly less frequent than in both random graphs and other social structures. NADA shows a significant deficit from expected frequencies in 19 of the 29 triads. In the case of SADA, the significant deficits from chance levels occur in 8 of the 29 ambivalent critical triads and in 7 triads for STRATFIELD. Furthermore, vis-à-vis SADA, NADA has a comparative deficit of 11 triads and a comparative

TABLE 13.3 Summary of Triad Census: NADA Compared With Comparative Cases of SADA and STRATFIELD[a]

Group	Triads	Surplus			Deficit			Comparative Surplus		Comparative Deficit	
		N^b	S^c	B^d	N	S	B	S	B	S	B
Rank-cluster	16	9	8	8	5	6	5	2	5	2	4
Cluster	11	5	5	5	3	3	3	2	2	2	3
Rank	23	8	4	5	13	14	10	5	5	1	6
Critical triads	20	7	5	5	12	14	8	4	6	2	9
Ambivalent rank-cluster	39	22	10	15	11	14	10	13	13	3	8
Ambivalent critical triads	29	7	6	6	19	8	7	3	5	11	13
Total	138										

a. Numbers indicate the number of times triads deviate from chance level at the .05 significance level or better.
b. N = NADA.
c. S = SADA.
d. B = STRATFIELD.

surplus in only 2. Together these two social structures differ substantially in 13 of 29 triads. Vis-à-vis STRATFIELD, NADA has a comparative surplus in 5 cases and a comparative deficit in 13 of the 29 ambivalent critical triads. NADA and STRATFIELD differ significantly in 18 of the 29 critical ambivalent triads.

Table 13.3 shows that the three social structures do not differ greatly in other domains, with the exception of the rank domain, which indicates that both NADA's and STRATFIELD's social structure are more hierarchical than SADA's. Moreover, in both NADA and SADA, the triad characteristic of breakdown, the 0-0-0 triad, where mutual conflict exists between the constituent organizations, occurs at chance level. Of the three cases, only STRATFIELD, representing a social structure at the brink of breakdown has a significant surplus in 0-0-0 triad, whereas all three, particularly NADA, contain significant surpluses of the asymmetric conflict triad, the 1-1-1 triad. The scapegoating triad (3-3-8-triad), in which B and C stand in mutual support relations to each other and direct a conflict tie to A, appears in both NADA and SADA at above-chance level but at chance level in STRATFIELD. The 0-0-8 triad, "coalition" triad, with one symmetric support and two symmetric conflict relations, also occurs in all three social structures at above-chance level.

Referring to H3, the comparative hypothesis, we find that none of the triads characteristic of other failures (i.e., scapegoating, coalition, or deterrence as the structural ingredients of factionalism nor mutual conflict, as the structural indication of breakdown) helps differentiate stalled social structure from a comparable case, SADA. Moreover, with the important exception of the 0-0-0 triad, triads characteristic of other failures are unable to discriminate between stalemate and breakdown (STRATFIELD). A similar conclusion can be drawn for the 4-4-4 triad (isolation), in which all relations are empty, and the 888 triad, which is required for all cliques with more than two members. To varying degrees, all three social structures have significant surpluses in both triad types. Thus, the structural states of isolationism and cliquishness are no distinctive features of stalemate.

In summary, the triad census confirmed the hypothesis that stalled social structures are characterized by a surplus of ambivalent rank-cluster triads that lead to substantial overlaps between conflict and support relations. The analysis also supported the deficit hypothesis, H2, which specified a deficit of critical ambivalent triads in stalled social structures. Finally, the third hypothesis, H3, was supported, too. STRATFIELD, as an example of a social structure in breakdown, showed a significant surplus of the 0-0-0 triad, the triad required for breakdown. Triads characteristic of other types of failures and states do not distinguish stalled social structures from those not in stalemate.

▓ TOWARD A THEORY OF STRUCTURAL FAILURE

This chapter began with a conceptual discussion of structural stalemate and other failures in terms of exit, voice, and loyalty. Coups, insurgencies, and mass movements represent voice processes, whereas breakdown and disintegration are exit phenomena. Although permanent failure is characteristic of loyalty, we suggested that in stalled social structures, neither exit, voice, nor loyalty presents clear and unambiguous alternatives.

Following a Simmelian approach, we emphasized the *form* of stalemate, the formal properties of stalled social structures, or what we called the signature element. We only marginally, if at all, considered the *content* of stalemate in terms of its cultural, ideological, historical, and economic components. However, by focusing on form, we can detect striking similarities across cases from very different societies. For example, Crozier (1974) describes a centralized, rigid system of French public enterprises, where endogamous status groups are locked into a social structure, apparently unable to dissociate. NADA, by contrast, represents a decentralized, heterogeneous case with multiple layers of conflict and competition. In NADA's case, individual organizations proved unable to form associational links for external coordination and collective action. Both the French administrative system and the Nigerian system of PVOs are capable of producing stalemate, even though they differ greatly in cultural, organizational, and economic terms. Both cases share the absence of rational administrative control, which enjoys legitimacy and loyalty by members and clients.

We suggest that stalemate is essentially a nonmarket phenomenon. Indeed, the various cases examined in the chapter suggest two likely scenarios for stalemate: On the one hand, a combination of homogeneity, absence of status and power competition, and overinstitutionalization (high degrees of routinization, regulation, and standardization), and on the other, a high degree of ideological heterogeneity, highly competitive organizational environments, and underinstitutionalization.

At the more general level, we follow Rokkan (1975) who argued that societies (and organizations, for that matter) must develop institutionalized exit and voice processes as "management tools." At the same time, they must create limitations on both exit and voice and institutionalize lower and upper bounds for the extent to which members engage in the organization or want to leave it. We can speculate that misspecifications of ceiling and floor levels for exit and voice can make the emergence of stalemate more likely. This may be the case in overinstitutionalized social structures, in which upper bounds are specified too rigidly, or in underinstitutionalized social structures, in which lower bounds are specified too loosely.

The clearest expression of organizations that institutionalize exit and voice processes are political parties in democracies (Hirschman, 1981, p. 228). Not surprisingly, given the central role that parties perform in exit and voice manifestations, political scientists have focused on stalemate in the field of politics. O'Donnell (1973) studied party competition in Argentina between 1955 and 1965 and identified what he calls the "impossible game," in which "both winners and losers must lose" (p. 175). We can hypothesize that the *Peronistas* and the numerous anti-*Peronista* parties were locked in a persistent, seemingly insoluble stalemate situation that led the country on a long road of decline. Compare this with the frequent crises of the Italian political landscape, in which parties find themselves in what we may call temporary stalemate. Within the context of Italy's electoral procedure, where it is easier to "predict which parties will not be part of government than which will,"

LaPalombara (1987, p. 128) argues that the "constant crises" of the Italian political system encourage rather than discourage political stability. Despite an average governmental life expectancy of about 10 months over the last 40 years, Italy represents one of the world's most stable democracies.

Although stalled social structures seem to be relatively rare occurrences, they are more likely in either over- or underinstitutionalized nonmarket social systems. In this context, the debate about governability (Habermas, 1985), the crisis of democracy (Crozier, Huntington, & Watanuki, 1975) or the clash of ideologies (Huntington, 1996) can contribute to our understanding of failures in societies: Many Western countries have institutionalized major social conflicts and regulated rather than solved social problems. Developing along conflict lines, such institutional settings may become social rigidities (Olson, 1982) and acquire an increased potential for stalemate over time.

Throughout, we emphasized the probabilistic nature of failures. Different types of failures are related to each other and share common features. Social structures can change from breakdown to stalemate if a significant increase of ambivalence is accompanied by decreases in mutual conflict and support as well as scapegoating tendencies. Likewise, stalled social structures may move toward factionalism by drastic decreases in ambivalent relations that change to scapegoating tendencies, combined with increases in mutual conflict and support. Stalemate, breakdown, and factionalism provide the cornerstones of a field within which concrete social structures can be located. This operational field is formed jointly by the voice and exit processes of organizations in terms of support, conflict, ambivalence, and indifference relations.

Within this framework, we can suggest an initial answer to the problem of recovery from stalemate. Voice processes may contribute to conflict resolution or coalition formations through the reduction of ambivalence and conflict. They can also move the social structure closer to other types of failures (rather than to recovery) by reducing ambivalence at the expense of increasing other exit indicators. However, we should recall that stalled social structures are not subject to great volatility. They tend to be inert and sometimes kept in some form of "uneasy equilibrium," making recovery from stalemate difficult. The reason for this may be, as Hirschman (1970) aptly put it, that "every recovery mechanism is itself subject to the forces of decay which have been evoked here all along" (p. 124).

APPENDIX

Description and Measurement of Ties T_i(NADA)

Questionnaires were personally administered. For all network questions, respondents had a list of all 60 member organizations in front of them (aided recall). Whenever possible, data relating to interorganizational social structure were cross-checked and validated through additional interviews and correspondence as well as official organizational documents and files. All names and acronyms used in this chapter for organizations are fictitious.

Content I

T_1 Personal membership of representative of PVO_i in PVO_j—includes membership on board of trustees, board of directors.

T_2 Organizational membership of PVO_i in PVO_j—includes official affiliations and cases where i is legally part of j.

T_1 and T_2 are based on document and file analysis, in addition to a question in a standardized questionnaire, administered to all NADA members:

"Besides working in this organization, are you member of any other organization, agency, club, or association?"

(If yes): "What other organizations do you belong to/are you member of? Since when? Do you hold offices there? Which one is the most important for you? And besides this one?"

The Boolean union of T_1 and T_2 form the membership tie.

T_3 PVO_i would give substantial funding to PVO_j.

"Now let's assume that you could give substantial funding to NADA member organizations. But you could give funding to only five organizations in NADA. What would be the five members you would give the money to carry out their projects?"

T_4 PVO_i expects PVO_j to play a leading role in NADA.

"Which organizations on this list do you expect to play a leading role in NADA in the future?"

Content 2

T5 PVO_i cooperates with PVO_j—includes information exchange, staff exchange, ad hoc problem solving, and general assistance.

"Is the kind of activity practiced by your organization also carried out by other groups in this area? Which ones? Have you made any attempts to establish some form of cooperation with these organizations? Which ones? Have these organizations made any attempts to cooperate with you? Which ones?"

"Do you work together with these organizations? Do you exchange clients, receive clients, exchange information, develop joint programs, provide or receive funding, engage in joint planning?"

"Besides these organizations you've mentioned so far, are there any other organizations you stay in contact with or organizations with which you have some form of cooperation? Which ones? What type of cooperation?"

"Of all the organizations you mentioned so far, which are the two most important ones for your organization?"

"Before the first meeting, or before you first heard about NADA, did you cooperate with some of those organizations present at the meeting? Which ones? Could you describe the nature of the cooperation?"

T6   Representative(s) of PVO_i are personally acquainted with representatives of PVO_j.

"Did you know some of the organizations that came to the meeting? Did you personally know some of the directors, members of the executive committee, or anyone else in high position in any of these organizations?"

T7 PVO_i intends to cooperate or to intensify cooperation with PVO_j.

T7   PVO$_i$ intends to cooperate or to intensify cooperation with PVO$_j$.

"Judging from your experiences so far, with which of the participating organizations on this list will you most likely cooperate in the future? What about the organizations you are presently cooperating with?"

T8   PVO$_i$ would vote for PVO$_j$ in NADA's executive committee.

"If there were elections for a general executive committee of NADA today and you were asked to pass five votes, each vote representing a different organization on this list, what would be the five organizations you would vote for to represent your organization?"

Content 3

T9   PVO$_i$ intends to exclude PVO$_j$ from membership in NADA.

"Were there any organizations present at the conference that you felt did not really fit the purpose of the conference? In other words, do you personally think that there were any types of organizations that you would rather not like to see as future members of NADA? What organization(s) are you thinking about?"

T10   PVO$_i$ expects PVO$_j$ to play an insignificant role in NADA.

"And which organizations on this list do you expect to play a less central—that is to say, minor—role in NADA in the future?"

T11   PVO$_i$ intends to decline or reduce cooperation with PVO$_j$.

"Are there any organizations on this list, where you would say that you find it difficult or less beneficial for your organization to cooperate with in the future? Which ones? What about the organizations you are cooperating with now?"

█ NOTES

1. Personal interview, Lagos, April 1985.

2. All names and acronyms used in this chapter for organizations are fictitious.

3. It has to be considered that several explanatory variables do not apply to the process of organizational formation. Threat-rigidity behavior (Staw, Sandelands, & Dutton, 1981), performance deficiencies, vacillating domain initiatives and slack deficits (Hambrick & D'Aveni, 1988), and contraction of environmental carrying capacity (Zammuto & Cameron, 1985) typically apply to organizational maintenance problems.

4. Data reported in this section are based on a survey of all of NADA's potential 60 member organizations; see section on "Data and Methodology."

5. Triad identification numbers follow the system suggested by Noma and Smith (1978). The first digit represents the dyad type from A to B; the second digit reports the dyad type from A to C, and the third digit gives the dyad type from B to C. For example, the 1-1-8 triad contains an asymmetric conflict tie (Dyad Type 1) from B to A and from C to A, and a mutual conflict tie between B and C (Dyad 8).

6. These included (a) personal visits to potential member organizations; (b) administration of a questionnaire to all organizations; (c) informal interviews and conversations with representatives, including follow-up correspondence; (d) attendance at several meetings of the organizing committee and two member conferences; and (e) relevant files, official documents, and reports whenever accessible.

7. Here, the case study of SADA serves comparative purposes only. The Senegalese federation can be described as a case of "retarded" organizational development. Although SADA encountered substantial difficulties during the first 3 years of its existence, it nevertheless did not develop into stalemate. We will report on SADA elsewhere.

8. As in the case of SADA, STRATFIELD serves as an additional scope condition for the hypotheses. For a detailed analysis of STRATFIELD see Romo (1986).

9. We wish to thank Ronald Burt for his assistance and advice in performing the coincidence analysis. Results of the coincidence analysis are available from the first author on request.

10. We would like to thank Randy Smith for his advice and assistance in performing the triad census and for making SHED available to us.

PART VI

Conclusion

Studying Organizational Failures   14

Helmut K. Anheier
Lynne Moulton

In the opening chapter of this book, we briefly outlined four relatively distinct approaches to the study of failure. The first approach, *organizational* studies, looks at creation, growth, decline, and death as part of the organizational life cycle and emphasizes the "fit" between organizational management and performance on the one hand and environmental conditions and changes on the other. According to the *political* perspective, organizations are seen as primarily political, rather than economic, entities that compete for advantages within a larger political economy inhabited by different institutions and constituencies. Legitimacy serves as the major explanatory variable in understanding organizational failures. In the *cognitive* approach, we emphasize aspects of definitions and perception of failure and focus on cultural blueprints and dispositions for declaring and managing breakdowns and other organizational catastrophes. Finally, the *structural* approach locates failures in the social fabric or relational patterns of organizations and institutions and stresses the combinatorial logic underlying different failure tendencies.

We also suggested that failure is a relative concept. In fact, failure is a relative term in two senses. First, organizational failure is relative to notions of organizational success, and at the least, to some understanding of a normal state of affairs, however defined. What is more, the definition and managerial consequences of failure are relative to the various interests and claims the various stakeholders put on the organization, leading us to ask, Success for whom? Failure for whom? In other words, one person's failure may be someone else's success.

Yet does the relativity of the term imply that we can reach no broad conclusions that yield a more general understanding of organizational failures, breakdown, and bankruptcies? We think not, and in the balance of the chapter, we summarize analytically what we regard as the lessons that can be drawn from the various contributions in this volume. We do so by posing four questions and then examining each of the approaches outlined above for answers. The four questions are these:

- ▥ *Concept:* What can we conclude about the concept and measurement of failure? How is failure defined?

- ▥ *Causes:* What do the approaches suggest about the causes of failure, breakdown, and bankruptcy? Why do organizations fail?

- ▥ *Process:* What conclusions can we draw about the process of failure? Are there specific triggering events or mechanisms, phases, and patterns in which organizations fail?

- ▥ *Implications:* Finally, what comes after failure? What are, according to the four approaches, the implications for failed organizations, and what afterlife awaits them?

Of course, neither all approaches nor all chapters in this volume pay equal attention to each of these questions. Taken together, however, they nonetheless allow us to identify some of the key insights that follow from this work, both in terms of management and policy implications and in terms of organizational theory. Table 14.1 offers a summary of the main points for each of the four approaches.

▥ ORGANIZATIONAL APPROACH

Concept

For the organizational approach, the concept of failure is not inherently ambiguous and problematic. Of course, the actual diagnosis of failure and different failure types may be difficult and frequently obscured by political influence and strategies of key stakeholders. Nonetheless, it should in most cases be possible to use economic performance and activity criteria to measure organizational failure. This does not necessarily mean,

TABLE 14.1 Approaches to the Study of Failure

Aspect	Approach			
	Organizational	Political	Cognitive	Structural
Core definition	Economic efficiency	Political *vs.* program failure	Social construction	Relational pattern
Prime cause	Fit between organizational performance and environment	Loss of legitimacy; failure to attract or maintain legitimacy claims of core constituencies	Impossibility of measurement; incongruence between task environment and organizational structure	Structure of conflict relations relative to interest configurations
Process/phases	Triggering events; downward spirals; coping	Strategic behavior among stakeholders to reap benefits and/or reduce costs from failure	Fantasy measures; fantasy plans; failures trigger more failures	Emergence of specific patterns of inter- and intragroup relations
Implications	Liability of newness; lack of slack; low degrees of embeddedness related to failure	Political legitimacy more important than economic performance	Lack of adequate measures and organizational models for failure-prone task environments	Probabilistic and combinatorial nature of failure and success; nonlinearity and threshold effects

however, that we treat organizational failure as a finite phenomenon. It can be the absolute end, or dissolution, of a firm. However, it can also lead to persistently low performance or profound reorganization. Most authors in the field distinguish between two types of failure: transformation and closure. Firms "transform" when they merge, lose independent control, and change ownership. "Closure" results from the loss of a corporate charter, bankruptcy, and mission completion.

Causes

Organizational approaches see the causes of failure in a complex genesis of factors that involve an initial threat and subsequent managerial responses. Usually, some triggering mechanism from either inside or outside the organization leads to perceived or actual low performance. Management tries to respond and puts in place recovery measures that may either lead to recovery or reinforce failure tendencies. The contributions in this volume examine the "causal chemistry" of failure from different, yet complementary, perspectives.

For Zucker and Darby in Chapter 2, the core argument addresses the degree to which organizations in a highly volatile field manage information—specifically, investments (or lack of) in costly information on developments in biotechnology. Indeed, for incumbent pharmaceutical companies, investment in information about, and adoption of, new breakthroughs in biotechnology can mean the difference between spectacular success and long drawn-out failure. In their study, failing or persistently low-performing firms were those less likely to invest in research and development of new technologies and were slow to adopt new breakthroughs in their field. In other words, passivity in volatile, rapidly developing organizational fields is associated with failure. By implication, active organizations that search the environment for strategic information are more likely to survive.

The organizational approach also sheds light on negative consequences of such strategic choices. Indeed, in Chapter 3, Wilson, Hickson, and Miller explore the nexus between key managerial decisions and outcomes in terms of failure and success. They look specifically at "big moves" from which firms cannot recover, employing the concept of managerial overreach to describe uncommon fatal mistakes that lead firms to closure or absorption by competitors, both of which they consider failures. In this case, failure is seen as the direct result of irreversible managerial decisions for expansion disproportionate to the organization's capacity to do so. Wilson et al. do not conceive of failure as resulting from bad day-to-day management, however, because "bad" strategic decisions are atypical for the managers making them. Failure in these rare occasions happens as a result of hasty decisions within firms with relatively little organizational slack. What is more, overfamiliarity with the product or service line may lead managers to overlook potentially problematic aspects of the decision that are outside the narrow confines of production and marketing considerations. Thus, failures result not only from inability to react appropriately to technical or market problems but also from managerial "overreach" that taxes organizational resources and narrows options for recovery.

In Chapter 5, Mayntz suggests that failure cannot be explained independently by environmental contingency or coping theories alone. Instead, external threats and managerial coping decisions work in consort to bring about organizational success or failure. In this case, failure can be seen as a potential organizational outcome situated within an ongoing historical process of environmental change and organizational response. Mayntz maintains that organizations generally succeed when they enjoy a good "fit" with their environment. Dramatic external changes that ruin this fit sets up conditions for failure. Whether failure occurs or not depends on organizational response to the changing conditions. According to Mayntz, historical context will not only help shape the meaning of the external changes but will also help shape (by enabling or constraining) organizational response and, therefore, the meaning of failure.

Process

Failures can be abrupt and sudden, but they typically involve a drawn-out process characterized by various attempts to rescue the organization. For Zucker and Darby, investment in new technologies in the pharmaceutical industry is a complex game of "lag and catch-up." A disproportionate amount of risk is taken up front by new small biotechnology firms, which tend to invest highly in research and development and subsequently tend to make most of the new discoveries in the field. Older, larger pharmaceutical firms then feed on these discoveries, either by eventually adopting the new breakthrough or by simply acquiring the biotechnology firm itself. Participation in this game at both ends tends to be necessary in preventing obsolescence or outright failure.

Looking at decision overreach (Chapter 3) also offers valuable insights as to what happens in the course of failure. For example, in one of the case studies that Wilson et al. describe, the failed firm was in operation during and long after its failed expansion. Failure in this case resulted in the firm's purchase by a competitor. The only difference between pre- and postfailure was loss of control by the firm's original owners. This case helps expand the concept of failure by demonstrating that failure can represent a discrete event within firms' *continuing* history. Thus, organizational failure does not always equal organizational death.

Finally, Mayntz looks at the process of failure and shows how the political history of the Central and Eastern European countries affected the way in which academies in each country coped with regime changes. The analysis also highlights the complexity of determining success and failure because some of the organizational deaths were not interpreted as failures because the dissolution was supported by the stakeholders involved. Likewise, some of the "survivors" looked more like "coping failures" because the quality of their research had dramatically declined since the regime change. Thus, changing definitions of what constitutes "failure" versus "success" have an impact of the process of organizational failure.

Implications

There are several implications we can draw for a theory of organizational failure. Zucker and Darby emphasize the importance of industry-specific stratification dynamics at the level of the organizational field. Thus, to help us understand both the causes and the process of failure within industries, we need to look at size and scope differences among firms and explore the different loci of innovation and new developments on an industry-wide level, including the accompanying information flows and the resulting strategic choices. Wilson et al. point to the need to separate the failure tendencies associated with routine management from risk factors of strategic decision making. Although the former may induce slow, gradual decline processes that may go unnoticed for some time, the latter frequently may lead to dramatic erosions of organizational resources and rapid narrowing of options available to management.

Hager et al. (Chapter 4) remind us that not all closures are failures. Particularly in the nonprofit sector, the prevalence of mission completion offers an important part of any explanation of organizational dissolution over time. The authors admit that declaring the organizational mission complete may be just a rationalization for failure. However, we should nonetheless acknowledge that a dissolving organization is not always a failing one. Hager et al. also confirm previous research claiming that two of the most salient explanations of organizational closure are youth and small size (Freeman, Carroll, & Hannan, 1983; Hannan & Carroll, 1992). The authors help specify the conditions under which newness is a liability. They find that small, young organizations tend to be disconnected and relatively isolated within their fields, two relational characteristics that are also inversely related to failure.

Finally, the study by Mayntz suggests just how dependent organizational studies are on the notion of an environment that is at least to some degree identifiable and predictable. Far-reaching and rapid political changes and upheavals can easily create havoc for even the most flexible and most "immune" of organizations. For her, the case in point is that we need to focus on the historical context of organizational dissolution, specifically when the political parameters in which organizational fields are located undergo profound changes. Similarly, the process of failure and the coping mechanisms available to organizations in reacting to such threats are subject to the same uncertainty introduced by the larger environment. In other words, beyond a certain expected degree of instability and uncertainty in organizational environments, any organizational analysis has to take account of political factors in explaining failures and breakdown—an approach to which we now turn.

▓ POLITICAL APPROACHES

Concept

For political scientists like Seibel, the very notion of failure is rarely a matter of economic efficiency, nor is failure necessarily based on low organizational performance or goal attainment. For him, failures can become successes, and success, failures. Indeed, in Chapter 6, Seibel turns the question of organizational failure around to ask why some failures survive to become what he calls "reliable failures." In spite of the value placed on efficiency and accountability as standards for success within modern organizational culture, Seibel claims that the dissonant persistence of low-performing organizations can be explained with the help of political factors. In the case of nonprofit organizations, he argues that their peripheral position, unique resource mobilization techniques, embeddedness in a political network of personal contacts, and supporting ideologies provide a unique operating zone for permanently failing organizations. In these "niches of inefficiency," the illusion that good work is being done helps principals (board members and the general public) deal with cognitive dissonance when performance reality consistently strays from norms of efficiency and accountability.

Delaney, too, challenges the efficiency-based notion of organizational failure (Chapter 7). He goes even further and prefaces his analysis by reframing the common understanding that bankruptcy is an indicator of failure. Instead, he argues that bankruptcy is often a strategic solution to a number of complex organizational and political problems, leading to organizational decline. Bankruptcy is often the 11th hour strategy employed to prevent liquidation, after other internal, network, and overt political strategies have failed. In this sense, when firms continue to operate during and after filing Chapter 11, bankruptcy is more an indicator of survival than of failure.

Bovens, 't Hart, Dekker, and Verheuvel, analyzing organizational failure associated with implementation of public policy (Chapter 8), make a fundamental distinction between program failure and political failure. They argue that an organization responsible for carrying out a particular policy mandate can fail to meet the goals of policy and still not become publicly defined as failing. In this arena, Bovens et al. contend that sometimes independent of performance, an organization is not truly failing until the public perceives it as such. In other words, for key stakeholders, public failure matters and becomes the necessary condition for failure among organizations charged with program implementation. In such cases, the loss of legitimacy becomes more important than the efficient use of resources. Thus, within the policy arena, failure, or fiasco as Bovens et al. describe it, is generally a political construction.

Causes and Processes

Within the political approach, the causes of failure are ultimately political and relate to questions of legitimacy, and compared with the management and organizational studies literature, most analysts make less of a distinction between an initial threat or triggering events and the processes that unfold. Indeed, within this approach, the origins of inefficiency are analytically less important than how impressions about them are managed.

For Seibel, organizational failure can be a permanent and understandable state of existence in certain zones of inefficiency in which the ideologies and the interests of the principals make the standards of efficiency and accountability "inappropriate." Similarly, in his analysis of various "megabankruptcy" cases in recent decades, Delaney describes the bankruptcy arena as a complex organizational field in which key players accumulate expertise and connections in their competition for advantage. In the legal and policy fields alike, failure is interpreted as created through a series of legal or rhetorical punches and counterpunches by the relevant actors trying to "weaken" each other. For example, Bovens et al. write that attribution of blame is integral in the construction of a political fiasco and that blame avoidance becomes a crucial strategy among the policymakers involved. Failure emerges from the process of defining an event, organization, or policy as a problem for which blame must be assigned.

Halliday and Carruthers (Chapter 9) show how the legal and political processes create the institutional environment in which corporate decline, reorganization, and failure occur. Although Mayntz argues that organizational failure is a function of organizational response to external transformations, Halliday and Carruthers claim that failure is also affected by environmental response to organizational decline. Looking at the professionalization of British insolvency practitioners through the 1986 Insolvency Act, the authors explain how the institutions set up to deal with corporate failure are partially a product of prevailing political ideologies and their interpretations of what causes failure in the first place.

In the British case, Thatcher-era conservatism and the attending commitment to move public goods to the private sphere shaped parliamentary action on insolvency legislation. The prevailing ideology at the time was that increasing rates of insolvency could best be dealt with by "statutorily guided self-regulating" professionals rather than by bureaucrats. During this time, the definition of organizational failure changed from a liquidation process dealt with by low-status "corporate undertakers" to the noble work of high-status professionals operating within a national ethos of "saving" companies at the margins.

Implications

Several implications flow from the political analysis of failure. First, the concept of failure is best understood through analysis of a competitive process. As organizations decline, the relevant stakeholders fight for political and economic advantage. For Delaney, the relevant question is not why organizations fail but for whom is it a failure when a firm employs bankruptcy as a survival strategy. His analysis highlights the complexity of the process of organizational failure in an important way. He concludes that "it may be misguided to talk about *organizations* failing at all, without first fully accounting for the roster of winners and losers in the organization's demise" (p. 120). For example, when a business shuts down, the owner may walk away with a substantial amount of money whereas employees lose their jobs. As Delaney demonstrates, bankruptcy is often a tool for corporate owners, managers, and creditors in what he describes as the "strategic chess match" that characterizes the process of organizational decline.

Moreover, failure tends to have human consequences in those arenas where blame has been assigned, either to individual policymakers or client groups. Bovens et al. suggest that the intensity of these consequences often depends on how well the policymakers involved employ defensive tactics aimed at preserving legitimacy. Failure may be a temporary inconvenience or a permanent career-ending disaster depending on how successfully the relevant actors shift blame from themselves.

Institutional changes in attitude toward failure feed back into organizational performance. This is a lesson we can draw from the study of bankruptcy law suggested by Halliday and Carruthers. The contents of the Insolvency Act and the new professional "policing of failure" place pressure on directors of failing firms to seek help sooner and intensify pressure on business in general to professionalize its activities. Whether or not the act has the desired effect on business performance and the occurrence of failure is an empirical question. Nonetheless, Halliday and Carruthers show how political process, driven in part by ideology, shapes the environment in which organizational decline occurs. But by implication, political process also changes the way we perceive and define failure and various recovery mechanisms in the first place, which is the central focus of the cognitive approach.

▦ COGNITIVE APPROACHES

Concept

Whereas the concept of failure is ultimately a political one for the political approach, the cognitive approach views the notion of failure as constructed, shaped by cultural conventions, power relations, even make-believe, as Clarke and Perrow suggest in Chapter 10. Nowhere does the concept of failure as a social construction become more evident than in Meyer's critique of performance measures (Chapter 11). Like Seibel, Meyer is concerned with what he calls "permanent failure" (Meyer & Zucker, 1989). He recognizes the inherent contradiction in the existence of persistently low-performing organizations. However, instead of trying to explain why some firms survive in spite of low performance, Meyer claims that the key to this contradiction is actually a measurement problem. He boldly argues that all performance measures are flawed because performance "lies largely ahead and beyond the reach of measurement." At best, managers and scholars can predict and project actual performance. But performance cannot be measured directly. Generally, we rely on "second-best" measures of past and current performance and hope they accurately predict the attainment of organizational goals. Burdened by inadequate measurement, and too much of it as Meyer points out, performance ends up being a poor index for failure and vice versa.

Cause and Process

Although the cognitive approach has most to contribute by making us aware of some of the complexities in measuring and identifying failures, it also leads to key insights when it comes to causes and processes. In contrast to those engaged in organizational studies, however, researchers taking a cognitive approach do not differentiate strictly between cause and processes. Rather, a cognitive approach emphasizes the very premise of using organizations to plan for specific types of contingencies. The incidents of organizational failure in the case of the Shoreham Nuclear Power Plant on Long Island, described by Clarke and Perrow, are almost too many to believe. The striking contribution this case makes to our understanding of organizational failure is in finding an explanation for such colossal failure under "the best of all possible conditions" for success. In the preparation of an evacuation plan, on which their organizational fate apparently rested, LILCO (Long Island Lighting Company) had acquired an abundance of expert knowledge, had extensively planned for years, was enormously invested financially in the success of the plan—and, subsequently, the opening of the plant—was cognitively prepared for the possibility of failure, and was under widespread scrutiny by every bureaucratic level from the Nuclear Regulatory Commission, down to individual Long Island residents. With so many contingencies "controlled for," how could the real-time simulation of the evacuation plan go so far awry, culminating in the eventual death of the Shoreham plant?

The answer to this question, and the key theoretical insight for organizational failure, lies in the straightforward claim by these authors that plans do not work unless organizational structures meant to implement them are appropriate for the task at hand. As Clarke and Perrow point out, "Organizations require that the problems for which they are planning recur on a more or less regular basis. Absent such recurrence, they cannot build the structural mechanisms that permit successful response" (p. 196). The authors describe how the conventional, centralized bureaucratic structure of LERO (Local Emergency Response Organization), the organization designed to deal with evacuation, was not appropriate to its task. Hence, its subsequent failure is not surprising. The lack of opportunity for routinization and the intraorganizational belief in their "fantasy plans" also help explain why LERO failed in its tasks. Although there may be no organizational structure that is both suitable and empirically possible to accomplish the tasks required of LERO, this case certainly helps specify the many contributions to failure of high-technology systems.

Implications

In a volume dedicated to exploring the concept and experience of organizational failure, the theoretical implications that follow from the cognitive approach are dramatic. Based on Meyer's insights, we suggest that whatever we can say empirically about the concept of failure, it is fundamentally limited by the flawed measures we employ. Pragmatically, of course, managers and scholars of organizational behavior must use the measures available to them. Hence, there may be no "elegant" solution to the problem of performance measurement, leaving us with multiple performance indicators in the hope that they capture aspects of true performance.

The implications of cognitive approaches reach beyond measurement aspects. From Clarke and Perrow, we learn about the complex relationship between the necessary lack of routinization in failure management and the need for a predictable, coordinated, well-tested and well-planned response. The latter, however, requires bureaucratization that can function effectively only in routine task environments—that is, precisely the opposite of the failure scenarios likely to confront the organization! This implication reminds us of Perrow's (1984) analysis in *Normal Accidents*, which linked specific types of disasters, technical failures, and man-made catastrophes to incompatibilities between organizational structure and task environment.

▦ STRUCTURAL APPROACHES

Concept

The structural approach differs from other work on organizational failure by going beyond the utilitarian, efficiency-oriented calculus of the management literature. The failures described here occur in the *social fabric* of organizations and groups, and such failures may not necessarily coincide with situations of economic distress and vice versa. Of course, notions of rationality are important, as Chapter 12 by Romo and Anheier shows, but rational action is shaped by the relational infrastructure in which it takes place. By developing a structural approach to failure, the study explores Simmel's thesis that the tendency of failure is the result of both simple and complex, sometimes counteracting, relational components of the social structure. In many ways, the structural approach to failures owes its origin to Simmel's sociology of conflict. In discussing the relationship between harmony and conflict in social groups, he compares the ideals of unanimity and peace that theologians and utopian philosophers have painted over the centuries to lifeless and unreal societies (Simmel, 1968, p. 187; 1984, p. 183). Likewise, he finds competition and antagonism equally ineffective as the sole constituting elements of organizing. Simmel continues to state that

> just like the cosmos needs love and hate, attractive and repulsive forces to attain a form, so must societies negotiate a quantitative relation between harmony and disharmony, association and disassociation, favor and disfavor, to achieve identifiable structures. (p. 187, first author's translation)

For Simmel, societies are conglomerates of conflict and support relations, as well as of positive and negative affect and indifference among participants. By implication, we can extend this reasoning to the study of organizations and institutions, as suggested in the work by Anheier and Romo in Chapters 12 and 13. Although the substantive meaning of the relative balance between harmony and disharmony, association and disassociation, and favor and disfavor certainly depends on the actual context and task environment, significant imbalances among these various relations may lead to failure tendencies. In this respect, the concept of organizational failure describes a specific structural pattern of complex social relations.

Causes and Processes

A structural approach establishes the *forms* of failure and thereby focuses on "how" social structure might fail. Little is usually said about the causes of failures or why a social structure fails in one particular way rather than another. The thesis that failure is the result of both simple and complex, sometimes counteracting relational components of the social structure that produce specific tendencies toward different types of failure should make it nonetheless easier to develop theories of why social structure or organizations fail. For example, Meyer and Zucker (1989) developed the somewhat counterintuitive notion of "permanently failing organizations," defined as the combination of low performance and high persistence. Permanent failure tends to occur through a dual process when the motivations to maintain an organization become both divorced from efficiency considerations and attached to different stakeholders in the organization. In other words, support and conflict relations become ambivalent and may accumulate to structural stalemate. Note, however, that the tendencies toward stalemate do not imply any indication as to the causes of failure.

A structural approach sets *failure tendencies* as collective processes analytically apart from *failures as outcome*. For example, intense antagonism among members of a subgroup (failure tendencies) may lead to splinter tendencies that, ultimately, make expulsion or secession (failure outcome) more likely. Similarly, withdrawals from organizational affairs, refusals to cooperate, and nonparticipation decrease interaction densities, and may, in the end, lead to disintegration and isolationism as outcomes. Thus, failure tendencies refer to the relational patterns among members of the organizations as they amount, in the aggregate, to specific propensities of the social structure toward different failure outcomes.

Implications

A structural approach offers a different look at the relationship between failure and success. In a way, this approach is already contained in Simmel's (1968) suggestion that societies must find a balance "between harmony and disharmony, association and disassociation, favor and disfavor, to achieve identifiable structures" (p. 187, first author's translation). In the nonlinear world of network analysis, this "quantitative relation" would be located in a neutral zone or "steady state" where the various failure tendencies are weakest or, in terms of the model developed in Anheier and Romo (Chapter 13), at chance level. Success, then, could be defined as the ability of a social structure to keep relational elements indicative of failure at random levels.

▨ CONCLUSION

The various chapters in this volume are testimony to the rich tradition and diverse currents in scholarship that have emerged around the topic of organizational failure in recent years. Specifically, research has moved beyond the confines of a narrow managerial orientation and examines failures in broader contexts and more varied settings. At the same time, the contributions also made clear that each of the approaches to the study of failure has specific strengths and shortcomings in providing answers to what we suggested as the four key research areas: What is failure? What are its causes? What is the process of failure? What are the outcomes and implications? The organizational approach is probably best at identifying the causes of failure and weakest when it comes to the issues of definition and measurement. The political approach improves on aspects of definition and process but is less clear as to the actual causal factors involved. The cognitive approach is most fruitful in dealing with issues of conceptualizations and measurement but remains somewhat mute on the actual "causal chemistry" that sets failure processes in motion. Finally, the structural approach usefully identifies different types of failure tendencies and outcomes and adds a welcome probabilistic framework to the discussion but does so by disregarding aspects of causality and political issues. We would argue, however, that the four approaches are in fact more complementary than rival.

This said, what can we say more broadly about the concept and experience of organizational failure? Economic reasoning leads us to expect that failure is a finite outcome resulting from irrational action on the part of organizations and managers. This logic also leads us to expect that failure is a *negative* outcome that individuals and organizations universally try to avoid. As the work in this volume robustly attests, the occurrence of organizational failure deviates from this expected logic in many interesting ways. In closing, we will briefly spell out some of the implications of this finding for our understanding of the different facets of organizational failure (see Table 14.1).

Failure as Outcome

In many instances, failure may not represent the negative outcome that the relevant stakeholders actively tried to avoid. We find evidence of this representation mostly within the organizational approach. The failures analyzed within this approach are often the result of rational action rather than irrational action on the part of the people involved. Indeed, firm closure and transformation often occur as a result of careful rational planning and decision making. What is more, some failures can be interpreted as a positive outcome of rational action, as in the transformation of the East German and Lithuanian academies of science, described by Mayntz. In these cases, various stakeholders recognized the misfit between the research organizations and their institutional environments after the regime changes in the 1980s, inspiring their purposive dissolution of these academies. Of course, understanding failure as an outcome of rational action does not imply that irrational and simply bad decision making play no role. To the contrary, as Wilson et al. demonstrate, failure can be the result of haste and overconfidence. We also saw that failure can be the consequence of irrational passivity within volatile organizational fields, as described by Zucker and Darby. Thus, at the very least, the contributions in this volume point to the conclusion that the relationship between rational action and organizational success or failure is more complicated than suggested by conventional management approaches.

Failure as Process

Throughout this volume, we also observe cases in which failure is not a finite outcome at all but a variable embedded within a reflexive process between organizations and their environments. The organizational approach and political approaches offer the richest evidence of this conception of failure. For example, Halliday and Carruthers show us that the definition of failure shapes, and is shaped by, aspects of the organizational environment such as political ideology and the legal remedies available to organizations in dealing with insolvencies. The dialectic relationship between failure and environment is also described by Zucker and Darby for a volatile industrial field in which routes to success or failure are at least partially determined by a firm's placement in the informational "food chain." Mayntz makes an even stronger case for the contingency of failure on the play between an organization and its environment by offering rich evidence of this reflexive process in the changing political economic environments of Central and Eastern European countries. These authors argue that failure cannot be fully understood as distinct from this reflexive process, and therefore should be defined as a process itself.

Failure as Negative Label

Contributions from the political approach treat failure as a negative label that is the object of political spin control and strategic deflection. In this sense, the *fact* of failure in terms of organizational goals is not always the most salient consideration. Bovens et al. offer the most blatant example of the political nature of failure in their discussion of the construction of the "Dutch crime-fighting fiasco." They argue that an organization's instrumental deficiency is not a sufficient condition for failure. Rather, a deficient organization and its members truly fail only when they are publicly labeled a failure and are unable to deflect this label. Delaney demonstrates the strategic uses of failure as a label. He shows that sometimes firms can use bankruptcy, *whether they actually file or not,* as both a shield against legal threats and as evidence of responsible problem solving with creditors. Seibel presents a more subtle example of failure spin control. He argues that nonprofit entities that might be labeled failures by conventional standards of efficiency and accountability can hide within "niches of inefficiency," in which the ideology of charity and political advantages of involvement in "good causes" buffer organizations and their members from the negative label of failure.

Failure as Construction

The third approach to failure in this volume shows us how failure can be perceived as a cognitive construction. From this perspective, failure may be a tangible outcome resulting from purposive action on the part of organizations and their managers, yet this outcome can stem from a particular flawed frame of mind. As Clarke and Perrow demonstrate, the prosaic organizational explanation for failure in their Shoreham case may lie in the misfit between the organizational structure and the task environment, but one of the *reasons* for failure may be that planners and managers, in an extreme version of groupthink (Janis, 1982), begin to believe their own "fantasy plans." Underlying faith in seemingly rational but ultimately misguided plans leads organizations to discard counterfactual experience and to ignore failure warning signs. Meyer puts a different emphasis on the cognitive construction of failure by arguing that because true performance is impossible to measure, any evaluation we do make about success or failure depends entirely on how we operationalize it.

Failure as a Structural Configuration

The conditions for organizational failure can also be defined as a structural configuration, found in the *social fabric* of a given organization. The structural approach shows how failure can be more of a potential, given certain combinations of relational elements. Anheier and Romo find higher probabilities for organizational failure in settings when combinations of support and conflict relationships are irreconcilable. From this perspective, failure can, and does, manifest in the outcome of organizational dissolution. Yet because this outcome is contingent on the structural configuration of the individuals and organizations involved, the instrumental causes and the actual outcome are not the analytic focus. Failure is best understood by looking at the structural *forms* that produce it.

Failure for Whom, Success for Whom?

Finally, let's return to one of our original questions: Who suffers and who benefits from the failure of an organization? From an organizational perspective, there are two answers to this question: In a narrow sense, shareholders, management, employees, and customers suffer, and in a broader sense, the other organizations and their stakeholders benefit, either by creating some sort of windfall opportunity or by changing parameters in the environmental carrying capacity by eliminating marginal elements. However, for the political and the cognitive approach, the question of who benefits is more complex. For example, a firm's bankruptcy and dissolution may greatly benefit its owners and creditors, while displacing its workforce and cheating wronged consumers. What is more, within the structural perspective, it may become unclear who the victims and who the beneficiaries are, just as it may be difficult to identify friend from foe in some political arenas. Thus, not all failures leave us with a clear understanding of who the losers and winners are. In summary, just as the occurrence of failure is contingent on many complex organizational, environmental, cognitive, and structural factors, so is failure outcome. We hope that future research will take the contingent nature of failure to heart and build on the conceptual and empirical work presented in this volume.

References

Abbott, A. (1988). *The system of professions: An essay on the division of expert labor.* Chicago: University of Chicago Press.

Abel, R. L. (1988). *The legal profession in England and Wales.* Oxford, UK: Basil Blackwell.

Abel, R. L. (1989). *American lawyers.* New York: Oxford University Press.

Akerlof, G. A. (1970). The market for lemons: Quality, uncertainty, and the market mechanism. *Quarterly Journal of Economics, 84,* 488-505.

Aldrich, H. E., & Pfeffer, J. (1976). Environments of organization. *Annual Review of Sociology, 2,* 79-106.

Amark, K. (1990). Open cartels and social closures: Professional strategies in Sweden, 1860-1950. In M. Burrage & R. Torstendahl (Eds.), *Professions in theory and history: Rethinking the study of the professions* (pp. 94-114). London: Sage.

Amburgey, T. L., & Rao, H. (1996). Organizational ecology: Past, present, and future directions. *Academy of Management Journal, 39*(5), 1265-1286.

Anderson, E. W., Fornell, C., & Lehman, D. R. (1994). Customer satisfaction, market share, and profitability: Findings from Sweden. *Journal of Marketing, 58,* 53-66.

Anheier, H. I. (1986). *Private voluntary organizations, networks and developments in Africa.* Unpublished doctoral dissertation, Yale University, Department of Sociology.

Anheier, H. K. (1987). Structural analysis and strategic research design: Studying politicized interorganizational networks. *Sociological Forum, 2,* 563-582.

Anheier, H. K. (1989). Private voluntary organizations and development in West Africa: Comparative perspective. In E. James (Ed.), *Non-profit organizations: Comparative perspectives* (pp. 339-357). Oxford, UK: Oxford University Press.

Anheier, H. K. (1994a, August). *Anatomy of organizational failures.* Paper presented in the session on Social Networks at the Annual Meeting of the American Sociological Association, Los Angeles, CA.

Anheier, H. K. (1994b). Non-governmental organizations and institutional development in Africa: A comparative analysis. In E. Sandberg (Ed.), *The changing politics of non-governmental organizations in African states* (pp. 139-168). Westport, CT: Praeger.

Anheier, H. K., Gerhards, J., & Romo, F. P. (1995). Form of capital and social structure in cultural fields: Examining Bourdieu's social topography. *American Journal of Sociology, 100*(4), 859-903.

Anheier, H. K., & Romo, F. P. (1992). Modelle strukturellen Versagens in Policy-Netzwerken. *Journal fuer Sozialforschung, 32*(1), 33-60.

Anheier, H., & Salamon, L. (Eds.). (1998). *The nonprofit sector in developing countries.* Manchester, UK: Manchester University Press.

Aris, S. (1985). *Going bust: Inside the bankruptcy business.* London: Andre Deutsch.

Arnold, U. (1990). *Entwicklung einer Marketing-Konzeption der Werkstätten für Behinderte. Forschungsbericht im Auftrag des Bundesministers für Sozialordnung. BMA-Reihe Sozialforschung 208* [Development of marketing concepts for workshops for handicapped persons]. Research report under the auspices of the Federal Ministry for Labor and Social Affairs (Report Series, Vol. 208). Bonn: Federal Ministry for Labor and Social Affairs.

Arrow, K. J. (1963). Uncertainty and the welfare economics of medical care. *American Economic Review, 53,* 941-973.

Bartol, K. M., & Martin, D. C. (1994). *Management.* New York: McGraw-Hill.

Baum, J. A. C., & Oliver, C. (1991). Institutional linkages and organizational mortality. *Administrative Science Quarterly, 36,* 187-218.

Baum, J., & Singh, J. (1994). Organizational niches and the dynamics of organizational mortality. *American Journal of Sociology, 100,* 346-380.

Berlant, J. L. (1976). *Profession and monopoly: A study of medicine in the United States and Great Britain.* Berkeley: University of California Press.

Best B schools. (1988, November 28). *Business Week,* p. 76.

Biddle, G. C., Bowen, R. M., & Wallace, J. S. (1996). *Evidence on the relative and incremental information content of EVA, residual income, earnings and operating cash flow.* Unpublished manuscript, University of Washington.

Bielefeld, W. (1992). Funding uncertainty and nonprofit strategies in the 1980's. *Nonprofit Management and Leadership, 2,* 381-402.

Bielefeld, W. (1994). What affects nonprofit survival? *Nonprofit Management and Leadership, 5,* 19-36.

Bilofsky, H. S., & Burks, C. (1988). The GenBank (R) genetic sequence data bank. *Nucleic Acids Research, 16,* 1861-1864.

Blau, P. (1955). *The dynamics of bureaucracy.* Chicago: University of Chicago Press.

Block, F. (1987). *Revising state theory.* Philadelphia: Temple University Press.

Bourdieu, P. (1975). The specificity of the scientific field. *Social Science Information, 14,* 19-47.

Bourdieu, P., & Wacquant, L. (1992). *An invitation to reflexive sociology.* Chicago: University of Chicago Press.

Bovens, M. A. P. (1998). *The quest for responsibility.* Cambridge, UK: Cambridge University Press.

Bovens, M. A. P., & 't Hart, P. (1996). *Understanding policy fiascoes.* New Brunswick, NJ: Transaction.

Bovens, M. A. P., 't Hart, P., Dekker, S., Verheuvel, G., & De Vries, E. (1998). The mass media and policy disasters: The IRT disaster and the crisis of crimefighting in The Netherlands. In P. Gray & P. 't Hart (Eds.), *Public policy disasters in Western Europe.* London: Routledge.

Bowen, W., Nygren, T., Turner, S., & Duffy, E. (1994). *The charitable nonprofits.* San Francisco: Jossey-Bass.

Braun, D. (1997). *Die politische Steuerung der Wissenschaft: Ein Beitrag zum "kooperativen" Staat.* Frankfurt: Campus.

Breedveld, W. (1996, February 17). Onbegrijpelijk dat ik zo stom heb kunnen zijn [How could I have been so stupid?] (interview with Ed van Thijn). *Trouw.*

Brint, S. (1994). *In an age of experts: The changing role of professionals in politics and public life.* Princeton, NJ: Princeton University Press.

Broszat, M. (1984). *Die Machergreifung.* München: DTV.

Brüderl, J., Preisendörfer, P., & Ziegler, R. (1992). Survival chances of newly founded business organizations. *American Sociological Review, 57,* 227-242.

Brüderl, J., & Schüssler, R. (1990). Organizational mortality: The liabilities of newness and adolescence. *Administrative Science Quarterly, 35,* 530-547.

Bryman, A. (1992). *Charisma and leadership in organizations.* London: Sage.

Burrough, B., & Helyar, J. (1990). *Barbarians at the gate: The fall of RJR Nabisco.* New York: Harper & Row.

Burt, R. S. (1983). *Corporate profits and co-optation: Networks of market constraints and directorate ties in the American economy.* New York: Academic Press.

Burt, R. S. (1983). A note on inferences concerning network subgroups. In R. S. Burt & M. J. Minor (Eds.), *Applied network analysis: A methodological introduction* (pp. 283-301). Beverly Hills, CA: Sage.

Burt, R. S. (1987). *STRUCTURE.* Technical Report TR2, Columbia University, Center for the Social Sciences.

Burt, R. S. (1992). *Structural holes.* Cambridge, MA: Harvard University Press.

Burt, R. S., & Schott, T. (1985). Relation contents in multiple networks. *Social Science Research, 14,* 287-308.

Bush, V. (1960). *Science, the endless frontier: A report to the president.* Washington, DC: National Science Foundation. (Original work published 1945)

California Department of Commerce. (1986, May). *Drugs and pharmaceuticals* (Report R-66A, prepared by the Institute for the Future). Sacramento: California Department of Commerce.

Cameron, K. S., Kim, M. U., & Whetten, D. A. (1987). Organizational effects of decline and turbulence. *Administrative Science Quarterly, 32,* 222-240.

Carroll, G. R. (1983). A stochastic model of organizational mortality: Review and reanalysis. *Social Science Review, 12,* 303-329.

Carroll, G. R., & Delacroix, J. (1982). Organizational mortality in the newspaper industries of Argentina and Ireland: An ecological approach. *Administrative Science Quarterly, 27,* 169-198.

Carroll, G. R., & Hannan, M. T. (1989). Density dependence in the evolution of populations of newspaper organizations. *American Sociological Review, 54,* 524-541.

Carroll, G. R., & Hannan, M. T. (1995). *Organizations in industry: Strategy, structure, and selection.* New York: Oxford University Press.

Carroll, P. (1993). *Big blues: The unmaking of IBM.* New York: Crown.

Carruthers, B. G., & Halliday, T. C. (1998). *Rescuing business: The making of corporate bankruptcy law in England and the United States.* New York: Oxford University Press.

Child, J. (1972). Organizational structure, environment and performance: The role of strategic choice. *Sociology, 6*(1), 1-22.

Clarke, L. (in press). *Mission improbable: Using fantasy documents to tame disaster.* Chicago: University of Chicago Press.

Cohen, M. D., March, J. C., & Olsen, J. P. (1972). A garbage can model of organizational choice. *Administrative Science Quarterly, 17,* 1-25.

Coleman, J. S. (1990). *Foundations of social theory.* Cambridge, MA: Belknap.

Collins, R. (1979). *The credential society: An historical sociology of education and stratification.* New York: Academic Press.

Collins, R. (1981). Crises and declines in credential systems. In *Sociology since midcentury: Essays in theory cumulation.* New York: Academic Press.

Cork, K. (with H. Barty-King). (1988). *Cork on Cork.* London: Macmillan.

Cork Report. (1982). *Insolvency law and practice: Report of the Insolvency Law Review Committee* (Cmnd. 8558). London: Her Majesty's Stationary Office.

Couderc, M-L. (1996). Adaptation of some former research units to the new economic environment in Russia. *Science and Public Policy, 23,* 375-384.

Cray, D., Mallory, G. R., Butler, R. J., Hickson, D. J., & Wilson, D. C. (1988). Sporadic, fluid and constricted processes: Three types of strategic decision-making in organizations. *Journal of Management Studies, 25*(1), 13-39.

Crozier, M. (1974). *The stalled society.* New York: Viking.

Crozier, M., & Friedberg, E. (1977). *L'Acteur et le systéme.* Paris: Seuil.

Crozier, M., Huntington, S. P., & Watanuki, J. (1975). *The crisis of democracy.* New York: New York University Press.

Cyert, R. M., & March, J. G. (1963). *A behavioral theory of the firm.* Englewood Cliffs, NJ: Prentice Hall.

Danzon, P. M., & Percy, A. (1995, July). *The effects of price regulation on productivity in pharmaceuticals.* Paper presented at the National Bureau of Economic Research Summer Institute on Productivity, Cambridge, MA.

Darby, M. R. (1976, June). Rational expectations under conditions of costly information. *Journal of Finance, 31*(3), 889-995.

Davis, J. A. (1979). The Davis/Holland/Leinhardt studies: An overview. In P. W. Holland & S. Leinhardt (Eds.), *Perspectives on social networks* (pp. 51-62). New York: Academic Press.

Davis, J. A., & Leinhardt, S. A. (1971). The structure of positive interpersonal relations in small groups. In J. Berger (Ed.), *Sociological theories in progress.* Boston: Houghton Mifflin.

Delacroix, J., Swaminathan, A., & Solt, M. (1989). Density dependence versus population dynamics: An ecological study of failings in the California wine industry. *American Sociological Review, 54,* 245-262.

Delaney, K. (1992a). Shifting risk during business bankruptcy. In J. Short, Jr. & L. Clarke (Eds.), *When organizations confront risk: Decision processes and outcomes* (pp. 103-118). Boulder, CO: Westview.

Delaney, K. (1992b). *Strategic bankruptcy: How corporations and creditors use Chapter 11 to their advantage.* Berkeley: University of California Press.

Delaney, K. (1994). The organizational construction of the bottom line. *Social Problems, 41,* 497-518.

Dezalay, Y. (1992). *Marchands de droit.* Paris: Fayard.

DiMaggio, P., & Powell, W. (1983). The iron cage revisited: Institutional isomorphism and collective rationality in organizational fields. *American Sociological Review, 48,* 147-160.

DiMaggio, P., & Powell, W. (1991). The iron cage revisited: Institutional isomorphism and collective rationality in organizational fields. In W. Powell & P. DiMaggio (Eds.), *The new institutionalism in organizational analysis* (pp. 63-82). Chicago: University of Chicago Press.

Dodd, J. L., & S. Chen. (1996). EVA: A new panacea? *Business & Economic Review, 42,* 26-28.

Dutton, J. E., & Duncan R. B. (1989). The influence of the strategic planning process on strategic change. *Strategic Management Journal, 8*(2), 103-116.

Edelman, M. (1977). *Political language: Words that succeed and policies that fail.* New York: Academic Press.

Edelman, M. (1988). *Constructing the political spectacle.* Chicago: University of Chicago Press.

Eisenhardt, K. (1989). Making fast strategic decisions in high-velocity environments. *Academy of Management Journal, 32*(3), 543-576.

Eisenhardt, K., & Bourgeois, L. J. III. (1988). Politics of strategic decision making in high-velocity environments: Toward a midrange theory. *Academy of Management Journal, 31*(4), 737-770.

Ellis, R. J. (1994). *Presidential lightning rods: The politics of blame avoidance.* Lawrence: University of Kansas Press.

Elsbach, K. D., & Kramer, R. M. (1996). Members' responses to organizational identity threats: Encountering and countering the *Business Week* rankings. *Administrative Science Quarterly, 41,* 442-476.

Emery, F. E., & Trist, E. L. (1965). The causal texture of organizational environments. *Human Relations, 18,* 21-32.

Enquêtecommissie Opsporingsmethoden. (1996). *Opsporing gezocht.* Den Haag, The Netherlands: SDU.

Erikson, K. (1994). *A new species of trouble.* New York: Norton.

Estes, C. L., Binney, E. A., & Bergthold, L. A. (1989). How the legitimacy of the sector has eroded. In V. A. Hodgkinson & R. W. Lyman (Eds.), *The future of the nonprofit sector: Challenges, changes, and policy considerations.* San Francisco: Jossey-Bass.

Fama, E. F. (1980). Agency problems and the theory of the firm. *Journal of Public Economy, 88,* 288-305.

Fayol, H. (1949). *General and industrial management* (C. Storrs, Trans.). London: Pitman.

Feder, B. (1990, December 13). The disputed deal at Eagle-Pitcher. *New York Times,* p. D2.

Federal Emergency Management Agency. (1986). *Post exercise assessment: February 13, 1986.* Exercise of the Local Emergency Response Organization (LERO), as specified in the LILCO Transition Plan for the Shoreham Nuclear Power Station, Shoreham, NY, April 17.

Feldman, D. C., & Arnold, H. J. (1983). *Managing individual and group behavior in organizations.* New York: McGraw-Hill.

Ferguson, K., & Blackwell, K. (1995). *Pensions in crisis.* New York: Arcade.

Festinger, L. N. (1957). *A theory of cognitive dissonance.* Stanford, CA: Stanford University Press.

Fisher, F. M. (1988). Accounting data and the economic performance of the firm. *Journal of Accounting and Public Policy, 7,* 256.

Flynn, J. (with J. Carey, J. Weber, & J. O'C. Hamilton). (1996, March 4). Is SmithKline's future in its genes? R&D Chief Poste is racing ahead in gene-based drugs. *Business Week,* pp. 80-81.

Freeman, J., Carroll, G. R., & Hannan, M. T. (1983). The liability of newness: Age dependence in organizational death rates. *American Journal of Sociology, 48,* 692-710.

Freidson, E. (1986). *Professional powers: A study of the institutionalization of formal knowledge.* Chicago: University of Chicago Press.

Galanter, M. (1974). Why the haves come out ahead: Speculations on the limits of legal change. *Law & Society Review, 9,* 95-160.

Galaskiewicz, J. (1985). *Social organization of an urban grants economy: A study of business philanthropy and nonprofit organizations.* Orlando, FL: Academic Press.

Galaskiewicz, J. (1990). *Corporate-nonprofit linkages in Minneapolis-St. Paul: Findings from a longitudinal study, 1980-1988.* Research report, University of Minnesota, Department of Sociology.

Galaskiewicz, J., & Bielefeld, W. (1990). Growth, decline, and organizational strategies: A panel study of nonprofit organizations, 1980-1988. In *The nonprofit sector (NGO'S) in the United States and abroad: Cross-cultural perspectives* (Spring Research Forum Working Paper). Washington, DC: Independent Sector.

Galaskiewicz, J., & Bielefeld, W. (in press). *Nonprofit organizations in an age of uncertainty: A study of organizational change.* Hawthorne, NY: Aldine de Gruyter.

Geertz, C. (1963). *Agricultural involution: The process of ecological change in Indonesia.* Berkeley: University of California Press.

GenBank, Release 65.0 [Machine-readable database]. (1990). Palo Alto, CA: IntelliGentics.

Glassman, R. B. (1973). Persistence and loose coupling in living systems. *Behavioral Science, 18,* 83-98.

Goodin, R. E. (1980). *Manipulatory politics.* New Haven, CT: Yale University Press.

Goss, K. A. (1993, June 15). A crisis of credibility for America's nonprofits. *Chronicle of Philanthropy,* pp. 1, 38-41.

Gould, S. J. (1988). Trends as changes in variance: A new slant on progress and directionality. *Journal of Paleontology, 62,* 326.

Gould, S. J. (1996). *Full house.* New York: Harmony.

Granovetter, M. (1973). The strength of weak ties. *American Journal of Sociology, 78,* 1360-1380.

Green Paper. (1980). *Bankruptcy: A consultative document* (Cmnd. No. 7967). London: Her Majesty's Stationary Office.

Greenwood, R., & Hinings, C. R. (1993). Understanding strategic change: The contribution of archetypes. *Academy of Management Journal, 36*(5), 1052-1081.

Grinyer, P., & McKiernan, P. (1994, September). *Sharpbenders revisited.* Paper presented at the British Academy of Management Conference, Lancaster University, England.

Gronbjerg, K. A. (1993). *Understanding nonprofit funding. Managing revenues in social services and community development organizations.* San Francisco: Jossey-Bass.

Habermas, J. (1985). *Die Neue Unübersichtlichkeit.* Frankfurt: Suhrkamp.

Hage, J. (1980). *Theories of organizations: Form, process and transformation.* New York: John Wiley.

Hager, M., Galaskiewicz, J., Bielefeld, W., & Pins, J. (1996). Tales from the grave: Organizations' accounts of their own demise. *American Behavioral Scientist, 39*(8), 975-994.

Hager, M., & Jorgensen, C. (1996, August). *Changes in the nonprofit sector, 1980-92: Evidence from four studies.* Paper presented at the annual meeting of the American Sociological Association, New York City, New York.

Hall, R., Clark, J., Giordano, P. Johnson, P., & Van Roekel, M. (1977). Patterns of interorganizational relations. *Administrative Science Quarterly, 22,* 457-474.

Halliday, T. C., & Carruthers, B. G. (1993, August). Redistributing property and jurisdictional rights across the public-private frontier: Professions and bankruptcy reforms in Britain and the United States. *Droit et Société: Revue Internationale de Théorie du Droit et de Sociologie Juridique, 23/24,* 79-113. (Reprinted in English translation, American Bar Foundation Working Paper 9314)

Halliday, T. C., & Carruthers, B. G. (1996). The moral regulation of markets: Professions, privatization, and the English Insolvency Act of 1986. *Accounting, Organizations, and Society, 21*(4), 371-413.

Halliday, T. C., Carruthers, B. G., & Parrott, S. (1993). *Legislating corporate failure: The structure of security and the politics of corporate reorganization in Britain and the United States* (American Bar Foundation Working Paper 9311). Chicago: American Bar Foundation.

Hallinan, M. (1974). *The structure of positive sentiment.* Amsterdam: Elsevier.

Halpern, S. A. (1992). Dynamics of professional control: Internal coalitions and crossprofessional boundaries. *American Journal of Sociology, 97,* 994-1021.

Hambrick, D. C., & D'Aveni, R. A. (1988). Large corporate failures and downward spirals. *Administrative Science Quarterly, 33,* 1-23.

Hannan, M. T., & Carroll, G. R. (1992). *Dynamics of organizational populations: Density, legitimation, and competition.* Oxford, UK: Oxford University Press.

Hannan, M. T., & Freeman, J. (1984). Structural inertia and organizational change. *American Sociological Review, 49,* 149-164.

Hansmann, H. B. (1980). The role of nonprofit enterprise. *Yale Law Journal, 89,* 835-901.

Hanson, G. H. (1995. May). Incomplete contracts, risk, and ownership. *International Economic Review, 36*(2), 341-365.

Hart, P. 't. (1993). Symbols, rituals, and power: The lost dimensions of crisis management. *Journal of Contingencies and Crisis Management, 1*(1), 36-50.

Hermann, C. F. (1963). Some consequences of crisis which limit the viability of organizations. *Administrative Science Quarterly, 8,* 61-72.

Hickson, D. J. (1987). Decision-making at the top of organizations. *Annual Review of Sociology, 13,* 165-192.

Hickson, D. J., Butler, R. J., Cray, D., Mallory, G. R., & Wilson, D. C. (1986). *Top decisions: Strategic decision-making in organizations.* San Francisco: Jossey-Bass.

Hickson, D. J., & Arruda, C. A. (1996). Sensitivity to societal culture in managerial decision-making: An Anglo-Brazilian comparison. In P. Joynt & M. Warner (Eds.), *Managing across cultures* (pp. 179-201). London: International Thompson.

Hickson, D. J., & Pugh, D. S. (1995). *Management worldwide: The impact of societal culture on organizations around the globe.* New York: Penguin.

Hilton, G. W., & Due, J. P. (1964). *The electric interurban railways in America.* Stanford, CA: Stanford University Press.

Hirschman, A. O. (1970). *Exit, voice, and loyalty: Responses to decline in firms, organizations and states.* Cambridge, MA: Harvard University Press.

Hirschman, A. O. (1981). *Essays in trespassing: Economics to politics and beyond.* Princeton, NJ: Princeton University Press.

Holland, P. W. (1971). Transitivity in structural models of small groups. *Comparative Group Studies, 2,* 107-124.

Holland, P. W. (1977). A method for analyzing structure in sociometric data. In S. Leinhardt (Ed.), *Social networks: A developing paradigm* (pp. 411-432). New York: Academic Press.

Holland, P. W., & Leinhardt, S. A. (1970). A method for detecting structure in sociometric data. *American Journal of Sociology, 75,* 492-513.

Huff, A. S., & Reger, R. K. (1987). A review of strategic process research. *Journal of Management, 13*(2), 211-236.

Hunsaker, P. L., & Cook, W. C. (1986). *Managing organizational behavior.* Reading, MA: Addison-Wesley.

Huntington, S. P. (1996). *Clash of civilizations and the remaking of world order.* New York: Simon & Schuster.

Huse, E. F., & Bowditch, J. L. (1977). *Behavior in organizations: A systems approach to managing.* Reading, MA: Addison-Wesley.

Impell Corporation. (1986). *Drill report for June 6, 1986 for LERO facilities, ECO, ENC, and Riverhead staging area.* Attachment 7 in USA, NRC, Docket No. 50-322-OL-5, March 20, 1987, Regarding Contention EX 50, Training of off-site emergency response personnel, October 31.

Insolvency White Paper. (1984). *A white paper: A revised framework for insolvency law* (Cmnd. No. 9175). London: Her Majesty's Stationery Office.

Ittner, C., Larcker, D., & Meyer, M. W. (1997). *Performance, compensation, and the balanced scorecard.* Unpublished manuscript, University of Pennsylvania, the Wharton School.

Janis, I. L. (1972). *Victims of groupthink: A psychological study of foreign policy decisions and fiascos.* Boston: Houghton Mifflin.

Janis, I. L. (1982). *Groupthink: Psychological studies of policy decisions and fiascoes.* Boston: Houghton Mifflin.

Johnsen, E. C. (1985). Network macrostructure models for the Davis-Leinhardt set of empirical sociomatrices. *Social Networks, 7,* 203-224.

Johnson, T. (1990, July). *Thatcher's professions: The state and professions in Britain.* Paper presented at the XII World Congress of Sociology, Madrid.

Jorion, P. (1995). *Big bets gone bad: Derivatives and bankruptcy in Orange County.* San Diego: Academic Press.

Kalu, O. (1978). *The divided people of God. Church union movement in Nigeria: 1875-1966.* New York: NOK.

Karylowski, J. (1982). Two types of altruistic behavior: Doing good to feel good or to make others feel good. In V. J. Derlega & J. Grzelak (Eds.), *Cooperation and helping behavior: Theories and research.* New York: American Economic Review.

Keller, M. (1989). *Rude awakening: The rise and fall for recovery of General Motors.* New York: William Morrow.

Kennedy, P. (1987). *The rise and fall of the great powers.* New York: Random House.

Kets de Vries, M., & Miller, D. (1984). *The neurotic organization.* San Francisco: Jossey-Bass.

Kimberly, J. R., & Miles, R. H. (Eds.). (1980). *The organizational life cycle: Issues in the creation, transformation, and decline of organizations.* San Francisco: Jossey-Bass.

Kingdon, J. (1984). *Agendas, alternatives, and public policies.* Glenview, IL: Scott Foresman.

Knoke, D. (1981). Commitment and detachment in voluntary associations. *American Sociological Review, 46*, 141-158.

Kocka, J. (1997). *Wissenschaft und Politik in der DDR*. Draft chapter for the final report of the working group, Wissenschaften und Wiedervereinigung of the Berlin-Brandenburgische Akademie der Wissenschaften.

Kreps, G. A. (1984). Sociological inquiry and disaster research. *Annual Review of Sociology, 10*, 309-330.

Kuran, T. (1995). *Private truths, public lies: The social consequences of preference falsification*. Cambridge, MA: Harvard University Press.

Labaton, S. (1990. June 11). Solving problems in the Manville trust. *New York Times*, p. D2.

LaPalombara, J. (1987). *Democracy Italian style*. New Haven, CT: Yale University Press.

Laroche, H. (1995). From decision to action in organizations: Decision-making as a social representation. *Organization Science, 6*(1), 62-75.

Larson, M. S. (1977). *The rise of professionalism*. Berkeley: University of California Press.

Larson, M. (1990). In the matter of experts and professionals, or how it is impossible to leave nothing unsaid. In R. Torstendahl & M. Burrage (Eds.), *The formation of professions: Knowledge, state and strategy* (pp. 24-50). London: Sage.

Laux, L., & Schütz, A. (Eds.). (1996). *"Wir, die wir gut sind": Die Selbstdarstellung von Politikern zwischen Glorifizierung und Glaubwuerdigkeit* ["We the great": The self-presentation of politicians between glorification and credibility]. München: DTV.

Lawrence, P. R., & Lorsch, J. W. (1967). *Organization and environment*. Boston: Harvard University Press.

Lee, K. B., Jr., & Burrill, G. S. (1995). *Biotech 95: Reform, restructure, renewal* (Ernst & Young Ninth Annual Report on the Biotechnology Industry). San Francisco: Ernst & Young.

Leibenstein, H. (1978). *Beyond economic man. A new foundation for microeconomics*. Cambridge, MA: Harvard University Press.

Lepsius, R. M. (1978). From fragmented party democracy to government by emergency decree and National Socialist takeover: Germany. In J. J. Linz & A. Stepan (Eds.), *The breakdown of democratic regimes: Europe* (pp. 34-79). Baltimore: Johns Hopkins University Press.

Levi, M. (1988). *Of rule and revenue*. Berkeley: University of California Press.

Levy, A., & Merry, U. (1986). *Organizational transformation: Approaches, strategies, theories*. New York: Praeger.

Lewis, P. (1990). *The crisis of Argentine capitalism*. Chapel Hill: University of North Carolina Press.

Lindblom, C. E. (1959). The science of muddling through. *Public Administration Review, 19*(2), 79-88.

Linz, J. J., & Stepan, A. (Eds.). (1978). *The breakdown of democratic regimes: Crisis, breakdown, and re-equilibration*. Baltimore: Johns Hopkins University Press.

Lipshitz, R. (1995). The road to Desert Storm. *Organization Studies, 16*(2), 243-263.

Lyles, M. A., & Mitroff, I. I. (1980). Organizational problem formulation: An empirical study. *Administrative Science Quarterly, 25,* 102-118.

Machiavelli, N. (1947). *The prince* (T. G. Bergin, Trans. & Ed.). Arlington Heights, IL: Harlan Davidson.

Makadok, R., & Walker, G. (1996). Search and selection in the money market fund industry. *Strategic Management Journal, 17,* 39-54.

Mallory, G. R. (1987). *The speed of strategic decisions.* Unpublished doctoral dissertation, University of Bradford Management Centre, England.

March, J. G., & Simon, H. A. (1958). *Organizations.* New York: John Wiley.

Marger, M. (1981). *Elites and masses: An introduction to political sociology.* New York: Van Nostrand.

Marple, D. (1982). Technological innovation and organizational survival: A population ecology study of nineteenth-century American railroads. *Sociological Quarterly, 23,* 107-116.

Mayntz, R. (1994a). Academy of sciences in crisis: A case study of a fruitless struggle for survival. In U. Schimank & A. Stucke (Eds.), *Coping with trouble: How science reacts to political disturbances of research conditions* (pp. 163-188). New York: St. Martin's.

Mayntz, R. (1994b). *Deutsche Forschung im Einigunsprozeß: Die Transformation der Akademie der Wissenschaften der DDR 1989-1992.* Frankfurt/Main: Campus.

Mayntz, R. (1997). Forschung als Dienstleistung? Zur gesellschaftlichen Einbettung der Wissenschaft (Akademievorlesung am 25. April 1996). In *Berlin-Brandenburgische Akademie der Wissenschaften. Berichte und Abhandlungen* (Vol. 3, pp. 135-154). Berlin: Akademie Verlag.

Mayntz, R., Schimank, U., & Weingart, P. (Eds.). (1995). *Transformation mittel- und osteuropäischer Wissenschaftssysteme.* Opladen: Leske & Budrich.

Mayntz, R., Schimank, U., & Weingart, P. (Eds.). (1998). *East European academies in transition.* Dordrecht, Netherlands: Kluwer.

McCaffrey, D. (1991). *The politics of nuclear power.* Boston: Kluwer.

Meyer, A. D. (1982). Adapting to environmental jolts. *Administrative Science Quarterly, 27,* 515-537.

Meyer, J. W., & Rowan, B. (1977). Institutionalized organizations. Formal structure as myth and ceremony. *American Journal of Sociology, 83,* 340-363.

Meyer, J. W., & Scott, W. R. (1983). *Organizational environments: Ritual and rationality.* Beverly Hills, CA: Sage.

Meyer, M. W., & Gupta, V. (1994). The performance paradox. *Research in Organizational Behavior, 16,* 303-363.

Meyer, M. W., & Zucker, L. G. (1989). *Permanently failing organizations.* Newbury Park, CA: Sage.

Michels, R. (1962). *Political parties: A sociological study of oligarchical tendencies of modern democracy.* New York: Free Press.

Middleton, M. (1987). Nonprofit boards of directors. Beyond the governance function. In W. Powell (Ed.), *The nonprofit sector. A research handbook* (pp. 141-153). New Haven, CT: Yale University Press.

Millar, B. (1991, February 12). United Way emphasizes donor choice. *Chronicle of Philanthropy*, pp. 23-25.

Millar, B., & Moore, J. (1991, July 2). Corporate gifts harder to obtain. *Chronicle of Philanthropy*, pp. 1, 12-14.

Miller, D. (1994). What happens after success: The perils of excellence. *Journal of Management Studies, 31*(3), 325-358.

Miller, P., & Power, M. (1993). Calculating corporate failure. In Y. D. Dezalay & D. Sugarman (Eds.), *Professional competition and the social construction of markets: Lawyers, accountants, and the emergence of the transnational state.* London: Routledge.

Miller, S. J. (1990). *Successfully implementing strategic decisions.* Unpublished doctoral dissertation, University of Bradford Management Centre, England.

Miller, S., Hickson, D. J., & Wilson, D. C. (1993, July). *Expansive gestures: Fancies and follies in strategic decision-making.* Paper presented to the 11th European Group for Organization Studies Colloquium, Paris.

Milliken, F. J. (1990). Perceiving and interpreting environmental change: An examination of college administrators' interpretation of changing demographics. *Academy of Management Journal, 33,* 42-63.

Milofsky, C. (1987). Neighborhood-based organizations: A market analogy. In W. W. Powell (Ed.), *The non-profit sector: A research handbook* (pp. 227-295). New Haven, CT: Yale University Press.

Mintzberg, H. (1990). *Mintzberg on management.* Englewood Cliffs, NJ: Free Press.

Mitchell, W., & Singh, K. (1995). Spillback effects of expansion when product-types and firm-types differ. *Journal of Management, 21*(1), 81-100.

Moody's Investors Service, Inc. (1988a). *Moody's industrial manual 1988.* New York: Author.

Moody's Investors Service, Inc. (1988b). *Moody's international manual 1988.* New York: Author.

Moody's Investors Service, Inc. (1988c). *Moody's OTC industrial manual 1988.* New York: Author.

Moody's Investors Service, Inc. (1995a). *Moody industrial manual 1995.* New York: Author.

Moody's Investors Service, Inc. (1995b). *Moody international manual 1995.* New York: Author.

Moody's Investors Service, Inc. (1995c). *Moody's OTC industrial manual 1995.* New York: Author.

Mucciaroni, G. (1990). *The political failure of employment policy, 1945-1982.* Pittsburgh: Pittsburgh University Press.

Murphy, R. (1988). *Social closure. The theory of monopolization and exclusion.* Oxford, UK: Clarendon.

Neumann, S. (1986). *Die Parteien der Weimarer Republik.* Stuttgart: Kohlhammer. (Original work published 1932)

Noma, E., & Smith, D. R. (1978). SHED: A fortran IV program for the analysis of small group sociometric structure. *Behavior Research Methods and Instrumentation, 10,* 60-62.

Nuclear Regulatory Commission. (1983). *Before the Atomic Safety and Licensing Board, in the matter of Long Island Lighting Company, Shoreham Nuclear Power Station* (Unit 1, Docket No. 50-322-OL-3). Emergency Planning Proceeding, Testimony of Matthew C. Cordaro, Russell R. Dynes, William G. Johnson, Dennis S. Mileti, John H. Sorensen, and John A. Weismantle on behalf of the Long Island Lighting Company on Phase II Emergency Planning, Contention 25 (Role Conflict), November 18.

Nuclear Regulatory Commission. (1986). *Emergency planning contentions relating to the February 13, 1986 exercise* (Docket No. 50-322-OL-5). In the matter of Long Island Lighting Company, Shoreham Nuclear Power Station, Unit 1, United States of American Nuclear Regulatory Commission, Before the Atomic Safety and Licensing Board, August 1, 1986.

Nuclear Regulatory Commission. (1987a). *Before the Atomic Safety and Licensing Board* (Docket No. 50-322-OL-5). Regarding Contention EX 50—Training of Offsite Emergency Response Personnel, March 20.

Nuclear Regulatory Commission. (1987b). *Before the Atomic Safety and Licensing Board, In the matter of Long Island Lighting Company* (Docket No. 50-322-0L-5) (EP Exercise). Direct testimony of Assistant Chief Inspector Richard C. Roberts, Inspector Richard Dormer, Inspector Philip McGuire, and Deputy Inspector Edwin J. Michel on behalf of Suffolk County regarding Contention EX 41—Mobilization and dispatch of road crew and removal of impediments from the roadways during the February 13, 1986, Shoreham Exercise.

Nuclear Regulatory Commission. (1989). *Nuclear Regulatory Commission, Before the Atomic Safety and Licensing Board, In the Matter of the Long Island Lighting Company* (Docket No. 50-322-OL-5R). Regarding Contention 20, Fundamental Flaws in LILCO's Training Program, February 2.

Nutt, P. (1986). Tactics of implementation. *Academy of Management Journal, 29*(2), 230-261.

O'Donnell, G. A. (1973). *Modernization and bureaucratic-authoritarianism.* Berkeley: University of California, Institute of International Studies.

Olson, M. (1971). *The logic of collective action: Public goods and the theory of groups.* Cambridge, MA: Harvard University Press.

Olson, M. (1982). *The rise and decline of nations. Economic growth, stagflation and social rigidities.* New Haven, CT: Yale University Press.

Organization for Economic Cooperation and Development. (1994). *Science, technology and innovation policies. Federation of Russia* (Vol. I). Paris: Author.

Parkin, F. (1979). *Marxism and class theory.* New York: Columbia University Press.

Pauly, M. (1968). The economics of moral hazard. *American Economic Review, 58,* 531-537.

Pension Benefits Guarantee Corporation. (1994). *Annual report.* Washington, DC: Author.

Perrow, C. (1984). *Normal accidents: Living with high-risk technologies.* New York: Basic Books.

Peters, B. G. (1992). Tragic choices: Administrative rulemaking and policy choice. In R. A. Chapman (Ed.), *Ethics in public service.* Edinburgh: Edinburgh University Press.

Peters, T., & Waterman, R., Jr. (1982). *In search of excellence: Lessons from America's top run companies.* New York: Harper & Row.

Pettigrew, A., & Whipp, R. (1991). *Managing change for competitive success.* Oxford, UK: Blackwell.

Pfeffer, J., & Salancik, G. R. (1978). *The external control of organizations: A resource dependence perspective.* New York: Harper & Row.

Pharmaceutical Manufacturers Association. (1993). 1993 Survey: 143 biotechnology medicines in development. In H. S. Price & R. Greenshields (Eds.), *The biotechnology report 1993/94.* Hong Kong: Campden.

Phillips 66. (1994, December 15). Transforming for the 1990s. HBS Case 9-194-022, rev., p. 15.

Powell, W. W., & DiMaggio, P. J. (Eds.). (1991). *The new institutionalism in organizational analysis.* Chicago: University of Chicago Press.

Pugh, D. S., & Hickson, D. J. (Eds.). (1976). *Organizational structure in its context: The Aston Programme I.* Westmead, Farnb.: Saxon.

Quarantelli, E. L., & Dynes, R. R. (1977). Response to social crisis and disaster. *Annual Review of Sociology, 3,* 23-49.

Quinn, J. B. (1978, Fall). Strategic change: Logical incrementalism. *Sloan Management Review,* pp. 7-21.

Quinn, J. B. (1980). *Strategies for change: Logical incrementalism.* Homewood, IL: Irwin.

Rajagopalan, N., Rasheed, A. M. A., & Datta, D. K. (1993). Strategic decision processes: Critical review and future directions. *Journal of Management, 19*(2), 349-384.

Robinson, J. E. (1992). *Freefall: The needless destruction of Eastern Air Lines and the valiant struggle to save it.* New York: HarperBusiness.

Rokkan, S. (1975). Dimensions of state formation and nation-building: A possible paradigm for research on variations within Europe. In C. Tilly (Ed.), *The formation of national states in Western Europe.* Princeton, NJ: Princeton University Press.

Romo, F. P. (1986). *Moral dynamics: A blockmodeling study of conflict in a mental hospital.* Unpublished doctoral dissertation, Yale University, Department of Sociology.

Romo, F. P., & Anheier, H. K. (1991). *The omega phenomenon: A social infrastructural study of social choice* (Russell Sage Foundation Working Paper, No. 16). New York: Russell Sage.

Romo, F. P., & Anheier, H. K. (1996). *Comparing network algorithms: Combinatorial and distance-based optimizations.* Working Paper series of the Institute for Social Analysis, State University of New York, Stony Brook.

Rosenthal, U., 't Hart, P., & Cachet, A. (1987). *Politiemanagement: Een Politiek-Bestuurlijke Visie.* Arnhem, The Netherlands: Gouda Quint.

Ross, J., & Staw, B. (1986). Expo 86: An escalation prototype. *Administrative Science Quarterly, 31*(2), 274-297.

Ross, J., & Staw, B. (1993). Organizational escalation and exit: Lessons from the Shoreham nuclear power plant. *Academy of Management Journal, 36*(4), 701-732.

Ross, S. A. (1973). The economic theory of agency: The principal's problem. *American Economic Review, 63,* 134-139.

Rueschemeyer, D. (1986). Comparing legal professions cross-nationally: From a professions-centered to a state-centered approach. *American Bar Foundation Research Journal, 3,* 415-446.

Sagan, S. (1993). *The limits of safety.* Princeton, NJ: Princeton University Press.

Salamon, L. M., & Anheier, H. K. (1996). *The emerging nonprofit sector: An overview.* Manchester, UK: Manchester University Press.

Schermerhorn, J. R., Jr., Hunt, J. G., & Osborn, R. N. (1988). *Managing organizational behavior.* New York: John Wiley.

Schimank, U., & Stucke, A. (Eds.). (1994). *Coping with trouble: How science reacts to political disturbances of research conditions.* Frankfurt/Main: Campus.

Schmidt, S., & Kochan, T. (1977). Interorganizational relationships: Patterns and motivations. *Administrative Science Quarterly, 22,* 220-234.

Schumpeter, J. A. (1976). *Capitalism, socialism, and democracy.* New York: Harper & Row.

Schütz, A. (1996). Selbstdarstellung in der Defensive Reaktionen in politischen Skandalen. In L. Laux & A. Schütz (Eds.), *"Wir, die wir gut sind": Die Selbstdarstellung von Politikern zwischen Glorifizierung und Glaubwürdigkeit* (pp. 114-140). München: DTV.

Seibel, W. (1989). The function of mellow weakness. Nonprofit organizations as problem nonsolvers in Germany. In E. James (Ed.), *The nonprofit sector in international perspective: Studies in comparative culture and policy* (pp. 177-192). New York: Oxford University Press.

Selle, P., & Oymyr, B. (1992). Explaining changes in the population of voluntary organizations: The roles of aggregate and individual level data. *Nonprofit and Voluntary Sector Quarterly, 21,* 147-179.

Shackleton, V. (1995). *Business leadership.* London: Routledge.

Sheppard, J. (1995, March). A resource dependence approach to organizational failure. *Social Science Research, 24,* 28-62.

Siegrist, H. (1986). Professionalization with the brakes on: The legal professions in Switzerland, France and Germany in the nineteenth and early twentieth centuries. *Comparative Social Research, 9,* 37-51.

Sills, D. L. (1957). *The volunteers: Means and ends in a national organization.* Glencoe, IL: Free Press.

Simmel, G. (1968). *Soziologie.* Berlin: Humboldt.

Simmel, G. (1984). *Schriften zur Soziologie.* Frankfurt: Suhrkamp.

Singer, M. I., & Yankey, J. A. (1991). Organizational metamorphosis: A study of eighteen nonprofit mergers, acquisitions, and consolidations. *Nonprofit Management and Leadership 1,* 357-369.

Singh, J. (1986). Performance, slack and risk taking in organizational decision making. *Academy of Management Journal, 29*(3), 562-585.

Singh, J. V., Tucker, D. J., & House, R. J. (1986). Organizational legitimacy and the liability of newness. *Administrative Science Quarterly 31,* 171-193.

Smelser, N. (1962). *Theory of collective behavior.* New York: Free Press.

Smith, D. (1995). The dark side of excellence: Managing strategic failures. In J. Thompson (Ed.), *The CIMA handbook of strategic management.* London: Butterworth-Heinemann.

Starbuck, W. H. (1982). Congealing oil: Inventing ideologies to justify acting ideologies out. *Journal of Management Studies, 19,* 3-26.

Staw, B. (1976). Knee-deep in the big muddy: A study of escalating commitment to a chosen course of action. *Organizational Behavior and Human Performance, 16*(1), 27-44.

Staw, B., Sandelands, L., & Dutton, J. (1981). Threat-rigidity effects in organizational behavior: A multilevel analysis. *Administrative Science Quarterly, 26,* 501-524.

Steinert, E. (1988). Interaktionsort Frauenhaus. Zur moralischen Entwicklung von Frauenhaus-Bewohnerinnen [Battered women shelter: Places of interaction. On the moral development of shelter occupants]. *Neue Praxis,* 275-290.

Sterngold, J. (1990). *Burning down the house: How greed, deceit, and bitter revenge destroyed E. F. Hutton.* New York: Summit.

Stinchcombe, A. L. (1965). Social structure and organizations. In J. G. March (Ed.), *Handbook of organizations* (pp. 142-193). Chicago: Rand-McNally.

Stoner, J. (1968). Risky and cautious shifts in group decisions: The influence of widely held values. *Journal of Experimental Social Psychology, 4,* 442-459.

Strebel, P. (1995). Creating industry breakpoints: Changing the rules of the game. *Long Range Planning, 28*(2), 11-20.

Suchman, M. (1995). Managing legitimacy: Strategic and institutional approaches. *Academy of Management Review, 20,* 571-610.

Swaminathan, A., & Wiedenmayer, G. (1991, March). Does pattern of density dependence in organizational mortality vary across levels of analysis? Evidence from the German brewing industry. *Social Science Research, 20,* 45-73.

Teitelman, R. (1994). *Profits of science: The American marriage of business and technology.* New York: Basic Books/Harper Collins.

Thompson, D. F. (1983). Ascribing responsibility to advisers in government. *Ethics, 93,* 546-560.

Thompson, D. F. (1987). *Political ethics and public office.* Cambridge, MA: Harvard University Press.

Topkis, M. (1996, December 9). A new way to find bargains. *Fortune,* p. 265.

Torstendahl, R., & Burrage, M. (1990). *The formation of professions: Knowledge, state and strategy.* London: Sage.

Tsoukas, H. (1991). The missing link: A transformational view of metaphors in organizational science. *Academy of Management Review, 16,* 566-585.

Tully, S. (1993, September 20). The real key to creating wealth. *Fortune,* pp. 38-50.

Turner, B. (1978). *Man-made disasters.* London: Wynham.

Tushman, M. L., & Anderson. P. (1986, March). Technological discontinuities and organizational environments. *Administrative Science Quarterly, 31,* 439-465.

Tushman, M. L., & Romanelli, E. (1985). Organizational evolution: A metamorphosis model of convergence and reorientation. In L. L. Cummings & B. M. Staw (Eds.), *Research in organizational behavior* (Vol. 7, pp. 171-222). Greenwich, CT: JAI.

Tversky, A., & Kahneman, D. (1974, September). Judgment under uncertainty: Heuristics and biases. *Science, 185,* 1124-1131.

U.S. Bureau of the Census, Department of Commerce, Economics and Statistics Administration. (1997). *Statistical abstract of the United States.* Washington, DC: Government Printing Office.

U.S. General Accounting Office. (1992). *Pension plans: Hidden liabilities increase against government insurance program.* Washington, DC: Government Printing Office.

Useem, B. (1985). Disorganization and the New Mexico prison riot. *American Sociological Review, 50* 677-688.

Valentin, E. K. (1994). Anatomy of a fatal business strategy. *Journal of Management Studies, 31*(3), 359-382.

Van de Ven, A. H., & Poole, M. S. (1995). Explaining development and change in organizations. *Academy of Management Review, 20,* 510-540.

Wasserman, S., & Faust, K. (1994). *Social network analysis: Methods and applications.* Cambridge, UK: Cambridge University Press.

Waterbury, J., & Gersovitz, M. (1987). *The political economy of risk and choice in Senegal.* London: Frank Cass.

Weber, M. (1978). *Economy and society: An outline of interpretive sociology.* Berkeley: University of California Press.

Weick, K. E. (1976). Educational organizations as loosely coupled systems. *Administrative Science Quarterly, 21,* 1-19.

Weick, K. (1995). *Sensemaking in organizations.* Thousand Oaks, CA: Sage.

Wernet, S. P., & Jones, S. A. (1992). Merger and acquisition activity between nonprofit social service organizations: A case study. *Nonprofit and Voluntary Sector Quarterly, 21,* 367-380.

Whetten, D. A. (1987). Organizational growth and decline processes. *Annual Review of Sociology, 13,* 355-358.

White, H. C., Boorman, S. A., & Breiger, R. L. (1976). Social structure from multiple networks 1: Blockmodels of roles and positions. *American Journal of Sociology, 81,* 730-780.

Wholey, D. R., Christianson, J. B., & S. M. Sanchez, S. M. (1992). Organizational size and failure among health maintenance organizations. *American Sociological Review, 57,* 829-842.

Williamson, O. E. (1975). *Markets and hierarchies.* New York: Free Press.

Williamson, O. E. (1985). *The economic institutions of capitalism.* New York: Free Press.

Wilson, E. K. (1985). What counts in the death or transformation of an organization? *Social Forces, 64,* 259-280.

Wolf, H.-G. (1995). An academy in transition: Organizational success and failure in the process of German unification. *Social Studies of Science, 25,* 829-852.

Young, R. C. (1988). Is population ecology a useful paradigm for the study of organizations? *American Journal of Sociology, 94,* 1-22.

Zald, M. N., & Berger, M. A. (1978). Social movements in organizations: Coup d'Etat, insurgency and mass movement. *American Journal of Sociology, 83,* 823-861.

Zaman, G., Sandu, S., & Dacin, A. (1995). *Transformation der Rumänischen Akademie.* Unpublished report, Bukarest.

Zammuto, R. F., & Cameron, K. S. (1985). Environmental decline and organizational response. In B. M. Staw & L. L. Cummings (Eds.), *Research in organizational behavior* (pp. 223-262). Greenwich, CT: JAI.

Zartman, I. W. (Ed.). (1983). *The political economy of Nigeria.* New York: Praeger.

Zucker, L. G. (1991a). Markets for bureaucratic authority and control: Information quality in professions and services. *Research in the Sociology of Organizations, 8,* 157-190.

Zucker, L. G. (1991b). The role of institutionalization in cultural persistence. In W. W. Powell & P. J. DiMaggio (Eds.), *The new institutionalism in organizational analysis* (pp. 83-107). Chicago: Chicago University Press.

Zucker, L. G., & Darby, M. R. (1995a, August). *Present at the revolution: Transformation of technical identity for a large incumbent pharmaceutical firm after the biotechnological breakthrough* (Working Paper No. 5243). Cambridge, MA: National Bureau of Economic Research.

Zucker, L. G., & Darby, M. R. (1995b). Sociological analysis of multi-institutional collaborations in space science and geophysics. In J. Warnow-Blewett, A. J. Capitos, J. Genuth, & S. R. Weart (Eds., with contributions by F. Nebeker, L. Zucker, & M. Darby), *AIP study of multi-institutional collaborations, Phase II: Space science and geophysics. Report No. 2: Documenting collaborations in space science and geophysics* (pp. 149-178). College Park, MD: American Institute of Physics.

Zucker, L. G., & Darby, M. R. (1996). Star scientists and institutional transformation: Patterns of invention and innovation in the formation of the biotechnology industry. *Proceedings of the National Academy of Sciences, 93*(23), 12709-12716.

Zucker, L. G., & Darby, M. R. (in press). Star scientist linkages to firms in APEC and European countries: Indicators of regional institutional differences affecting competitive advantage. *International Journal of Biotechnology, 1(1).*

Zucker, L. G., Darby, M. R., & Armstrong, J. (1994, December). *Intellectual human capital and the firm: The technology of geographically localized knowledge spillovers* (Working Paper No. 4946). Cambridge, MA: National Bureau of Economic Research.

Zucker, L. G., Darby, M. R., & Brewer, M. B. (1994, February). *Intellectual human capital and the birth of U.S. biotechnology enterprises* (Working Paper No. 4653). Cambridge, MA: National Bureau of Economic Research.

Zucker, L. G., Darby, M. R., Brewer, M. B., & Peng, Y. (1996). Collaboration structure and information dilemmas in biotechnology: Organizational boundaries as trust production. In R. M. Knumr & T. Tyler (Eds.), *Trust in organizations: Frontiers of theory and research* (pp. 90-113). Thousand Oaks, CA: Sage.

Index

Bankruptcy, 3, 4, 11-12, 105-106
  failure and, 119-120
  political tool, 106-113, 107 (table), 109 (figure), 282
  structured organizational field, 114-119, 115 (figure), 116 (table)
Biotechnology:
  entities, new biological, 27-30, 28-29 (table)
  national levels in, 21-24, 23 (table)
  patent production, 24-26, 26 (table)
Blame avoidance, 123-124, 282
  argumentative tactics, typology, 140-145, 142 (table)
  case study: Netherlands, crime fighting in, 129-140, 132-133 (table)
  policy fiascoes, political construction of, 124-126, 145-147
  tactics for, 127-129
Breakthrough discoveries, 30-32

Coping, 72-73, 86
  environmental challenges, 80-82, 87
  institutional changes, 77-80
  regime reform, radical, 76-77
  socialist societies, academies in, 73-76
  strategies for, 82-85
  See also Successful failure
Corporate insolvency, 149-150
  civil service/self-regulation, 159-161

English Insolvency Act 1986, 153-155, 282
government sponsored professionalization, 169-172
insolvency legislation, 161-164
insolvency practitioners, 155-159
professionalization, hybrid model of, 164-168
professionalization, politics of, 151-153
reorganizational infrastructure, 150-151
See also Permanent failure; Planning to fail
Crozier, Michel, 241-242

Decision overreach, 35-36, 276-277
  cases of, 36-40
  components of, 40-41
  contributory factors, 43-47
  genre of failure, distinct, 41-43
  model of, 48-49, 48 (figure)
Development. *See* Institutional development; Research and development

English Insolvency Act 1986. *See* Corporate insolvency
Environment as factor, 55-57
  resource-dependence model, 71-72

structural contigency model, 71
See also Coping

Failure. *See* Government failure; Organizational failure; Permanent failure; Planning to fail; Successful failure
Fantasy documents, 180-182, 191-192, 193-196
Fiascoes. *See* Blame avoidance

Government failure, 4, 5-6
See also Socialist society

Information, 8-9, 17-19
asymmetry, 92-93
gathering mechanisms, 21
See also Intellectual human capital; Research and development
Insolvency practitioners, 155-157
civil service, 159-161
collective organization of, 157-158
government involvement, 168-172
hybrid model, 164-168
quality guarantee, 158-159
standards/disinterestedness, 161-164
transprofessional community identity, 168
Insolvency. *See* Bankruptcy; Corporate insolvency
Institutional development, 237-239
attitudes, free riding vs. oligarchy, 227-232, 228 (table), 230 (table)
blockmodels, NADA/SADA, 223-227, 224-225 (tables)
case studies, Nigeria/Senegal, 217-219
free rider hypotheses, 220, 222-223
oligarchy in, 215-217, 220-221
organizational elitism hypothesis, 221-222
social infrastructure and, 232-236
social networks, blockmodeling analysis, 219-220, 221
Intellectual human capital, 18-19
corporate productivity and, 26-30, 28-29 (table), 31 (table)

corporate ties to, 21-24, 23 (table)
star scientists and firms, 24-26, 25 (table), 26 (table)
See also Research and development
Investment:
information/technology, 8-9, 17-19, 276, 277
intellectual human capital, 18-19
See also Research and development

Liquidation. *See* Bankruptcy; Corporate insolvency

Management, 6, 35-36, 276-277
Michels, Robert, 215-216, 221-222

Nonprofit mortality, 51-52, 54, 92, 100-104, 278

Oligarchy thesis, 13, 215-217
Olson, Mancur, 216, 222-223
Organizational death, 51-52, 67, 69, 278
concept of, 52-53
external causes, 55-57, 64-66, 65 (table), 277
internal causes, 54-55, 62-64, 63 (table)
predictors of survival, 60-62, 61 (table)
research on, 57-59, 58 (figure)
size/age factors in, 66-67, 68 (table)
See also Organizational failure
Organizational failure, 3-5, 13-14, 273-274, 274-279, 275 (table)
bankruptcy and, 119-120
cognitive aspects, 6, 12, 275 (table), 282-284
decision overreach, 35-49, 276-277
environmental influences, 55-57, 71-73
facets of, 287-290
phases of, 5
political aspects, 5-6, 9-10, 275 (table), 279-282
structural perspective, 7-8, 12-13, 71, 275 (table), 284-286
theory of, 278-279

See also Bankruptcy; Corporate insolvency; Organizational death; Organizational success; Planning to fail; Stalemate; Successful failure
Organizational success, 8-9
predictors of survival, 60-62, 61 (table)
response, structural mechanisms of, 283-284
See also Coping; Successful failure

Patents, 24-26, 26 (table)
Performance measurement. *See* Permanent failure; Productivity
Permanent failure, 179, 197-198, 246, 282-283, 286
invention of measures, 207-210
managers/researchers, measurement choices, 210-212, 284
performance measures, 198-199, 199-201
second-best measures, 201-204, 202 (figure), 203 (table), 283
stalemate as, 247
variance loss in measurement, 204-207, 206 (figure)
See also Planning to fail; Stalemate
Planning to fail, 179-180
case study: Shoreham Nuclear Power Station, 180-196, 283
failure and fantasy, 193-196
fantasy documents, 180-182, 191-192, 194-195, 196
freeplay messages, 189-191
organizational breakdown, 185-189, 193
simulation exercise, 182-185
Policy fiascoes. *See* Blame avoidance
Productivity:
development, linear model of, 75
intellectual human capital and, 26-30, 28-20 (table), 31 (table)
patents, 24-26, 26 (table)
performance measurement, 198-199
performance outcomes, 12
See also Permanent failure

Research and development:
investment in, 19-21, 20 (table)

national levels, 22-24, 23 (table)
socialist countries and, 75
star scientists and firms, 24-26, 25 (table), 26 (table)

Shoreham Nuclear Power Station, 180-196
Socialist society:
academies, 73-76, 278
coping strategies, 82-85, 86
environmental challenges, variety of, 80-82, 87
institutional change, tendencies in, 77-80
regime reform, radical 76-77
Stalemate, 13, 241-243
case study: Industry Financing Project, 243-245
case study: Nigerian Association of Development Agencies (NADA), 248-252
characteristics of, 252-253
conflict/support overlap, 253-259, 254 (figures), 256 (figure), 257 (figure), 258 (figure), 285
data/analysis, 259-261, 261 (table)
exit phenomena, 246, 265
loyalty, false, 247
network, description/measurement of, 267-269
permanent failure, 246-247
recovery from, 266
structural failure, theory of, 264-266
triad hypotheses, 259, 261-264, 262 (table), 263 (table)
voice, 245-246, 265
Successful failure, 91-92
Autonomous Women's Houses, 93-94
failure/ignorance, interest in, 95-99, 96 (table)
nonprofit sector and, 100-104
prerequisites, structural/ideological, 99-100
resource contribution, 92-93
Workshops for Handicapped Persons, 94-95

Triggering events, 6, 276

About the Editor

Helmut K. Anheier is Associate Professor of Sociology at Rutgers University, a Senior Research Associate at the Johns Hopkins University Institute for Policy Studies, and the incoming Director of the Centre for Voluntary Organisation at the London School of Economics. Prior to this, he was Social Affairs officer at the United Nation's International Narcotics Control Board and has held research appointments at the Program on Nonprofit Organizations, Yale University; the University of Cologne; and the Science Center in Berlin. He is involved in research on a comparative study of the size, scope, and role of the private nonprofit sector in 30 developed and developing countries and is founding editor of *Voluntas,* the international journal of research on nonprofit organizations. His most recent publications include *The Emerging Sector: An Overview* (1996) and several volumes as part of the Johns Hopkins Comparative Nonprofit Sector Project. He has also authored numerous journal articles. A graduate of the University of Trier in Germany, he holds a Ph.D. in sociology from Yale University.

About the Contributors

Wolfgang Bielefeld is Associate Professor of Sociology and Political Economy at the University of Texas, Dallas. He has also taught in the Sociology Departments at the University of Minnesota and Stanford University as well as in the Public Policy Program at Stanford. His research interests include the relations between organizations and their environments, the dynamics of nonprofit sectors, the development of human service delivery systems, and the social impacts of government human service policies and spending patterns. He is currently conducting research on the nonprofit sector in the Dallas-Ft. Worth metropolitan area. Publications from a recently completed 12-year longitudinal study, with Joseph Galaskiewicz, of changes in the nonprofit sector in the Minneapolis-St. Paul metropolitan area include *The Social Organization of an Urban Grants Economy* (1985) and *Nonprofit Organizations in an Age of Uncertainty: A Study of Organizational Change* (in press). He received his Ph.D. in Sociology from the University of Minnesota.

Mark Bovens is Professor of Legal Philosophy at Utrecht University in The Netherlands. He studied Law, Political Science, and Philosophy at Leiden University and at Columbia University School of Law in New York. Before coming to Utrecht in 1997, he was lecturer in the Departments of Political Science and Public Administration at Leiden University. His research interests include political and legal philosophy, government, policy analysis, and public administration. Some of his most recent books are *Understanding Policy Fiascoes,* with Paul 't Hart (1996), and *The Quest for Responsibility: Accountability and Citizenship in Complex Organizations* (1998).

Bruce G. Carruthers is Associate Professor of sociology and director of the graduate sociology program at Northwestern University. His books include *City of Capital: Politics and Markets in the English Financial Revolution* and *Rescuing Business: The Making of Corporate Bankruptcy Law in England and the United States,* coauthored with Terence Halliday. He is currently writing a book on economic sociology and has previously published articles on accounting, stock markets, bankruptcy, money, and American welfare and fiscal policy during the 1930s.

Lee Clarke teaches sociology at Rutgers University. His early work concerned how decision makers choose among risks in very uncertain environments. Publications include *Acceptable Risk? Making Decisions in a Toxic Environment; Organizations, Uncertainties, and Risk;* "Explaining Choices Among Technological Risks," *Social Problems;* "Oil Spill Fantasies," *Atlantic Monthly;* "Sociological and Economic Theories of Markets and Nonprofits," *American Journal of Sociology;* and "The Disqualification Heuristic: When Do Organizations Misperceive Risk? *Research in Social Problems and Public Policy.* Clarke's most recent book is *Mission Improbable: Using Fantasy Documents to Tame Disaster.* He is currently writing about the Y2K problem and also about the idea of worst cases in modern societies.

Michael R. Darby is the Warren C. Cordner Professor of Money and Financial Markets in the Anderson Graduate School of Management and in the Departments of Economics and Policy Studies at UCLA, Director of the John M. Olin Center for Policy in the Anderson School, and Research Associate of the National Bureau of Economic Research. He is the author of eight books and monographs and numerous other professional publications. He edited the *Journal of International Money and Finance* and was elected Vice President and President-Elect of the Western Economic Association in 1998. He and Lynne Zucker are currently publishing on productivity in basic science and its commercialization, and production of trust in science.

Sander Dekker is a graduate student in public administration at Leiden University. He is specializing in crisis management, more specifically, in the crisis of crime fighting in The Netherlands. Furthermore, he is affiliated with the Crisis Research Center (COT) at Leiden University, where he is doing research after the Dutch police and public prosecution.

Kevin J. Delaney is Associate Professor of Sociology at Temple University. He is author of *Strategic Bankruptcy: How Corporations and Creditors*

Use Chapter 11 to Their Advantage (1992) as well as articles on bankruptcy strategy, the creation and use of financial documents as strategic instruments, and business restructuring published in *Social Problems, Law & Society Review,* and other leading journals. His current research is on the formation of local networks and financial expertise.

Joseph Galaskiewicz is Professor of Sociology and Strategic Management/ Organization at the University of Minnesota. He has a long-standing interest in community organization and nonprofits, social networks, organizational theory, and prosocial behavior. He is the author of *Exchange Networks and Community Politics* (Sage, 1979), *The Social Organization of an Urban Grants Economy: A Study of Business Philanthropy and Nonprofit Organizations* (1985), and *Nonprofit Organizations in an Age of Uncertainty: A Study of Organizational Change,* with Wolfgang Bielefeld (1998). He also coedited, with Stanley Wasserman, *Advances in Social Network Analysis: Research in the Social and Behavioral Sciences* (Sage, 1994). He received his B.A. from Loyola University of Chicago and his M.A. and Ph.D. in Sociology from the University of Chicago.

Mark Hager is Assistant Professor of Sociology at Indiana University of Pennsylvania. His research interests include failure processes in individual organizations and populations of organizations, especially nonprofit organizations. He recently completed his Ph.D. at the University of Minnesota with a dissertation titled *Explaining Demise Among Nonprofit Organizations.*

Terence C. Halliday is Senior Research Fellow at the American Bar Foundation, Chicago, and President, National Institute for Social Science Information. He has taught at the Australian National University and the University of Chicago. He has served as chair of the section on the Sociology of Law, American Sociological Association; on the Boards of the Research Committee on the Sociology of Law, International Sociological Association; and the Onati International Institute for the Sociology of Law. He has been an editor of *Law and Social Inquiry* and general editor of the monograph series, Onati International Studies in Law and Society. His books on professions, law, and organizations include *Beyond Monopoly: Lawyers, State Crises and Professional Empowerment; Sociology and Its Publics: The Forms and Fates of Disciplinary Organization,* edited with Morris Janowitz; *Rescuing Business: Making Bankruptcy Law in England and the United States,* coauthored with Bruce Carruthers; and *Lawyers and the Rise of Western Political Liberalism,* edited with Lucien Karpik.

Paul 't Hart is Professor of Public Administration at Leiden University in The Netherlands. He studied Political Science at the Erasmus University Rotterdam and has a Ph.D. in Public Administration from Leiden University. Before becoming a professor of Public Administration in 1998, he was a Fellow of the Royal Dutch Academy of Science and lecturer at the Leiden Department of Public Administration. His research interests include crisis management, political and social psychology, government, and policy analysis. Some of his most recent publications are *Groupthink in Government* (1994), *Understanding Policy Fiascoes,* with Mark Bovens (1996), and *Beyond Groupthink,* edited with Eric Stern and Bengt Sundelius (1997).

David J. Hickson is Research Professor of International Management and Organization at Bradford Management Centre, England. His principal research interests are how societal culture affects managerial decision making in different nations and what influences the success of major decisions. He has published numerous research papers and is author or editor of eight books—most recently, *Management Worldwide: The Impact of Societal Culture on Organizations Around the Globe* (1995, with D. Pugh). He is a Fellow of the British Academy of Management.

Renate Mayntz founded the Max-Planck-Institute for the Study of Societies (MPIfG) in Cologne in 1985 and was Director of the institute until her retirement in 1997. After receiving a Ph.D. from the Free University of Berlin, she did full-time research work at the UNESCO Institute of Social Research, Cologne, followed by grant-financed research work in Berlin and a year as a Rockefeller Fellow in the United States. She was appointed Full Professor of Sociology at the Free University of Berlin in 1965, at the Postgraduate School of Administrative Sciences in Speyer in 1971, and at the University of Cologne in 1973. She has also had teaching assignments at Columbia University and the New School for Social Research in New York; at FLASCO (Facultad Latino-Americana de Ciencias Sociales) in Santiago de Chile; and at Stanford University in California. She served on the German Council for Educational Reform, the Commission for the Reform of Public Administration, and the Senate of the German Research Council. Her research interests include sociological macrotheory, comparative social and political research, organizational and administrative sociology, and the sociology of technology.

Marshall W. Meyer is Professor of Management in the Wharton School and Professor of Sociology at the University of Pennsylvania. His work on organizational performance includes "The Performance Paradox" in *Research on Organizational Behavior* (1994), "Measuring the Performance of Economic Organizations" in the *Handbook of Economic Sociology* (1994), and a forthcoming book, *Finding Performance: The New Discipline in Management*. Meyer was Associate Editor of *Administrative Science Quarterly* from 1987 to 1995 and has served on the editorial boards of journals including the *American Sociological Review, Contemporary Sociology, Social Forces, Organization Studies,* and *Social Science Quarterly*. He is author, co-author, or editor of nine books, including *Permanently Failing Organizations,* with Lynne Zucker.

Susan J. Miller is Lecturer in Organizational Behavior and Strategic Management at Durham University Business School, England. Her research interests include strategic decision-making processes and managerial/clinical interfaces in the health sector.

Lynne Moulton is a doctoral student in the Department of Sociology at Rutgers University, where she earned her M.A. in 1997. She has presented work on homelessness and welfare policy at regional conferences. Her current work on microcredit programs focuses on organizational structures and social networks of community economic development.

Charles Perrow is Professor of Sociology at Yale University and is currently working on a study of the role of large organizations in shaping U.S. society. His recent publications in this area are "A Society of Organizations, " in *Theory and Society* (1991) and "The Bounded Career and the Demise of the Civil Society," in *Boundaryless Careers* (in press, edited by Arthur and Rousseau.)

Joel Pins is both a Research Assistant in the Department of Sociology and a doctoral student in the Department of Epidemiology at the University of Minnesota, Minneapolis, where he received his M.S. in sociology in 1996 and his M.P.H. in nutrition in fall 1997. His current research and writing interests include the study of methodological issues associated with organizations.

Frank P. Romo is Associate Professor of Sociology at the State University of New York, Stony Brook. His research interests are structural analysis, organizational sociology, research methods and statistics, and economic sociology. Recent contributions have appeared in the *American Sociological Review* and the *American Journal of Sociology*.

Wolfgang Seibel is a Professor of Political and Administrative Science at the University of Konstanz. His current research focuses on institutional reconstruction in post-1989 Eastern Germany. Recent books include *Funktionaler Dilettantismus: Erfolgreich Sheiternde Organisationen im "Dritten Sektor" Zwischen Markt und Staat* (Funtional Dilettantism: Successfully Failing Organizations in the Third Sector, 1994). And *Verwaltungsaufbau in den Ostdeutschen Bundeslaendern: Zur Kommunikativen Logik Staatlicher Institutionenbildung* (Administrative Reconstruction in the East German States: On Communicative Logic of State-Institution Building, 1996).

Gerdien Verheuvel is a graduate student in public administration at Leiden University. From 1991 till 1996, she studied at the Institute of Higher European Studies in The Hague. In 1996, she received a bachelor's degree in Politics and Public Administration of the European Union. For the Crisis Research Center (COT) at Leiden University she took part in a "crisis and media" project. For that, she did research after the media influence on the crisis of crime fighting in The Netherlands (IRT affair) and the tactics that key players used in the affair. This project has resulted in four publications.

David Wilson is Professor of Strategic Management at Warwick Business School. He is Director of the Research Centre for Creativity, Strategy and Change. His research interests include decision-making processes and organizational change. He has also conducted research in the U.K. voluntary sector on strategy, structure, and change. He is coauthor of five books, the most recent of which are *A Strategy of Change* (1992) and *Strategy and Leadership* (1994, with B. Levy). His is a fellow of the British Academy of Management.

Lynne G. Zucker is Professor of Sociology and Policy Studies, Director of the Organizational Research Program at the Institute for Social Science Research, and Director of the Center for International Science, Technology, and Cultural Policy in the School of Public Policy & Social Research at UCLA. She serves as Research Associate, National Bureau of Economic Research and as Consulting Sociologist, American Institute of Physics. She is author of four books and monographs and numerous articles on organizational theory. With Michael Darby, she is currently publishing on productivity in basic science and its commercialization, and production of trust in science.